THE MASTER IN BONDAGE

The Master in Bondage

Factory Workers in China, 1949–2019

HUAIYIN LI

STANFORD UNIVERSITY PRESS
Stanford, California

STANFORD UNIVERSITY PRESS
Stanford, California

© 2023 by Huaiyin Li. All rights reserved.

No part of this book may be reproduced or transmitted in any form or by any means, electronic or mechanical, including photocopying and recording, or in any information storage or retrieval system without the prior written permission of Stanford University Press.

Printed in the United States of America on acid-free, archival-quality paper

Library of Congress Cataloging-in-Publication Data

Names: Li, Huaiyin, author.
Title: The master in bondage : factory workers in China, 1949-2019 / Huaiyin Li.
Description: Stanford, California : Stanford University Press, 2023. | Includes bibliographical references and index.
Identifiers: LCCN 2022046054 (print) | LCCN 2022046055 (ebook) | ISBN 9781503634541 (cloth) | ISBN 9781503635289 (paperback) | ISBN 9781503635296 (epub)
Subjects: LCSH: Manufacturing industries—China—Employees—History. | Factories—China—Employees—History. | Industrial relations—China—History. | Management—Employee participation—China—History. | Labor productivity—China—History. | Working class—China—History.
Classification: LCC HD8039.M2252 C65 2023 (print) | LCC HD8039.M2252 (ebook) | DDC 331.7/670951—dc23/eng/20230106
LC record available at https://lccn.loc.gov/2022046054
LC ebook record available at https://lccn.loc.gov/2022046055

Cover design: Derek Thorton / Notch Design

Cover art: Zhong Zaiben, *Let the "Sputnik" of High Production Circle Around the Sky Forever*, 1958. 73x52 cm

Typeset at Newgen in 10/14.4 Minion Pro

Contents

Preface vii

Introduction 1
1 The Making of the Masters: Disciplining Workers through Identity Building 28
2 Beyond Masterhood and Democracy: Worker Participation in Factory Governance 62
3 Everyday Power Relations in State Firms 102
4 Worker Performance in Everyday Production 132
5 The Frustrated Masters: Workers before and during the Cultural Revolution 167
6 The Master of One's Own Labor Only: Workers in the Reform Era 206
Conclusion 246

Glossary 259
List of Interviewees 271
Notes 281
References 285
Index 307

Preface

There is no doubt that the Chinese economy grew much faster in the reform era than before; this was true in agriculture as well as in the nation's industrial sector on the whole. However, if we focus on the performance of the state sector, which dominated industrial production in Maoist China, a different picture emerges. During the first two decades of the reform era, the output of the state-owned industry increased from 367.36 billion yuan in 1979 to 3,557.1 billion in 1999 (Guojia tongjiju 2005: 64), or 12 percent a year, which was striking. But the record of the Maoist era is no less impressive. In the twenty-five years before the reform, the industrial output of the state sector also grew by 12 percent a year, from 19.37 billion yuan in 1953, the year when Chinese economy was fully recovered from war devastation and when the first five-year plan started, to 328.92 billion in 1978, the last year of the Maoist era (Guojia tongjiju 2005: 63–64). Needless to say, many factors influenced the performance of state-owned enterprises, and these factors varied before and during the reform; therefore, the growth rate of the state sector alone cannot sufficiently explain the efficiency or inefficiency of the enterprises involved or the effectiveness of industrial institutions in different periods. Nevertheless, the fast expansion of the state sector in the Maoist era suggests that the systems and institutions underlying the state firms should not simply be dismissed as a failure, as many have assumed in the past.

To understand how the state-owned factories operated in post-1949 China, this study explores the micro-level mechanisms that constrained as well as motivated the labor force in state firms. My goal in this book is to reconstruct the realities of worker performance in everyday production and participation in factory governance. For that end, we have to first of all put aside the ideological assumptions that have influenced the conventional wisdom about labor relations and factory politics in contemporary China. We should not take it for granted, for example, that the absence of market mechanisms or private property rights would necessarily result in chronic inefficiency in production or that the lack of material incentives would inevitably lead to widespread shirking among the workers, as the pro-reform elites in China or the neoliberal intellectuals in the West have suggested. Nor should we yield to the Maoist state's claim that the Chinese workers, as the leading class in society, were fully dedicated to production and enthusiastic for exercising their power as the *zhurenweng* or "masters" of the factory. Instead, I propose to bring the Maoist factory back to history, that is, to historicize the context in which the workers engaged in economic and political activities and reconstruct the reality of factory politics as it actually took place. Institutions are important for understanding the context in which the labor force worked and lived. But my discussion is not limited to the formal institutions, such as state policies and regulations as well as a whole set of factory organizations that involved the workers. Equally important in my analysis are the informal factors and practices that were invisible yet ubiquitous in the workplace and beyond, such as interpersonal relations, group consensus, peer pressure, collective sanctioning, and, most important, one's personal character and self-consciousness that were influenced by past experiences, family backgrounds, and personal standing in the group. It was the interaction between the formal and informal institutions that shaped the work norms within a particular factory or workshop and conditioned the dispositions of the workers in everyday factory life. The workers' strategies for engaging in production and factory politics thus were complex, dynamic, and changing over time and space.

Thus the approach that I employ in this study is microhistorical. Unlike the past studies on Chinese factories that have tended to focus on the state's macro-level policies or the governing bodies at the factory level or above, and that have interpreted workers' behavior and choices as resultant and deducible from those policies and systems, this study centers on the workers.

It foregrounds the role of ordinary workers and explains how they formed their identity as individuals and as a group in the workplace, how they performed production tasks, and how they dealt with the people around or above them in the process of factory governance. I hope that the findings from this study will help reduce existing distortions, in which the industrial workers of post-1949 China were either caricatured as slackers on the shop floor and powerless in factory politics or exalted to the glorious producers of the socialist enterprise. Studying the Mao-era factory politics from the microhistorical perspective will also shed light on the dynamics of enterprise reforms and the rebuilding of labor relations in the post-Mao era, which I will explicate in the last part of this book.

A worker-centered history of factory governance cannot be done without the voices of those who personally experienced factory life in post-1949 China. This work is largely based on the oral narratives of the retirees from state-owned enterprises. In 2012–2013, I collaborated with my colleagues at several universities in China to interview a total of ninety-seven retired factory workers and cadres in different cities. These colleagues include professor Di Jinhua of Huazhong University of Science and Technology; professor Jiang Manqing of Huazhong Normal University; professor Yong Suhua of Nanjing University of Information Science and Technology; professor Zhuang Yiping of Shanghai Jiaotong University; research fellow Zhang Chunlong of Jiangsu Province Academy of Social Sciences; and the late research fellow Huang Yingwei of the Institute of Economics, the Chinese Academy of Social Sciences. I am indebted to the aforementioned individuals and their students for participating in the interviews. I also thank the staff at the Nanjing Municipal Archives for assistance in my use of the archival files on the factories of the city.

At the University of Texas at Austin, I am indebted to the College of Liberal Arts for a Humanities Research Award (2011–2014) and a Faculty Research Assignment (2015–2016), and to the Department of History for its annual Scholarly Activity Grants, which facilitated my research and writing of this book. Chapters 3 and 4 are based respectively on two previously published articles, "Everyday Power Relations in State Firms in Socialist China: A Reexamination" (*Modern China*, vol. 43, no. 3, 2017) and "Worker Performance in State-Owned Factories in Maoist China: A Reinterpretation" (*Modern China*, vol. 42, no. 4, 2015); I thank the publisher for allowing them to be incorporated into this book. Parts of previous drafts of this book were presented at the following two conferences hosted or co-hosted by UT Austin's Center for East Asian Studies, of which I served as director: the international symposium on "Rethinking Socialism and Reform in China" in October 2016, and the conference on "China's Reform and Opening Up: Four Decades of Legacies and Lessons" in February 2019. I am thankful to the participants at these conferences for their comments on my presentations; among them were professors Joel Andreas, Marc Blecher, Xiaoping Cong, Alexander Day, Bryan DeMare, Joshua Eisenman, William Hurst, Fangchun Li, Dorothy Solinger, Brantly Womack, Wu Chongqing, and Yafeng Xia. The detailed comments and very constructive suggestions from the two anonymous reviewers helped me greatly in preparing the final draft of this book. For their discussions and suggestions on the chapters of this book that were taught in my graduate seminars on contemporary China, I thank my former or current students John Harney, James Hudson, Kazushi Minami, Ben Yeager, Jing Zhai, and Zhaojin Zeng. All errors that remain are my own.

My greatest thanks go to my wife, Guiyun, and our two children, Cathy and Daniel. Their understanding and support made the writing of this book a pleasant experience.

H. L.
Austin, Texas
March 2022

THE MASTER IN BONDAGE

INTRODUCTION

ON APRIL 20, 1959, at a mass gathering celebrating the tenth anniversary of the Liberation of Nanjing, Xia Shuiliu, president of Nanjing General Trade Union, declared:

> "On April 24, 1949, Nanjing was liberated. From that time on, the workers of Nanjing have been transformed from the slaves of the old society into the master of the new society. They have shaken off forever the yoke imposed by reactionaries, gotten rid of the sufferings of hunger and unemployment, and ended a life that had been worse than that of beasts of burden." (NJ6001-2-279)[1]

Xia's speech, eloquent as it was, in fact only reiterated the Maoist rhetoric about industrial workers. In the three decades following the founding of the People's Republic in 1949, the state's propaganda elevated factory workers to the status of *zhurenweng* or the "masters" of the country. Indeed, as a privileged group, workers of state-owned factories were entitled to a full range of benefits unavailable to the rest of society. In return, they were expected to "treat the factory as home" (*yi cang wei jia*), take good care of its properties, and work diligently in everyday production. As the "leading class" (*lingdao jieji*) of socialist China, they were encouraged to participate in the "democratic management" (*minzhu guanli*) of the factory and take initiatives in technological innovation. The workers, in other words, were more than the employees of an industrial firm in the state's representation; they had the inalienable rights to own and run the place where they labored every day.

In sharp contrast, to justify the initiation of economic reforms in the late 1970s and the 1980s, the official discourse of the post-Mao era downplayed the economic performance of the Mao past. It underscored the inefficiency of production and chaos in labor management in state firms before the reform, attributing the poor performance in industry to the policies of egalitarianism, excessive centralism, and ultra-leftism of the radical leadership that prevailed in the late Maoist era, known notoriously as the "Gang of Four" (*sirenbang*). Workers of state firms, in this light, appeared to be shirking and slacking on the shop floor because of the lack of material incentives, and they seemed disinterested in participating in factory governance due to factory cadres' arbitrary leadership. So wrote Hu Qiaomu, a key propagandist of the post-Mao leadership, in an editorial of *The People's Daily*:

> "Under the reign of the Gang of Four, it made no difference for workers to produce more or less, to work hard or slack off, and to perform well or poorly, when the system of economic accounting was badly damaged. In other words, there was no calculation and supervision of labor input at all. At some work units, workers were paid even if they did not work year-round. Still at some work units, production was up to temporary workers; regular workers never went to work, or only worked privately for personal gain, or just loafed around." (Hu Qiaomu 1978)

In a similar vein, a divide exists in the Western literature on Chinese workers and factory politics under Mao. Based on their readings of the official publications from China or guided visits to the Chinese cities, some researchers in the 1970s noted the rapid growth of Chinese industry and the effectiveness of worker participation through formal or informal channels of factory management.[2] Other scholars, however, portrayed Maoist China as yet another totalitarian society modeled largely after the Soviet Union, and emphasized the party-state's total control of all aspects of the social, economic, and political lives of its people.[3] The factories in urban China, in this light, appeared to be atomized units in which the workers, as well as urban residents at large, existed as victims living in fear and dependent on their supervisors; recurrent political campaigns and the stifling of personal expression arguably further enhanced the state's effective control of local communities without having to use secret police rule (Whyte and Parish 1984, 295, 367; Whyte 1999, 177–178). Despite the state's promotion of "democratic management" of factories and its attack on bureaucratism and hierarchy during the Cultural Revolution, what prevailed in Maoist China and continued into the post-Mao era remained "patrimonial" leadership (Kraus 1983; Burns 1989; Lü 2000a, 2000b) or "neotraditionalism" (Walder 1986, 1987, 1989). This was evidenced by the factory cadres' arbitrariness in dictating workers' well-being, the workers' dependence on and personal loyalty to their supervisors, political particularism in cadre-worker relations, and a subsequent split between the privileged activists and the rest of the labor force.

Recent studies have definitely departed from the paradigms of totalitarianism, patrimonialism, and neotraditionalism. Together they reveal a more dynamic and complicated picture of factory politics in the Maoist era. Based on their fieldwork at a state-owned liquor distillery, Jonathan Unger and Anita Chan (2007) documented, for instance, a prevalent consensus in the enterprise that all workers who had contributed to its growth for years or decades were entitled to its resources. This shared notion of "economic justice," the researchers contend, functioned to regulate the relationship between factory leaders who continued to act in a paternalist style and the workers whose rights were well respected in the early reform era. In another instance concerning state-owned enterprises in Northeast China, the workers, who suffered unemployment and marginalization in the 1990s, tended to nostalgically remember the Maoist years as a time when they had enjoyed a privileged social status and overall economic and political equality at workplace, as Ching Kwan Lee (2007a, 2007b) found through her extensive interviews with local residents. In both studies, the researchers noted that the workers being interviewed tended to emphasize their commitment to the enterprise and their hard work in production during the Maoist past despite the severe economic shortages and poor living conditions they had endured. The researchers interpreted this as resulting from multiple factors involving the workers, such as fear, anxiety, and compulsion on the one hand and consent, identity, and loyalty on the other, although these elements function differently for workers depending on their generation, locality, and industrial sector. My own preliminary studies leading to this book further questioned the assumptions about widespread shirking among industrial workers and their systematic dependence on, and victimization by, factory leaders in the Maoist era. Instead, I found a set of strategies in the workplace that served the workers' interests and a pattern of power relations between cadres and workers that is best described as "symmetric" in nature (Li 2016, 2017). More recently, inspired by Guy Standing (2009, 2010), who observed a global phenomenon of "industrial citizenship" in the postwar decades in which workers' secured employments came with various practices of workplace democracy, Joel Andreas (2019) saw labor relations in China under Mao as no exception, where the workers' permanent employment in state-owned enterprises enabled them to participate in various forms of "democratic management" of the workplace, but he also underscored the Chinese workers' lack of autonomy under the party's monopoly of power at all levels. He thus described labor politics in the Maoist factory as a form of "participatory paternalism."

What, then, exactly were the actual experiences of Chinese workers in state-owned enterprises during the Maoist decades? Were they truly motivated to improve productivity and participate in factory governance, living up to their public image as the maters of the enterprises? Or, to the contrary, did they routinely slack on the shop floor in the absence of mobility and freedom to improve their career opportunities, fall victim to the violence of recurrent campaigns characteristic of Maoist politics, and frequently succumb to the abusive and corrupt cadres because of the failure or lacking of supervisory mechanisms, as the pro-reform discourse has assumed since the 1980s? Finally, what does a comparison with worker experiences in the post-Mao era reveal about the operational realities of factory governance before the reform?

Needless to say, these questions are key for understanding the Chinese economy under Mao and the origins of post-Mao reforms. For the Maoist state, the micro-level management of labor relations was as important as macroeconomic planning in shaping the overall performance of the socialist economy. In other words, the extent to which its goal of economic growth could be achieved depended not only on how its macro growth strategy for different sectors was implemented on the national level but also on the efficiency of day-to-day production in every factory. A thorough examination of the micro-process of labor management at the factory level, therefore, will help explicate how economic growth took place under Mao and why the

Maoist approach eventually yielded to post-Mao reforms. Moreover, labor relations at the factory level were at the core of the entire process of factory governance, which is key to understanding state-society relations in Maoist China. An examination of the practices and institutions of labor politics at the industrial enterprises, therefore, will shed light on the actual functioning of the Maoist approach to grassroots governance and its impact on the mechanisms of social control in the post-Mao era.

Unlike the existing scholarship on Chinese workers that has been done mostly by social scientists in sociology, anthropology, and political science, what follows is a systematic study of workers' everyday experiences in factory governance using a historical approach. It begins with a scrutiny of the formation of workers' personal identity through the classification of family status, admission into the party, pursuit of honorary titles, and involvement in political study sessions. It was, after all, through this process of identity formation that the workers defined who they were, perceived how they related to one another in the workplace and beyond, and determined what they could do and what they must avoid. I will then examine workers' involvement in the institutionalized channels of interest articulation, such as the staff and workers' congress (SWC), the trade union, and the appeal system, as well as their participation in recurrent political events that culminated in the Cultural Revolution. Through a detailed analysis of these routine mechanisms as well as unusual events, we will discover how the workers formed their choices and strategies in expressing their concerns and defending their interests as individuals and as a group. I will emphasize workers' day-to-day interactions with the cadres and the pattern of power relations that conditioned the functioning of an entire set of systems and practices in factory governance. I will pay equal attention to how those systems and practices motivated as well as constrained the workers in everyday production; after all, the single most important goal for the socialist state and its agents in labor management was nothing less than the timely and complete fulfillment of production tasks. To what extent the workers were willing and able to finish the assigned tasks was also the best measurement of the effectiveness of factory institutions.

As a historical study, the goal of this work is to reconstruct the realities of factory production and management in the Maoist era and compare them to worker experiences after Mao. My ultimate concern is to conduct a bottom-up inquiry into the dynamics, and their limitations, underlying the growth of China's industrial economy during the Maoist era and the logic behind China's transition from a planned economy to a market-based economy in the post-Mao era.

THE MAOIST PAST AS HISTORY

As I have argued elsewhere, a constant challenge to historians is how to reconcile between their shared commitment to objectivity in reconstructing the past and the inevitable subjectivity or personal preference in their selection of the object of investigation and the approach to interpreting it. Such preferences reflect more or less one's intellectual inclination and even ideological bias, which in turn have to do with the influences of the paradigm that prevails in a given discipline or field as well as the ethos of the society or age in which the researcher is situated (Li 2013). "Subjectivity" is particularly an issue in the studies of economic and political policies of Maoist China. During the height of the Cold War years in the 1950s and 1960s, ideological and geopolitical confrontations between capitalist and socialist countries led many in the West to characterize Maoist China as a totalitarian state and therefore repudiate its economic institutions and policies. The escalation of the Vietnam War and the rise of antiwar agitations in the United States in the late 1960s and 1970s, however, caused a growing number of leftist intellectuals to be critical of U.S. foreign policies and the underlying modernization theory and at the same time sympathetic to the nationalist and socialist movements in the non-Western world (Latham 2000; Gilman 2003). Maoist China, in this light, emerged as a model for the rest of the Third World for its impressive records in industrialization, elimination of epidemics and extreme poverty, promotion of public health and literacy, and improvement of women's status in the family and workplace by the late 1970s.[4] Nevertheless, the inception of "Reform and Opening Up" in post-Mao China, the liberalization of intellectual and political lives that culminated in the student protest movement of 1989 and its tragic ending, and finally the collapse of the Communist states in Russia and East Europe by the end of the Cold War period—all these developments contributed to the predominance of neoliberalism in Western countries and beyond in the post-Cold War era. Many in the West, therefore, attributed China's vigorous economic growth and prosperity in the reform era to the forces of the market and privatization;

in sharp contrast, their writings reduced the Maoist past and its legacies to nothing more than repeated failures and endless tragedies.

More recently, however, China's meteoric rise as a global manufacturing center and the quick improvement in the living standards of Chinese people since the turn of the twenty-first century have caused scholars to reexamine Maoist legacies. These include the central role of the socialist state in engineering China's phenomenal economic growth, and the impressive durability and adaptability of the state itself despite the Western media's repeated predictions of its coming collapse. Unlike the literature about Maoist China up to the 1990s, which had been largely a product of area studies conducted by scholars in social sciences, the new generation of scholarship on Maoist China since the 2000s has been primarily a result of the emerging discipline of the history of the People's Republic of China (PRC) as a subfield of modern Chinese history, and most of its contributors are historians rather than social scientists.[5] Furthermore, unlike the earlier scholarship, which tended to be policy studies by social scientists centering on aspects of the Maoist state's top-down process of policy-making, the new generation of scholarship has focused largely on the bottom-up process of history, that is, the events that actually took place at the local level or the experiences of the individuals who actually participated in those events. With the ideological confrontation of the Cold War era left far behind, it is more likely than ever before that researchers will put aside the highly polemic and ideologically charged controversies and focus on the objective reconstruction of the Maoist past as history. This study joins the recent efforts of historians to reexamine post-1949 China.

The biggest barrier to the objective study of Maoist China, therefore, is no longer so much about the influences of contemporary geopolitical concerns or ideological biases among the researchers as the problem of subjective preferences or biases found in the sources that inform their research. By and large, recent studies on this subject have relied on two types of sources, namely, government archives that have been recently declassified and made accessible to researchers, and oral histories narrated by those who lived through the Maoist era. Unlike the official publications (primarily newspapers at national, provincial, or local levels and the documents of the CCP) that have informed many of the earlier studies on Maoist China, government archives reveal much about the actual implementation of the state's policies at regional or local levels. But the archives have their own shortcomings. First, the scope of topics covered by the archives is usually limited, covering only the parts to which government policies were directly applied and focusing only on a select group of people who actively participated in the implementation of such policies, thus obscuring the experiences of ordinary people. Equally problematic are the reports by local government officials, as well as the confessions (or "self-examinations") by the targeted individuals of their "wrongdoing," which cover only the facts that were believed to prove the correctness of the policies and omit the aspects where the policies did not work. This study is no exception in using government archives. Much of its discussion about worker participation in factory governance draws on reports generated by the state-owned enterprises in Nanjing, currently preserved at Nanjing Municipal Archives. The problems with government archives previously discussed also exist in the records from this locality.

To complement, and offset the problems of, government archives, this study relies primarily on interviews with retirees from major industrial cities who worked in state-owned enterprises during the Maoist years. In 2012–2013, I collaborated with a team of researchers from different universities in China to interview a total of 97 retirees from different state-owned enterprises in Shanghai (19), Beijing (11), Jiangsu (14, mostly from Nanjing), Hubei (28, mostly from Wuhan), Zhejiang (5, all from Ningbo), Liaoning (5), Guangdong (3, all from Guangzhou), and other localities. Participants in this collaborative project are researchers, university faculty members, and graduate students from the institutions located in the aforementioned cities who selected the interviewees from their family members, relatives, friends, or acquaintances. The interviewees were identified to meet a basic requirement: having worked as regular, full-time workers or cadres in a state-owned enterprise between 1949 and 1976. Among the 97 interviewees, 39 were cadres at certain points during their careers in the state firms (5 factory heads, 7 workshop foremen, 11 group leaders, 1 party branch secretary, 1 trade union chair, 2 engineers, 3 technicians, 2 quality-controllers, 6 office clerks, and 1 teacher) and the rest were ordinary workers. They were employed in enterprises of different sectors (18 in machinery, 15 in textiles, 8 in metallurgy, 7 in electronics, 9 in petroleum, 4 in chemical industry, 4 in mining, 5 in construction, 5 in transportation, 6 in food processing, 3 in chemical fertilizer, 3 in tools, 2 in rubber, 1 in pharmacy, 1 in printing, 1 in plastic products, 1 in lighting, and

4 in various logistic services). The interview conducted with the 97 retirees was based on a standard questionnaire, consisting of 43 questions, that surveyed their personal experiences in factory production and political activities during different decades and specific movements. Each interview resulted in a written transcript varying from approximately three to ten thousand characters in length.

It should be noted that interviewing the retired workers and cadres in the early 2010s was very different from doing so decades earlier. Having just lived through the Maoist era and with vivid memories of factory life behind them, those who were interviewed by researchers from the West in the late 1970s and early 1980s, mostly in Hong Kong as emigrees or refugees, could certainly provide more accurate and detailed information about their personal experiences and observations of grassroots politics in urban China. However, what they told more likely reflected the most recent developments in their work units than those back in the 1950s, 1960s, or early 1970s, and their memories and judgments were necessarily tinted by the striking contrast between Hong Kong and mainland China in living conditions and sociocultural environments as well as by the propaganda of the reform-oriented state in the early 1980s, which underscored the myriad of problems with state firms in production and management in order to justify its reform agenda that departed from the Maoist past.

By contrast, interviewing the workers more than three and a half decades after the inception of the reform era has its own advantages and disadvantages. The disadvantage is that for many informants, now in their seventies or eighties, details about their factory experiences have faded from memory; it was also hard for some of them to specify the exact year or time range of certain events. Nevertheless, recollecting their factory life decades after the Mao era could also dilute the color caused by the sharp contrasts that shocked the interviewees who had just emigrated or escaped from China around the end of that era. What the more recent interviewees described is more likely about the entirety of their overall career as workers or cadres in the factories throughout the Maoist period rather than their experiences only in the last years of that period; their judgments could be more "well-rounded" than the testimonies of those newly arrived in Hong Kong decades ago. At the same time, however, the stark contrast between the Maoist era and the 2010s (i.e., decades after marketization and privatization of the industrial economy) in workers' social status and in their relations with enterprise management could also affect the informants' subjective reading of the past; from time to time, some of the interviewed retirees displayed a sense of nostalgia or strong aversion toward what they witnessed or lived through before the reform.

Added to the complexity of how to use the information provided by the interviewees of different backgrounds and experiences is the necessity and difficulty in distinguishing between the different years or periods of the Mao era or the different historical backgrounds to which the information refers. Many changes occurred to the economic organizations and grassroots politics in industrial firms throughout the three decades of the Maoist era as a result of the major shifts in the state's macroeconomic strategies and industrial policies. These shifts accounted for the recurrent alternations between the state's emphasis on material stimuli and prioritization of moral or political standards in incentivizing the workers, between its use of bottom-up initiatives and top-down implementation of regulations to boost productivity, and between its reliance on professional "expertise" (*zhuan*) and promotion of political "redness" (*hong*) in selecting the "activists" from among the rank and file for promotion or other rewards in state-owned enterprises. All these changes had an immediate impact on the everyday politics in state firms, thus causing the balance of power to tilt toward the rank and file at one time and toward the management at another. Therefore, when quoting our informants, this study will be as specific as possible on the backgrounds of the informants or any other individuals involved and the time period in which the events or phenomena being discussed took place, with an aim to make sense of factory politics under the state's different policy orientations at different times.

Nevertheless, many of our informants' comments do not specify a particular year or period. Instead, they described their experience of factory life in a general way. The value of such generalized observations should not be discounted. After all, there were some basic institutions in the state-owned enterprises that remained unchanged throughout the three decades of the Maoist era and essential to the formation of power relations in the industrial firms. These included: the standard three- or four-tiered hierarchy of production organization in a regular state-owned factory, which we will describe later; the state's definition of industrial workers as the "leading class" in society in its ideology and as the "masters" of the factory in relations to the cadres; regular workers' entitlement to lifetime employment and a full package of welfare benefits that was guaranteed by the state and out of the factory management's control; and the lack of periodical increases in their wage level and the use of seniority as the primary criterion in determining their eligibility for a raise when it did occur nationwide. These institutions were no doubt the most important factors in shaping the historical context of factory politics, in which the workers developed their self-consciousness and everyday strategies for interaction with the cadres and among themselves during the "normal" times of the Maoist era, especially the 1970s when the chaos of the Cultural Revolution was over and of which our informants' memories were the clearest in relation to the earlier periods. Therefore, wherever the years or the particular period is not specified, it is assumed in this study that our informants' comments generally refer to the 1970s and sometimes the Maoist era as a whole.

All in all, despite the exceptional richness of government archives and personal narratives in revealing the actual implementation of government policies and workers' everyday experiences in factory governance, it is necessary to caution against possible distortions in our examination of this process caused by the biases inherent to these two types of sources, including the highly selective and one-sided representation by factory cadres or government officials in line with state policies and the equally selective memories of the retirees that have changed over the past decades from being resentful to nostalgic of the Maoist past. To minimize such distortions, therefore, this study emphasizes the use of two analytical approaches: (1) to distinguish between the ideologized and highly formalist representation of the official institutions in factory governance on the one hand and the substantive approach to factory governance as seen in the actual functions and efficacy of these institutions on the other; and (2) to distinguish between the formal institutions that shaped the official framework of factory governance and the informal institutions that created the social context in which the formal institutions operated. Let us begin with a discussion of the first approach and its application to our analysis.

SUBSTANTIVE GOVERNANCE UNDER SOCIALISM

A standard but complex set of systems existed in all state-owned factories throughout Maoist China that defined the rights and duties of individual workers, ranging from regulations about their employment, classification of personal background and standing, and entitlement to welfare benefits offered by the factory, to requirements of their performance in day-to-day production and involvement in various events and organizations at different levels. Ideology played a key role in the state's formulation and justification of the purposes of these systems and regulations. In a fashion of "high modernism" (Scott 1998, 87–102) commonly found in the ideologies of authoritarian states, Maoist China embraced the goals of industrializing the nation on a larger scale and at a faster pace than its capitalist counterparts, building an egalitarian society by eliminating inequality and hierarchy between different classes, and making the socialist state more democratic than its capitalist rivals by encouraging the laboring people to participate in the management of factories and the entire country. It was on the basis of Maoist ideology that the state developed its factory system, such as the classification of workers into various categories ranging from the ordinary "masses" (*qunzhong*), the more desirable "Advanced Producers" (*xianjin shengchanzhe*) or other honorary titles, and the politically reliable "party members" (*dangyuan*), to the undesirable "backward elements" (*luohou fenzi*), "bad elements" (*huai fenzi*), or "elements of the Four Categories" (*silei fenzi*, namely, landlords, rich peasants, counterrevolutionaries, and bad elements; expanded to "Five Categories" to include rightists after 1957). It was also based on Maoist ideology that the workers were required to attend daily sessions of political study, join the labor union, elect their representatives to the SWC, participate in factory management and technological innovations, and fight bureaucratism by appealing to government authorities. Maoist China, in a word, was no different from other "totalitarian" states in its heavy reliance on an ideology to legitimize its apparatus at every level and its programs of social transformation. Not surprisingly, for decades since the founding of the PRC in 1949, much of the debates among researchers and policymakers in China and beyond about factory management of the Maoist era have centered on the questions of whether or not, and to what extent, the workers were able to exercise their "democratic rights" versus succumb to the arbitrary leadership and abuse of power by factory cadres.

But the importance of ideology in the formation and operation of the factory system should not be overstated. By centering on an analysis of worker participation in everyday production and management, this study demonstrates a striking disjunction between the ideological goals of factory institutions and their instrumental functions in actual practice. To put it bluntly, the Maoist ideology lost a lot of its original purpose and meaning as a theoretical guide for action in the Communist revolution or socialist construction as it was designed; in its everyday application, this ideology became nothing more than a convenient tool for the factory to regulate production and discipline the workers. Key to understanding this disconnect is an understanding of the functional versatility of the Maoist ideology. In his monumental work *Ideology and Organization in Communist China* (1968), Franz Schurmann distinguished between what he termed "pure ideology," or a set of ideas to guide one's formation of a unified worldview, such as the doctrines of Marxism and Leninism, and "practical ideology," or a set of ideas to guide one's actions in the real world, such as the "Mao Zedong Thought," which was derived from connecting pure Marxist and Leninist ideology to the Chinese revolution (22–34). In its actual application to the realities of factory governance in the Maoist era, however, not only did the pure ideology of Marxism and Leninism lose much of its relevance to workers' daily experiences, but Mao Zedong Thought as the party-state's practical ideology also failed to function as it was originally designed. Rather than a set of rich and sophisticated ideas derived from the experiences of the Communist revolution, when relating to the daily practice of factory governance, Maoist teachings were reduced to a set of quotations completely detached from their original contexts. Ideological indoctrination became nothing more than the daily routines of reciting Mao's quotations or reading party documents based on Mao's instructions.

Nevertheless, through the repeated sessions of political study and after years of recurrent political campaigns, workers did indeed grow a collective consciousness about who they were, how to distinguish between "us" and "others," what the "correct" ways were to speak and behave, and what was "wrong" and how to avoid it. In other words, the party's ideology, even though it deviated from its original context and lost much of its intended meaning, firmly established its "hegemony," to borrow from Antonio Gramsci (1976, 328), in Chinese society and came to shape the political consciousness and everyday expressions of factory workers as individuals or as a group. It was in the language of the party's ideology that different groups of people were identified and classified; this highly ideological language further defined power relations among these groups and fashioned their everyday operation. Ideology, in the final analysis, functioned merely as a practical instrument for labor control. It generated a pervasive discourse characteristic of the Maoist society that separated its real-world functions from ideological ends but worked effectively to mediate the complex relations among the state, cadres, and ordinary workers. This is clearly seen in the discussion of various factory institutions in the following chapters.

Chapter 1 examines the day-to-day operation of various factory systems and practices in shaping workers' identity and status. Unlike the conventional wisdom that interprets the state's stress on ideological goals as the very end of the party's state-making efforts, this chapter reveals the use of ideology or its conversion into a workplace discourse as a pragmatic means to discipline the labor force. Thus, while the Maoist teaching was used to justify the classification and labeling of factory workers based on their family origins, in actuality, this chapter argues, such groupings functioned only to cultivate the workers' consciousness of self-discipline and compliance with the state's institutions of social control. Much of the same can be said about the effects of political study sessions. While ideological consideration seemingly served as a key factor in identifying workers for the political rewards of party membership or other honorary titles, this system of moral incentives turned out to be more cost-effective than material stimuli in motivating the workers and mitigating popular resentment during times of severe economic shortage.

Chapter 2 further investigates the institutions for worker participation in factory management, including the SWC, the trade union, and the appeal system. Contrary to the state's ideological definition of these institutions as tools for workers to exercise their rights or as channels to promote democracy in factory management, workers found few chances to participate in their factory's decision-making process by those means. The conventional wisdom about the perfunctoriness and ineffectiveness of these institutions in promoting "democratic management" in the factories thus was valid in this sense. Nevertheless, through an in-depth examination of their day-to-day operations, this chapter argues that these institutions operated to serve a wide array of practical purposes that have been largely overlooked in past studies. They turned out to be quite effective and indeed indispensable ways for workers to express practical needs for improved conditions of production and livelihood as well as to vent their discontent against irresponsible and abusive cadres. Government authorities and factory leaders also allowed, and sometimes encouraged, workers to use these channels, and leaders frequently satisfied worker demands in order to assuage disgruntlement and keep the labor force in good spirits. None of these demands had to do with the workers' role as the masters of the enterprise or with democracy in factory management, but they did satisfy day-to-day needs in the workplace and beyond.

The Maoist approach to labor management and factory governance thus was pragmatic and substantive in nature. For the socialist state, the most important goal in running the factories was ensuring their smooth operation. For that end, it had to keep the labor force disciplined in the most cost-effective way, that is, to rely on the means of moral and political incentives while reducing the use of material rewards. At the same time, it also had to satisfy workers' reasonable demands to ensure that their subsistence needs were met and that they performed their production tasks as expected. Despite its commitment to workers' rights as factory masters and democracy at the grassroots level, the state had to rely on experienced cadres and engineers to effectively manage the state-owned factories while limiting the scope of workers' participation in management to avoid chaos and inefficiency in production, a lesson it learned repeatedly from the Great Leap Forward and the Cultural Revolution. For the Maoist state, the practical needs of factory production were more important than its ideological claims. In fact, in most of the Maoist era, the state had to use its fractured ideology to serve its goals of production rather than the reverse.

The key to understanding the prevalence of substantive governance in Chinese industry lies in a profound contradiction that was inherent to the Maoist state, namely the incompatibility between its ideology that had bolstered its rise to power and its new mission of industrialization after it came to power. The Maoist state was in essence a mobilizational one. It won the civil war against the Nationalist regime by appealing to the masses in rural and urban China. Central to its mobilization was the making and popularization of a revolutionary ideology that promised economic and political liberation of the peasantry and the working class. Therefore, after the founding of the PRC in 1949, the Maoist state defined itself as a government based on the alliance between peasants and workers, with the latter as the leading class in society. It was this ideology that led the Chinese Communist Party (CCP) to designate industrial workers as the factory masters who supposedly had the innate right to participate in enterprise management; this same ideology drove some of the idealistic policymakers to promote democracy in factory management. Nevertheless, the most important and challenging task for the socialist state after 1949 was economic reconstruction, central to which was the quick recovery of the devastated industry in the cities. After the completion of economic recovery in 1952, the state faced the even more urgent and daunting task of full-scale industrialization, which required the institutionalization and bureaucratization of the state apparatus to run the increasingly complex and ever-expanding economy and society.[6] Thus, throughout the decades under Mao, the Communist state struggled to strike a balance between its commitment to the revolutionary ideology and its need to institutionalize. From time to time, this balance tilted to the former, resulting in radicalism against the privileged elites; but most of the Maoist era maintained a delicate balance, tolerating the hierarchy and inequalities in the socialist society. Not surprisingly, in the day-to-day management of state-owned factories, experienced cadres and technical experts dominated; worker participation and workshop democracy were greatly curtailed or nonexistent.

THE WORK-UNIT EQUILIBRIUM AND WORKER PERFORMANCE

Aside from the differences between their ideological representation and instrumental utilities, to understand the operational realities of factory institutions, we should further distinguish the formal, official institutions from informal and unofficial practices that were usually invisible yet indispensable in shaping the social context in which the formal institutions functioned. It was the interaction between these formal and informal institutions, I shall argue, that generated a low-level equilibrium in the political and economic relations in state-owned factories, which worked to maintain industrial production during the Maoist era. Rapid industrial growth, in other words, was not merely a result of the Maoist state's macroeconomic strategizing, as numerous studies have demonstrated in the past, but also had to do with the functioning of the complex and nuanced microeconomic mechanisms on the shop floor, an element that has been largely overlooked in previous scholarship about the Chinese economy under Mao.

The term "formal institutions" here refers to a wide range of official systems and policies that were universally implemented in every factory in Maoist China. By and large, there were two sets of such formal institutions.

One set was administrative and political, including: (1) the management personnel of a factory, ranging from the party secretary and factory director at the top, to workshop directors in the middle, and production group leaders at the bottom; (2) political organizations that had their branches and members in the factory, namely the CCP and the Communist Youth League; (3) organizations open to worker participation, namely the SWC and the trade union; (4) the appeal system, also known as the system of people's letters and visits; and (5) the daily, weekly, or periodic sessions of political study. The other set concerned factory production and labor management, including: (1) permanent employment for the vast majority of factory workers; (2) their entitlement to a full range of welfare benefits, ranging from maternity leave, childcare, children's education, and hospitalization to housing, food and grocery supplies, weekend or holiday activities, and retirement pensions; (3) rules and regulations on workers' duties and performance in production; (4) regulations on workers' relocation, change of jobs, and so forth; (5) the wage system, including the regulations about wage grades, eligibilities for wage upgrading, and the criteria in using time-rate or piece-rate systems; and (6) regulations about the selection of workers for honorary titles and rewards, etc.

"Informal institutions," on the other hand, refers to practices and relations in the workplace that were not prescribed in official regulations yet remained prevalent in and outside the factory to condition the functioning of the formal institutions. Some of them deviated significantly from, and even ran counter to, state ideology or factory regulations, such as the practices of favoritism, nepotism, patron-client ties, or personal connections (*guanxi*) that have been covered well in past studies on industrial organizations and the party-state in Maoist China (Walder 1986; Yang 1994; Lü 2000a). However, the range of informal institutions to examine in this study is much broader; it covers the informal or invisible institutions that directly influenced the operation of the formal institutions and includes workers' identity or self-perception about who they were and how they were related to the factory and all others at the workplace; personal relations between cadres of different levels and the rank and file in the factory; work norms or shared expectations among the workers about what constituted an acceptable job in production; cultural values and customs that the workers had learned in their growth to adulthood; and social networks that the workers developed in and outside the factory.

This study scrutinizes the operation of industrial organizations in Maoist China by taking into account both the formal and informal institutions outlined here. It postulates that the formal and informal institutions interacted to form a social milieu in which factory workers chose an action that best served their interests when participating in everyday production and dealing with people around them. The picture of industrial production and factory politics in post-1949 China that emerges from this perspective thus differs from the conventional wisdom that accentuates inefficiency in production and worker dependency on cadres. My findings also disagree with a neoliberal assumption that sees China's industrial economy under Mao as a "failure" and attributes this to the lack of incentives motivating the labor force (Lin et al. 2003; Wu 2009; Coase and Wang 2012).

Chapter 3 examines everyday power relations in industrial factories. Instead of focusing on the obvious formal institutions, this chapter emphasizes the various informal institutions that worked to constrain both workers and cadres. Recruited from the rank and file, most of the grassroots cadres, including production group leaders and workshop directors, held power and influence over the workers not only because of their appointments by the superiors but, more importantly, due to workers' recognition of their leadership and capabilities. To effectively perform their duties as managers and supervisors, as well as to ensure the timely completion of routine production tasks, cadres of different levels had to win over workers' respect in order to gain their voluntary cooperation in the workplace, unlike the managers of private firms of the post-Mao era, who could enforce work discipline by firing a slacking worker. While the cadres were always in a position to protect a select group of workers who showed personal loyalty to them, they had to avoid flagrant favoritism and subsequent damage to their reputation among the workers. This was especially true during the recurrent political campaigns that invariably targeted any misconduct of the cadres. The workers, for their part, normally showed no hesitation to confront a wrongdoing cadre and defend themselves for two basic reasons. First, they did not have to worry about losing anything key to their livelihood in the Maoist era because of their right to permanent employment and guaranteed entitlement to the factory's welfare benefits. Second, and more important, workers enjoyed a particular discursive and psychological advantage over the cadres in the Maoist era, when the party-state's ideology designated the workers as the leading class of the country with the innate power to supervise the corruptible cadres through political campaigns as well as the routine mechanisms of appeal to superior authorities. Thus, rather than the one-sided dependence of workers on cadres, as the conventional wisdom has suggested, this chapter reveals an equilibrium in cadre-worker relations. The workers interacted with the cadres on an equal footing by and large, and they were definitely more powerful in relation to the cadres than past studies have suggested.

Chapter 4 turns to workers' everyday experiences in production. It challenges the received wisdom that worker performance in Chinese factories under Mao was plagued with the problems of widespread shirking and perennial inefficiency because of the egalitarian wage system, which minimized income differentiation among the workers, and further because of the policy of permanent employment, which prevented factory leaders from firing workers due to poor performance. Without denying the existence of shirking as a problem in poorly managed factories and during times of disorder, this chapter underscores the role of work norms in shaping workers' everyday performance on the shop floor. Work norms, I shall argue, were not merely the result of enforced disciplines and cadres' on-site supervision, nor were they just the workers' response to the pressure of political campaigns that forced them to conform or to the incentives of spiritual rewards that motivated them to work hard. This chapter highlights the role a set of informal factors played in shaping the work norms, including workers' self-consciousness of their personal position in relation to those outside the state-owned factories, identification with their work units, and peer pressure from co-workers. The interaction between the formal and informal elements, this chapter suggests, shaped workers' perception of their workplace, defined what they thought to be a decent job, and formed their subsequent attitudes toward routine tasks. Under normal circumstances, neither flagrant shirking nor utmost diligence was a wise choice for the majority of workers; instead, the best strategy was to avoid being alienated by their peers or censured by the cadre, so they conformed to what they believed to be the proper way or acceptable level in performing their daily tasks—hence the prevalence of an equilibrium in everyday production. Rather than a sign of "innocence" or "simplicity," as many of our interviewees believed when talking about their commitment to the factory in the Maoist era, what dictated their performance in the workplace, I shall argue, was a shared disposition, or habitus, to borrow from

Pierre Bourdieu (1976; 1977, 72, 80), among the workers that was conditioned by their self-perception as a privileged group as well as their awareness of the objective environment in which they worked. The workers in Maoist factories were indeed rational actors who prioritized their self-interest over anything else, but they pursued this self-interest by taking full consideration of the social context and forming the best strategy of action.

A dual equilibrium thus prevailed in labor management and power relations in state-owned enterprises during the Maoist era. Far from passive and apathetic in production, or submissive and powerless in relation to the cadres, the workers were strategic and calculating when pursuing their interests as individuals or as a group by taking into account all formal and informal factors within their economic and sociopolitical universe. Without having to seek personal protection or favor from supervisors, most workers chose to keep what they thought to be a "normal" relationship with those in power, as their employment and livelihood were secured by the state; they would not hesitate to defend themselves by turning to the readily available means of appeal, formal or informal, when suffering unfair treatment at the workplace. An overall symmetry thus characterized the power relations between labor and management. In their everyday production activities, likewise, most workers habitually chose to do what they believed to be a "decent" job that met the expectations of those around them. Their criteria for being "normal" or "decent" certainly changed over time and from factory to factory, varying from strict compliance with official regulations and requirements to open defiance, depending on how the formal and informal institutions interplayed to shape the workers' shared attitudes and expectations. Usually, however, being "normal" meant maintaining a stable working relationship with those above them and delivering the timely and full completion of production tasks as scheduled. Both the cadres and the workers were subject to a set of shared dispositions that functioned to motivate as well as constrain them. The dual equilibrium in the workplace, more than any other factor, enabled the necessary degree of efficiency in production at the micro level, which accounted in large measure for the impressive growth of China's industrial output: at the rate of 9.4 percent per year between 1953 and 1978, if both the state-owned and collectively owned sectors are included (Guojia tongjiju 1987, 36), or 12 percent a year during the same period for the state sector only (Guojia tongjiju 2005, 63–64).

But the dual equilibrium in labor relations and power politics was fragile. Underlying it was a set of economic and social institutions that bespoke inequality and division within the factories and threatened to undermine the status quo. Chapter 5 shows that, despite its rhetorical commitment to social equality and the well-being of the laboring people, the Maoist state pursued a policy in the 1950s and the first half of the 1960s that resulted in a striking differentiation between social classes and between different groups within the working class in particular. Not surprisingly, the most conspicuous phenomenon in the factories at the beginning of the Cultural Revolution was the agitation of radical workers, who demanded higher wages. Temporary and contract workers who had been marginalized also joined the rebels to demand the conversion of their status into permanent workers, despite the state's quick suppression and condemnation of these requests as the "wind of economism." The Cultural Revolution itself had a huge impact on the existing equilibrium in the workplace. Most of the cadres at the factory or workshop level lost their positions due to seizure of power by radical workers, who came to control their factory and thus became its masters in a real sense during the first few years of the Cultural Revolution. The existing regulations in the workplace also lost their effectiveness in constraining the labor force when the workers were divided into different factions and when their violent confrontations caused chaos and disrupted production. Nevertheless, as the turmoil of radicalism subsided in the early 1970s, the dual equilibrium was gradually restored over the rest of the Maoist era, as a result of the rehabilitation of senior cadres, the marginalization and eventual expulsion of the most active rebels from the reestablished factory leadership, the recovery of the SWC and the trade union, the enforcement of working disciplines, and the restoration of all other factory institutions that had been paralyzed during the height of the Cultural Revolution. As the number of informal workers increased steadily throughout the 1970s, their gap with formal workers widened, despite the state's efforts to absorb most contract workers into the regular labor force in 1971 and 1972. In the final analysis, what really mattered to the Maoist state was not the party's ideological commitments but its practical concern with industrial productivity, which was key to its viability, and, for that end, maintaining the dual equilibrium in the workplace.

It is worth emphasizing that the existence of this equilibrium was based on the insulation and stability of the work unit (*danwei*)—that is, a factory or a workshop—as a microeconomic entity bolstered by a series of institutional links. Each of these links was indispensable for the existence and functioning of the equilibrium; the malfunctioning or disappearance of any of these links would necessarily cause the equilibrium's damage and eventual collapse. Among these links are the following:

- The enterprise existed only as a "factory" of the state, subject to the state's centralized planning of every aspect of its operation, without being affected by any factors that made up a "market" and without "competition" from any other enterprises.
- Workers' employment in a factory was permanent; the factory management had no right to fire any of them, and at the same time the workers also lost the freedom to exit the factory and choose a job on their own.
- The recurrent political campaigns and the regularly repeated study sessions, together with other means of identity-building, generated a constant pressure for all individuals in a factory to comply with its work disciplines.
- Workers received a wage that was low by the standard of the post-Mao era but higher than the contemporary wage level for cohorts of comparable age outside state-owned factories.
- Workers had an all-inclusive welfare program that guaranteed their livelihood; this was also better than the benefits for workers outside state-owned enterprises.
- Employment opportunities at state-owned enterprises were limited, and getting into these firms was competitive.
- Workers in state-owned enterprises enjoyed a superior social standing compared to laborers in other economic sectors.
- The bonuses that the workers received in certain Maoist years served primarily as supplements to their wage income and were not linked with their performance in production.
- Workers had no opportunities to earn extra income outside their work unit.
- Honorary titles were the major or even the only incentives for workers who performed extraordinarily well in production.
- Upgrading workers' wage levels was based on government regulations. The factory management had no autonomy in making its own policy in this regard.

- The allocation of the essential "commodities" for livelihood, especially housing, clothing, and staple foods, were primarily based on workers' family size and the state's ration policies; factory cadres had little or no room to exercise their discretion.

These factors worked together to form a sealed and isolated "ecosystem" in which the equilibrium prevailed. Entitled to a full range of rights and privileges unavailable to the working population outside the system, hailed as the leading class in the socialist society, and shielded by various means, formal or informal, against possible cadre abuse, the workers had good reason to assume themselves the masters of the place where they labored every day. Few felt the need to seek particular favor from the cadres above them; when they encountered unfair treatment, they did not hesitate to speak out and fight back. On the other hand, unable to change their job, the workers had to count on the work unit for nearly all subsistence needs. Their perceived and imagined masterhood within a work unit was thus inextricably linked to a complete dependence on it. This paradox of being the master yet in bondage explains in large measure worker performance in factory production and attitudes toward workplace politics. While they saw no reason to show personal loyalty to a particular cadre, the workers' dependence on the work unit nevertheless led them to strongly identify with it, which in turn generated group solidarity among the workers within the unit. Given the tenuous link between labor and reward in production, they saw no reason to work exceptionally hard, but they did care about personal standing within their unit or group and therefore avoided conspicuous shirking and the resultant group sanctioning. For both cadres and workers, the best strategy for being a "normal person" (*zhengchang ren*) or to "live a normal life" (*guo zhengchang rizi*) was to do what they were supposed to do and avoid mistakes. How the workers performed in production and dealt with cadres depended on the extent to which the work unit was insulated and the equilibrium remained in place. They would choose to do a decent job as long as the ecosystem remained tightly sealed, and they would prefer shirking or exiting the ecosystem when the latter began to crack and collapse in the end, which eventually did happen in the post-Mao years.

THE FATE OF CHINESE WORKERS IN THE POST-MAO ERA

To show how the dual equilibrium yielded to a new dynamic in labor relations and factory politics in post-Mao China, Chapter 6 explores Chinese industrial workers' experiences in enterprise reforms under the leadership of Deng Xiaoping and his successors in the 1980s through the 2000s. This chapter shows that each of the links that sustained the equilibrium suffered severe damages or collapsed one after another over the course of the reforms that led to the privatization of most state-owned enterprises. Faced with competition from the emerging rural township and village enterprises and foreign or joint investments, most state-owned enterprises witnessed loss of profitability in the 1980s, which, together with the state's worsening fiscal situation, triggered a series of reforms that destroyed those links and the equilibrium they bolstered: the introduction of the contracted responsibility system that greatly increased factory leaders' power in labor management; the wide use of bonuses to incentivize workers when many of them were attracted to money-making opportunities outside the factory; the conversion of all workers from permanent to contract employees with fixed terms of employment; and finally bankruptcy and privatization of most state firms or their transformation into shareholding corporations in the late 1990s. Workers' self-perception underwent huge changes during this course, from the proud "masters" of factories with a secured livelihood, superior social standing, and strong identity with their work unit, to contract workers vulnerable to management's abuses, or laid-off individuals living on subsidies and suffering the mental impact of marginalization. Gone was their identity with the workplace, together with the loss of group solidarity, peer pressure, and political pressure to conform. As a result, shirking and declining productivity became severe problems in many state firms before they were privatized. After privatization, the workers became nothing more than wage laborers who earned more than before but at the cost of their job security and commitment to the workplace.

Equally noticeable was the disappearance of the equilibrium in power relations between factory cadres and workers. Gone was the workers' political superiority as the leading class of society and as the masters of the factory, together with the cadres' dependence on workers' collaboration for timely fulfillment of production tasks. In the 1980s and 1990s, favoritism and clientelist ties became rampant among the cadres in state firms undergoing enterprise reforms that greatly increased their power in employment and labor remuneration. After the privatization of most state firms, the relationship between enterprise managers and workers was simplified into that between bosses and employees. The institutional tools that the workers had used to express their grievances and address injustice in the workplace lost much of their functionality or did not exist at all; in their stead was the establishment of the new governing bodies in privatized firms, in which the ordinary employees were marginalized.

Needless to say, workers responded to enterprise reforms with resistance, as many studies have documented.[7] Of particular interest here is how the legacies of worker participation in the Maoist era influenced the employees of the post-Mao era in articulating themselves and choosing their actions. Chapter 6 underscores two features of worker activism in the restructuring of state firms in the 1990s and early 2000s. One is the workers' use of the Maoist discourse equating workers with the masters of their factories to justify their actions against the corporatization, merging, or outright selling of their factories when these changes failed to meet their expectations for compensation and reemployment. Nostalgic for the old days before the reform, workers felt disgruntled over the dire situation they encountered after the waves of massive layoffs. Their protests ranged from petitions to the government and traffic obstruction to occupying factory buildings and beating up the managers of the companies that now owned their factories. Behind their resistance was the workers' shared belief in their right to subsistence that was inextricably linked to the factory where they had worked for years or decades. No matter how morally justified, however, worker protests invariably ended in their yielding to the logic of the market economy and acceptance of their new fate as the master of their own labor only. The other feature of worker resistance in connection with Maoist heritage is the workers' use of the SWC to build consensus and legalize their actions. It was typically through the SWC that the workers vetoed the management's plan to sell all or part of the factory or demanded full compensation or reemployment opportunities. For the first and last time, the SWC did indeed function as a critical organ in making decisions with and for the workers themselves. Unfortunately, the SWC soon yielded to the shareholders' meeting as the decision making organ for restructured enterprises, in which ordinary employees had no say at all.

As striking as the passing of the Maoist generation of industrial workers was the rise of a new type of labor force in China's industries, namely rural migrant workers, which has quickly come to dominate the manufacturing sectors since the late 1990s. After decades of massive flow into the cities, migrant workers have seen drastic changes in their own rank and abilities. Unlike the first generation of the 1980s and early 1990s, who worked only temporarily in the cities and therefore tended to tolerate the harsh working conditions and minimal wages as long as they earned more in the factory than in the countryside, the second generation of migrant workers, mostly born after 1980 and with a better education, has shown a stronger willingness to integrate into the cities where they work and live. And unlike the workers of state-owned enterprises, whose resistance to enterprise reforms centered on better treatment by the existing or new employers, the migrant workers since the late 1990s have struggled for equal treatment with their urban counterparts, particularly in wages, working conditions, healthcare, social security, retirement, residential status, and their children's education. Most of such grievances targeted foreign or private firms, where migrant workers were largely concentrated and abuses at the workplace were severe.

Gone was the Maoist legacy of substantive governance in these firms; workers could no longer use the trade union or the SWC as effective tools to address problems concerning their working or living conditions, for the trade union did not exist in most private and foreign firms. Where it did exist, the trade union was subject to the firm owner's control, thus tending to side with the management rather than representing the workers when a dispute arose between the two sides. Interestingly, the higher the level of the trade union above the firms, the more likely it was to act autonomously in relation to the enterprise involved. This meant that in many cases the union intervened in favor of workers, even helping them establish their own trade union or reelect union leaders. The conflicting roles of the multilayered trade union system reflect the party-state's dilemma in managing labor relations throughout the reform era: While encouraging and protecting foreign or private investments for the sake of economic prosperity and tax revenue, the post-Mao state was also committed to rebuilding its legitimacy by reinventing the Maoist heritage of worker participation in factory governance.

All in all, Chinese workers underwent a profound transformation in their relations with the workplace during the enterprise reform of the 1990s and 2000s. Before the reform, they were exalted as the masters of the factory and privileged with a full range of rights and benefits. The institutions intended for their participation in factory governance were functional and substantive to the extent that they were indeed able to address their concerns with working and living conditions through these channels. But their status as the most privileged group of the entire labor force in Maoist China came with the loss of freedom to choose their employment and negotiate for higher wages. Working for a state-run firm in Maoist China meant at once empowerment and deprivation. After the reform, workers became free in many ways: They could migrate anywhere for a new job and could quit a job they disliked, and indeed they changed their employers frequently. But their freedom came with a loss of job security and protection at the workplace. As the master of their own labor only, the new generation of the working class in private or restructured state firms continued to live in a state of bondage, entrapped in dire distress of low pay, long hours, and harsh working environments, and denied access to formal, independent organizations to effectively represent them. A new equilibrium in labor relations will not come into place until the migrant workers, as the major labor force in China's industry today, are entitled to a full range of legal protections, which would enable them not only to sell their labor freely but also to sell it for a good price and on their own terms.

1 | THE MAKING OF THE MASTERS

Disciplining Workers through Identity Building

THE WORKERS OF STATE-OWNED enterprises were the most privileged among the entire working population in urban and rural China during the Maoist era. Once recruited into a state firm, a worker was guaranteed a permanent job that would last until retirement; unless the worker was convicted of a crime and incarcerated, they would never be fired no matter how dissatisfactory their performance was in everyday production, and furthermore, a criminal was still allowed to return to their original unit after being released from prison (Whyte and Parish 1984, 33; Wemheuer 2019: 17, 241–242; Andreas 2019, 57). The workers' wages were low and remained largely unchanged in most of the Mao era, to be sure. Nevertheless, their work unit provided them with almost all the necessary resources and services to accommodate their subsistence needs, including dormitories or other forms of housing that came with only a nominal rent, free healthcare and hospitalization, free education for their children in public schools or schools run by their own work unit, free provision of groceries during holidays or other occasions, free tickets to movie theaters, free tours and other events organized by their work unit's trade union, and, most importantly, a guaranteed pension plan for all retirees. So complete and generous was the benefits package for the formal workers of state firms that it has been properly termed "state paternalism" (e.g., Walder 1986, 248; Unger and Chan 2007; Lee 2007a, 15, 38). In return, however, the socialist state expected the workers to perform well, demonstrate their commitment to the work unit, and be loyal to the state itself.

The materialization of the mutual obligations between a state firm and its workers, or the so-called "socialist social contract" (Tang and Parish 2000, 3; Lee 2007a, 12, 15, 34–68), however, rested on the state's effective cultivation of workers' identity with the workplace. Instead of relying on administrative coercion and material incentives, as seen in contemporary Soviet Union and other Communist states, the Maoist approach to disciplining factory workers was rather "soft" or introspective, centering on the promotion of workers' self-consciousness as the ruling class of the country and as the masters of their factories. This chapter scrutinizes four devices that functioned to form and enhance the workers' identity and status in the factory and beyond: the classification of all individuals into certain categories for the creation of a new hierarchy in society; political study sessions routinely attended by all workers; the recruitment of workers into the party; and the selection of motivated workers as role models or activists and their promotion to cadre positions. While ideologically driven, all these institutions and practices worked to serve the state's practical goal of controlling the labor force.

WHO ARE THE MASTERS, AND WHO ARE NOT?
The Masters

Not all industrial workers could be called the "masters" (*zhurenweng*) in Maoist China. From the 1950s through the 1970s, the labor force was made up of people from various backgrounds whose economic, social, and political standings varied from factory to factory and from person to person. Those who proudly claimed themselves the masters of the workplace were primarily the full-time regular employees of state firms, whose number grew from 15.8 million in 1952 and 22.49 million in 1957 to 42.11 million in 1960 during the peak of the three-year Great Leap Forward (GLF) campaign (1958–1961); this decreased to 30.74 million in 1963 as a result of the post-Leap economic adjustment, and then mounted steadily to 62.78 million by 1978, the last year of the Maoist era (Guojia tongjiju 1983, 123; 1987, 33). As registered urban residents, once recruited into a state-owned factory, these workers were guaranteed a permanent job. They were paid a monthly wage according to age of employment and corresponding wage scales set by the state's universal policy. They were entitled to a full range of fringe benefits provided by their work units, including housing, healthcare, retirement pension, maternity leave, childcare, and children's education. And by the state's policies, as members of the factory's labor union, they had the right to vote in the election of factory leaders and make decisions pertaining to the factory's production and their personal well-being. In other words, they were enfranchised; their rights and standings in the factory resemble what is known as "industrial citizenship" that prevailed in postwar industrial societies (Fudge 2005; McCallum 2006; Andreas 2019).

To a lesser degree, full-time workers with urban residential status in factories under "collective ownership" (*jiti suoyou*) could also be called the masters of their own work units. Unlike state-owned factories whose procurement of raw materials, production, and allocation of manufactured goods, as well as recruitment and remuneration of workers, were subject to the state's centralized and unified planning, these factories were established and operated by a street residential committee (hence called a *xiaojiti* or "small collective") or by a local municipal or district government (thus called a *dajiti* or "big collective"). There were about 6.5 million such workers in 1957, 10 million in 1963, and 22.7 million in 1979 (Guojia tongjiju 1983, 123, 134). Depending on its the size, ownership level, and profitability, a collective paid its workers on a wage scale that differed from factory to factory but was in general lower than that of a state-owned enterprise. Welfare benefits also varied remarkably in different collectives but again were less generous than those of a state firm. As these collectives were subject to frequent restructuring and even shutdowns, employment was rarely permanent and secure. Workers in these firms also participated in trade unions and other mass organizations, if their firm was large enough, but compared to their counterparts in state firms, their voices were overall much weaker or nonexistent in factory governance due to the greater decision-making power vested in local government authorities or factory leaders.

Depending on their political performance, the formal workers of state or collective firms can be grouped into three categories. The first is those who were active in political events and/or superior in production, hence known as "activists" (*jijifenzi*). Small in number, they were likely to be admitted into the party, promoted to the rank of cadres, or awarded with various honorary titles such as "Model Laborers," "Advanced Producers," or "March 8th red banner bearers" (for females only). The second is ordinary workers, who constituted the majority of the labor force and did an average job in production. They had membership in the trade union of their own work unit and attended the SWC and other political activities that were open to all workers, but they rarely spoke out. The last group was no different from the second except for their poor performance in production or political events. They were likely to be censured or punished by the cadres for frequent failure to perform production tasks or recurrent violations of factory policies, hence known as the "backward elements" (*luohou fenzi*). Counting on their status as the formal employees (i.e., the masters) of the factory, however, they could also be pugnacious in defending their interests and among the first to confront the cadres whom they hated. Therefore, some of them were also known as the "toughs" or troublemakers in the workplace.

The Marginalized
Aside from the full-time regular workers with an urban residential status, both state-owned and collective firms hired a large number of informal workers, including "contract workers" (*hetonggong*) with a fixed term of employment that ranged from several months to years, and "temporary workers" (*linshigong*) whose employment lasted for only a short period (up to a few months). Before the installation of a nationwide household registration system in January 1958, each year as many as two to four million rural residents migrated into the neighboring cities to look for employment opportunities in the early to mid-1950s. The enforcement of the household registration system effectively stalled the "blind inflow" of population into the cities, by controlling the grain market and linking the provision of grain rations with one's urban residential status. But the launch of the Great Leap Forward in May 1958 and the accompanying measures of decentralization in economic planning resulted in the mushrooming of new industrial enterprises throughout the provinces, leading to a skyrocketing number of newly hired workers, mostly from rural areas. The total number of informal workers, therefore, reached 11.78 million in 1958, mostly concentrated in construction and mining (55 percent) as well as manufacturing (29.5 percent). The unprecedented burden of supporting the enlarged urban population

caused the government to prohibit hiring new workers from rural areas in 1959 and 1960, and a total of twenty million workers would be laid off in the next two years, mostly contract or temporary workers who had to return to their home villages. After 1963, when China had economically recovered from the damages caused by the Great Leap Forward, new investments in industrial projects again expanded labor force. Under the state's policy of "hiring more of temporary workers and fewer of permanent workers," the number of informal workers in state firms increased from 2.5 million in 1963 to 5.1 million in 1965, 6.66 million in 1970, and 11.73 million (or 15.7 percent of the entire labor force in state-owned enterprises) in 1978 (Guojia tongjiju 1987, 26–27, 33; Lin Chaochao 2014).

Informal workers were second-class citizens in state-owned enterprises. Their annual wage averaged 462.6 yuan per person in 1959, or 88 percent of what regular workers made. During the three years prior to the Cultural Revolution, their annual wage steadily declined, from 563 yuan in 1963 to 475 yuan in 1964 and 403 yuan in 1965, or only 87 percent, 72 percent, and 62 percent of regular workers' average levels in those three years, respectively. After the outbreak of the Cultural Revolution, their income declined further, averaging 383 yuan in 1967 and 372 yuan in 1969, or only 57.95 percent and 57.98 percent of regular workers' average earnings, respectively. This occurred primarily because of the reduced demand for labor, which in turn was a result of social chaos and subsequent reduction and even suspension of factory production. After 1969, when the height of the Cultural Revolution was over and economic growth gained momentum, the number of informal workers increased steadily year after year, and their average wages also recovered to 504 yuan in 1971 and 507 yuan in 1977, or 87 percent and 84 percent of regular workers' average levels, respectively (Guojia tongjiju 1987, 122–123). Without urban residential status, however, most informal workers were denied the fringe benefits intended for regular workers only. Unable to join the trade union or other mass organizations in the factory, they were marginalized and even excluded from the various events that regular workers participated in. While some informal workers, especially those under long-term contracts, were luckily converted into regular workers, such opportunities were rare in most of the Maoist era; most contract and temporary workers had to return to their home villages when their contracts expired or when their seasonal jobs were done (Zhang Xuebing 2014; Song and He 2020).

The Pariahs

In addition to creating a hierarchy among the workers of different economic and social standings, another measure the government took to promote workers' identity with the socialist state was classifying them into different political categories that privileged the "good" over the "bad." As an official guide to this process of political labeling, the central government promulgated "The State Council's Decision on Differentiation of Class Statuses in the Countryside" in August 1950, which classified urban residents into poor residents (*pinmin*), intellectuals (*zhishifenzi*), staff members (*zhiyuan*), vagrants (*youmin*), and religious practitioners, while dividing rural residents into the classes of landlords, rich peasants, middle peasants, and poor peasants (*WXXB* 1, 382–407). This measure of social categorization, coupled with three political campaigns in the 1950s (namely the Suppressing Counterrevolutionaries Campaign from December 1950 to October 1951; the Cleansing Hidden Counterrevolutionaries Campaign of 1955; and the Anti-Rightist Campaign of 1957), established a political hierarchy in China. At the bottom were the so-called "Four Categories" (namely landlords, rich peasants, counterrevolutionaries, and social dregs) or "Five Categories" (with rightists added in 1957). They constituted pariahs in the Maoist society. It was against these stigmatized categories that the "people" of the socialist country were defined. To cultivate workers' awareness of their status as the masters of society and their identity with the workplace, therefore, the state made ceaseless efforts to distinguish them from people in the undesirable categories.

It should be noted, however, that while class labeling was a powerful tool for the state to discipline workers, a degree of flexibility and practical care existed prior to the Cultural Revolution in dealing with members of the Five Categories. The aforementioned Decision by the central government clearly stipulated that the class statuses included in the document would not apply to children and students who were eighteen years old or younger; they would be assigned only a "family origin" (*jiating chushen*) rather than a class status (*WXXB* 1, 406). Official publications during this period (from the 1950s to 1966) frequently cautioned against confusing one's family origin with the class status of one's parent or treating the members of the Five Categories and their family members equally. The political judgment of any student or young person should be based on the person's own "performance in reality" (*shiji biaoxian*) rather than their family origin. A recent study of job assignments for college graduates in 1965 found that one's family origin mattered little in this regard; a student's good family origin did not guarantee a good job after graduation, and vice versa (Shen Jianpeng 2019).

During the Cultural Revolution, however, political radicalization resulted in the widening of the categories of class enemies to include former private business owners, or "capitalists" (*zibenjia*), who had been included in the general category of the "people" in the 1950s and early 1960s and were allowed to receive dividends or interest payments from the government after their businesses were nationalized in 1956. During the Cultural Revolution, not only did the government stop making payments to them, but the rebel groups frequently directed their attacks at the capitalists because of their history of exploiting workers. Not surprisingly, one's class status or family origin mattered more than anything else in shaping one's standing in the workplace and society. The Cultural Revolution itself, as Mao intended, was chiefly a movement to attack government bureaucrats and party cadres at different levels who had adhered to the "capitalist road" (hence known as *zouzipai* or "capitalist roaders," implementing policies that stressed material incentives and strict regulations in economic activities while embracing elitism and hierarchy in social and political orders). Nevertheless, the radicalization of grassroots politics often led the various factions of Red Guards, regardless of whether they were radical or conservative, to aim their attacks at the Five Categories in everyday political agitation, especially after the capitalist roaders had been expelled from office. Individuals with the undesired class labels or family origins thus became victims of Red Guard violence. At Datong Bedding Factory in Nanjing, for instance, two employees, who were former businessowners (*zibenjia* or "capitalists"), suffered the worker rebels' search of their homes and the confiscation of their silver ingots and gold bullions. Unable to bear the shame of being beaten and paraded on the street or the hardship caused by separation from family members sent to the countryside, both committed suicide by swallowing sulfuric acid or some other chemical liquid (L6).

In another instance, a group leader of the compressing workshop at Huaqiao Sugar Mill in Guangzhou who was a technician at a factory previously owned by the Nationalist government and a member of the Nationalist Party before 1949, thus falling into the category of "counterrevolutionaries." Nevertheless, he was recruited into the sugar mill after 1949 because of his expertise in production, and he had been in charge of the factory's technological operations for years. Unfortunately, according to our interviewee, who joined the mill in 1955 and later became a technician in the same workshop, the group leader "always appeared aloof and arrogant," counting on his technical expertise, thus "having a poor relationship with the masses." The director of the mill had to tolerate this person because of his knowledge and capability in managing production. Later in the early 1960s, when the "Four Cleanups" campaign started, his background as a former Nationalist made him an easy target, so all kinds of evidence, including his membership in the Nationalist Party and misconducts as a group leader at the mill, were put together against him. Subsequently, he was fired and sent to a labor camp for three-year reform. He finally died of suicide by drowning (N10).

Young workers with a capitalist or landlord family background also fared badly in their work units if they "did something wrong" (*fan cuowu*). One of the workers in the concrete-casting group at the Lijiao Dock in Guangzhou, for example, was the son of a former capitalist and thus was also sent to a labor camp. According to his co-worker's recollection, this person had been dismissed from a university because of an affair with a female student, which violated the school's ban on dating, before he joined the concrete-casting group. While hired by the dock as a temporary worker, he dated and had sex with another female student. After the girl's parents reported the affair to a local police station, the male worker received the penalty of "reform through labor" (*laojiao*). In his co-worker's view, this person's repeated tragedies had to do with not only his family background that subjected him to harsh punishment but also to his personal problems. As the co-worker aptly remarked:

> A small group like ours is often a mix of all kinds of people. There were those who had the perfect background of Poor-and-Lower-Middle Peasant family, and there were also those who had fallen from the top to the bottom of society. At that time when "class struggle" was the buzzword, your family background determined what you would be in society. Nevertheless, another opinion also existed in society: Children of the elements of the Five Categories could be reformed; to what extent you could be reformed, however, depended on your personal efforts, as seen in their performances in production, politics, personal relations, and so forth. What impressed me the most in those years as a worker was this: No matter what kind of society in which you live, your personal efforts are

very important and even the most decisive. At that time when political pressure was high, one's family background often determined what you would be, but that did not mean you were doomed. If you made efforts, you could change yourself.

Unfortunately, this co-worker, according to our informant, not only had a "family background that was not good" but also a tendency to "abandon himself to vice" (*zigan duoluo*), and he "repeated the same mistake and behaved himself like a bum" (N7).

It should be noted, however, that among the workers with an undesirable family background or political label, those who continued their "bourgeois" attitude or lifestyle at the risk of severe punishment, such as the examples described here, were the exception rather than the norm. Most kept a low profile. Chang Shouzhong (b. 1932), who joined Wuhan Steel and Iron Work in 1956, described himself as someone with "the problem of family status": "My family background is bad, belonging to the 'rich peasant' category. Therefore, in many ways I was treated differently. With a diploma from a vocational school, I should have been appointed to the position of technician, but I was always used as a worker because of my family background. I never dared to argue with the factory over this issue and had to tolerate, remaining a worker for life. If I had a good family status, I would have argued with the leader using the method of 'free airing of views through big-character poster and public debate.'" Nevertheless, Chang added, "I was fortunate. I was enthusiastic when doing things at that time and never said high-sounding words. And I appeared sincere and honest. Therefore, nobody ridiculed me as the son of someone of the Five Categories. So I survived all movements" (H14).

The same was true for Song (b. 1937), a female weaver at Xinghuo Cotton Mill since 1950 and retiring as a doctor from the clinic of Datong Bedding Factory in Nanjing in 1990. Because her father was a former member of the Nationalist Party, she "never participated in the activities of 'Beating, Smashing, and Plundering'" during the Cultural Revolution: "I was always among the first when performing a task but would stay behind when involved in politics." As a result, she recalled proudly, "neither me nor my family suffered the impact (of political movements)" (L6).

As these instances suggest, labeling all individuals with a class status or family origin served two purposes. One was to facilitate the state's external control of the entire population by applying a standardized yet oversimplified method to judge one's political standing and thereby make the society "legible." This approach was essentially no different from the technique used by many modernizing states in other parts of the world for the "administrative ordering of nature and society" (Scott 1998, 2–3, 88). The other was to establish the internalized control of individuals within a given organization or community in two different yet supplementary ways. First, those belonging to the category of "us" (people with a desirable class status or family origin) would develop a sense of superiority over the "others" (those of the Five Categories) and would commit to the rules and regulations of the factories where they were supposed to be the masters. Second, members of the Five Categories also had to conform to state policies and factory discipline because of their internalized guilt and pressure from society. In other words, not only did the state need to make the society it ruled legible, but ordinary people also had to act cautiously within the grid of social ordering imposed by the state. The end result was the state's effective control of the entire society at a minimal cost.

PARTY MEMBERSHIP
Requirements and Procedures

Compared to a good family background, which ensured one's standing as an ordinary individual with the same rights as all others in education, employment, and other aspects of social, economic, and political life, becoming a member of the Communist Party would distinguish one from "the masses" (*qunzhong*) because of the assumed qualities that came with party membership. From the party's point of view, being its member meant that the person in question was politically reliable and trustworthy. A party member thus would have a better chance than a nonmember of surviving political campaigns. Because of their assumed loyalty and credibility, party members also had more opportunities to serve in government office and party organizations at different levels. In fact, almost all government officials and party cadres were selected from party members. Party membership, in other words, was a necessity for anyone aspiring to be part of the political elite in post-1949 China.

Understandably, the procedure for obtaining party membership was complex and difficult. To become a party member, a worker had to demonstrate excellence in performing daily production tasks, maintain a good relationship with co-workers, and, most importantly, win the favor of factory leaders. Procedurally, the quest for party membership began with writing and submitting an application, a task that had to be done repeatedly over a long period of time. Zhou Meizhen (b. 1936), a female worker at a military bedding factory in Wuhan since 1960, for example, submitted a total of eighteen application letters, and she recalled that "each letter was lengthy." But she never gave up and eventually succeeded in 1983, when she was already forty-seven years old (H5). In another instance, Yang Zhixiong (b. 1929, who participated in the Korean War in 1951 as a soldier of the Chinese People's Volunteer Army and later worked at a power station in Dangyang of Hubei province, described how he "kept submitting a party membership application every year for fully twenty years from 1952 to 1972." He eventually joined the party after he became a technician and hence a "targeted candidate" (*zhongdian peiyang*) in 1971 (H20).

After receiving the applications, the factory's party branch had to periodically screen them and select a few as candidates for serious consideration, putting the applicants into a "period of examination" (*kaochaqi*). During this time, which would last for a year or two, a thorough investigation would be done into the applicant's family background. Mr. Fan (b. 1942) of Zhongxingyuan Silk Mill in Nanjing, who joined the party in 1985 after trying for many years, thus recalled the situation in the 1960s and 1970s: "At that time, the investigation covered one's family history back to three generations (oneself, parents, and grandparents), including the wife's family. If the wife's side had any problem, then the husband's probability would be affected. The official policy at that time was to emphasize one's performance rather than family background, but in reality, one's family background mattered a lot" (L2; see also H2). The investigators, who were usually members of the party branch from the factory at which the applicant worked, then had to travel to the applicant's birthplace. There, they verified the local records and spoke with local cadres and neighbors, thus ensuring the accuracy of information submitted about the applicant's family relations (B12; H13).

Family Origin Mattered

It is no surprise, then, that individuals with "bad" family backgrounds were denied the chance to become party members in the Mao era. Among them was Shen Ning (b. 1952), who started his job at the canteen of Shanghai No.

1 Steel and Iron Work in 1976. As Shen said, "Politics mattered the most in the past, and family background was critical. Therefore, it was totally irrelevant to me when it came to joining the Communist Youth League or the Communist Party," because his father had been an "instructing director" and secretary-general of the Nationalist Government's Whampoa Military Academy in Nanjing before 1949 (S1). The aforementioned Song of Datong Bedding Factory, too, had to give up the idea of becoming a party member because her father had been a Nationalist Party member before 1949, despite her own "outstanding performance in work." "At that time," she complained, "the requirements for party membership were highly restrictive, including an investigation of one's family history back to three generations. Burdened with this concern, I always told people that I was ineligible for party membership and had to work harder. As a result, I never submitted an application" (L6). Song was not alone among the workers with a family background problem who chose not to consider party membership. Mr. Han (b. 1938), a graduate from Hebei Institute of Engineering and a technician at the Military Factory No. 768 since 1960, never submitted an application during the Mao era because of his grandfather's status as a former landlord who once owned about 100 mu (roughly 17 acres) of land before 1949 (B8). So too did Mr. Yao (b. 1957), a miner at the Zhongshan Mine in Nanjing since 1972, who was from the family of a "small trader or peddler" (*xiaoshang xiaofan*). As he recalled, "They would investigate all the way back to three generations and won't allow me to join the party. So I did not apply at all" (L7).

Mr. Chang (b. 1933) of Wuhan Steel and Iron Work, however, thought differently. He was indeed "fortunate," as mentioned earlier, in that he not only survived the recurrent political campaigns but also succeeded in becoming a member of the Communist Youth League in 1958, just two years after he joined the factory, despite being from the family of a former rich peasant. Therefore, he had a strong willingness to join the party as a step up on the political ladder. "After submitting my application," he said, "the League organization watched me for about a year before allowing me membership in the League. I thus received a League badge and a certificate after I swore my loyalty at the ceremony. Afterward, each year I kept submitting an application for party membership. However, because of the problem with my family background, I have never been able to join the party, which is my lifelong regret. When the Cultural Revolution started, my chances to join the party became even slimmer. Nevertheless, I have always behaved myself by the standards and consciousness of a party member" (H14).

In sharp contrast, workers with "good" family origins fared differently. They included those whose families fell into the categories of "Poor-and-Lower-Middle Peasants" (*pinxiazhongnong*) or "Urban Poor Residents" (*chengshi pinmin*). But having a good family background alone, while essential for party membership, was far from enough to guarantee one's entry into the party. One had to "perform well" (*biaoxian hao*) on the shop floor and stand out from the rank and file. For instance, a repair worker at the port machinery factory of Ningbo Port Affairs Bureau became a party member in 1959, only three years after he entered the factory. His origin as the son of a Poor-and-Lower-Middle Peasant family definitely helped in his quick success (he had grown up as a cow herder and a farmer for five or six years before he joined the factory). But the most important factor behind his party membership was his work performance. As he recalled it, "I worked very, very hard, and I kept working day and night during the Great Leap Forward. Therefore, my application for party admission was approved, which was in late 1958. Next year I officially became a party member" (N4). Other informants from different localities also emphasized the importance of one's performance in production: "[The requirements for] joining the party were very restrictive. You have to be outstanding in production, and you must be really outstanding" (S2); "You must take the lead in doing everything" (C1).

Performance and Interpersonal Relations

No less important than performance in production, however, was one's relationship with co-workers. After all, whether or not an applicant performed well on the shop floor was judged chiefly by people in the same production group or workshop. Thus, when a local party cell decided to seriously consider an application, the party branch secretary would speak to the co-workers individually to verify the applicant's actual day-to-day performance. Having a good "relationship with the masses" (*qunzhong guanxi*)—or in other words, a good reputation among co-workers—was therefore just as important as one's real performance in production (N4; H7). From the party's point of view, only when a party member had a good reputation and good working relations with the people around them could they be expected to play an exemplary role and take the lead in performing the tasks assigned to a group of workers.

Nevertheless, the most critical factor affecting one's chances of becoming a party member was the attitude of local party branch leaders. As Wang Gang (b. 1956), who joined Shanghai Silicon Steel Factory in 1975, aptly described it, "Your writing (of a party membership application) alone was useless. It all depended on the party secretary's willingness to invite you for a conversation. Only when those above you expressed their willingness through the conversation, then could you submit a report on your thinking (*sixiang huibao*) every six months. In addition, the party branch had to seek opinions from below, which would take a month or merely two weeks. So a meeting to solicit opinions would be ritually conducted, and nobody would say no. If someone had a troubled relationship with you, that person would not be invited to the meeting at all. Thus, when the party secretary invited you for a talk, that meant that your application had already been approved" (S2).

Our informants from different factories had similar observations about the process. In the words of Zhu Delong (b. 1948), a welder at Shengli Oil Field since 1965, "A lot of young people wanted to progress and join the party, but the quota was limited. Only when the leader expressed his intention for you to write (an application), then you would indeed have the hope and should start writing" (Y1). So too said Yan Longyou (b. 1949), a worker at Liaohe Oil Field who joined the party in 1969: "When I applied for party membership, I performed well. Then the leader said, you should move closer to the (party) organization. So, I wrote an application for party membership, and succeeded after a period of observation" (Y4).

Given these strict and complex requirements, it is small wonder that most factory workers lost interest in joining the party. As Mr. Liu (b. 1941), a worker at Nanjing Steel and Iron Work since 1965, admitted, "The requirements for party membership are just too high, I didn't apply at all" (L1). Mr. Yang (b. 1942), who became a worker at Qingyun Aerospace Instrument Factory in Beijing at age eighteen, thus described his own experience: "I hated to join it. Early on, I did submit my applications several times, but the party organization always told me that it's going to put me on the list for observation, and so on. So frustrated, I stopped writing anymore. Later I was assigned a new job at the warehouse of defective products. Again, the branch secretary there approached me and said, 'How about writing an application?' I was disinterested at all. Why another application? And what to write about? I have written so many before, but all of them were treated as trash and thrown away. So I refused, despite his invitation. What on earth were the benefits to write it? Nothing at all" (B1).

Others gave up the idea of joining the party because of their unwillingness to periodically submit a "thought report" on what they had been thinking about and doing recently. So complained Mr. Guo (b. 1942), who joined the Military Factory No. 768 for wireless equipment in 1961: "I am particularly sick of joining the party. You had to keep writing a thought report to criticize yourself, if you want to join the party or the youth league. The more I watched it, the more disappointed I became. To join the party or the league, you have to pretend and deceive, claiming that you picked a screw or an iron wire on the street and handed it over to an officer or that you voluntarily cleaned up the floor or fetched hot water, and so on, to prove your unselfishness. All things became highly formalistic in the end. So I refused to apply" (B7).

Obviously, the importance of the party organization lay not only in the existence of the organization itself as a tool for the party-state's top-down control of the working force, but also in the way the grassroots party cells exercised their influence through the ongoing process of recruiting new members. In other words, applying for party membership as a process for candidates to constantly demonstrate their loyalty to the party was no less important than performing one's duties as a member after joining the party. In fact, it was during the application for party membership and the following period when one was granted probationary membership, rather than after obtaining the formal membership, that the candidates' behavior and words came under the party cells' close monitoring. Throughout this process, what really concerned the party cell and the applicants was not so much the applicant's true faith in the party's doctrine as their actual performance at the workplace; the candidate had to outperform all others in daily production and get along well with everyone around or above them. Ideology still mattered in this process, but ideology as the applicants and formal party members understood it was neither the "pure ideology" as formulated in the classic works of Marx or Lenin nor the "practical ideology" represented by the writings of Mao, as defined by Franz Schurmann (1968, 24–34). What really made sense to the party members and applicants was the usefulness of the practical ideology, or how Maoism served their everyday needs on the shop floor.

PURIFYING THE MIND
Political Study Sessions

In addition to categorizing people based on family origins and party membership, factory governance in the Mao era also attached the utmost importance to political indoctrination through regularly held study sessions. The study session served two purposes. One was political. Studying the party's documents or Mao's messages was believed essential in cultivating workers' consciousness, making them the "socialist new man" (*shehuizhuyi xinren*) who would be free of "incorrect, non-proletarian ideas" and committed to the party's revolutionary cause. The other was practical. The study session functioned as another tool to discipline the workers.

The study session usually had a fixed schedule, with a guaranteed time slot that "could never be altered under any circumstance" (H13). At some factories, it took place every Monday, Wednesday, or Friday for one to two hours (C6; C7; S7) or fifteen to thirty minutes in the early morning every day (C2; N5). At a metallurgical enterprise in Wuhan, for example, "there was a fixed time for participation in political study on contents such as Chairman Mao's 'Three Famous Essays' and currently circulated political documents. Because it was planned by the factory, every worker had to participate. Political campaigns took place one after another at that time, especially in 1974 to 1976, such as the campaigns of 'Criticizing Lin Biao and Criticizing Confucius' and 'Striking Back the Rightist Wind of Reversing Verdicts.' Therefore, political study was particularly intense during this period, and it was seriously conducted, rather than a formality," recollected Yan Shanfa (b. 1948), who worked for the factory as an electrician since 1965 (H9). Political study also became a priority during the months following the death of Lin Biao on September 13, 1971. As miner Zhou Dexian (b. 1950) of Shitouzui Mine in Daye put it, "After the September 13 Incident, political study became especially intense. For half a month, we stopped working and studied documents from early morning to the evening every day, and no late arrival or early leave was allowed. Everyone participated in it seriously" (H13). Qiu Baohua (b. 1956), a worker at the military's Hongwei Machinery Factory since 1973, also emphasized the importance of political study in his unit: "During the Cultural Revolution, political study lasted for two to three hours in an afternoon once a week. Political study was a very serious task and its time could never be squeezed by production activities. So was the slogan, 'grasp the revolution and speed up production' (*zhua geming, cu shengchan*). Unless one was ill or had any other kind of particular situation, everyone had to participate." Much of the session, recalled Qiu, was for the workshop director to "read a newspaper editorial and sometimes also the documents from superior authorities." The director was selective in reading the newspaper; he only picked an article or a paragraph that was relevant to the problems in his factory. "When he felt tired reading a lengthy article, he would ask someone else to continue in his stead" (C7).

Therefore, the pressure was huge for workers to participate in study sessions, which were linked to one's "political performance" (*zhengzhi biaoxian*). "Whenever there was a movement," said Hu Shixiang (b. 1950) of Jinhu Steel and Iron Work in Daye, "we had to stop working and attend study meetings every day. At that time, politics was above everything else. One's political performance mattered a lot at that time. Therefore, whenever there was a study task, everyone was very serious about it" (H16). Political performance was important because it determined in large measure one's chance to join the Youth League and the party or to be selected as an Advanced Producer (*xianjin shengchanzhe*), as Li Changjian (b. 1952) and Zhao Li (b. 1951) of Wuhan Steel and Iron Work explained (H10; H12). On the other hand, "if one performed poorly in the study sessions," as Tian Chunsheng (b. 1951) of the same work unit pointed out, "the person would likely be accused of being politically problematic" (H15). Yang Xiaofeng (b. 1943), who was once named an Advanced Producer at Yimin Food Factory in Shanghai, thus explained the consequences of failure to attend a meeting: "At that time of the 1970s, too many meetings were held, in addition to the rituals of 'seeking advice (before the plaster statue of Mao) in the morning, reporting back in the evening, and performing episodes of the exemplary operas at lunch hours.' When people were too busy with production tasks and no regular hours were available (for a study session), an after-hours meeting had to be held when the production tasks were finished. If you did not show up at the meeting, that meant you had a problem in political thinking, and you would be summoned for questioning. Therefore, few dared not to attend the meetings. People who had experienced the Cultural Revolution were just frightened and no one could ask for an absence" (S8). "You had to participate (in the study session), no matter you liked it or not. There was no way not to attend it," said Mr. Cao (b. 1939), a technician of Changshou Chemical Plant in Chongqing who worked there since 1967 (C2).

To what extent, then, was the study session effective in influencing workers' thinking and performance in production? Organizers of such meetings, to be sure, did want participants to actively engage in the study sessions. At Xinghuo Cotton Mill in Nanjing, for example, "everyone had to speak at the meeting, and the meeting would not be dismissed until everyone had said something." Such meetings, as Song (b. 1937), a production group leader, recalled, were held for one to two hours after work. "To ensure that the workers actively participate, sometimes I had to administer a quiz to see if they had listened attentively," she remembered. But she was disappointed that "some were not attentive at all, often appearing sleepy because they had been working too hard or looking absent-minded because they were obsessed with things at home" (L6). In fact, workers' indifference on such occasions was common in the last years of the Cultural Revolution. "During the times of the Criticizing Lin Biao and Criticizing Confucius campaign," recollected Sun Aiting (b. 1955), a production group leader at Shanghai Artistic Carving Factory, "political study became a mere formality. A senior worker thus fell asleep at the meeting, for example. Workers just did what they wanted, and when the task was done, they did knitwork for themselves" (S6). Thus, unless pressured to speak, most workers remained silent at such meetings. At Ningbo Port Machinery Factory, workers' apathy in the last years of the Cultural Revolution was in sharp contrast with their enthusiasm at the beginning of the Great Leap Forward: "During the Great Leap Forward, when a task was announced at an evening meeting, everyone was motivated, including me. Everyone knew that the task had to be done, disregarding material incentives" (N5). The aforementioned Yang of Yimin Food Factory attributed workers' disinterest in political study to the boredom that the workers widely experienced in those years: "Having survived the high tide of the Cultural Revolution, there was little to say. People were not interested in it at all. Their daily routines were merely 'two points and one line' (*liangdian yixian*), the two points being factory and home; after getting the job done at the factory, they just wanted to hurry back home" (S8). So too were the observations of informants from other factories: "Everyone was exhausted" (L2); "People were just too tired ... they returned home as late as 7 p.m. Then they started cooking, and they had to burn honeycomb briquets by fanning the stove for a long while until the briquets were lit, which could make you crazy! By 8 p.m., they eventually sit down for dinner. After finishing food and washing, they went to bed immediately, without TV or any other kind of entertainment. They were so tired. Next morning, they had to wake up early to catch the bus" (C1).

The Utility of Political Study Sessions

Despite workers' apathy toward political study, the study sessions nevertheless served some practical purposes that benefitted the factory. In addition to reading Mao's essays or newspapers and party documents, an essential part of the study meeting was to link the readings with the actual problems that concerned the cadres of a workshop or production group. Most of the issues had to do with workers' daily performance, such as slacking, unexcused absence, late arrival, or early departure. Thus, the workshop director or group leader would shout at the workers in question like this: "Never loaf on the job! People keep an eye on you whenever you are slacking. Everyone knows well whether you are lazy or not. For what reason in hell did you shirk your duties? You are paid no less than everybody else!" So recollected Mrs. Chen (b. 1927), a warehouse shipping worker at the Xiaguan Railway Station in Nanjing since 1958 (C4). To make sure the newly hired, inexperienced workers learned production skills within a time limit, apprentices at Yimin Food Factory were not allowed to date. If anyone violated the ban on dating, once discovered, they would be openly censured at the factory-level meeting. The person had to further make a "self-examination" (*ziwo jiantao*) at the workshop's study meeting. Finally, at the production group's study meeting, co-workers had to "help him improve his political consciousness." Materially, the violator would be subject to the penalty of the lowest level of wage raise (S8).

Mrs. Song (b. 1937) of Xinghuo Cotton Mill in Nanjing thus believed in the effectiveness of factory regulations on worker performance because of the routinely held study meetings: "By the regulation of our factory, if someone failed to come to work without an excuse for a couple of days in a row, it's likely that he would be fired, thus losing his source of income. Each of us therefore had to participate in political study, because there were very restrictive regulations. For instance, I had to run when going back and forth to the toilet. I ate meals very quickly, and had to refrain from drinking water before work. I drank water only during the lunch time when I also stopped by the toilet. To concentrate on work and save time, I did my best to avoid a trip to the toilet" (L6). Firing a worker simply because of shirking, however, was by no means an easy punishment to mete out. At the port machinery factory of Ningbo Port Affairs Bureau, for instance, the factory director failed to fire a worker who "had often been late to work" because the director had to first seek approval from the Bureau to do so; the Bureau, after approving it, had to further seek approval from the Labor Bureau of the Municipal Government, which rejected it in the end (N4).

The study meeting at the production group level was also the occasion for workers to make a "personal review" (*geren zongjie*) or a "report on personal thinking" (*sixiang huibao*), usually at the end of each quarter, and a major review at the end of a year. In these reviews, workers had to identify "where they have done well and where they have done poorly, and how they will improve in the future," and the group leaders would then select what they believed to be the best reviews and publicize them (L3). Everyone was expected to show their self-denial and commitment to the factory on such occasions. Understandably, it was inappropriate and indeed "embarrassing," for instance, for workers to ask for a wage raise on such occasions, as Yang Wanru (b. 1933), a retiree from Nanjing Precast Concrete Plant, mentioned when talking about the annual reviews (C5). A popular saying in the 1960s and 1970s thus was "Fight Selfishness, Repudiate Revisionism" (*dousi pixiu*). As a worker at the Lijiao Dockyard in Guangzhou since 1969 explained, "People's mindset was highly politicized—or controlled—at that time. Fight Selfishness and Repudiate Revisionism means that even a flash of selfish thinking has to be seriously criticized. Indeed, selfish ideas were less likely to prevail among us at that time. Even if they did exist, nobody dared to admit them. They all wanted do a good job on the shop floor" (N7). Not surprisingly, workers were encouraged to expose "bad people and bad things" (*huairen huaishi*) at the study meetings or by writing a "big character poster" (*dazibao*) during the Cultural Revolution. At Xinghuo Cotton Mill in Nanjing, for example, "workers were not allowed to go back home unless each of them wrote something. If they couldn't find anything wrong with themselves, they had to at least mention something wrong with the factory.

When a problem was exposed, everyone was nervous. So we had to be very cautious and careful" (L6). The wrongdoer, once exposed, would likely be brought to the front of the audience at a study meeting for people to criticize (H23). In fact, the pressure for workers at the Filature of Huanggang Region to expose "bad people and bad things" was so high that one of them had to falsely accuse a co-worker of drinking a bit of the honey from the factory's canteen; in actuality, the accused only "touched a honey jar" but did not drink any, as Dai Zhenhua (b. 1942), a canteen worker, recalled (H1). Nevertheless, the regularly held political meetings and the pressure they generated did function to discipline workers and curb violations against factory regulations, as many of our interviewees observed.[1]

The Workers of Nanjing

The records about study meetings at the factories in Nanjing, currently preserved at Nanjing Municipal Archives, offer us another perspective to view how political study functioned to improve productivity in these factories. It was reported, for example, that study sessions had a positive effect on production techniques. At the third section of the No. 1 Workshop of Gulou Machinery Factory, more than seventy workers participated in "small-scale political lectures" every two weeks in 1963. Each time, the director or party secretary of the workshop delivered a lecture on topics such as "Leap Forward and its relationship with us" or "How to handle the relationship between collective and personal interests." Shen Chongyi, a young worker in the section, thus explained how his performance changed because of these lectures: "My job is about thermochemical treatment of metals. Because of the danger of poisoning, I always wanted to change my job to a different workshop or go to school. The more I did my job during the Leap Forward, the more I was worried. This is wrong! How could I quit my job and let others do it that has the danger of poisoning? I must learn the advanced practices from other factories and improve the technologies of thermochemical treatment." He thus submitted a "proposal of rationalization" and changed the materials, instruments, and procedures. Eventually, he succeeded in making the treatment harmless (NJ6001-2-395).

Political study was also believed to be effective in helping workers perform well in production. At the military No. 103 Factory, for instance, workers participated in the "100-day competition for reducing the use of materials" while studying Mao's two essays, "The Foolish Old Man Removes the Mountains" and "The Struggle in the Jinggang Mountains," and succeeded in reducing a filtering plate to one to five square centimeters less than the standard size in April 1963 (NJ6001-2-415). In another instance, at Nanjing Instruments Factory, the twelve workers of the electroplating group formed the "Red Flag Theoretical Study Group" in 1963. Studying Mao's "On Practice" and "On Contradiction" reportedly helped them in production. For instance, a worker named Li Chenggui, who tended to make defective products—hence his nickname "the prince of waste" (*feipin dawang*)—dramatically improved his performance after studying these texts, despite his prior nine years of work experiences (NJ6001-2-395). At Nanjing Valve Factory, a group of young workers, motivated by political study, decided to challenge Ye Yufa, a senior worker who was highly skilled but at the same time "careless, slobby, and conservative." One of the young workers, named Huang Ren, produced 1,200 porcelain clippers per day, far surpassing Ye's level, which was 900 per day. Ye was stimulated in turn and later set the record of producing 1,230 pieces per day (NJ6001-2-395).

Finally, political study was also believed to help change the workers' lifestyles and interpersonal relations. A certain worker at Nanjing Teaching Instruments Factory, for instance, used to keep a "cabbage-like hairstyle" (*baocaitou*), wear a pair of pointed dress shoes, and spend his spare time ballroom dancing or strolling around the streets. He often failed to finish his production tasks. By studying Mao's "Serve the People," however, he changed a lot. "Since the beginning of 1963, he has finished his tasks every month, and he also lives a plain life" (NJ6001-2-415). At Xiaguan Power Plant, two group leaders in the carrier room had long failed to get along with each other. After studying Mao's "Combat Liberalism," one of them admitted his mistake: "I should be responsible for having failed to get along with comrade Sun Sanfu. For long, I have assumed that I had a higher level of education and therefore looked down upon Master Sanfu. As a graduate from a secondary vocational school, I saw my diploma as an advantage and gave myself airs, looking down upon all others." Subsequently, he rebuilt his friendship with Sanfu (NJ6001-2-415).

The most characteristic feature of labor management in the Maoist era, therefore, was the routinely organized political study sessions. For both the cadres, who organized these study sessions, and ordinary workers, as participants, what mattered was never the cultivation of faith in the party's ideologies; the theoretical doctrines of Marxism, Leninism, and Maoism were rarely included as readings for such meetings. When Mao's writings were indeed included, which happened frequently during the Cultural Revolution, they were limited to the few essays that were directly linked to workers' attitudes and performance in production. These meetings, therefore, served only one practical purpose: ensuring the workers' compliance with the disciplines of the factory, thus preventing any shirking or disobedience, by connecting their everyday performance in production with their political consciousness. From the state's point of view, this method of worker discipline was not only cost-effective compared to the use of material incentives, which would require the factories' extra spending on them, but it was also more effective overall. It made the workers' conformity a seemingly voluntary choice rather than a result of administrative compulsion or material incentivization.

BECOMING WORKER ELITES
Composition of the Worker Elite

Another method used to incentivize the workers was awarding the best-performing individuals with various honorary titles. Among these, the most prestigious title was "Model Laborers" (*laodong mofan*), which was usually awarded by the government at the local, provincial, or national level to a very limited number of individuals. In Shanghai, for instance, 659 individuals were selected as municipal-level model workers from among the 1.9 million workers in 1955, or one model worker out of every 2900 workers. By 1979, the selection of model workers had become even more restrictive; there were only 966 out of 4.3 million workers, or one model worker per 4,450 workers. To be a model worker, a candidate had to meet a number of criteria, such as "making a special contribution to production and economical use of materials," "inventing or improving production technologies," or "having rich work experiences and significant achievements in training apprentices and teaching techniques." The requirements for an Advanced Producer were similar in kind but at a lower level. Therefore, there were more Advanced Producers than model workers. In Shanghai, again, there were 1,336 Advanced Producers in 1963 and 1,280 Advanced Producers in 1977, or about one Advanced Producer per 1,200 and 3,200 workers, respectively. Unlike model workers that were selected only at the municipal level or above, Advanced Producers were also awarded by individual enterprises and in large numbers. In addition, in 1963 and 1965, a new honorary title, called "Five-Good Workers" (*wuhao gongren*), was made available to an even larger number of workers throughout the country. The so-called "Five-Good" means "good in political thinking, completion of tasks, study of literacy and skills, fraternity and mutual aid, and conformity with disciplines." In Shanghai alone, a total of 26,974 individuals received the Five-Good Worker award in 1963, or twenty times the number of Advanced Producer awardees. In 1965, the number of Five-Good Workers increased to 131,955, or nearly one recipient out of every five ordinary workers in Shanghai (Li Jiaqi 1997, Part 15, Chap. 4).

A similar picture of the worker elite is found in Nanjing. In 1960, for example, the municipal government awarded a total of 2,273 model workers and Advanced Producers; in addition, individual enterprises also awarded 72,811 Advanced Producers (NJ6001-1-75). In 1965, among the 17 factories under Nanjing Telecommunication Instruments Industrial Company, 47 workers received various honorary titles, including 14 Advanced Producers and 20 Five-Good Workers. Of the 47 recipients, 34 were male and 13 were female; 15 were party members and 16 were league members in terms of political background; and in terms of occupation, there were seven production group leaders, one section head, one workshop director, and all others were ordinary workers (NJ5088-2-43).

By receiving an honorary title, one was immediately set apart from other workers. Recipients of the city-level titles enjoyed special privileges and at the same time were burdened with additional duties. It was reported that among the city-level model workers and Advanced Producers in Nanjing, there were the problems of "four more" and "four less": They had "more concurrent appointments, meetings, after-hours activities, and invitations" and "less time to work, to connect with the masses, to study, and to rest." One of such model workers was Yang Houfa, who had fourteen appointments, such as member of the municipal Youth League committee, delegate to the city-level people's congress, member of the city-level Association of Science. He thus spent 121 days on meetings or trainings in the first 238 days of 1960, and each day he could only get four or five hours of sleep. Wang Fengqi, in another instance, as a country-level Advanced Producer, spent 167 days on meetings, traveling, rehabilitation treatments, and trainings during the same period, thus having only 71 days to work (NJ6001-1-75).

The Technical Geniuses

How, then, did the workers become recipients of the honorary titles? And what do their experiences tell about the approach to labor management and factory governance in the Maoist era? The records from Nanjing Municipal Archives about the Five-Good Workers in the factories in Nanjing in 1965 are illustrative. Let us begin with Advanced Producers who made exceptional contributions to production by inventing or improving technologies.

Xue Ru'ai (b. 1926) was named an Advanced Producer in Nanjing Radio Components Factory first in 1956 through 1959 and again in 1964 and 1965. To overcome the backwardness of the technology in making carbon diaphragms in his factory, Xue visited a factory in Shanghai for a vocational training, where he "persuaded some technicians to give up their conservativeness." After coming back, he spent six months and a total of 4,000 yuan to invent more than ten new instruments for the factory's production line, which would have cost more than 20,000 yuan if they had to be purchased, and some of them were not available for purchase at all. All these instruments "played an important role in improving the quality of products," as a report about him described. Moreover, the report went on, Xue was "known for consistently working hard, thriftily, and intelligently." He was particularly good at "utilizing waste materials and substitutes to make inventions and troubleshooting the problems in processing equipment with smart methods," and he "often worked for several days in a row without sleep in order to finish a job."

In the same factory, another worker named Zheng Wengang was also on the list of Advanced Producers in 1965. In a matter of half a year, the report claimed, he made "more than ten technical innovations." Most importantly, "he designed and built by himself an automated 15-kilovolt direct-current experimental platform in only three months by utilizing waste materials and outdated equipment, thus overcoming a major difficulty in the factory's production that had never been solved for years." The platform was "not only well designed and in the size of only a standing cabinet but also safe and convenient to operate." The total cost for Zheng to build it was only about 2,000 yuan, compared to the price of 15,000 yuan to purchase one from elsewhere. He also graciously declined an award of 100 yuan that the factory offered him.

A third example is Yu Shengxuan from Taiping Ceramic Components Factory. He improved the technique for making electric capacitors by reducing the stack inside the capacitor from five to three ceramic layers, thus saving a third of the material and improving productivity by 30 percent.

In addition to those who made significant contributions to technological inventions or innovations, winners of the honorary titles also included those who demonstrated superior skills and experiences in production, thus known as *nengshou* among the workers. One of such technological gurus was Xu Zhongtao (b. 1928) from Nanjing Light Bulb and Valve Factory, who was able to make ordinary and special bulbs and repair relays, valves, semiconductor devices, and so forth. "It is well known throughout the factory," a report about him claimed, "that wherever a trouble occurs to a key equipment, Master Xu will appear and the problems will be solved immediately." In the absence of a complete system of equipment and tools, the report continued, "Master Xu took the initiative in renovating a number of processing techniques and inventing new methods in manufacturing, thus saving a lot of funds and materials for the factory."

Sun Yonggen (b. 1932) was another Advanced Producer from the same factory. Sun was a crackerjack at blowing bulbs and pulling tubes. "Though he is still a young worker, Sun has already shown his superior craftmanship. He is particularly good at blowing bulbs, large and small, and pulling tubes, ordinary or special. He never rejected the toughest jobs that the workshop assigned to him." Productivity increased by two- or threefold after he headed the group for pulling tubes. And he never kept his skills a secret: "When blowing a big jar of 5,000 cc in volume, he explained without reservation the key steps to do it, and he also helped others to grasp the skills in making tiny bulbs."

All these Advanced Producers, as the reports typically affirmed, not only excelled in technological renovation and production but also showed their unusual altruism in daily activities. Xue Ru'ai, for example, was described as someone who "treats the factory as home" (*yi cang wei jia*). To save money for the factory, for instance, "he preferred to walk and carry the materials on his shoulder, instead of riding a bus, when traveling outside to obtain materials for processing." Sun Yonggen, likewise, typically came to work one hour earlier than everyone else in order to prepare the materials for making bulbs and tubes: "When he is not on shift, Sun still stands by the furnace to help this or that worker, though there is no regulation that requires him to do so" (NJ5088-2-43).

The Ordinary but Committed Workers

Without being geniuses in innovation or experts in production, ordinary individuals also had a chance of being honored with the title of Advanced Producer by simply following the factory's rules and performing their duties fully. One such recipient was Fu Liangmiao (b. 1944), a young worker in Nanjing Telecommunication Equipment Factory, who was able to "keep the record of full attendance and have no accident in production year-round." More specifically, as a report described him, "in the past year [1964], his record shows no absence, late arrival, or early leave. He volunteered to work extra hours when there was an urgent task, and sometimes, after finishing his daytime shift and regardless of the fatigue, he continued to work into the night and even until dawn in order to get the job done. He rarely made defective products even if the products were experimental and therefore short of a well-designed blueprint and well-developed craftmanship." The report also noted that Fu "never wears fashionable clothes and instead lives a plain and simple life. He hands over his wages and bonuses to his parents every month, keeping only a small sum of pocket money and yet still participating in making savings."

A similar example is found in Jinchuan Power Meter Factory, where Zhu Shuzhen "manifests the spirit of 'treating the factory as home' by working extremely hard and coming to work early and leaving late, without taking a break at noon. She never complains no matter how busy her job is. Each month, she makes tens of thousands of clipper axles, magnetic steel bolts, and bearing caps. She finishes her task always ahead of schedule and her products pass quality control by almost 100 percent." "Besides, she pays attention to safety in production. Every day, she wears the hat to fully cover her hair and never forgets wearing the security glasses. Each time when she leaves, she always makes sure that the power switch is off." She was quoted as saying: "If the power switch remains on after work, the motor is likely to be burned, and the factory's property will be damaged. I rely on the factory for making a living, so the factory is equivalent to my home, and the machines should be well taken care of. Every day before I leave the factory, I always clean up everything, wipe the lathe carefully and apply some lubricant to it."

The title of Advanced Producer could be awarded even to those located at the bottom of factory labor force. Chang Yuzhen, for instance, was an illiterate woman and an "odd-job worker" (*qinzagong*) at the aforementioned

Jinchuan Power Meter Factory whose duty was to boil drinking water and deliver it to different sites of the factory: "No matter whether it is freezing in winter or scorching in summer, she works hard to guarantee the supply of hot water for the convenience of the masses." In addition to performing her assigned work, Chang volunteered to heat or cook the lunch boxes for more than one hundred individuals. "Whenever the workers leave, she would have the lunch boxes steamed and covered well in winter, to make sure the workers can eat a hot lunch. Sometimes when a worker rushes to the factory without enough time to wash the rice in the lunch box, she would do so instead. If there are rice grains that spill over from the lunch box, she would pick them up from the floor, leaving the dirty rice to herself, and add clean rice of her own to the box. She is thus known as a voluntary cook."

A more interesting case is that of Liu Ruzhen, a component assembler and party member at Nanjing Telecommunication Equipment Factory. Liu was named a Five-Good Worker in 1965. Known as the Big Sister (*dajiejie*), Liu was good at mediating between couples or individuals in a troubled relationship. Upon hearing that a co-worker named Tai had "a problem in lifestyle" (denoting involvement in extramarital affairs), Liu immediately talked to her, "offering her suggestions on how to handle personal issues." Tai refused her suggestions and was even resentful of Liu's intervention. Later Tai became ill and stayed home. Liu visited her repeatedly and helped her with home chores. This way, Liu was able to chat with her and "eventually knew where the problem was." Both Tai and her husband were grateful to Liu for her efforts to save their marriage. In a similar instance, a worker named Liang was upset because of a "troubled conjugal relationship." Liu again intervened by talking to the people around Liang and "for many times" directly to Liang himself in order to know the facts about the couple. She then started mediation by visiting Liang's home and talking to his wife. As a result, the couple "were eventually reconciled with each other." But Liu's interventions were not limited to troubled couples. After hearing that the "study group head" in the No. 1 Production Group had a poor relationship with the "production group head," Liu talked to each of them individually several times during weekends and holidays. Thanks to her mediation, the tension between the two "was mitigated somehow." It was reported that, because of her skills at mediation, "people all treat her as a bosom friend (*zhixinren*), willing to share with her whatever they think about, and listen to her words."

It turned out that the Big Sister was not only an adept mediator but also a caring person, ready to help anyone in need. "Whenever someone in the production group was ill," a report about her thus described, "she would accompany the patient to a hospital, assist in registration and diagnosis, and then send the patient back home. Once upon a time, a co-worker named Zhong fell ill at the same time when his wife was sick too. She thus helped both of them to do the paperwork, comforted them, and took care of them." She also paid several visits to a worker named Tong, who was hospitalized, and after learning that Tong wanted to taste glutinous rice, she gave him a portion of rice that she had brought from her hometown. In another instance, a newly graduated college student named Zhang, from the province of Hunan, was assigned a job in the factory and always felt homesick during holidays. The Big Sister always invited Zhang to her home for dinner and even gave Zhang her own clothes.

It should be noted that Liu was not alone in showing exceptional care to people around her. The reports about Advanced or Five-Good Workers frequently mention how these people helped those who encountered difficulties in everyday life, such as illness, poverty, troubled marriages, or even "incorrect views of courtship," as seen in the examples of Ni Zhongliang and Ding Yaqin, who were both Five-Good Workers from Jiangsu Wireless Equipment Factory (NJ5088-2-43).

Cadres as Activists

About a quarter of the winners of the honorary titles were cadres of different levels, such as production group leaders, workshop directors, and factory heads, as suggested by the statistics from the seventeen factories under Nanjing Telecommunication Equipment Company (NJ5088-2-43). To make sense of how these cadres were selected to receive these titles, consider the following examples.

The first is Wang Changmei, a production group leader from Nanjing Light Bulb and Valve Factory. His group was singled out as a "five-good group" (*wuhao banzu*) for four reasons, as outlined in an official report. First, Wang Changmei organized competitions for production in his group. For that end, he identified the most skilled workers for different tasks, such as Wang, who excelled at putting together the coiled filament within a bulb; Tao, who operated machines so well that few defective filaments were found; and another Wang, who was an expert at repairing machines. He then let each of them lead other workers to "practice hard the basic skills," and he set high standards for each task. For example, the wire that supports the filament must be a single straight line, and the time for the entire process of producing such a wire must be limited to ten minutes. Second, Wang Changmei did a great job of "learning from the advanced" (*xuexi xianjin*). For instance, he sent a number of workers to Shanghai Light Bulb Factory for training and thus upgraded the production of wires from manual to machine operation, with the help of an experienced worker from another bulb factory. Third, Wang Changmei managed production in his group by the principle of "careful calculation and strict budgeting" (*jingda xisuan*). By recycling used parts and waste, his group collected a pile of copper wires that was worth 754 yuan. Finally, Wang Changmei contributed to the "cultivation of the good styles of communism," or mutual care, within his group. He never allowed his group to delay their work, which would cause the postponement of the next tasks for another group on the same production line. For the conducting wires made for other factories, Wang Changmei always had each of the wires thoroughly examined to ensure that no defective products were shipped out. In the last quarter of 1964, he allocated five workers from his group to another group to help the latter finish its task on time. Likewise, Wang showed personal care to his group, such as visiting them when they were on sick leave. As a result, the workers around him reportedly had the feeling of belonging to an intimate community, where "everyone takes care of the group and the group takes care of everyone."

The next examples concern two workshop directors. Lu Yongkang (b. 1929) was a workshop director of Xianfeng Hardware Factory. He stood out from many other middle-ranking factory cadres in that he always participated in manual work together with the rank and file. According to a report about him, "He never eschews tasks that are dirty and laborious, and is always among the first to take on the toughest jobs, completely forgetting that he is a cadre. Therefore, workers always address him as 'our Master Lu' instead of 'Director Lu.'" It was further reported that Lu worked several extra hours each day, arriving earlier and leaving later than everyone else, and whenever there was a night or weekend shift, he was always present. No wonder there was this saying among the workers: "Master Lu indeed treats the factory as home—he is seen in the factory all the time."

Another example is Huang Xiuying, a female workshop director and vice factory director of Nanjing Wireless Components Factory. Huang had been an Advanced Producer several times at municipal, provincial, and national levels since 1956, and she once witnessed Chairman Mao when attending the National Conference of Advanced Producers in 1956. Compared to Lu, she was more of an entrepreneur, committed to maximizing the factory's business opportunities, rather than a hands-on manager on the shop floor. Her factory, small in size, was not on the state's procurement list of the manufacturers of mica sheets and was therefore ineligible for the unified supply of mica by the government. In 1962, there was a nationwide shortage of capacitors, and mica was an essential material for making this product. To search and procure mica on her own, Huang traveled to Danba, a county on the Tibetan Plateau, where she persuaded a local mica mine to sell a certain amount of the mineral to her factory on the eve of the Chinese New Year, even while she was ill at the time. To minimize waste, she took the lead in splitting, cutting, and washing the mineral, thus saving about 380 kilograms of mica (worth 80,000 yuan) in the few months after the factory obtained it. As a committed cadre, Huang cared about the well-being of the workers and the factory. It was reported that she volunteered to clean up a women's toilet every day. She never had her expenses reimbursed on night meals when working extra hours, sometimes until midnight. When traveling to Beijing for a meeting or to Shanghai for business, she preferred to stay in a small inn instead of a luxurious hotel and buy a train ticket for a regular seat rather than a sleeping berth. She thus won workers' respect, and they called her "Sister Huang" (*Huang dajie*).

The last example is about a factory head named Zhu Xiaoshu, from Taiping Ceramic Wares Factory. She was selected as an Advanced Producer for "democratic management of the factory" (*minzhu banchang*). For instance, she allowed workers of each production group to elect by vote eight committee members, and each member was in charge of a specific task, such as setting production quota, accounting, technology, storage, quality control, and so forth. Each committee member reported directly to one of factory's offices that was in charge of the same duty. Each of the eight committee members was responsible for assigning tasks to individual workers, so that "everything is taken care of by someone, and everyone is responsible for something" (*shishi you ren guan, renren you shi guan*). More specifically, she allowed workers to have a "full discussion" before the factory's production goals were finalized; she then assigned production tasks every month, every ten days, and every day to specific workers and publicized the assignments. "Since the workers set the production goals on their own, they did their best to finish the tasks no matter what kind of difficulty they encountered." In addition, Zhu was praised for "thrifty management of the factory" (*qinjian banchang*). For example, to reduce the cost of the production of ferroelectric capacitors, she reduced the stack of a capacitor from five to three layers without compromising the quality and functionality of the product. She also took measures to increase the rate of products that met quality requirements from 15 percent to 85 percent and reduce the cost of ceramic layers from more than 1 yuan per piece to 0.43 yuan per piece (NJ6001-2-431).

SUBSTANTIVE MAOISM

Just like many other institutions in post-1949 China, the factory system in state-owned factories was established and operated by heavily borrowing from the Stalinist models that had prevailed in the Soviet Union from the 1930s to the early 1950s (Filtzer 1986, 2002). Therefore, there were many similarities in factory governance between the two countries. Yet, as some researchers have noted, the Maoist approach to social control was also significantly different from the methods widely used in Russia. Unlike the latter, which relied primarily on various forms of terror (including the omnipresent surveillance, unexpected arrests by secret police, and purges against political dissidents on a massive scale), the Maoist style, while also resorting to coercion and violence, tended to be rather "introspective," emphasizing the use of education and persuasion to ensure conformance to the party-state (Schurmann 1968, 311–315; Bianco 2018, 63).

To make sense of the Maoist approach to factory governance, it is important to distinguish between the formal and substantive parts of Maoism as an ideology. The formal part of Maoism refers to the original ideas of Mao, which Schurmann defines as "practical ideology" or Mao's application of Marxism and Leninism to the realities of the Chinese revolution. In contrast, what was indoctrinated among the workers in Maoist China was neither the pure ideology of Marxism and Leninism nor the practical ideology of original Mao Zedong Thought (*Mao Zedong sixiang*). Instead, it was the substantive part of Maoism, or a unique set of ideas that served the real-world purpose of disciplining the labor force, such as its emphasis on the distinction between "us" and "the others" on the basis of a new hierarchy of class categories, its assumption of workers as masters of the country and the factory (*dangjia zuozhu*), its denial of self-interest (*dagong wusi*) and prioritization of collective goals, and the concomitant idea of equal status and equal rights for all (*renren pingdeng*), etc. These moral principles had little to do with the party-state's pure ideology and were only tenuously linked with Mao's original thoughts on conducting a revolution in China. Termed "substantive Maoism" for convenience of discussion here, this set of moral principles should be distinguished from Mao Zedong Thought, which was much more sophisticated with rich historical origins. At best, substantive Maoism functioned only as an oversimplified application of several of Mao's sayings that were detached from the entirety and historicity of Mao's original thoughts. In its application to disciplining the work force, substantive Maoism had little to do with either the pure or practical ideology of the Maoist state.

Nevertheless, through its repeated and ubiquitous propagation at the workplace and beyond, substantive Maoism functioned as more than an externally imposed ideology; its hegemony was firmly established to shape workers' identity, political consciousness, and behavior. It was in the discourse of substantive Maoism that power relations in the factory were articulated and mediated. Workers' status as masters of the factory was more than a false rhetoric in this context; their rights and privileges became real and tangible when compared to the stigmatized and marginalized individuals of the Five Categories. In the absence of immediate material incentives, ideological indoctrination and political mobilization turned out to be the only viable and effective tools to curb shirking and inefficiency in production. The selection of motivated workers as activists and party members also generated pressure on ordinary workers by privileging the few with political rewards that could be easily converted into material benefits, such as greater chances for a wage upgrade, a better housing allocation, or a promotion to cadre. All in all, substantive Maoism was more than an ideology; it turned out to be a powerful tool to control the workers.

Finally, the Maoist state's preference for the introspective approach to disciplining the workers and controlling society, instead of directly copying the Stalinist model, had in part to do with the fact that China in the 1950s through the 1970s remained a largely agrarian society, which made it difficult to implement the extreme form of totalitarianism that worked only in a modern industrial society (Pye 1968, 235). Equally important in the genesis of substantive Maoism, however, were the cultural traditions that the Maoist state inherited from China's past. The expectation was that workers would treat their work unit as a family, act as the master of the family, and remain completely devoted to the interest of the family. All these ideas, central to substantive Maoism as a set of principles of socialist morality, had their roots in Confucian paternalism rather than the pure ideology of Marxism and Leninism. Another heritage that added to the popularity of substantive Maoism was pragmatism, or concern with practical solutions to real-world challenges rather than commitment to transcendent causes. Pragmatism was a cultural tradition that had undergirded Confucian values for thousands of years and influenced Mao's thoughts on the revolution in China. In the final analysis, what really mattered to the Maoist state was how to ensure workers' compliance and productivity by using the most feasible and effective set of ideas and institutions. Ideology served only as a means, rather than an end, in its quest for industrialization.

2 | BEYOND MASTERHOOD AND DEMOCRACY

Worker Participation in Factory Governance

THROUGHOUT THE MAOIST ERA, several official channels existed in state firms and beyond for workers to express their concerns and participate in the process of factory governance, including the staff and workers' congress (SWC), the trade union, and the system of appeal by letters and visits (*xinfang*) to government authorities at different levels. Behind the establishment and functioning of these institutions was a set of driving forces, each of which had its own historical origins and unique traditions of political culture. The first was radicalism, a tradition that had its roots in the Communist revolution in the 1930s and 1940s. What distinguished this revolution from the rebellions or actions of collective violence before it was chiefly its organizers' tremendous abilities of mobilization, which in turn had to do with the revolutionaries' creation of an ideology that promised to subvert the existing economic and social orders, liberate the laboring people from the oppression by landlords and capitalists, and make them the masters of the new society. After the establishment of the People's Republic, therefore, that ideology prevailed in society and served as the most important basis on which the new state was legitimized. The socioeconomic measures that the new state implemented right after the revolution, including the land reform, agricultural collectivization, and the nationalization of private industry and commerce, also made people believe that the government was serious in delivering what it had promised. But the revolutionary ideology soon came into conflict with the practices in state-owned factories under the "one-man system" (*yizhangzhi*) transplanted from the Soviet Union. The one-man system entailed a highly bureaucratized mode of governance on the basis of a strict hierarchy of management personnel, complicated and detailed regulations, and, most importantly, the centralization of power in the hands of the factory head, thus leaving little room for workers to participate.[1]

After copying the Soviet model for a few years, therefore, the Chinese Communist Party (CCP) leaders increasingly realized the incompatibility of the Russian systems with the conditions in China and decided to explore their own path to socialism after 1956, in the wake of de-Stalinization in Russia. Beginning with the relaxation of political control, Mao's initiative was unexpectedly met with workers' protests and strikes in cities (Perry 2002, 206–237). Part of worker disgruntlement had to do with the perfunctory role of the workers' council (*zhigong daibiao huiyi*) and the lack of effective channels for them to express their voice under the one-man system. They demanded the direct election of factory heads by themselves and the elevation of the workers' council to a status parallel to that of factory management. After the outbreak of the Cultural Revolution in 1966, the radical workers who joined rebel organizations succeeded in taking control of their factories after ousting former factory leaders; many of them believed that, as worker representatives, they became the true masters of their factories (Sheehan 1998, 130–132). As shown later in Chapter 5, however, the seizure of power at the height of the Cultural Revolution quickly yielded to the creation of a revolutionary committee in every factory, in which the rebel leaders were marginalized and eventually ousted when the Cultural Revolution ended. The political chaos in the early years of the Cultural Revolution further caused the paralysis and disappearance of the SWC and the trade unions. The radical vision of workers as masters of the factory, in short, never came true throughout the Maoist era.

Rationalism, as an alternative tradition in China's political culture in the twentieth century, also played a role in shaping factory politics in the Maoist era. This tradition had its origins in the May Fourth period from the late 1910s to the early 1920s, when the so-called "enlightenment" intellectuals embraced individualism and liberalism under the slogan "wholesale Westernization" and envisioned the transformation of China by replacing cultural conservatism and political autocracy with the advanced civilizations of Europe (Chow 1960; Fung 2010). Unfortunately, rationalism quickly receded from the center stage of Chinese politics due to surging nationalism, triggered by Japanese aggression in the 1930s and the rise of the Communist movement that targeted primarily the Nationalist regime. But it never vanished among the liberal intellectuals; many of them sympathized with, supported, and even personally joined the Communist movement precisely because of their aversion to the Nationalist regime's dictatorship and corruption. After 1949, a large number of such liberal individuals or liberals-turned-revolutionaries came to leadership positions at different levels. While staying in line with the party in ideology and action, they turned out to be more independent and critical in thinking than the rest of party cadres, and whenever possible they adopted a practical approach in promoting popular participation in government (Li 2013, 200–203). In the early 1950s, when a large number of private firms were yet to be nationalized, for instance, they emphasized organizing workers into trade unions and enhancing the role of the unions to defend workers' rights and interests; meanwhile, they also stressed the relative autonomy of the trade unions in state-owned enterprises (Sheehan 1998, 23–24; Perry 2007). After the nationalization of private firms in 1956, they made efforts to reorganize the workers' council into the SWC, which by design would play a greater role than its predecessor in supervising the performance of factory cadres, especially their decision-making activities. Therefore, they were among the most enthusiastic and supportive in response to the party's call for "promotion of democracy" (*kuoda minzhu*) at the grassroots level in the 1950s. During the Cultural Revolution, they were branded as "bourgeois democrats" (*zichanjieji minzhupai*) or "powerholders taking the capitalist road" (Chi Heng 1976) and came under the rebels' attack. When the Cultural Revolution was over, many of them were rehabilitated and reappointed to key government positions. Once again, they proposed the "democratic management" (*minzhu guanli*) of factories as one of the priorities of industrial reforms, hence the advent of the "golden age" of the SWC and trade unions in the history of labor relations in contemporary China (Zhu and Chen 2003; Andreas 2019, 168–178). This development, in conjunction with promoting the election of village councils, accounted for the growing faith among liberal intellectuals and reformers in the rise of "grassroots democracy" in China. For them, both village-level elections and the democratization of factory management served as preliminary steps leading to the long-term objective of building a democracy in modern China, rather than temporary solutions to problems in grassroots governance (Shi 1999).

Unfortunately, neither the ideals of radicalism nor the principles of rationalism came true in practice throughout the Maoist era. For instance, when workers requested the direct election of factory leaders, which they understood as the pinnacle of promoting democracy in the factories, the government refused on the grounds that every factory in the country belonged to "all the people," not just to the workers of a specific factory; therefore, the head of the factory should be appointed by the government that represented the interests of the entire people (*Renmin ribao*, 05/29/1957). In a similar fashion, the government rejected worker-rebels' appeal to turn temporary and contract workers into regular workers and reprimanded this request as "economism" (Perry and Li 1997, 97–117). Nor could the party-state tolerate the idea of making the SWC and trade union independent of enterprise management, which it criticized as "extreme democratization" or "absolute democracy" based on "bourgeois democracy and individualism" (Huang Xin 1958). Not surprisingly, the existing literature on the SWC and trade union generally emphasize their failure to function as the true organs to speak for workers.[2]

Instead of an inquiry about whether the SWC and trade union functioned in line with the principles of radicalism or rationalism—that is, to make the workers the "masters" of the factory or to promote "democracy" in factory management—this chapter is concerned chiefly with the practical purposes and real-world functionalities of these institutions and their informal alternatives. More specifically, the following discussion centers on these questions: To what extent did the formal participatory channels (i.e., the SWC, trade union, and the appeal system) as well as the informal options work to satisfy the actual needs of enterprise management and the demands of ordinary workers? What did the enterprises and the workers need to ensure the factory's normal operation and the workers' livelihood? And what can be learned from an examination of these issues for understanding the nature of factory governance and labor relations in the Maoist era?

THE STAFF AND WORKERS' CONGRESS (SWC)
Origins and Purposes

The creation of the staff and workers' congress (*zhigong daibiao dahui*) (SWC) in state-owned enterprises was first proposed by the CCP at its eighth national congress, held in September 1956, as part of a package of "democratization" in response to the rebellions in eastern European socialist countries, namely Poland and Hungary. The SWC were later widely established in the wake of strikes and petitions in Chinese cities in late 1956 and early 1957. A fundamental way to prevent the recurrence of such strikes and protests, according to a directive of the CCP central committee in March 1957, was to "overcome bureaucratism" and "expand democracy" by promoting "bottom-up supervision." A key measure of "bottom-up supervision" was establishing the SWC system in factories (*WXXB*, 10, 156–157) to replace the preexisting "staff and workers' meeting" (*zhigong daibiao huiyi*) (SWM) that had existed in state-owned enterprises since the early 1950s (Wang and Li 1992, 61–64). This meeting was usually held for a factory leader to announce a new task and for workers to promise their completion of the assignment; its role in offering suggestions and consultations to the factory administration under the "sole leadership system" was limited. It was almost impossible for the meeting to interfere with the factory's decision-making process and supervision of administrative activities (An Miao 1990, 121).

The transition from the SWM to the SWC also had to do with the fact that, after the completion of the "socialist transformation of industry and commerce" in 1956, the role of the party committee in industrial enterprises shifted from supervising factory leaders to making decisions in place of the leaders. Therefore, the SWM, which had *periodically* convened before, had to be elevated to the status of a *standing* SWC to play the supervisory role previously performed by the party committee. The aforementioned CCP directive and a subsequent notice of April 1957 thus explicitly defined the SWC as a "power-possessing institution for the masses to participate in enterprise management and to supervise the administration" (*WXXB*, 10, 157). They both allowed the SWC power in the following areas: (1) auditing the enterprise's plans for production, finance, technology, and labor, and periodically examining their implementation; (2) making decisions on incentive funds and the budget for welfare, healthcare, labor protection, and other programs relating to the well-being of employees; (3) recommending a change of enterprise leaders to the enterprise's superior authority; and (4) offering alternative suggestions to the superior authority for regulations with which the congress disagreed (*WXXB*, 10, 157, 168).

The famous "Industrial 70 Articles," promulgated by the CCP central committee in September 1961 to restore order to industrial production and management after the chaotic Great Leap Forward, defined the SWC as an organ to "discuss and resolve" problems in enterprise management and problems that "concerned the masses of employees the most"; it granted the SWC "the rights to criticize any leaders, to suggest to superior authorities punishment and removal of some of the leaders for their severe malfeasance and misconduct, and to make accusations to higher authorities by skipping the administration immediately above it" (*WXXB*, 14, 676).

What we need to examine here is the extent to which the SWC performed its duties as prescribed in the party's documents. A traditional view in this regard is that the functioning of a SWC, from preparation for the meeting and the choice of its topics for deliberation to the selection of its representatives and the arrangement of proceedings, was completely subject to the party committee's control; the representatives, therefore, had little autonomy and reputation among the masses. Without real power and unable to truly represent the workers, the SWC was only a formality operating in a perfunctory manner (An Miao 1990, 124). This remained true in the 1980s: A nationwide survey of workers in 1986 showed that 45.4 percent of respondents believed the SWC to be perfunctory in deliberating the enterprise's major decisions and supervising cadres (An Miao 1990, 198).

Selection and Qualification of Worker Representatives

The representatives of the SWC, by official regulation, should be reelected once a year, and the SWC should be held at least four times a year (*WXXB*, 14, 676). How to elect the representatives and who would run for election, therefore, were key to the functionality of the SWC. Two reports from the 1950s showed that the methods varied from case to case. Some factories adopted the so-called "equal quotas system," under which the number of candidates for voting equaled the number of representatives to be elected; voters, in other words, had no right to elect anyone other than the candidates prepared by SWC organizers (*CBJY*: 37). More factories, however, chose the "different quotas system," under which the number of candidates was usually 5 percent more than the number of representatives elected, so that the voters were allowed a small margin to make a choice (*CBJY*: 53). To select the candidates, again there were two ways: nomination by factory leaders or by ordinary workers. When the SWC was just introduced, it was usually up to the leaders to nominate the candidates so that the SWC would be "under control." Later, the method of "nomination by the masses" prevailed in most enterprises, as factory workers widely believed the first method to be "undemocratic" (*bu minzhu*) and insisted on the second, believing it to be a true way to "promote democracy" and the representatives thus produced to be "most democratic" and "responsible" to the workers (*CBJY*: 44, 53, 62). Local provincial authorities, too, urged factory leaders to "let the masses select those satisfactory to them to be representatives, and the leaders should not interfere in the process" (*CBJY*: 36); to ensure a "free election," factory leaders "should not nominate candidates, prescribe any conditions for candidacy, or name anyone as 'designated representatives'" (*CBJY*: 57). The representatives were usually elected from the candidates through an anonymous vote by workers (*GZJY*: 38), and the number of representatives was usually one-fifteenth of the total number of factory employees (*GZJY*: 5). To ensure that ordinary workers dominated the body of representatives and to prevent the SWC from becoming a conference of party members and factory cadres, a common practice was to limit the number of party members and factory cadres to around one-third of the total number of SWC representatives (*CBJY*: 10); in some factories, party members were limited to half of the SWC representatives (*CBJY*: 54).

Most of our interviewees confirmed that the SWC representatives in their factories were selected by workers through a vote (e.g., L6). Fang Hao (b. 1938), who had worked at Xi'an Instrument Factory for forty years since 1959 and served as a representative for multiple years, thus said that "the representatives were not selected by the factory leaders, but elected from bottom up and level by level, in the same way as the election of delegates to the People's Congress" (S10). Zhu Delong (b. 1948), a welder at the Shengli Oil Field since 1965 and a representative for fifteen years, also confirmed that the representatives in his work unit were "elected by workers but approved by the leaders" (Y1). But there were also instances where the representatives were actually "first picked by the leaders and then voted by the masses," as seen in the General Machinery Factory of Wuhan Steel and Iron Work (H15).[3]

Procedurally, the elections typically took place within small groups. At the No. 17 Cotton Mill in Shanghai, for instance, each group normally had about ten to twenty workers and thus produced one or two representatives by a vote, while a large group of fifty to sixty workers would have five or six representatives. "When it came to an election," recalled Zhang Yiping (b. 1955) who joined the mill in 1971, "workers elected the representatives by secret ballot, and the results of the election had to be publicly announced and formally registered if there was no dispute over the elected" (S7). Alternatively, as seen in the Zhenjiang Mine, workers elected their representatives simply by a show of hands at a small group meeting, and, as our informant recalled, "you raised your hands if you agreed, and you would not if you disagreed" (N2; see also W4). It should also be noted that, while it was officially required that workers account for no less than 60 percent of all representatives elected, in reality, cadres at different levels could occupy as many as half of the seats in the SWC, as Mr. Feng (b. 1940) of Wuhan Pharmaceutical Factory witnessed in his work unit, having worked there for twenty-nine years since 1958 (W3).

To be elected as workers' representatives, the candidates had to meet certain qualifications. The first was their reputation among fellow workers. They had to, as Mr. Yang (b. 1933) of the carrier equipment factory of Nanjing Telecommunication Bureau explained, "perform well in daily activities and follow the orders of task assignments"; moreover, he added, "they got along with others very well and were truly outstanding" (C1). At the machinery factory of Ningbo Port Affairs Bureau, workers elected their representatives "on the basis of their impressions about the candidates." "If they believed that the candidate was not bad, they would vote for him," our interviewee explained, "and three or four such candidates would be elected. They would be there to be entertained while attending the meeting, where fruits and candies were served" (N5).

Another important qualification was that the candidate had to be able to speak on behalf of fellow workers. Workers preferred to vote for those who "were able to speak out for the ordinary people" (S6), or those who "spoke for workers and spoke fairly" (W3). At the Wuhan Pharmaceutical Factory, for instance, workers "tended to vote for those who dared to make suggestions and complaints to the leaders. Those who were unwilling to do so would not be considered and elected. There were just too many people who remained silent even though they knew well that the leaders did something wrong.

Those who dared to speak out in front of the leaders were rare but truly wanted" (W4). Sun Aiting (b. 1955) of Shanghai Artistic Carving Factory thus explained workers' expectations of their representatives: "People voted for you and you should speak for them. When an issue arose, you should speak out as a worker representative. There were lots of issues, such as how to deal with the unfair assignment of duties, how to handle the problems of late arrival or early departure, whether or not a wage deduction should be made for a two-day sick leave, or to whom the subsidies should be distributed or not" (S6).

Submitting Propositions

The next step in preparing the SWC was collecting propositions from the elected representatives, which could be criticisms or suggestions on anything concerning the representatives that they wished to discuss in the forthcoming congress. The SWC organizers would usually receive hundreds to even more than a thousand proposals before or during the meeting, depending on the size of the enterprise and the particular situation in a given factory (*CBYJ*: 12, 23, 60; *GZJY*: 12, 54). The propositions generally fell into two categories: those about production and management, which were encouraged by factory leaders and usually accounted for about 80 percent or more of the proposals; and the rest about employees' working and living conditions. Not surprisingly, when determining the topics for deliberation and resolution at an upcoming conference, a divide often appeared between factor leaders and employees: The former preferred to focus on issues pertaining to "increasing production and saving costs," while the latter insisted on discussing issues affecting their well-being or problems with the leaders' "working style" (*CBYJ*: 45).

Let us start with the first category, propositions about production and management. Wu Binquan (b. 1942), who worked at the Bedding Factory of Huanggang Region for twenty-one years since 1967, recalled that, as a representative, he submitted two propositions: one about the "realistic appraisal of the quality of products" and the other about "how to reduce waste in production" (H8; see also B2). Another representative, Sun Guolong (b. 1952), who joined the Huaibei Power Plant as an examiner in 1968, made propositions on "improving the skills and procedures in production" and "issues concerning safety in production" (S14). Zhang Zhongbo (b. 1935), who worked for Shanghai General Petrochemical Plant for forty-three years since 1952, submitted propositions on "improving the quality of production" and "solving key technological issues," as he was an engineer and worker representative of the factory (S20).

The other category of propositions covered a wide range of issues concerning workers' working and living conditions. Ms. Fan (b. 1948) of Nanjing Telecommunication Equipment Factory, for instance, submitted proposals to "provide a work meal at noon" and "build a shower room," both of which were later "adopted by the leaders and implemented" (L5). A proposal from Mr. Sun (b. 1958) of Nanjing Housing Management Bureau concerned the "free distribution of gloves, hand towels, and safety helmets," which, too, was "adopted by the leaders" (L3). Fang Hao (b. 1938) of Xi'an Instrument Factory proposed to "build shelters and improve their management to prevent random parking and theft of bicycles" (S10). His second proposition was about enhancing safety protection, to which the leaders of the factory responded by adding a second firetruck and increasing the crew of firefighters from twelve to twenty-four (S10). At Shanghai Compressor Factory, representative Luo Guiling (b. 1936) proposed "the construction of a basketball playground and the promotion of sports and performing arts activities," and all these proposals "were implemented" (S11).

At some factories, the SWC also played a role in deciding punishments for disqualified workers and factory cadres. Two of our informants confirmed that, while it was up to factory management to fire a worker who had made a grave mistake, its decision in this regard was invalid until the SWC approved it (H5; H7). Likewise, while the SWC had no right to remove a wrongdoing factory leader, as Fang Hao of Xi'an Instrument Factory confirmed, it could nevertheless "be active in recommending to the administration the removal (of the disqualified cadre)" (S10), as the "Industrial 70 Articles" of 1961 prescribed (*WXXB*, 14: 676).

A full session of the congress usually lasted for two or three days. To guarantee that the representatives had ample opportunities to air their opinions, and to prevent factory leaders from using too much time to report on their work, a common practice was to reserve at least half of the meeting time for individual representatives' speeches, with the rest divided between leaders' reports and group discussions. Those who were interrupted by the presiding chair because of the time limit complained that the interruption was "undemocratic" and requested time for "additional speech" or "free speech" (*CBJY*: 28; *GZJY*: 43). Some factories allowed as much as 80 percent of the meeting time for representatives and audience members to speak (*CBJY*: 38, 63). As a result, more than half of the representatives would find time to speak out in those factories, and some of them could speak two or three times during the same meeting (*CBJY*: 43; *GZJY*: 43). To let the representatives freely air their opinions, the SWC organizers in some factories placed no limits on the topics of speeches (*CBJY*: 63), and the attending factory leaders would offer no explanations or defenses in the middle of the representatives' speeches (*CBJY*: 58). Compared to the SWM under the "sole leader system" before 1955 that was dominated by factory leaders' reports, the SWC representatives from factories in Hebei province claimed that the atmosphere of their meetings was "truly democratic" (*CBJY*: 44).

Handling Propositions
Although SWC representatives had more opportunities and greater freedom to speak out than their counterparts under the prior "one-man system," what really mattered to them was how their propositions were handled. There was, to be sure, no shortage of instances in which their propositions were adopted, and substantial measures were taken by factory administrators to address the representatives' concerns (*GZJY*: 62, 70). But the factory management dismissed without serious consideration the vast majority of propositions, often in the hundreds and even thousands, despite the representatives' request that "each and every piece has to be answered and handled" (*jian jian you dafu, tiao tiao you jiaodai*) (*CBJY*: 46). Leaders at Shijiazhuang Truck Factory, for example, processed the 900-odd propositions in a matter of six hours; in other words, they spent less than one minute per proposal on average. The representatives thus complained that the leaders' attitudes toward the propositions were "inappropriate" (*CBJY*: 47). After the SWC passed its resolutions or after factory leaders responded to propositions with solutions, how they implemented the suggested measures would become a serious concern to the representatives. Therefore, when a session ended, an "examination group" of representatives would form to see that the follow-up measures were properly carried out (*CBJY*: 16, 27, 39, 54–55, 59, 76). However, the official reports offer no indication of how the examination groups performed their duties.

What interests us here is factory leaders' real attitude toward the SWC. A report by the CCP Wuhan city committee admitted that the cadres in local factories were worried about the possibility of electing "unruly" workers as representatives, about the examination groups' inspection that would "impede" production, about workers' "endless complaints," and about workers' excessive demands on improving their welfare through the meetings (*CBJY*: 31). Likewise, the CCP Hebei provincial committee found that the administrators of local factories "had many worries"; they were concerned "about being criticized by the masses and losing face; about the workers' disobedience to their command in production under the expanded democracy; and about their inability to deal with so many complaints and suggestions from the masses" (*CBJY*: 41). The CCP Anhui provincial committee, too, admitted in its report that the cadres in three local factories where the SWC was first introduced adopted a "skeptical attitude" toward the SWC; some of them "were nervous and worried about being accused" at the beginning, and therefore "were unwilling to listen to criticism by the masses, believing that the workers were only interested in embarrassing the cadres and showed no understanding of the cadres' difficulties" (*CBJY*: 50). Reports from individual factories revealed similar concerns among factory administrators over worker disobedience and accusations against them under the SWC system (*GZJY*: 1, 36, 53).

Given the factory administrators' widely shared skepticism and resistance to the SWC, it was no surprise that they would make every effort to divert the representatives' attention from demanding improvements in their livelihood and criticizing the cadres' misconduct or poor performance to issues concerning production. Indeed, as mentioned earlier, most of the representatives' proposals were about how to increase production and cut costs through innovations and improvements (see, e.g., *CBJY*: 45; *GZJY*: 10, 20, 21, 47), and proposals about the workers' income and life accounted for no more than a fifth of all proposals in most cases. Still fewer were accusations about problems with cadres; the only two examples found in the official reports concern factory cadres' "excessive occupation" of housing (*CBJY*: 42) and favoritism in recruiting employees (*GZJY*: 10). It was likely, therefore, that the entire process of the SWC, from electing representatives and soliciting proposals to deliberating and making resolutions during a congress session and inspecting the implementation of resolutions after the session, was under the party committee's control. Workers, in other words, had little or no autonomy in shaping the proceedings of the congress.

This does not necessarily mean, however, that workers or their representatives were entirely powerless in articulating their interests through the

SWC or that the SWC proceedings were completely perfunctory and fruitless. While worker representatives were cautious in criticizing the cadres, they showed much less hesitation in expressing their concerns with issues that directly affected their income or living and working conditions. The representatives' propositions submitted to the SWC thus covered a wide range of topics in this regard. They complained about, for example, poor ventilation and high-level humidity in the dormitories; the poor quality and high price of foods in the canteen; the bad attitudes of staff at the clinic; or the need to lower the temperature in the workshop (*GZJY*: 10, 46, 77). Factory leaders did act quickly to address some of these problems (*CBJY*: 45). For example, in response to one representative's request, a new window was added at a woolen textile factory's canteen in Harbin specifically for mothers with children, thus saving them time on waiting in lines with other workers to get food (*GZJY*: 13). Cadres at a power plant in Shijingshan, in another instance, responded to representatives' proposals by adding a skylight to the roof of a building for better ventilation and building a shelter to protect workers from rain and sunburn (*GZJY*: 43). At Shanghai Machine Tool Factory, workers' biggest issue was their decreased income after introducing "three new systems" (new time rates in labor remuneration, new classification of working objects, and new methods of compensation); their subsequent shirking and lethargy caused an increase of defective products. After receiving many complaints about this, the party committee of the factory formed a special "work group" to investigate the situation. As a result, about 60 percent of the working objects were reclassified, and workers were reportedly satisfied with the result (*GZJY*: 62).

Another issue that concerned workers was fairness in distributing public goods. Division existed among workers in the same factory or different factories over their need for or access to various welfare programs. For example, while some workers who had become parents wanted a kindergarten in their factory, unmarried and older workers without this need would oppose the proposal; likewise, some workers enjoyed the nominal rent of housing units allocated by the factory, while others who owned an apartment or lived in dormitories would propose an increase in rent (*GZJY*: 23, 31). Similarly, while young workers wanted to change a pond into a swimming pool, older co-workers opposed it; and while those living in a dormitory enjoyed the sheltered hallway where they could set up a kitchen, those without this shelter proposed adding additional rooms as cooking space and faced opposition from the former (*GZJY*: 47). At the aforementioned Shanghai Machine Tool Factory, some newly hired employees proposed the cancellation of meal stipends available only to senior employees, but to no avail; in the same factory, all pregnant women had the privilege of receiving half a pound of free milk every day from the factory, but the "municipal federation of trade unions" soon ordered the factory to terminate the program due to opposition from other factories where pregnant workers had made similar requests (*GZJY*: 59–60).

The SWC, as these instances suggest, was more than a tool for factory leaders to enlist workers' conformity with party lines, as conventional wisdom has implied. To be sure, the SWC was far from performing the state-designated roles of participating in factory management, supervising factory administration, and promoting workers' awareness of being the masters of their own factories. From the official reports of the SWCs in various factories, we did not find a single case in which the SWC was involved in making decisions on the factory's production or welfare programs for workers, impeaching an unqualified factory leader and removing them from leadership, or reporting abusive leaders to authorities above the factory. There is no evidence to suggest that the SWC succeeded in playing its supervisory role in most enterprises. On the other hand, however, the official reports cited thus far do suggest that workers used the SWC as a means to express their concerns over various issues that immediately affected their income and their working or living conditions. They also used the SWC to air their dissatisfaction with inequity in the distribution of public goods between workers of different age groups, rankings, or factories. The SWCs, in other words, functioned to represent factory workers more in an economic than in a political sense. And the effectiveness of the SWCs in representing workers' economic concerns varied significantly from factory to factory. Many elements came into play in this regard, including the enterprise's size and number of employees, the profitability of its production and hence its fiscal condition, its employees' education and preparedness for participating in the SWC, and its factory administrators' willingness to incorporate the SWC into everyday management. It is thus not unlikely that the SWC was more effective in articulating workers' interests in large-scale state-owned factories, where the party's regulations on the SWC were more seriously implemented, and in industrial centers such as Shanghai where workers had a long tradition of struggle for economic and political rights. On the other hand, the SWC could be entirely perfunctory in factories where the workers were under the factory leaders' tight control or had no prior exposure to collective action.

THE TRADE UNION

Widely established in the early 1950s under the Trade Union Law of 1950 and the Trade Union Regulations of 1953, the trade union (*gonghui*) officially served as "the mass organization of the worker class on the basis of voluntary grouping" (*WJXB*: 4). Most of the trade unions at the grassroots level collapsed in the first few years of the Cultural Revolution that started in 1966, reemerged gradually after 1972 under different names, such as *qungongzu* ("mass work group") or *gongdaihui* ("worker representatives' council"), and became officially reestablished in most work units after 1974 (H13; also Shi Tanjing 2002).

In both the "Industrial 70 Articles" of 1961 and the "Provisional Regulations on the Staff and Workers' Congress in State-Owned Enterprises" of 1981, the trade union was defined as the "working institution" of the SWC, responsible for preparing and organizing the SWC while serving as the congress's standing office when the congress was not in session. By paying an annual due, which was 1 percent of one's monthly wage, all employees were eligible to become members of the trade union in their work unit upon approval by the union committee; a trade union at the grassroots level had at least twenty-five members (*ZYWJ*: 87).

The trade union's leadership was comprised of one chairperson and several deputy chairpersons. Together, they formed the trade union's working committee, and all committee members were "democratically elected from bottom up by union members" (*GHZC*: 2–3). To ensure that the trade union had enough power to function as the executive organ of the SWC, the 1981 Provisional Regulations further specified that the chairperson of the trade union should be selected from cadres at the rank of vice secretary of the party's committee or vice leaders of the factory (*WJXB*: 1318). Our informants confirmed that the chairperson of the trade union at their factories was a vice secretary of the factory's party committee (S1) or a vice factory head (H6), and that in the 1980s the trade union committee further became one of the "four sets of leadership" (*si tao banzi*) at their work units, along with the factory's party committee, factory head office, and disciplinary inspection committee (S2).

The routine duties of the trade union, according to the 70 Articles, fell into one of three categories. The first was about production: The trade union was to organize workers for competition in production, promote among them advanced working skills and experiences, and therefore ensure the completion and over-fulfillment of production tasks. The second was about education: The trade union was to educate workers with the state's policies, laws, and regulations, to make sure that the workers were disciplined and well organized; workers should also be taught how to help and learn from one another to promote a spirit of unity. The third category, which mattered the most for workers and constituted the most important tasks of the trade union, was about workers' well-being. The trade union was responsible for operating factory canteens, dormitories, bathrooms, childcare centers, and clinics; offering subsidies to workers in need; solving the concrete difficulties in workers' daily lives; organizing workers to study new knowledge and technologies; and organizing cultural, entertainment, and sports activities (*WXXB*, 14: 675).

When asked what the trade union did at their work units, our interviewees' answers were largely in line with the official duties of the trade union outlined above. At Shanghai Medical Equipment Factory, for instance, "the trade union was responsible for the welfare program and after-hours activities, such as arts and sports activities, or a tour out of town on the weekends or holidays. The factory covered the cost of the tour. When conditions allowed, they would organize a hiking to places such as the Shanghai Zoo. When the weather was hot, they would get the workers together for swimming," recalled a retiree from the factory. He further explained that "the factory usually used three percent of its annual profits for arts and sports activities, and five percent (of its profits) for the trade union's welfare things, such as a hand towel or a bar of soap. Therefore, the better the production was done, the more welfare benefits there would be; there was always a link between them" (N3). Mr. Sun (b. 1958) of the Nanjing Housing Management Bureau enumerated the trade union's activities at his work unit:

(1) Organized workers to watch a movie once a month or twice a month;
(2) Distributed labor protection products such as hand gloves and helmets;
(3) Provided subsidies and care for employees in difficulties, including funerals and weddings of the employee's family;

(4) Organized us for a visit to the mausoleum of the revolutionary martyrs at Yuhuatai to receive an education on the revolution;
(5) Annually organized the workers for a long-distance running in the Lake Xuanwuhu Park; and
(6) Offered classes on social dances and choirs of revolutionary songs after 1976. (L3)

Other factories saw similar trade union activities, such as organizing a competition in production (H5)[4] or activities in the performing arts, sports, or tourism (B7).[5] According to Mr. Liu (b. 1941) of the Nanjing Steel and Iron Work, his factory's basketball team won first place in the city-level championship in Nanjing in the early 1970s; as it turned out, some of the team members had joined the factory after retiring from provincial-level professional basketball teams (L1).

A key task of the trade union was to support "workers in difficulties" (*kunnan zhigong*). When a worker, a retiree, or a worker's family member died, for example, the trade union of the worker's unit would normally send someone to visit the worker's family to express condolences, organize a funeral to be attended by all former co-workers of the deceased, and present a wreath, or offer a subsidy to the worker if their family member had died (H15).[6] If a worker or a worker's family member was ill, the patient would be eligible for a subsidy of 10 yuan or so from the trade union to cover part of the medical costs (C5, H1, H18), and the trade union leaders would also pay a visit to the hospitalized worker and offer them a bag of fruits or foods worth 20 to 50 yuan (H4, Y1). The trade union would do the same for workers who gave birth or had a miscarriage (S8). If a sick worker's family was unable to look after them, it was up to the trade union to organize workers to take care of the patient in turns. "What impressed me the most," recalled Ms. Yang (b. 1938), who worked at the Nanjing Textile Company after 1962, "was when a worker of my factory was diagnosed with colorectal cancer and thus had to be treated at the Workers' Hospital in 1969 at the moment when the Party's Ninth Congress was held. Upon the trade union's call, we all enthusiastically and spontaneously participated in attending the co-worker" (L8). If a worker suffered an injury at the workplace, they would first seek help from the trade union; upon verification of the injury, the trade union leader would raise the issue to the leader of the work unit and ask for a certain amount of compensation (N2, S8). "The trade union indeed played a role in speaking for the injured worker and offering a certain kind of assistance," remarked an interviewee from the Zhenjiang Mine (N2). Finally, it was also up to the trade union to offer relief to workers who lived in poverty. Mr. Zhao (b. 1935), who joined the Jiangnan Clock Factory in 1956, described himself as having a longtime "household in difficulties" (*kunnanhu*) and living on "relief grain" (*jiujiliang*). With three children who were born one after another, his monthly wage was far from enough to feed the mouths in his family. He thus kept submitting requests for subsidies (C3). The trade union annually evaluated the economic situations of all employers and paid a visit to the families who were most in need during the Spring Festival, providing them with a limited amount of subsidy in cash or in kind (H2, N10, S13).

The trade union was also responsible for mediating disputes among workers and within workers' families (C1, H1). For instance, workers would complain to the trade union if they believed they "received unfair treatment" at the workplace (H19) or if they encountered "anything that made them unhappy" (L7). Part of Mr. Feng's (b. 1940) duties as a group leader of the trade union at Wuhan Pharmaceutical Factory was to visit a worker's family and help resolve disputes between a couple or even between a mother-in-law and a daughter-in-law. "If a female (worker) started a quarrel, I had to find someone to go with me for a mediation, and we would have a conversation with both the mother-in-law and the daughter-in-law. Our work was so meticulous in this regard." He added, "Whenever we heard of a quarrel taking place in a worker's family, and if the worker belonged to my group, the chair of the trade union would immediately send me to that family (for a mediation), and I would say yes in response" (W4). Mr. Yue (b. 1949) of the Gongnong Garment Factory in Wuhan, too, observed that the trade union cadres often visited a worker's family whenever a dispute took place there, especially when a couple quarreled with each other for a divorce (W5). Mediation itself, Mr. Yue emphasized, was an art that entailed the careful choice of words and delicate balancing of the requests and complaints from both sides. An important reason the chair of the trade union in his factory failed to be reelected, he explained, was precisely because he did a poor job mediating a dispute, and this made him unpopular among the workers. The female worker involved in the disagreement, Mr. Yue recalled, insisted on a divorce after the chair "uttered an improper sentence" during the mediation that made her furious. Even worse was that the chair released some of the details about the couple's dispute that should have been kept confidential. "Being a trade union chair," Yue concluded, "you should stand with your workers and speak for the interests of your workers" (W5).

Obviously, the trade union in Maoist China functioned very differently from its counterpart in a free market economy, in which workers move freely between jobs and bargain for labor price or wage level. With lifetime employment and a wage level that was fixed or, when there was a wage upgrade, based on one's seniority, the trade union in Maoist China lost the basic functions of those in a capitalist economy, namely protecting workers' employment rights and bargaining for better terms of labor remuneration and protection. To curb "bureaucratism" (*guanliaozhuyi*) among factory cadres and mitigate the discontent among the workers, as seen in the widespread strikes in the major industrial cities in late 1956 and early 1957, the party did want to "expand democracy" (*kuoda minzhu*) and promote "bottom-up supervision" (*you xia er shang de jiandu*) in factories by enhancing the roles of the SWC and the trade union in "listening and discussing" the factory head's work report; "checking and discussing" the factory's plans about production, finance, technology, and labor wages; "periodically examining" the implementation of such plans; and "when necessary, proposing to the higher-level administrative institutions the replacement of certain leading personnel of the enterprise" (*WXXB*, 10: 157). But the trade union's power stopped there; its influence on factory leadership and its participation in the decision-making process was very limited. Not surprisingly, the workers had mixed and often contradictory images of the trade union in their work unit. Sometimes they denied that the trade union had "real power" at all:

- "The trade union did not have so much influence. It had no real power, being a *qingshui yamen* [a government office without much income] idling with light duties." (H11)
- "It could participate in the discussion of administrative issues, but had no real power." (S15)
- "The trade union surely spoke and acted for workers, but whether or not it was effective was another thing." (S9)
- "[The trade union] had no say over the major issues." (Y1)

- "Workers usually turned directly to the workshop director or the factory head when they had something to deal with. The trade union had no final say, but it could speak for workers." (L6)

Others, however, had a positive impression of the trade union in their memory:

- "In general, it was still able to speak for workers, taking workers' opinions back to higher-ups, and pass on the leaders' opinions down." (S13)
- "The trade union did have the right to speak out and forward to factory leaders all kinds of requests and concerns in production, and handle issues such as subsidies for workers in difficulties and housing allocation, etc." (S10)
- "The trade union had to work to ensure the completion of production tasks under the party's leadership and at the same time struggled for the interests of workers." (S7)
- "The trade union was indeed able to act and speak for workers, showing care for workers during normal times and, when there was a work shift during holidays, visiting the workshop with gifts, thus making the workers feel warm and treat the trade union as home." (B2)
- "The trade union is like a window; workers used it to speak out and do things for themselves. It had to work to defend workers' legitimate rights and interests." (H23)

In fact, both versions could be true. The trade union did indeed have little influence over the factory leadership's making of key decisions on production, spending, or personnel appointment. Yet it played a key role in satisfying the workers' everyday needs on the shop floor or at home. It worked in improving workers' everyday working and living conditions and implementing the propositions passed by the SWC concerning these areas. It organized a variety of after-hours activities to satisfy workers' diverse needs outside the workplace and provided support to the workers having difficulties. It played a key role in factory businesses that directly affected the workers' livelihood, including the adjustment of wage levels and the construction and allocation of housing units. Obviously, most of the duties performed by the trade union in Maoist China did not fall into the range of those done by the trade unions in a free market economy, yet they were indispensable for the workers to improve their well-being at the workplace or in their everyday lives.

APPEAL BY LETTERS AND VISITS

To more effectively air their grievances, criticize local cadres, or make suggestions on government policies, factory workers could also write letters to state or party authorities at different levels or appeal to such authorities by paying a personal visit. Compared to expressing their opinions on formal occasions, such as at the SWC or complaining to the trade union within the factory, writing a letter or paying a visit to a government office at the municipal level or higher had obvious advantages. First, letter writing involved minimal risk and was most cost-effective. Letter writers, who could choose to reveal their identity or remain anonymous, were free to criticize any cadres of their factory that they were dissatisfied with but unwilling to criticize openly at formal meetings for fear of possible retaliation. And the only cost of writing and mailing a letter was a stamp of a few cents and a trip to a mailbox or post office. Second, letter writing was also the most convenient and accessible option to ordinary people. A letter could be written at any time and addressed to government authorities at any level above the writer's own factory; in contrast, at the SWC meetings workers had to wait until the meeting was held and express their opinions through the representatives who did not necessarily speak for them, and the representatives could only speak to their own cadres and the audience from their own factory. Third, unlike the proposals submitted to the SWC, which had to be about the shared well-being of a group of people or about the collective interests of the work unit, letters could cover just about anything, and indeed were primarily about letter writers' personal grievances that they could not express publicly. Finally, the government welcomed letter writing, deeming it a "democratic right" of the people and a means for them "to participate in the political life of the state and to supervise the work of government institutions"; for party and state leaders, reading such letters was believed to be a reliable and timely way to get to know the real situation at the grassroots level and the true concerns of the people (Diao Chengjie 1996, 4, 389).

What we need to address here are the following three questions: First, when did the workers write letters or pay visits to government agencies, and what did they write or complain about? Second, how did the government handle such letters and visits? Third, how effective were the letters and visits in reflecting and redressing workers' grievances, and to what extent did the letters and visits contribute to popular participation in political life and in supervising the government as the state intended?

Letters and Visits: When, Why, and What

Several factors influenced one's decision to write and what to write about: one's own economic condition or social/political standing in a given period, the state's economic or political policies that immediately affected the individual's well-being, and the overall political atmosphere that encouraged or discouraged writing. Thus, the frequency of letter writing or personal visits and the motivations behind these activities varied significantly over different periods. In the early 1950s—right after the civil war—letters and visits came primarily from unemployed workers, intellectuals, and students seeking jobs, or from retired soldiers in need of government relief. Letters and visits from ordinary citizens increased rapidly during the "Three-Anti" and "Five-Anti" campaigns in 1952 and 1953 to inform against corrupt cadres and illegal businessmen, and continued to increase until 1956. In that year, nearly 72 percent of the letters or visits handled by the State Council's Secretariat, for example, were about employment, education, relief, or other personal issues; criticisms and accusations against the wrongdoing government officials or others accounted for 5.51 percent, and the rest were various suggestions (Diao Chengjie 1996, 23, 56, 80).

But the number dropped quickly after October 1957, when the oppressive political atmosphere of the Anti-Rightist Campaign caused people to refrain from making criticisms or complaints, and later, when local government authorities detained a large number of letters and arrested letter writers to prevent the central government from learning about local famine and casualty caused by the Great Leap Forward. Most of the letters and visits during the Great Leap Forward were about food shortages and requests for relief, about reemployment after losing one's job as a factory worker, or about local cadres' use of coercion and arbitrariness (Diao Chengjie 1996, 121–124).

When the Great Leap Forward ended in complete failure in 1961, a wave of criticism against the radicalism of the preceding few years prevailed in official media and public discourse; the government also took measures to rehabilitate the greatly impaired economy and to reestablish order in social and political life. As a result, letters and visits increased by leaps and bounds in the following years; those handled by the State Council Secretariat, for example, increased to nearly 130,000 in 1962, more than twice the number it processed in the previous year, and further to almost 210,000 by 1965 (Diao Chengjie 1996, 165). Similar trends are also observable at the local level: The number of letters and visits handled by Tianjin municipal authorities, for instance, increased from merely 5,793 in 1959 to 16,300 in 1961 and about 30,000 in the following two years (XFZ: 187). People complained of various issues in letters or during visits, including reemployment or reappointment after being laid off from factories or "trimmed down" from government offices during the later stage of the Great Leap Forward; compensation of economic loss and retroactive payment of salaries from the government; or removing the label of "rightist" and terminating labor reform that had been inflicted on the victims of the successive political campaigns in the preceding years. Later, when the Socialist Education Movement started in 1963, an increasing number of letters and visits were about disputes over the classification of one's family status as landlord or rich peasant or concerning political disciplinary actions against convicted cadres or citizens.

Overcoming Post–Great Leap Forward Difficulties
The records on "people's letters and visits" (*renmin laixin laifang*) preserved at the Nanjing Municipal Archives allow us a glimpse of how local workers expressed their grievances through these channels. All these records originated from the General Trade Union of Nanjing Municipality (*Nanjing shi zonggonghui*). The reason why workers turned to the general trade union to seek justice and express their demands is obvious. Unlike a local branch of the trade union at the factory level, which tended to be subservient to factory leadership and scarcely acted independently on behalf of the workers, the general trade union at the municipal level was above the factory in the administrative hierarchy and free of the influences from the leaders of individual factories in the city. It thus was able to investigate the workers' appeals rather objectively and respond to their claims independently. The number of

appeals received by the general trade union varied from year to year, typically surging when a nationwide movement ended and the pressure of mass mobilization had dissipated; those who had suffered thus sought solutions to the distresses that they had experienced during the movement. One such moment of rising complaints was the period of several years following the Great Leap Forward.

In the first quarter of 1963, for example, the General Trade Union of Nanjing Municipality received 174 letters and 195 visits, or 369 cases in total, compared to only 117 in 1962. Among the 369 complaints, 95 were about compensation to workers who had been "trimmed off and sent down" (*jingjian xiafang*) from their original work units, and 103 were about the reduced wage rates and welfare benefits for existing workers. As a correction to the problem of excessive employment of new workers during the peak of the Great Leap Forward (1958–1961), the adjustment policies of the central government in the post-Leap years (1962–1965) focused on cutting down employment in state-owned enterprises and reducing the rates of labor remuneration, in addition to slowing the expansion of heavy industries and shrinking the scale of infrastructural construction. Most of the "trimmed-off" workers had been rural residents before they were hired at state-owned factories; therefore, after being laid off, they were sent back to their home villages under the slogan of "return to the countryside and support agriculture" (*huixiang zhinong*). Although each of them should receive a subsidy upon departure, and the subsidy was determined by the number of years in employment at the work units, the laid-off workers often received much less than they deserved due to miscalculation of their employment history. After leaving Nanjing Brick and Tile Factory in 1963, Xie Muquan, for example, found that the official report of his employment history at that factory was eight years less than the actual length (ten years) of his work experience there. He thus complained to the General Trade Union. The latter intervened, and Xie eventually received a full payment from his former work unit. He personally visited the office of the General Trade Union to express his gratitude (NJ6001-2-425).

The General Trade Union also gave special consideration to workers who had personal difficulties in accepting the layoff plan. Jiang Zhengxin, a worker at Nanjing Steam Navigation & Electric Machinery Factory, for instance, lost two fingers because of an accident in the factory back in 1959. He thus wrote to the General Trade Union in 1963, requesting the removal of himself from the list of employees to be "sent down" to the countryside, on the ground that having lost two fingers made it difficult for him to do farming tasks. In response, the General Trade Union cadres consulted the Municipal Party Committee's "trimming-off office" (*Jingjian ban*) and further discussed the issue with the leaders of Jiang's factory. They reached a solution, and Jiang was removed from the list of workers to be laid off (NJ6001-2-425).

Workers who had been urban residents before employment were not completely exempt from the trimming-off program, and those of old age were among the first to be let go. Among such victims was Feng Youde, a worker at the warehouse of Xiaguang Grain Processing Factory. According to the factory, Feng was laid off in 1963 because he was "too old and ineligible for work assignment." With seven members, however, Feng's family had huge difficulties in making ends meet after he lost his job. Feng thus turned to the General Trade Union for help. After an investigation, the General Trade Union concluded that, though in his old age, Feng "is in good health condition and has never been ill." The General Trade Union thus suggested that the factory "reconsider its handling of old-age workers." Similarly, Chen Hexian, a female worker at Nanjing Qinfeng Cigarette Factory, was laid off only a few months before she reached the official retirement age (fifty-five years old) in 1963. She requested that she be allowed to work for a few more months so that she would be qualified for retirement benefits. The factory leader refused on the ground that "it is difficult to assign her a job after the factory transitioned from manual to mechanized operation." After receiving Chen's complaint, the General Trade Union suggested that the factory "conduct an investigation on this kind of cases; otherwise old-age workers would encounter difficulties in their livelihood" (NJ6001-2-425).

As these instances indicate, the General Trade Union's reactions to worker grievances varied. It actively intervened only when the workers involved were obviously maltreated, as seen in the cases of Xie and Jiang. In the cases of Feng and Chen, the General Trade Union only responded by making "suggestions" to relevant factory leaders without endorsing the victims' requests, obviously because the decisions made by the factories were justified by economic necessity from the factory's point of view and backed by policies that did not target Feng or Chen specifically. Not surprisingly, for complaints from workers about the reduction of wage rates, the General Trade Union came up with no suggestions at all. At the warehouse mentioned above, for instance, the workload for a fixed amount of labor remuneration in repairing the packaging bags increased from 170 to 220 bags under the piece-rate system. Workers from Nanjing Cotton Textile Factory also complained that their income declined after the application of the piece-rate system and thus demanded adjustments of workloads and wage rates. These changes reflected a nationwide trend in economic "adjustments" in the wake of the Great Leap Forward rather than factory-specific policies against workers. The General Trade Union thus refrained from responding to such complaints. For letters or visits that came up with an "unreasonable request" (*buheli yaoqiu*), the General Trade Union would endorse the factory's decision but nevertheless would also settle the case by offering a suggestion to alleviate the difficulties of the letter writer or visitor. A good example is the case of Tang Lingbang, a worker from a coal mine construction company, who was fired in February 1963 because he had "engaged in market speculation" and sold the lumber that the work union had allocated to him for repairing his house, thus making an illicit profit of 80 yuan. The General Trade Union rejected his request to keep his job at the company but suggested that the company offer him a subsidy of 30 yuan and assist him in obtaining a peddler's license to make a living.

Grievances over Cadres' Workstyles

The General Trade Union of Nanjing Municipality handled no fewer letters and visits during normal times than the years of adjustment or rehabilitation following a vehement movement such as the Great Leap Forward, as seen above. In 1965, for instance, it received 716 letters and 1,061 visits, or 1,777 cases in total, which fell into the following categories: "lingering issues relating to the trim-off and send-down program" (507 cases); "labor protection" (421 cases); "cadres' workstyle and democratic life" (120 cases); "all kinds of appeals and requests" (521 cases); and "hardship in livelihood and requests for subsidies" (181 cases). What stand out from these records are the various complaints about factory cadres' "workstyle" (*gongzuo zuofeng*), or the way they performed their duties and dealt with workers, an issue central to the Socialist Education Campaign that lasted from 1963 to the first half of 1966. The General Trade Union noticed a difference before and during the campaign in workers' accusations against the cadres: "In the past, workers usually wrote us anonymously, and when they visited us, they refused to tell their real names." After the socialist education campaign started, however, the workers were emboldened, and "most of them are brave enough to disclose their real names when exposing the cadres' problems of privileging themselves, overspending on meals and excessive occupation of public goods (*duochi duozhan*), and incorrect workstyle." Zhai Xingyi, a "sent-down student" working at the state-owned Nanjing Farm, thus accused Kong Xiangan, a cadre of the trade union of Jianye district (part of Nanjing), of "extravagant consumption" and purchasing "luxurious commodities" such as a wristwatch, bicycle, and radio. The General Trade Union conducted an investigation shortly after receiving Zhai's letter and found that Kong had embezzled more than 5,000 yuan of public funds. In another instance, Zhang Baiyu, a female guide at the Yahuatai Memorial Park of Revolutionary Martyrs, visited the General Trade Union several times to complain that the cadres of her work unit refused to reimburse her for her daily commute; even more intolerable, she complained, was that the cadres brutally treated her by "gripping her legs and pulling her on the ground for one or two meters" when they tried to get her to leave the management office. The General Trade Union responded by conducting a "criticism and education" on the cadres involved and asked them to "solve the subsidy issue."

A more telling case about factory cadres' workstyle problem came from Shuguang Cotton Textile Factory, a state-owned enterprise. In May 1965, at an order from Nanjing Municipal Textile Industry Company, the factory decided to send Waang Xiuying and nine other workers to the spinning group of the recently established Diaoyutai Textile Factory, to provide technical support to the new factory, which would open on June 2. Waang refused to go there, while the other nine workers all accepted the decision after an "education." Waang's biggest concern was that once she was sent to the new factory, which was a collectively owned business and therefore inferior to her current work unit in terms of wage rates and welfare benefits, it was likely that she would stay there forever and never be able to come back. In addition, she was in poor health because of being overweight and complications from a surgery. On June 10, both Waang and her husband, Lu Youshui, a worker of Nanjing Vegetable Oil Mill and also a party member, visited the General Trade Union, expressing that Waang would be willing to go to the new factory only if the party secretary of her current work unit guaranteed in writing that she would be allowed to come back three months later. The party secretary, a female named Wang, rejected their request. She further withheld wage payment to

Waang and disallowed her to work in the factory. Unable to work, Waang continued sitting in front of the factory office to get their attention. A few days later, a cadre in charge of personnel affairs from the factory visited the General Trade Union and complained that Waang's resistance to the new appointment and her "troublemaking" (*nao*) had caused "bad influences" among workers; because of her "unjustified refusal" to the new job, she had been treated as "being absent from work without good reason" (*kuanggong*) since June 2.

In response, Ma Zhaoying, a female cadre of the General Trade Union, visited Waang's home on June 17 and assured Waang that she would be allowed to go back to her current factory with her wage and benefits unchanged three months later. Two days later, Waang's husband and brother visited the General Trade Union. The husband accepted the new appointment on behalf of Waang but insisted that the current factory pay her the wages they had withheld since June 2. Ma agreed, believing this to be a "reasonable request," and phoned Waang's current factory accordingly. But the party secretary of the factory, who took her call, was infuriated and resentful, saying "you should not listen to the one-sided words from the worker only. We cannot continue the discussion on the wage issue if you think so."

Waang went to the new factory on June 19 because of Ma's promise, but her husband, Lu, phoned the General Trade Union on June 22 because Waang's former factory had not yet paid her the withheld wage for seventeen days (June 2–18). The General Trade Union replied: The withheld wage should be paid back to Waang, but Waang should also make a self-criticism for resistance to the new appointment at a meeting of the "small production group" to which Waang belonged. Lu was angered: "She [Waang] won't do a self-criticism even at the cost of the withheld wage. If she has to make a self-criticism, then the factory leader should do so first, because the leader paid no attention to the worker's health condition." Lu nevertheless brought his wife's written self-criticism to the General Trade Union on July 10, after Ma contacted Lu's factory for this purpose. But Waang's former factory refused to pay the withheld wage on the ground that Waang's self-criticism was "insufficient," insisting that she had to come back to the factory to make a self-criticism at a meeting.

The meeting was held on August 7. Instead of a meeting at the level of "small production group" as the General Trade Union suggested, it had nearly twenty attendants from different workshops. A factory cadre in charge of personnel questioned Waang at the meeting: "Why did you resist work reappointment? Why did you turn your back on the party secretary? What would you want to be after coming back?" Another cadre chimed in: "Why did you ask your husband and brother to make trouble with the General Trade Union? Troublemaking did not help solve the problem." Waang refused to criticize herself at the meeting, believing that she had already written a self-criticism, and she was surprised by the level of the meeting. Afterward, the factory's trade union chairman, named Guo, visited the General Trade Union and complained to Jiang Peihua, a cadre of the General Trade Union: "Waang behaved badly at the meeting and the participants were dissatisfied. The withheld wage will not be paid to her." He justified the factory's escalation of the meeting from the level of small production group to the level of workshops: "The higher-level trade union cannot put a constraint on the form of our meeting. It's a decision made by our factory leader." He blamed Waang for bringing this issue to the General Trade Union and even blamed the General Trade Union for "backing" her. Jiang's reply: "Workers have their democratic rights. Your words are incorrect!" Upon hearing Jiang's remark through Guo, the factory's party secretary Wang was unhappy: "The General Trade Union has treated me as a capitalist (*zibenjia*)!"

The General Trade Union thus had to forward this case to the Party Committee of the City. At the intervention of the latter and the instruction from the Party Committee of Nanjing Municipal Textile Industry Company, the head of the factory visited Waang's home, paid her the withheld wage, and admitted the factory's mistake of "paying insufficient attention to the worker's health condition." In its report on the handling of this case, dated August 27, 1965, the General Trade Union made the following conclusion:

> Waang Xiuying was wrong from the very beginning because of her refusal to job reassignment. But the Factory disallowed her to work, suspended wage payment, and held a large-scale meeting to "educate" her. All these methods are incompatible with the instructions of Chairman Mao. Chairman Mao said, "As long as they do not persist in wrongdoing, we should not ridicule them with a bias and take a hostile attitude toward them"; Chairman further said, "So long as the problem is just about different ways of thinking and so long as the problem belongs to the

category of disputes among the people, we can only solve it with a democratic method, or the method of discussion, criticism, persuasion and education, instead of the method of coercion and compulsion." The masses of the people are bold enough and willing to express their own opinions and demands to higher levels. We should realize that this fact alone is a vivid manifestation of popular democracy in our socialist country, evidence that the masses have unlimited trust in the party and the government, and a deep reflection of the close relationship between our party and government on the one hand and the masses of the people on the other. Therefore, we should welcome opinions that reveal real situations. Unfortunately, some of the comrades at the Shuguang Factory adopted a biased attitude and even brazenly required the worker to "confess" why she had visited the Trade Union for "troublemaking." Strictly speaking, this is a sign of suppressing workers' democratic rights. Secretary Wang of the factory said that the City's General Trade Union "treats her as a capitalist," the factory's personnel cadre said that the "higher-level trade union cannot limit the form of the factory's meeting," and the factory trade union chairman said that the worker had someone "backing" her. All these words are inappropriate. It was even more inappropriate that the factory delayed wage payment to Waang to August 19 despite the City Party Committee's intervention on August 17 and that it failed to truthfully report to the City Party Committee by claiming on August 17 that the wage had already been paid. Furthermore, we believe that it is against moral integrity that the Shuguang Factory "provides support" to another factory by sending a worker in poor health condition. This is irresponsible for both the receiving factory and the masses of workers. (NJ6001-2-425)

The Triangular Relationship among Worker, Factory, and High-Level Trade Union

The above instance illustrates the triangular relationship among workers, their factories, and the trade union above the factories. For workers with grievances, the trade union within the factory was obviously unreliable, because it tended to side with factory leaders when the latter were confronted with the disgruntled workers, as best evidenced in the attitude of Trade

Union Chairman Guo of the Shuguang Cotton Textile Factory. The workers, therefore, chose to appeal to the General Trade Union at the municipal level, which was far above the factory and thus free of the personal influences from factory cadres. Unlike the factory-level trade union that discouraged workers to challenge factory leadership, the general trade union usually welcomed the letters and visits from workers; how quickly and how successfully they handled such letters and visits directly shaped the records of their performance of duties. Not surprisingly, its annual and quarterly reports always emphasized the number of letters and visits it received as well as the number of the cases it had successfully handled, hence the so-called "rate of settled cases" (*jie'an lü*), which was, for instance, 89.2 percent, 78.81 percent, and 85.47 percent in the first three quarters of 1963 (NJ6001-2-425).

But the General Trade Union responded to different kinds of complaints in different ways. For cases that apparently involved unjust treatment of workers by factory cadres or the cadres' abuse of power at the expense of the "masses of the people," the general trade union would intervene, but its intervention was always measured and "principled." In other words, it had to carefully weigh the complaints and claims from all parties involved and make sure that its responses considered both the merits and faults in each party's words and deeds; most importantly, it had to form a judgment and decision by adhering to the party's policies and Mao's instructions. Given its status as a government organ at the municipal level, most factories involved in such cases had to respect the General Trade Union's intervention and accept its decisions, but they did not necessarily welcome its involvement, especially when its decision or suggestion was against the factory leadership. Party Secretary Wang of the Shuguang factory thus resisted the General Trade Union's intervention by accusing the latter of equating her with a "capitalist." Under this circumstance, when the factory explicitly refused to cooperate and even resisted its intervention, the General Trade Union's only option was to forward the case to the municipal government's relevant administrative division, such as the aforementioned Nanjing Municipal Textile Industry Company, and even bring the case to the attention of the city's party committee. It was only under the pressure from the city's party committee and the government body in charge of the textile industry that the leaders of the Shuguang factory eventually conceded.

Finally, it is worth noting that Waang Xiuying, the protagonist in this case, was neither a model worker favored by factory leaders nor a "backward element" (*luohou fenzi*) who performed poorly in everyday production activities. She was only an ordinary worker or, more exactly, the "weak" among ordinary workers. Given her poor health condition, Waang was less willing than her co-workers to accept the new appointment. For her, what really mattered was the security that came with her current job at a state-owned factory. Her request that the factory guarantee her right to come back to her original job after the three-month support thus appeared to be reasonable from the General Trade Union's point of view. The final settlement of this dispute reflected a balanced reconciliation of demands from the three parties: The factory saved face after Waang eventually accepted its decision to work at the new factory for three months; the worker received payment of the withheld wage and obtained the assurance to come back to her original factory after three months; and the General Trade Union intervened and succeeded in the end despite resistance from the factory. Unlike the grassroots trade unions that were subject to factory leadership (Andreas 2019, 9, 81), the trade unions at higher levels, free of influences from the factory involved, did show a degree of autonomy, as this instance suggests.

INFORMAL METHODS OF GRIEVANCE REDRESS

In addition to the formal and legal channels discussed so far, workers also employed various informal means to express their grievances and seek redress. For instance, a discontented person may visit the office of their factory cadre for a "conversation" (*lilun*). Depending on the worker's personal temperament, the complaint involved, and their relationship with the leader (*lingdao*, which usually means the factory head or workshop director), the conversation could be polite and peaceful, but it could also develop into a quarrel, in which the worker would argue with the cadre and even call the latter names. If a conversation like this did not work out, the worker may find every possible opportunity to speak tenaciously and pugnaciously to the cadre until the latter conceded. At the Shitouzui Mine of Daye, Hubei province, for example, a miner "treaded on the heels of the leader everyday" because the latter had failed to handle the worker's complaint. According to Zhou Dexian (b. 1950), who entered the mine in 1971, that miner "followed the leader wherever the latter appeared, and even pursued the leader all the way to his home. He visited the leader's home almost every day and even ate there. He bugged him endlessly. So exhausted was the leader that he eventually yielded and satisfied the miner's request" (H13). Le Shuiyuan (b. 1951), who joined the same mine in January 1971, also observed that "there were always a few who tended to argue with the leader whenever they had a problem." Once they "made a scene" (*nao*), Le added, "the issue would be quickly solved, that's why there is a saying, the crying baby gets milk first" (H11). Zhu Delong (b. 1948), a welder at Shengli Oil Field since 1965, described himself as someone who "had no fear of the leader." Around him were a group of co-workers who were always ready to "argue and even quarrel" with the cadres whenever any of them faced "unfair treatment." Vexed with the cadre's apathy toward their grievances, for example, the boldest among them could even stop working by shouting: "I quit!" (Y1; see also Y2 for a similar observation).

Workers were discontented for various reasons. For example, they would be unhappy with injustice in the annual selection of Advanced Producers. At the Yimin Food Factory in Shanghai, it was up to the head of a production group to nominate a worker from the group to the workshop director for approval, and the latter in turn submitted the approved list of candidates to the factory for finalization at the end of a year. As Ms. Yang (b. 1943) explained, "If fifteen candidates were nominated but only ten could be approved, then the factory head had to delete five. The five who had to be dropped were usually those that the head disliked. The head disliked them because they had been the most troublesome and contentious." Predictably, the head had to face protests from those who had been removed from the list (S8). At Wuhan Rubber Plant, in another instance, evaluating one's performance was highly subjective in the process of nominating an Advanced Producer. According to our informant, a candidate could easily argue with all cadres above them over their qualifications: "He would pick a quarrel with the group leader, and if that didn't work out, he would argue with the factory head or the party secretary" (W2). A quarrel was most likely to happen when any of the nominees was obviously unqualified in the eyes of their co-workers. According to Mr. Yue (b. 1949) of Gongnong Garment Factory in Wuhan, the Advanced Producers in his factory were usually selected from those who worked exceptionally hard "on the front line" and also got along with co-workers very well, always willing to help others after finishing their own shifts. "No one would dispute such candidates," he went on, "if, however, you nominated someone who was bad or who tended to perform poorly, then workers would have an opinion. Though they themselves were unqualified, the workers would protest the injustice by all means" (W5). The most frequent complaint among the workers about the nomination of Advanced Producers, as a retired technician of the Huaqiao Sugar Mill in Guangzhou put it, thus was: "Why the title is given to him, not me?!" (N10).

Another common reason for discontent was factory leaders' mishandling of workers' bonus payments or wage raises. Mr. Feng (b. 1940) of Wuhan Pharmaceutical Factory described himself as a "senior worker" and "rebellious person." One of the moments when he "rebelled" was when the party secretary of his workshop decided to cancel a bonus payment to all workers of his production group for the current month after the secretary found a worker in his group taking a nap during work hours. Instead of arguing with the secretary, Feng, as the head of the production group, complained directly to the trade union president of the factory: "That worker alone made a mistake and he alone should be punished. You shouldn't cancel the bonus for the rest of us in the group. It's unacceptable that all of us are to be punished when only one of us made a mistake." Furthermore, he argued, "the worker took a nap only after he finished his work. For that mistake, you can educate him in whatever manner you like, but you should not cancel his bonus, which didn't work at all, because economic punishment has only limited effects, compared to education that can really move him." He then eloquently blamed the secretary for his incorrect handling of this issue: "There is no such a thing as the backwardness of the masses. There are only backward cadres who failed to perform their duties." He threatened that he would continue to "make trouble" (*nao*) all the way to the leader of the factory until he won (W4).

Yang Xiaofeng (b. 1943) of Yimin Food Factory also described how her co-workers reacted to an injustice in pay raise, in which the "work shift coordinator" (*zhibanzhang*), who oversaw the activities of different production groups in a workshop, played a key role. The raise in the early 1970s was on the level of 3, 6, or 9 yuan for workers of different qualifications. In her factory, she recalled, "only two out of every one hundred workers were allowed for a raise. Who would be the two? The coordinator would prefer those who had good relationship with him" and therefore crossed the rest off the list that had been recommended by production groups under his supervision. Those who had been removed from the list would pick a fight. "They would quarrel with you, shout slanders about you, or stop working, loitering out there. One of them who was one generation older than me kept shouting abuses everywhere and uttering all kinds of swearwords. He would not stop until he fully vented his anger. He never knew how to defend his rights" (S8). For our interviewee from Hefeng Yarn Mill in Ningbo, one of the biggest disadvantages to being a workshop director was precisely being prone to workers' cursing, especially when determining pay raises. "At such moments," she explained, "workers cared about nothing. They were straightforward when making a complaint. If a worker is resentful of you, she would dig out anything that is bad about you, including things that are very personal and irrelevant to your work, such as your husband's wrongdoings, or anything that had happened to you before. All of the family members of the workshop director or group heads are subject to her cursing. Workers cared about nothing indeed. After all, a pay raise is of one's personal interest. Sometimes you missed the opportunity only because you are a bit behind the criterion" (N1). Zhong Yunping (b. 1954), who started working for a local labor service company in 1972, agreed that the most common reasons for workers' disgruntlement were pay raises or bonus payments: "The bonus was as little as five yuan a month at that time, but nevertheless there was injustice. Sometimes you lost your bonus for a month simply because you arrived late" (S9).

Workers could be resentful and boisterous when they were faced with other kinds of unfairness in the workplace. Take the assignment of tasks within a production group. It was usually up to the leader of the production group to assign the daily or routine tasks to individuals in the group. "If any unfairness occurred in the assignment," recollected Sun Aiting (b. 1955) of Shanghai No. 1 Artistic Carving Factory, "those below him would rebel immediately" (S6). For instance, the factory once had a party secretary who was notorious for his "stubborn bias." He would appoint whomever he liked to their desired position regardless of the candidate's abilities. Workers thus protested (*nao*), causing the authority above the factory to conduct an investigation and censure the secretary (S6). Workers were also likely to argue with the cadres when their request for a leave or change of job was rejected (L6), or when they found unfair distribution of opportunities for vocational training, which happened to Mr. Yue (b. 1949) of Gongnong Garment Factory in Wuhan in 1973. After being hired in 1965 and working in the factory for eight years, he believed that his work experiences qualified him to be one of the factory's two candidates to receive training in making woolen cloth at a garment company. Unfortunately, he had a difficult relationship with the party secretary of the factory because of his inclination to criticize the latter. Not surprisingly, he was not included on the secretary's list. When questioned, the secretary explained to Yue: "Your political consciousness is not that good." Yue was angered: "What's wrong with my consciousness? You have selected me as the head of the study group, so I am surely better than all others in this regard. Besides, I am a member of the Youth League branch committee, so why am I not qualified enough? I have also worked for eight years in the factory. Why then did you not allow me to go and study?" He thus kept "making a fuss" (*nao*) with the secretary. The latter did not yield in the end on the ground that the number of candidates was limited, but he nevertheless tried to placate Yue by promising him an opportunity next time (W5).

It should be noted, however, that contentious workers such as Yue were in the minority. When confronted with different forms of injustice in the workplace, most workers chose to be "forbearing and silent" (*renqi tunsheng*) and adopted the attitude of "submitting to the will of Heaven" (*tingtian youming*); only a few of them were bold enough to argue with the cadres, as Chen Zhiping (b. 1946) of Shanghai Light Bulb Factory confirmed (S4). Luo Guiling (b. 1936) had a similar impression of the situation in Shanghai Compressor Factory, where he worked initially as an apprentice in 1951 and later became a workshop director: "People usually chose to forbear when their opinions and complaints were ignored. Of course, there were also people who wrote a letter or pay a visit to a government office at higher levels, or even quarrel with the leaders. All these did happen to my work unit, but they were very rare. I never did so, though I did once argue with a leader" (S11). For workers with a "bad" family background, such as Zhou Meizhen (b. 1936), who worked at a military bedding factory in Wuhan and whose father had served the Nationalist government before 1949, arguing with factory leaders was never an option. Zhou described herself as someone who "never thought about personal gains or losses and quarreled with any leaders." "At that time when the class status of one's family mattered the most," she explained, "young people with a bad class status had to keep a low profile by all means" (*jiazhe weiba zuoren*) (H5).

Finally, the propensity for workers to quarrel with cadres also depended on the nature of the workplace and the composition of the workforce. For example, miners and oil field workers appeared to be among the most pugnacious, as evidenced in the cases cited earlier, obviously because most of them had been peasants in suburban areas or veterans who were peasants before being enlisted. Socially known as "uncouth fellows" (*dalaocu*), they were less educated and less restrained by the traditional social codes of forbearance and submission than the rest in urban China. In sharp contrast, workers in the military factories were subject to the strictest discipline; therefore, their disputes with cadres were nearly nonexistent. Zhang Qishan (b. 1942) of the abovementioned military bedding factory thus remarked that "the political consciousness (of workers) in military factories was of high level in general, so they won't argue with leaders, thanks to the existence of the person-to-person dialogue (*tanxin*) system, the working of the mediation committee and the livelihood committee, and the practice of cadres' periodical visit to worker families (*jiafang*)" (H6).

SUBSTANTIVE GOVERNANCE

The operational realities of factory governance in industrial enterprises under Mao departed remarkably from the ideological assumptions of both radicalism and rationalism. It was true that the SWC was officially intended for workers to supervise factory leaders, practice grassroots democracy, and eliminate bureaucratism in factory management. By design, the SWC had the right to "discuss and solve" major issues in business management, "criticize" factory leaders, and make suggestions to superior authorities on disciplinary actions against the incompetent cadres, including removal from office. In reality, however, the SWC was far from a legislative or decision-making body within a state firm as the advocates of grassroots democracy would assume, and its supervisory roles as designated by the state were mostly perfunctory in practice. Likewise, the trade union in Maoist China was in fact part of the factory management, rather than an independent organization representing workers. Equally disappointing was the actual record of worker participation from the perspective of radicalism. While by definition all state-owned factories belonged to the people, and the workers, as the leading class in the socialist society, were supposed to be the masters of the factories, their masterhood was nevertheless limited to the discursive level and rarely institutionalized in practice. The state forbade workers' direct election of factory leaders and quick improvement of their wages and living standards, as Chapter 5 will discuss. Despite the radical or rational assumptions underlying the state's policies on factory governance, neither the masterhood of the working class nor the promotion of democracy came true in state firms throughout the Maoist era.

This does not mean, however, that the institutions for worker participation failed, as the conventional wisdom has long suggested. To make sense of the real purposes and functionality of these institutions, we have to take into account two basic facts about the state-owned factories in Maoist China. First, production and employment in a state firm were completely subject to the unified planning of the central government. The state firm could only perform whatever production tasks it was assigned, and it could not make any decisions on its own; in other words, no autonomy existed among the factories, not to mention the SWC or the trade unions within them. Therefore, it was practically impossible for these institutions to play a key role in the firm's decision-making activities, if any. Second, the regular workers of state firms were entitled to a full range of benefits and rights to guarantee their permanent employment and meet their needs in education, subsistence, and recreation. Without workers' freedom to choose a job and the firm's flexibility to determine wages, the trade union within the firm was never in a position to bargain with the factory on behalf of the workers as was its counterpart in a market economy based on private ownership. The idea of a trade union's independence and autonomy made no sense to the Chinese workers at all.

This, however, should not lead us to conclude that the SWC and trade union were useless and nonfunctional. For factory cadres, a key issue in labor management was how to keep the workers in good spirits. Workers' attitudes and performance on the shop floor shaped the quality and quantity of production. The leaders knew well that ideological indoctrination and political pressure alone were insufficient to keep the workers motivated; they had to provide them with the necessary material means to satisfy their needs in production and everyday life. It was precisely in this regard that the formal institutions for worker participation as well as the informal alternatives came into play and functioned as they were *actually* intended. The factory leaders did pay attention to SWC proposals about providing safety protection in production or facilities to accommodate workers' needs, and they acted accordingly in many cases. Whenever workers encountered problems in employment or difficulties in family life, they sought help from the trade union within their work unit or above; alternatively, they petitioned to government authorities by letter or visit. On many occasions, their complaints were heard and requests were handled. If any of these formal channels did not work as expected, the workers would turn to informal means for a solution to the problems that confronted them, and from time to time, such informal options worked as well. The effectiveness of these practical functions of the participatory institutions contrasted sharply with the formality of their officially stated objectives, be they the manifestation of workers' status as masters of the factory or the promotion of democracy at the grassroots level.

The term "substantive governance," therefore, best characterizes the realities in which the institutions governing labor relations and factory production actually operated. This substantive mode of factory governance departed from the formalist assumptions underlying the official representations of labor politics in the Maoist era. Alternating between radicalism and rationalism, those assumptions, be they about elevating workers' status or promoting democracy, were largely detached from the complex and ever-changing realities of factory politics and irrelevant to the rank and file. In sharp contrast, substantive governance emphasized the use of a variety of formal institutions as well as informal practices to manage labor relations and satisfy the everyday needs of both cadres and workers. What mattered in this mode of governance was how practical and effective those institutions and practices were in solving the real-world problems that concerned the workers as well as the cadres, rather than how consistent they were with the state's ideology or the state firms' regulations. In other words, substantive governance functioned primarily to ensure the workers' satisfactory performance in production and the smooth operation of state firms instead of prioritizing the unrealistic and impractical objectives of formalist ideologies. By ensuring the normal operation of state firms at the micro level, the substantive mode of governance contributed to industrial growth in Maoist China no less than the obvious macro-level factors that have been well observed in past studies, such as the adjustment of development strategies, the making of economic planning, the massive input of labor force, etc. Exactly how workers performed in everyday production and fared in the network of power relations will be the subjects of the following chapters.

3 | EVERYDAY POWER RELATIONS IN STATE FIRMS

CLIENTELISM IS ONE OF THE KEY concepts in the existing literature on power relations at the grassroots level in post-1949 China. Unlike the use of pure coercion under a totalitarian state, clientelism denotes the bargaining and reciprocity between a power holder (the "patron") who provides protection and benefits for their followers ("clients") and the latter's loyalty to the former, as anthropologists and political scientists have widely observed since the 1960s in their studies of power relations and local politics in African, Latin American, and Southeast Asian societies.[1] The thriving of patron-client networks, as James Scott describes in his analysis of Southeast Asian societies, rests upon "the persistence of marked inequalities in the control of wealth, status, and power" and "the relative absence of firm, impersonal guarantees of physical security, status and position, or wealth" (Scott 1972, 101).[2] In his research on industrial enterprises in contemporary China, Andrew Walder also underscores the prevalence of patron-client ties. Factory leaders at the workshop level, he contends, ensured workers' compliance in production by implementing "principled particularism," that is, to reward "activists" or loyal workers with opportunities in promotions, pay raises, bonuses, admission into the party, or priority in housing allocation and job assignments. This practice resulted in the workers' organized dependence on the leaders, given their de facto life-employment in the factory and lack of job opportunities outside the work unit. Instead of stratification based on education, seniority, or skills, Walder finds the split of the workforce into the minority of activists and the majority of non-activists, depending on their relationship with workshop leaders; hostile to the privileged activists and their "official patron-client network" with the leadership, ordinary workers, he further suggests, cultivated "instrumental-personal ties" with individual factory cadres for survival because of scarcity (Walder 1986).

Critics of the clientelist model do not deny the existence of patron-client networks in Chinese society at large and the industrial factories in particular, but they dispute the extent to which this network prevailed on the workshop floor, the applicability of this model to the analysis of the entire factory system (Davis 1988), and the split between activists and non-activists in factory politics (Perry 1989). For them, equally important in understanding cadre-worker relations in Maoist China were the formal and informal institutions that empowered the workers and constrained the cadres (Blecher 1987; Womack 1991). Unfortunately, these critiques are mostly based on the commentators' general observations and inferences; few substantiate their criticism with solid evidence from field research.

This chapter begins with an overview of the structure of factory leadership and then addresses three issues. The first is the overall relationship between factory leaders and workers, as seen in their everyday interaction in production and political activities; we pay particular attention to the various formal and informal constraints on the leaders in their decision-making process and relations with workers. The second is the operational reality of the mechanisms by which the material goods and political incentives were distributed. The central question here is whether they were distributed only to the small and fixed group of "clients" according to their loyalty to the leaders or to all eligible workers on the basis of announced rules and regulations, and to what degree the cadres were able to practice favoritism in the process. The third is the relationship between the activists and non-activists, and the question here is whether a split and mutual hostility widely existed between the two. This chapter ends by discussing the implications of the findings here for conceptualizing everyday social and political relations in state firms of Maoist China.

THE CADRES AND WORKERS: AN OVERVIEW
The Three-Tiered Leadership

The factory head and the secretary of the Chinese Communist Party's committee at the factory were the top leaders of a state firm; while the former carried out the specific tasks of production, the latter was in charge of political and ideological matters in principle. Both of them normally did not interact in person with ordinary workers. This was the case in large-scale factories with more than ten thousand employees, where the workers knew who their factory leaders were only "from the photos displayed on the glass-fronted billboards," as Mrs. Zhang Yiping (b. 1955), who entered the No. 17 Cotton Mill in Shanghai in 1971, recalled (S7), and where "the factory head did not come down to the shop floor at all" (*genben bu xialai*), as Mrs. Yang Xiaofeng (b. 1943), who joined the Yimin Food Factory in Shanghai in 1968, witnessed (S8). This was also true in small firms with only hundreds of workers, where the factory heads "did not deal with workers at all" (*he gongren bu daga*), according to Mr. Yue (b. 1949) of the Gongnong Garment Factory, which had only about 280 workers in 1970 (W5; also W1).

Next to the factory head and party secretary were the workshop directors (*chejian zhuren*) and the party's branch secretaries at the workshop level, who were normally promoted from lower-ranking cadres; most of them started as ordinary workers and later were promoted because of their "hard work, good skills, and outstanding performance" (*ken chiku, jishuhao, biaoxianhao*), explained Mrs. Fan (b. 1948), a former accountant of Nanjing Post and Telecommunication Equipment Factory (L5).[3] The workshop director was to see to it that the workshop achieved or surpassed its production goal within a time limit and the workers performed well inside and outside the workshop. The director was responsible, for example, for finding a replacement if a worker in charge of a specific task was absent because of illness or another reason (W5). If a worker was accidentally late or absent and no other alternates (*beiyonggong*) were available, the head had to do the task of the absent worker (*dingban*) (N1, W3). If the workshop had an urgent task that had to be done within a time limit, the head as well as all other factory office staff had to join the workers in completing the rush task, such as the seasonal job of processing tomatoes and mushrooms in large quantities before the produce spoiled, as seen in a food processing factory in Shanghai during the harvesting season (S8).

But the workshop leader's most important jobs were to coordinate with the leaders of production groups, to apportion the tasks to each of the groups, and to oversee their performance. The head thus had to be present on the shop floor all the time (*genban*) (H4), unless they had other engagements such as attending a meeting or conferring with the factory head. In addition, the head had to spend much of their energy on workers' various personal issues, such as illness, family violence, divorce, or illicit sex, and on any conflicts or problems among the workers that the subordinates were unable to handle (B8).

Below the workshop director were a number of group leaders (*zuzhang*), each responsible for dozens of workers that formed a "production group" (*shengchan xiaozu*). Above the group leaders, there might also be shift foremen (*zhibanzhang*), in factories where production continued twenty-four hours a day in three eight-hour shifts, or section chiefs (*gongduanzhang*), in factories where production was divided into several sections with each section responsible for one stage of the entire production line. A group leader's basic duty was to assign specific tasks to each individual. During the height of the Cultural Revolution, the leader also presided over a study session for fifteen to thirty minutes before the shift started. When the eight hours of work ended in the late afternoon, the leader normally convened the group members for a meeting (*pengtouhui*), usually less than ten minutes, in which the leader would discuss "how the production had been done, how much had been manufactured, what problems had occurred, who and what deserved a praise, and what the workers should pay more attention to tomorrow, etc." (N10).

The Costs and Privileges of Being a Cadre

Other than the duties outlined above, the group leader performed the same tasks as ordinary workers in production. Therefore, they were believed to be the least powerful yet the "most hard working" (*zuikude*) among all cadres of a factory (S1, S6). A group leader had to "take the lead" (*shenxianshizu*) (S4) when confronted with the most difficult and dangerous tasks, such as handling an accident or an emergency situation in the factory (W1, W2); otherwise they would lose popularity (*shiqu minxin*) among the group members, and the latter would "not respect and obey" (*bufu*) the leader (N7). When the group's shift was over and all other members were gone, the head had to stay to clean up the floor and examine the tasks done by its members; if anyone left early or was absent, the group head had to work in their stead. According to the aforementioned Yang Xiaofeng (b. 1943), the group leader was "the most capable yet suffering the most" (*zuinenggan, zuichikui*) among the workers (S8), yet their earnings were no higher than the ordinary members' of the same wage grade (see also S2, S5). When it came to a group discussion on the amount of bonus payment for each group member, the leader had to yield to others if the total amount for bonuses was limited (N7). As an ordinary miner under the Shanghai Metallurgical Bureau observed, "Only after you give up and take the loss, you can mobilize others and make them motivated in production. This was called to 'suffer at the beginning and enjoy later' for the cadres" (N2). Not surprisingly, it was widely believed that being a lower-level cadre meant to "lose (or suffer)" (*chikui*) (W1, N1).

In contrast, workshop directors were somewhat privileged because they did not have fixed tasks in the production line, and most of time they did not have to work together with ordinary workers. However, they, too, had to join the group heads to "lead in a charge" (*chongfeng zai qianmian*) when the workshop had an urgent or dangerous task. A former group leader at the Shanghai No. 17 Cotton Mill thus said: "Being a cadre, you have to take the lead. Otherwise, the task cannot be done, and you surely won't be able stay in your position for long. When you go down to the bottom level, you have to make people convinced and respectful of you (*baiping renjia*) by demonstrating yourself first. You have to take the lead to make them convinced. Moreover, you have to treat them with sincerity" (S7).[4]

The cadres of different levels had to show their unselfishness and superior morality when deciding wage raises, bonus distributions, apartment allocations, or nominations for advanced workers. On these occasions, they were invariably expected to yield their opportunities to the most qualified workers and "not to compete with the masses" (S10).[5] At the Nanjing Post and Telecommunication Equipment Factory, for instance, the cadres were normally allocated the "worst" apartment units, as a former factory accountant witnessed (L5). In another instance in 1976, at a housing service unit in Nanjing, a workshop director's wife quarreled with her husband because he had repeatedly given up opportunities to receive an apartment; in the end, the work unit decided to give the head an apartment (L3). Such instances, to be sure, may be considered the "best practices" expected of the cadres, but they do suggest the cadres' concern with their reputation and public image and their eschewal of overt and excessive malfeasance, if any.

The cadres fared no better when there was a wage raise. At the machinery factory of the Port of Ningbo, for example, the wage was increased by 5 yuan for workers but only 2 or 3 yuan for the cadres, when their wages were upgraded by one level in 1971, which explained why our informant from this factory was reluctant to accept the workshop director position (N4). So too was the situation at the General Machinery Manufacturing Factory of Wuhan Steel and Iron Work, where "the wage increased less for the cadres and more the workers" during a wage raise (H12). When determining the level of bonuses to be distributed, again the cadres had to yield. Mrs. Song (b. 1937), a retiree from the Xinghuo Cotton Mill in Nanjing, thus recalled, "If the total amount of bonuses was insufficient to be paid to all workers of the same workshop, usually the leaders had to automatically reduce their rates. At the end of a year, when nominating recipients for a year-end bonus, which had to be publicized, workers had better opportunities than the cadres to get the first-grade bonus, while the cadres, if truly outstanding, only received the second- or third-grade bonuses" (L6). During the most difficult years following the Great Leap Forward, the cadres of state firms were required to take the lead in returning coupons for cloth, meat, and grain to the government to help relieve the shortage of supplies in the market, as a former workshop foreman of Shanghai Compressor Factory confirmed (S11). When promoted to the position of workshop director or any other positions as cadres "detached from production" (*tuochan ganbu*), the grain ration was reduced from the standard amount of 31 catties (1 catty = 0.5 kilogram) for ordinary workers to that of 26 catties for cadres (H7). In state-owned mines, the standard grain ration was 46 catties for miners and 32 catties for all cadres (H13). Hence a popular saying among the cadres: "Promotions come with a reduced grain ration rather than getting rich" (*shengguan bu facai, liangshi jian xialai*) (H6). Workers had a good reason to joke that "the cadres are idiots!" (*ganbu shi sazi*) (C6).

Of course, the hardest times for the cadres were during the political campaigns. Unlike ordinary workers who were "free of troubles" (*meishi*) when a campaign came into the factory, the cadres were invariably the targets of repeated investigations and struggles (H11); they had their worst period during the first few years of the Cultural Revolution, when most of them were struggled against repeatedly and even beaten up by the radical youth (H14). Throughout the rest of the Cultural Revolution, the cadres "feared the masses" (*haipa qunzhong*) (S6) and therefore had to "keep a low profile" (*suo zhe tou zuo*) when dealing with them (S5). When assigning an extra task to the workers, such as an after-hours shift (*jiaban*), the factory leader had to first discuss it with the group head and let the group head "consult" (*shangliang*) the workers to obtain their consent, instead of imposing on the latter a compulsory order (*mingling*), as a retiree from the Shanghai Medical Equipment Factory explained (N3). If a cadre did something that irked the workers, causing "wide complaints among the masses" (*qunzhong yijian da*) (N5), that cadre would be subject to either protest from the latter, in the form of open "big character posters" (*dazibao*) in the most visible parts of the factory compound or the clandestine "letters of the people" (*renmin laizin*) addressed to higher authorities, or an investigation from their superior and, if verified, subsequent disciplinary measures.

The Maoist state's stress on curbing the cadres' privileges and narrowing their gaps with the rank and file can be seen in part as a continuation of the party's pre-1949 revolutionary tradition, central to which were its cadres' practices of austerity and equality with the masses on the one hand and the masses' voluntary participation and initiatives on the other hand (Selden 1995). Mao's own preference for voluntarism, his profound faith in mass mobilization, and his aversion to elitism and hierarchy (Schram 1989) accounted for the continuity of the revolutionary tradition after 1949 and its triumph over the short-lived attempt in the 1950s to adopt the elitist approach of the Soviet Union, which allowed the cadres and skilled workers a full range of privileges and therefore gave rise to a striking inequality between the cadres and workers as well as among the workers of different skills and wage grades. A more fundamental reason behind the Maoist state's limitation of cadre privilege and its promotion of equality between cadres and the masses, however, had to do with a combination of two factors: the state's strategy that aimed to maximize its extraction of resources for state-led industrialization, and the constraints of resource endowments. The latter forced the state to prioritize the survival of the entire urban population by guaranteeing its full employment, precluding the option of cultivating a privileged bureaucracy and elite workers that would compete with the state and the rest of the population for limited resources. To motivate the workers in production, the state could only emphasize the use of political or non-material incentives instead of material awards, thus narrowing the gap between cadres and workers in production and income distribution. It is in this context that the relationship between the cadres and the workers can be appropriately understood.

Relations with the Workers

One of the biggest concerns for factory leaders of the Mao era was to maintain good "relations with the masses" (*qunzhong guanxi*) or to "mix up with the masses" (*yu qunzhong da cheng yipian*) (H20). Our interviewees generally agreed that, except for the few who were arrogant and indifferent, the leaders at their factories were "fairly considerate" (*hen tiliang*) (C1) and "quite active in taking care of those below them" (S8), or that they "cared a lot about their relations with the rank and file" (H3; also L3). A retiree from Hefeng Yarn Mill in Ningbo thus described her shop head:

> The head visited our workshop very often, partly to get close to the workers and partly to see how they performed.... The head was faced with the pressure to meet the production target, so he had to please the workers. When it was getting hot, for instance, the head would bring to us a basin of cool water so that we could wash our faces—that's how to take care of the workers! Otherwise, we would complain: how comfortable you are sitting in your office, while we sweat blood in the workshop, which is so hot in the summer! The workshop head had to keep a cordial relationship with the workers, or it would be very difficult to keep improving production. (N1)

Given the importance of worker cooperation in factory production and management, it is not surprising that the cadres at different levels managed to find supporters among the workers, who would take the lead in responding to orders and completing tasks. To have followers was especially important for the cadres who were recently promoted or those who came from outside the factory. The new leaders were particularly interested in finding supporters from among the newly recruited workers, who tended to be obedient, unlike some of the senior workers, who appeared to be defiant, counting on their seniority or connections with other cadres (N5). Motivated workers, too, were likely to seek favor and protection from their superiors. As our informants all pointed out, however, those who deliberately pleased the cadres by flattering, gift-giving, or outright bribing (together known as *paimapi*) were very few (W1, N1, N2). Most of the interviewed retirees denied that flattering was a common phenomenon in their relations with shop leaders. They claimed that "there was no need to flatter the leaders at that time" (*nashi buxuyao taohao lingdao*), in the words of a retiree from the Nanjing Post and Telecommunication Equipment Factory (L5), or that "it was unnecessary to flatter the leaders" (*yongbuzhao taohao*), as an interviewee from a labor service company in Shanghai put it (S9).[6]

As for why most of the workers in state firms shunned fawning on the cadres, the interviewees offered different explanations. Some of them found the reasons in their personality (H1).[7] Other informants emphasized the larger social and institutional context to explain why cultivating personal ties was not as important in the Mao era as nowadays. A retiree from the General Machinery Factory of Wuhan Steelworks, for instance, explained that few workers in his firm flattered the cadres because "the social atmosphere at that time was fairly good" (*dangshi fengqi bijiao hao*), which contrasted sharply with rampant corruption in the reform era (H10). The retirees of other firms stressed the relatively good quality of the leaders in their factories. Promoted mostly from the rank and file, the cadres were believed to be hardworking and "totally different from [the leaders] nowadays" (*gen xianzai wanquan bu yiyang*) (L3). The workers, for their part, kept "fairly normal relations" (*guanxi bijiao yiban*) (H10, S18), "good relations" (*guanxi manhao*) (L5, S9), or "very harmonious relations" (*guanxi feichang rongqia*) (L3) with the cadres; they respected the cadres and, therefore, did not feel the need to flatter them (H13, H15).

A more common reason behind the limited importance of personal ties in state firms, as most of our informants stressed, was the gross "equality" between the shop leaders and ordinary workers. When talking about their relationship with the cadres, the informants repeatedly stressed that it was "equal" (*pingdeng*) (S10, S18, Y1, Y4), "fairly equal" (*bijiao pingdeng*) (S8, S11), "completely equal" (*yilu pingdeng*) (S11), "on equal footing" (*pingqi pingzuo*) (L2), or "fairly good" (*hai bucuo*) (B9, L4, N4). However, the interviewees each define "equality" differently. For some of them, equality was primarily political and social, which was felt only when they were off duty; while on duty, workers "had to obey the leaders, because it was widely accepted at that time that to obey the leaders was to obey Chairman Mao, and to accept the state's arrangements" (B2; also S4). Other interviewees defined equality in an economic sense. For Mr. Fan (b. 1941), a retiree from the Zhongxingyuan Silk Mill in Nanjing, the workers were equal to their leaders because their wages were paid in the same way, determined primarily by one's seniority; those who had longer employment and better performance were paid more, regardless of whether they were cadres or workers (L2; also Y1, B9).

The most important reason behind the perceived equality between cadres and workers, however, lay in the fact that the former had only limited power in influencing the well-being of the latter (L2).[8] According to Mr. An (b. 1930), a retired physician from the No. 2 Company in Nanjing under the Ministry of Petroleum Industry, the workers in his factory "normally did not flatter" because "the leaders back then did not have as much power as the leaders have nowadays, and most people just needed to work honestly and seriously" (L4). So too was the view of a retiree from the Port of Ningbo when explaining why the workers there fared well with the cadres: "There were only a limited number of things that the leaders could handle on their own. Our food was rationed and administered by the grain department of the government, our grocery coupons were distributed by the street residents' committees, and the wages were paid according to the state's regulations, which the leaders had no right to deduct. Nor did the leaders have the right to lay off workers, which had to be approved by the superior authorities" (N4).

To recapitulate, two institutional arrangements central to labor management in the state firms shaped the relationship between cadres and workers. First, the workers' lifetime employment and guaranteed entitlement to a full range of benefits on the one hand and the limited power of cadres regarding employment and income distribution on the other precluded the necessity for the vast majority of workers to seek protection from and develop loyalty to individual cadres. Second, instead of the workers' dependence on the cadres for the security of their livelihood, the cadres depended on workers' cooperation for the timely fulfillment of production targets, in the absence of the ability to offer material incentives at their own discretion to motivate the workers. These two features were in turn a result of the state's transplantation of the Soviet factory system model and its adaption to the Chinese context of resource endowments in the 1950s. In China, the huge size of the labor force and the limited job positions precluded the possibility for workers to freely change jobs between different firms and accounted for their lifetime dependence on their employing enterprises, contrasting with the shortage of labor and hence the high turnover rate in the Soviet factories (Filtzer 1992; Whyte 1999). On the other hand, the limited availability of capital and resources for the industrializing state prevented it from relying on material incentives (e.g., frequent wage upgrades, bonus distributions, or housing allocations) to motivate the workers. The cadres' limited discretion in rewarding the workers, their dependence on the latter for production, and the narrow gap between the cadres and workers in income levels and living conditions all contributed to the rise of a shared consciousness among the workers of being equal with the cadres, which again contrasted sharply with the stark hierarchy and inequality in Soviet society (Lane 1985, 177–194; Filtzer 1986, 101–102).

WAGE UPGRADE AND HOUSING ALLOCATION

To determine whether the relationship between workers and cadres was characterized by a general equality, as many of our interviewees claimed, or whether a split existed among the workers, as the clientelist model suggests, we must look further into how much discretion workshop cadres had in making decisions concerning the workers' material well-being and political standing in the workplace. A key issue that has to be addressed here is to what degree the cadres were subject to a full range of institutional constraints and whether they had "wide discretion" in determining the workers' wage raises, bonuses, promotions, job assignments, and entitlement to various political honors, as Walder claims (1986, 96–97, 160, 163, 166). For Walder, these factors constituted the necessary conditions for worker dependence on their supervisors and the rise of clientelist ties in the factories. So powerful and arbitrary were the cadres, Walder writes, that "discretion can be used to punish workers by refusing to exercise it in their favor. Selected individual can be denied bonuses and raises to which they might otherwise be entitled based on their work performance" (ibid., 100). To illustrate the cadres' personal power and preference, he quotes a description of the foremen at a Budapest tractor factory and suggests that this depiction mirrors the situation in China: "They are emperors here. They hold us all in their hands. They dole out favors as they see fit. . . . The foreman doesn't just organize our work:

first and foremost he organizes us. The foremen fix our pay, our jobs, our overtime, our bonuses, and the deductions for excessive rejects" (ibid., 102). Were the Chinese workshop cadres truly as powerful and arbitrary as their counterparts in Hungary? Let us first look at how wage raises and housing allocations were determined in the Chinese firms.

Upgrading the Wage Level

Wage raises were rare in the Mao era. Since a standardized wage system was introduced nationwide in 1956, there were only three upgrades in the rest of the Mao era: first in 1959 and 1960, when the upgrade was limited to 50 percent (30 percent in 1959 and another 20 percent in 1960) of the workforce in state firms, and priority was given to workers who excelled in production and technological innovation; second in 1963, when 40 percent of workers, primarily those of lower wage grades for the longest period, benefited from the upgrade; and third in 1971, which again gave priority to workers of the lowest grades, including all first-grade workers hired by the end of 1966, second-grade workers hired by the end of 1960, and third-grade workers hired by the end of 1957. In 1977, a similar upgrade took place nationwide, targeting primarily all first-grade workers hired by the end of 1971 and second-grade workers hired by the end of 1966. Therefore, it was unusual for workers to have a raise in the Mao era (H9), and when a raise did take place, it involved almost everyone or all workers of the same seniority, in a method known to them as "pushing all ducks to cross the stream" (*gan yazi guohe*) (H13).

The most important criterion in determining the workers' eligibility for a raise, as the state's policies made clear for the upgrades in 1963, 1971, and 1977, was their seniority, or years of employment (*gongling*), which was confirmed repeatedly by our informants (e.g., H15, N5, N10, W1). In the memory of a retiree from the machinery factory of the Port of Ningbo, for instance, "The evaluation of wage grade was based on one's total scores, which in turn was determined by one's work performance, workload, seniority, and assessment by the masses. So it was conducted reasonably well, and the major criterion in the evaluation was one's seniority. If you have only fifteen years, while someone else has thirty years, then that person's score was certainly higher than yours. Seniority was the primary standard, and other criteria were considered as well" (N5). A former technician at the Huaqiao Sugar Plant had a similar memory: "After the superior authority imposed a plan, the factory would have a discussion, which usually took into account these factors: seniority, attendance, work attitude, achievements, relations with the masses, and political performance. Politics mattered at that time; if you were politically backward, you had no chances. Seniority was the primary criterion for workers of the fifth grade and lower; if there was nothing wrong with you, then your eligibility would be determined by your seniority. For those of the sixth, seventh, and eighth grades, your performance would be the primary determinant" (N10).

Most of our informants agreed that the determination of one's eligibility for a wage upgrade was "fairly open and transparent" (*bijiao gongkai touming*) or "very democratic" (*hen minzhu*) (N10).[9] The process typically involved several rounds of discussions and the publicizing of the results (H15, L6). At the aforementioned machinery factory at the Port of Ningbo, the determination was done by an "evaluation committee" consisting of the factory leader and several activists. Part of the committee's job was to consult "quite a few" individuals about one's eligibility: "If someone was obviously ineligible, the masses would take him down. There was the so-called practice of 'three ups and three downs' (*sanshang sanxia*). Once the superiors formed a tentative list of the finalists [eligible for a wage upgrade], it would be sent to the masses for a discussion, with feedback returned to the leaders, a process to be repeated three times like this" (N4). At the Xinghuo Cotton Mill in Nanjing, the results of each round of discussion were announced on a large red poster for public examination. "Favoritism and malfeasance were not completely absent, but very rare. Overall, [the evaluation] was done well," our informant from the factory confirmed (L6). Instead of manipulating the wage raise to their own advantage or protecting the individuals under their patronage, the cadres as well as the activists among the workers were expected to give up their own opportunities to the workers of the lowest grades or highest seniority (B7, L8). Mr. Luo (b. 1936), a former workshop director at the Shanghai Compressor Factory, recalled that he reduced his own raise by "half a grade" when it was required that all cadres had to "give up out of modesty" (*qianrang*). During another round of upgrades, he recalled, the cadres were not allowed to have a raise at all (S11). Another policy guiding the cadres' salaries during the Cultural Revolution, as a former vice leader of the Guangzhou Fountain Pen Factory recollected, was that their average wage level could not exceed the average wage level of workers, and his own wage as the vice factory head was 65.2 yuan, equivalent to the wage of a fourth-grade worker (N9).

Ordinary workers, too, were expected to be modest when they were to receive a wage raise. Yang Wanru (b. 1933), a retiree from a factory of prefabricated concrete components in Nanjing, thus described the situation in her workplace: "At that time, everyone appeared to be well-mannered indeed. It would be embarrassing for one to say, for instance, 'This time I should get a raise!' No, no one said so. Everyone seemed to be modest, and nobody would make a fuss over it." In sharp contrast, in the last two rounds of wage raises in the same factory before she retired in 1985, Yang observed that workers became increasingly discontent; those who did not get a raise would shout, "Why did they get a raise and I didn't?" or "I do deserve a raise but they don't!" (C5).

The tense relationship between the cadres and workers over wage raises in the late 1970s and early 1980s was also pronounced in places where factory leaders' discretion played an important role. In Shanghai, for instance, a large proportion of workers hired after 1960 were not assigned a wage grade on the standard eight-grade scale, and all new employees after 1968, amounting to more than 1.7 million by 1983, had no fixed wage grades at all. Instead, their wages were determined by a different scale that increased by 3 yuan at each level, known as "the single dragon" (*yitiaolong*) system (*Shanghai laodong zhi*: 4.3.1). When it came to a wage upgrade, the leaders of state firms that adopted the non-standard wage system had the discretion to increase their employees' wage levels by 3, 6, or 9 yuan, individually. It was thus likely, as Mrs. Yang (b. 1943), a retiree from the Yimin Food Factory, said, that the workshop foreman "would increase the monthly wage by nine yuan for those whom he believed to be excellent but others would not necessarily think so." She further explained, "There were also a certain kind of people who were really competent for all kinds of tasks but they often arrived late or left early. So how much should their wages be raised? If you had a good relationship with the leaders, you could get six yuan, and if it was bad, then just three yuan. So here is where the leaders' power lay, if any. This is something that is very subtle and hard to explain" (S8).

But the cadres who were suspected of practicing favoritism had to face protests by the frustrated workers (*dage baobuping*) (W5). At Hefeng Yarn Mill in Ningbo, for instance, "those who did not get a raise would shout abuse. There were always some who did not receive a raise; no one could guarantee a raise with one-hundred percent certainty. So they would shout abuse face to face. Sometimes the workers did not care about anything. They were straightforward when making complaints. If someone was resentful against you, she would dig out everything that was bad about you, including your private matters that had nothing to do with the work [of the factory]. She just wanted to make you notorious; she would say, for instance, how bad your husband had been before or what kind of nasty things you had done in the past. All of the adults and children of the workshop director and group heads were subject to her cursing. The workers cared about nothing indeed" (N1).

Housing Allocation

Unlike wage raises in the 1960s and 1970s that prioritized one's seniority, when allocating housing units, the most important criterion was the per capita size of the preexisting residence of a worker's household; priority was given to those who had the smallest quarters or the most difficult living conditions. This was understandable. In the Mao era, the state's economic strategy was to maximize investments in manufacturing and infrastructure at the expense of the livelihood of the workforce. Therefore, construction of new apartment buildings was rare, and the factory-wide allocation of housing units never happened for most of the state firms. Workers and their families had to rely on their private residences or else be crammed into the compounds forfeited from former capitalists or wealthy families or into the dormitories that had been designed for unmarried workers. By the 1970s, it had become common for a worker's household of three or more generations to live under one roof, where married couples had no private space at all. Therefore, in the late 1970s and more commonly in the 1980s when the state firms started the construction of apartment buildings, the "difficulty level" of workers' living conditions became the most important factor in housing allocation; whether a worker was an activist, a party member, or a cadre did not affect their eligibility ranking. The room for factory leaders' favoritism was very limited (L4). At the Guangzhou Fountain Pen Factory, for instance, workers had to first fill out an application form for housing allocation in 1979. The applicants were ranked by difficulty level: "Those who were the most difficult were ranked at the very top; the number of your family members, the size of the leased residence, and its location were all taken into account."

The ranking was done by a "housing allocation group" consisting of nine members, with each member representing the workers of a workshop. The ranking was then announced for public examination, and allocation started only when no one disputed the ranking (N9).[10]

Therefore, most of our informants agreed that housing allocation in their work units was fair, involving several rounds of publicizing and discussing the ranking of eligible applicants (e.g., N7, N15, S3); when describing the process, many used phrases such as "transparent" (*toumingde*) (S6), "open and transparent" (*gongkai touming*) (N5, N7), "fairly open and transparent" (*bijiao gongkai touming*) (L5), "very transparent and allowing no room for favoritism and malfeasance" (*hen touming, meiyou baobi wubi de kongjian*) (H15), "pretty fair and no favoritism or misconduct" (*bijiaogongzheng, meiyou baobiwubi de xingwei*) (L3), "no favoritism" (*meiyou baobi xingwei*) (H17), and "no backdoor deals in general" (*jibenshang meiyou shenme kaihoumen*) (S3). Given the limited availability of housing units and strong pressure against abuse of power, the cadres had to refrain from overt misconduct in housing allocation; instead, they had to appear altruistic, giving up their opportunities to the neediest workers in the same manner they did a wage upgrade (B7, L5). Not surprisingly, at the railroad bureau in the Xiaguan District of Nanjing, an ordinary female retiree recalled that she received an apartment with more bedrooms than the one assigned to a cadre above her before she retired in 1982 because she had more children than the latter (C4).

All these do not suggest, however, that personal relations were irrelevant in this process or that the leaders were free of favoritism. Our informant from a company in the Putuo District of Shanghai admitted that "personal relations surely factored, but always in a covert manner and within an acceptable limit." "Let's say," she explained, "there is such-and-such a person whose living condition is a bit difficult and whose personal relations [with the leader] are a bit better, then he'll get an apartment first. This is just perfectly normal; after all, there is always a bit of personal relations there" (S9). The workers, however, were not powerless when confronted with the leaders' potential abuse in housing allocation. At the Shanghai Artistic Carving Factory, for instance, whenever the workers suspected their leaders of doing "little tricks" (*xiaodongzuo*), "they would rebel, and they were brave enough to protest" (S6). Mr. Yang (b. 1942), a retiree from the Qingyun Aerospace Instruments Factory in Beijing, made a similar remark: "The leader was afraid of showing favoritism when allocating apartments. Once he showed favoritism, those below him would rebel. Everyone looked closely at one another and knew one another very well, having lived together for long. Once the masses believed there was a wrongdoing, they would write a big-character poster, and expose it to higher levels, and those at the higher levels will take care of it" (B1). The workers protested especially when they believed that the leaders' backdoor deals threatened their opportunity to get an apartment. The only option for them was "to protest and shout" (*qu nao qu chao*): "If you protest in a proper manner, you'll get it; and if you protest in an improper manner, you won't," as Mrs. Yang (b. 1943) from the Yimin Food Factory testified (S8). A good example of this kind of protest was found at the Zhenjiang Mine under the Shanghai Bureau. As our informant from the mine recalled, two or three miners who were ineligible for an apartment firmly demanded one, and they quarreled fiercely with the leader. The leader had no choice but to concede, because he wanted to make sure everyone under him was "satisfied" (*baiping*); however, this could only result in "squeezing" some individuals off the list of eligible members or reducing the size of apartments for the more eligible miners (N2). Alternatively, when such protests did not work at all, the workers would only take action to "occupy an apartment" (*zhanfang*) by force without the factory's authorization if they believed that they would not be qualified under normal procedures (H18). At the Filature of Huanggang Region, for instance, one had to be "aggressive" enough to get a desirable apartment, which was especially true for female workers, who were normally ineligible for housing allocation. "If the woman was very aggressive," our interviewee commented, "she'd get one. If you are a bit aggressive, your apartment would be a bit better; if you are too honest, you'll get a poor one" (H1).

The workers' resistance thus mattered a lot when confronted with cadre abuses. Legitimate or not, their actions of defiance were grounded in their identity as the members of their work unit and the subsequent belief that they were entitled to the rights of subsistence; therefore, it was *righteous*—if not *rightful* by official regulations—for them to take any actions that they deemed appropriate and effective, including shouting abuses and occupying apartments, to defend what they deserved. More often than not, the cadres, too, had to yield to the pressures from the rank and file and accommodated the workers' demands, hoping to avoid an escalating confrontation and to save their own reputation as competent and paternalist leaders able to solve problems to the satisfaction of all. Instead of the disciplined, impersonal relationship between superiors and subordinates, here both the cadres and the disgruntled workers behaved more like members of the same community living their everyday lives together, where the subsistence needs and the "faces" of all members involved dictated their mutual relations more than anything else.

ACTIVISTS AND POLITICAL REWARDS

As discussed earlier, in most of the Mao years when material incentives, such as wage raises or bonus payments based on work performance, were largely absent, state firms had to rely on political incentives to motivate the workers, such as selecting the most active of them for the various honorary titles ("Advanced Producers," "Model Laborers," and the like), promoting them to higher positions, or admitting them into the Communist Party. According to the clientelist explanation, the criteria used by the factory leadership in selecting the workers for awards, material or non-material, did not have much to do with the recipients' actual performance in production or moral quality as it did with the clients' "concrete loyalty" or "personal loyalties" to the leaders (Walder 1986, 100, 124, 131). The questions that need to be further addressed, therefore, are how the activists were selected for the political incentives, to what extent the selection was based on the activists' loyalty to the cadres or on their abilities in production, and what exactly the relationships were between cadres and activists and between activists and ordinary workers.

Advanced Producers and Model Laborers

The selection of "Advanced Producers" (*xianjin shengchanzhe*, alternatively called *xianjin geren* or "advanced individuals") took place within every production group, with each group producing several candidates from the dozens of group members. Winners of the title were usually those who "showed strong enthusiasm for work and engaged in production with superior quality and quantity" (L1). The material rewards for them were minimal and symbolic, typically including a certificate plus a daily item such as a mug, hand towel, basin, or notebook (e.g., W3, Y1); later, in the late 1970s and early 1980s, being an Advanced Producer also entitled the recipient to a one-time bonus payment, when this was used as a new incentive in some factories (L4). The "Model Laborer" (*laodong mofan*) title was more selective, usually limited to only a few in a factory. Both the advanced and model workers were given priority when applying for membership in the party and the Youth League or being considered for promotion to a cadre's position (L8, S6); in some factories during the Cultural Revolution, they had the opportunity to join the "workers' propaganda team" (*gongxuandui*), which included a free trip to a different city or a training program for one or two months during which they did not have to work (N6). Being a model worker further qualified the recipient for a wage upgrade by one level when it was allowable in the late 1970s and thereafter in some of the state firms (H15, N6, W4).

As for exactly how the advanced individuals and model workers were selected, our informants almost unanimously emphasized that they were nominated and elected by their peers primarily because of their hard work and dedication to production. Those who won the titles, therefore, were the individuals who "worked every workday throughout the year without absences, never asked for leave when falling ill, saved energy and raw material, exceeded the production quota, and completed in eight hours the work that normally would have required ten hours," as Mrs. Fan (b. 1948), a retiree from Nanjing Telecommunication Equipment Factory described, (L5); the workers who "excelled in production, did not care about the time they spent on work, pretended to be fine and continued to work when they were ill, and sometimes also acted as a mediator when their peers quarreled with each other," as a retiree at the Renfeng Fabric Mill explained (N6); or the workers who "never made troubles and never arrived late or leave early," who "did more volunteer tasks," and who "spoke when there was a meeting," etc., as seen at the Wuhan Rubber Plant (W2). The few who were selected as model workers were exceptionally hardworking. The retiree from Wuhan Pharmaceutical Factory thus described a female model worker in the factory: "She worked more than just eight hours a day. Being a group head in our workshop, she worked even during lunch hours at noon. In addition to her own shift from early morning to the noon, she worked an extra shift in the evening. She turned herself a model worker by working hard (*zuochulai de laomo*). All of the model workers then and now were those who work extremely hard (*sizuo*)" (W4). The advanced workers at the No. 6 Oil Refinery in Jinzhou of Liaoning province, according to a female retiree, "became what they were by hard work, and [they were] hardworking indeed!" (*douzhi gan chulai de, zhen gan*) (C6). At a bedding and clothing factory in Wuhan, a worker by the name of Zhang Xiangwen, who died in 2012 at age eighty-three, was selected as the "National Model Laborer" in 1959. "How was he selected?" Our informant explained, "By the quality of his work. His record at that time was making 190,000 pieces continuously without defective products. In 1982, he made another record: making 220,000 pieces without defects, and again became the model worker of the city of Wuhan. He worked so hard that his fingers deformed" (H6). Chen Fangfang, a worker for more than ten years at Hefeng Yarn Mill in Ningbo, was named a model worker at the city level, and finally the president of the General Trade Union of the city, because she "was so skilled in production that no one else could compete with her" in tying up the broken yarns as smoothly and quickly (N1). So too was Wang Jiafang at the No. 17 Cotton Mill in Shanghai, who "had good work skills, making products in better quality and larger quantity than others without defects" and always won first place when there was a production competition (S7). Likewise, Ye Guiying, a worker at the filature in Huanggang of Hubei province, was named a model worker of the firm and later a model worker at the provincial level. Her job was to have the cocoons boiled and delivered to the reelers, and "every day, she arrived at the factory earlier and left later than all others" (H4). Mr. Cui, a retiree from the Shijiazhuang Chemical Fertilizer Plant in Hebei province, described the model workers in his factory as "truly skilled and competent, and truly excellent in work" (*queshi you zhen benshi, queshi gande bucuo*), which contrasted sharply with the so-called model workers nowadays who earned their titles by "using personal connections and going through the backdoor" (*la guanxi zou houmen*) (B2).

Relations with Co-workers
In addition to excellence in production, another indispensable quality of advanced and model workers was maintaining "good relations with the masses" (*qunzhong guanxi hao*). Our informants thus typically characterized them as the individuals who were "hardworking and popular" (*gongzuo hao, renyuan hao*) (S19), "enthusiastic for work and popular among the masses" (*gongzuo jiji, qunzhong jichu hao*) (Y1), or "easygoing" (*jiang suihe*) and "getting along well with everyone, or they won't get elected" (C1). The aforementioned informant from the pharmaceutical factory in Wuhan particularly stressed the importance of popularity for the activists: "They were elected by the workers, rather than selected by the leaders. The leaders did not have the

guts to select on their own. They were elected level after level, first at the small group level, then at the team level, and finally at the workshop level. They were thus determined through different levels. It was impossible for any leader to appoint and decide on any of them. Again, they were selected through elections. Those who had superior qualifications won" (W4). So too was the opinion of a former welder at the Shengli Oil Field in Shandong: "The advanced individuals were elected by the masses; without good relations [with co-workers], was it possible for them to get elected?" (Y1). Mrs. Yang (b. 1943) of the Yimin Food Factory in Shanghai put it bluntly: Those who became advanced and model workers "got along with the masses fairly well; otherwise, no one would vote for you" (S8). Similarly, at the machinery factory of the Port of Ningbo, those who were selected as the activists "usually had a reasonably good basis of popular support, or they won't be able to be elected. If the workers all had a low opinion on someone, they would protest and topple him down even if he was elected" (N4).

One of the central procedures in selecting the activists, therefore, was a discussion (*ping*) and competition (*bi*) among the workers that took place at every level, and candidates had to demonstrate their particular abilities in front of their co-workers (L6, N1); the winners were all produced "through a competition" (*doushi bi chulai de*) and by an "election by the workers" (*kao gongren xuan chulai de*) (W4). Those who competed to become model workers, therefore, had to show their exceptional abilities by "specific numbers that were convincing enough" (*yaoyou nadechu de shuju*) (S7). Thus, once they were selected, the rest of the workers respected the winners. Our interviewees typically described their attitudes toward the winners as "being sincerely convinced" (*xinfu koufu*) (L5), "all convinced" (*dou hen fuqi*) (S3), "all convinced and respectful" (*doushi futie de*) (N1), or "all admired them" (*dou hen peifu tamen*) (L4, S4).

Upon being announced as advanced or model workers, the winners were expected to show their appreciation for the support from co-workers by spending money on some candies or other treats to distribute to the members of their group (S8); in the words of a retiree from the No. 768 Factory in Beijing, "You can't have both fame and profit" (B9). Afterward, throughout the year until the next round of competition for the honors, the winners felt compelled to "mix up with the masses," to keep a low profile, to take the lead in production, to be altruistic and ready to help others, and to be active in volunteering activities, such as cleaning the public toilets (L4).[11]

There were, to be sure, co-workers who were unconvinced, resentful, and envious toward the winners. Mr. Fang (b. 1938), a retiree from Xi'an Instrument Factory, believed that those who were "unconvinced and contemptuous" (*bu fuqi, kanbuqi*) of the activists certainly existed, but they were limited to the few (S10). So too was the situation at the Shanghai Artistic Carving Factory, where some "cynical words" (*lengyanlengyu*) about the winners were unavoidable after the results were announced (S6). Likewise, Mrs. Yang of the Yimin Food Factory commented that "it was perfectly normal that there were some workers who were jealous, just like there were workers who admired [the activists], but the jealous ones were very few," and she pointed out a reason why it was impossible for the activists to get along well with everyone: "Because you are so skilled in production, it was likely that you would always blame others who were unskilled and slow-paced. Those who were blamed were certainly resentful of you." However, Yang denied that this was a serious problem among the workers as to cause antagonism between the activists and ordinary workers; after all, she explained, "people at that time were not really that resourceful and malicious" and "people at that time were not as quibbling and contentious as they are today" (S8). Resentment was also likely to occur among the workers who failed in the competition for the honors, especially if the margin was narrow between two possible candidates who were equally qualified for the titles (W5). As Mr. Guo (b. 1942), a retiree from the No. 768 Factory in Beijing, described, "Among the workers, there were indeed some who particularly cared about it [the honors]. They won't feel good throughout the year if they did not get something they coveted. Let's say that he failed in the nomination and election [of the activists], then he would appear picky and resentful from the beginning to the end of a year. He would quibble over this and that with everyone" (B7). There were workers who were resentful because they actually worked harder than the winners and they failed in the competition only because "they did have the perfect family background" or because they "did not have good relations with the leaders" (H15). In a few cases, the activists won their honorary titles by flattering the leaders (*paimapi shangqu de*) (L1) or because of their personal ties with the leaders (*kao guanxi shangqu de*) (W1), and they would find it difficult to get along well with the co-workers who "had a low opinion of them and refused to collaborate" (W1). Nevertheless, these instances were exceptions rather than the norm in the selection of the activists. To infer from these instances that hostility widely existed among ordinary workers toward the activists and that a split prevailed between the small number of loyal clients and the rank and file in Chinese industry (Walder 1986, 26, 164–170) exaggerates the divide, if any, between the activists and non-activists in most of the state firms.

Relations with the Cadres

Nearly all our interviewees denied that the advanced and model workers received their honorary titles primarily because of their personal connections with factory leaders; instead, they stressed performance in production as the most important factor leading to those titles (S4).[12] This does not mean, however, that the leaders were unimportant in selecting the activists. Quite the contrary, our informants emphasized the decisive role of the cadres in determining the finalists. A precondition for the candidates to be selected, as a retiree from the Gedian Chemical Plant stressed, is that "the leaders deem highly of you" (*lingdao kanzhong ni*); "if the leaders did not think of you highly and paid no attention to you, you won't be named as a pace-setter, no matter how hard you've worked." To be considered by the leaders, he added, "you have to demonstrate yourself and perform well. The most important thing is that you did a good job, so that the leaders valued you" (W1). Mr. Wang (b. 1956), a retiree from the Shanghai Silicon Steel Factory, had a similar view: "First of all, you got to make sure that the leaders valued you. Otherwise, no matter how hard you worked, you just can't do anything about it, if the leaders did not think of you highly. So is the saying: thirty percent by effort and seventy percent by luck." To be considered by the leaders, the would-be activists had to "play a leading role, doing everything ahead of all others, and they then would have the chance to be selected. Without exceptional contributions, no one was able to be selected" (S2). Mr. Le (b. 1951), a retired miner from the Shitouzui Mine of Daye, Hebei province, observed a similar situation in his firm, where the miners were grouped in military units during the Cultural Revolution: "When all of them looked almost the same [in terms of their qualifications], the selection [of the candidates] was mainly up to the leaders for a final decision, which in turn was based on the company commander's impression of you. Although there were procedures at the meetings of teams and groups, the power for a final decision lay in the hands of the company commander." The reason that the leaders "admired" the selected candidates and "designated" them as the activists was because the candidates "used to play a leading role and get along well with ordinary workers" (H11). In other words, the activists maintained good relations with the leaders primarily because of their outstanding performance in production, rather than their cultivation of personal ties with the leaders through flattery or bribery. As a retiree in Shanghai who had worked at an electronic instrument factory in Xingan county of Jiangxi province described it, "The leader surely like you if he finds you working hard. As long as you show your abilities, the leaders surely like you" (S5).[13]

There were, to be sure, indeed "a few" (*shaoshu*), "very few" (*jigebie*), or "a small proportion" (*shaobufen*) of the activists who obtained their honorary titles by flattery or by counting on their particular personal ties with the leaders, and they thus found themselves in an awkward relationship with their peers on the shop floor (L1, S18, W1), as mentioned earlier—a situation that became more common in the post-Mao era (B1, B2). Nevertheless, as many of our informants quickly pointed out, while one's particular relationship with the leader was important and sometimes even critical to being selected as an activist, that relationship alone was never sufficient enough to warrant an honorary title. More important than the leader's personal preference was the "collective consent" (*gongren*) of the workers as a group. "If the group members do not consent, it is impossible for one to be selected by counting on the leader only. Otherwise, they will rebel," so explained Mrs. Yang, our informant from the Yimin Food Factory in Shanghai. She added that "the masses would disagree" (*qunzhong yaoyou yijian*) if the leader blocked someone they personally disliked from being selected who was nevertheless competent and fully qualified. Thus, overall, those who were eventually selected truly deserved the titles. "At that time," she averred, "the leaders were acceptable by and large. After all, what they did could be put on the table [for public examination]" (*neng zai taimian shang jiajian guang*) (S8). Mrs. Zhong (b. 1954), a retired cadre from a service company in the same city, had a similar view: "If someone is named as an advanced worker simply because of [their] particularly good relationship with the leader, all others will be resentful once it is announced" (S9). So too is the view of the retiree from Hefeng Yarn Mill in Ningbo. To be named as an activist, she explained, "one has to get through the test of the leaders. Without the leader's approval, it is impossible to be selected. However, it does not work either if one counts on his or her relations with the leader only. The leader has to think about this: If selected, would this person be exemplary enough and have the basis [of support from other workers]?" (N1).

The promotion of workers to the position of cadres in state firms was a bit different from the selection of activists that prioritized one's performance in production. To be promoted to a cadre, merely working hard was not enough; one had to have necessary education and enough literacy to perform the cadre's tasks. Most important, the candidate had to demonstrate their leadership abilities, as a former factory head and party secretary at the Jiefang Plastic Factory in Shanghai explained (S3). This was especially true for leaders at the workshop level, who, as mentioned earlier, had to not only oversee production activities of all teams and groups in the shop but also the personal issues of the employees, such as marriage, divorce, family violence, any issues involving couples (*nannu guanxi*), or even criminal activities and charges that involved the workers (B8). Not surprisingly, there were those who were qualified and nominated by the superiors to be shop leaders but chose not to accept the positions. This was exactly what happened to a maintenance worker at the Zhenjiang Mine under the Shanghai Metallurgical Bureau. As he recalled it, "The factory wanted me to be a shop head, but I was unwilling to accept it. I only wanted to do some assistance work. The reason was that I was not a good speaker. Yes, I worked hard. But it would be against my will if I was asked to supervise others. I just wondered why I had to supervise others. People are different. Some wanted to climb upward, and they would feel more comfortable once promoted. For people like me, however, to be promoted like this would only make me a sufferer" (N2).

When appointing the cadres at different levels, the factory leaders, too, had to first consider the candidates' abilities; they could not make appointments merely because they had a personal relationship with a candidate without also considering their competence. As an ordinary worker who retired from Hefeng Yarn Mill remarked, "When it comes to promotion, one's abilities matter! Otherwise, people will have rumors over those who were promoted but incompetent. They would say: Look! What kind of abilities that person has? He does not know how to work at all! . . . So they would be subject to rumoring" (N1). Concerns with the possible disgruntlement among the workers was only part of the reason why the factory leaders had to prioritize one's abilities when promoting a candidate to the cadre position. More important was the reason that, as shop head and team or group heads, the middle- and lower-level cadres' competence in coordinating and supervising the activities of individual workers and communicating with them was key to maintaining efficiency in production, which in turn was linked with the factory leaders' own performance rating and possible promotion to higher levels of the bureaucratic hierarchy. Therefore, for the factory leaders, the first and foremost criterion when appointing cadres to the middle and lower levels was the candidates' competence. In the words of Mrs. Yang, who was a former group head at the Yimin Food Factory in Shanghai, the candidates "must be able to stand the ordeal" (*yao neng cheng de qilai de*). "It just won't work if they can't stand," she added. "How could it be if you are unable to command others and if you yourself are unskilled and incompetent? This is something serious that cannot be glossed over. You have to be competent enough to be promoted. At any rate, one's ability counts. He has to be at least sixty or seventy percent competent, if not one hundred percent" (S8). Mr. Han (b. 1938), formerly the vice lead of the No. 768 Factory in Beijing, has a similar view: "You have to demonstrate yourself in work (*gongzuo yao na de qilai*). No matter how successful you are in building personal connections with those above you, you have to demonstrate yourself; you cannot be just an idiot. When it is up to you to take action, you have to roll up the sleeves and work right there immediately, and you have to make the workers below you convinced with respect and awe (*yao zhen de zhu xiamian de gongren*). This was especially true when selecting workshop leaders; they had to be tough enough" (B8). Not surprisingly, even in the two cases mentioned above where personal ties with the factory leaders played a key role in the promotions, the promoted person had to work extremely hard (H18) and "had to be capable enough and performed fairly well" (H16).

Clearly, unlike selecting recipients for honorary titles, which was primarily based on workers' consent and objective criteria of performance in production, granting promotions did allow the factory leaders a greater degree of discretion, since it involved no nomination or voting by the workers. It was likely, therefore, that personal ties and loyalty played a role. Nevertheless, the cadres' choices of who to promote were still subject to certain constraints, including the requirements of the candidate's family background or competence for the desired position. The candidates' personal ties with their superiors could be a key factor only when they met the other requirements. The cadres could never grant their followers promotions merely because of personal loyalty, disregarding their actual qualifications.

THE EQUILIBRIUM IN POWER RELATIONS

For the workers in state firms in Maoist China, the factory or workshop was not only a place where they labored eight hours a day, but it was also the very site where the security of their job and livelihood resided. The identity they developed with their work unit (*danwei*) was as strong as what the villagers in pre-1949 China had with their community or clan. Just as these villagers assumed their subsistence rights as superseding the claims by any authorities in or outside their community (Scott 1976), the workers took for granted their entitlement to the rights and benefits provided by the firm or state. For them, the cadres' legitimacy lay not only in their appointment by the government as the supervisors and managers in production, but it was also tied to their abilities and impartiality in distributing material and nonmaterial benefits to ensure worker' subsistence. So too was the self-perception of the cadres, who had to not only perform their duties in production and labor management but also take care of workers' everyday needs outside the workshop. The work unit, in a word, was not just a workplace but also a community where the cadres and workers lived together side by side. The workers would not hesitate to defend themselves against potential abuse by the cadres not only because of their taken-for-granted rights as full members of the work unit, but also because of two state-firm institutions that were central to the workers' formation of self-identity and attitudes toward the cadres. One was the Maoist discourse that upheld the workers as the leading class with the correct political consciousness and juxtaposed them with the cadres, who were perceived as corruptible and inclined to be "power holders taking the capitalist road" (*zouzipai*); in theory, therefore, the workers had the innate right to supervise the cadres and correct their mistakes. The other was workers' secured livelihood in the state firms, with the state's guarantee of permanent employment and full entitlement to fringe benefits. Unless they were motivated for upward mobility, ordinary workers saw no reason to seek favoritism from the leaders or to worry about the security of their subsistence when fighting against abusive cadres.

In sharp contrast, the cadres were politically and discursively disadvantaged. They were invariably the targets of political campaigns, including the Three-Anti Campaign (against corruption, waste, and red tape) and the Anti-Rightest Campaign in the 1950s, the Socialist Education and the Cultural Revolution in the 1960s, and the One-Strike, Three-Anti Campaign in the early 1970s. It was no wonder that the cadres who suffered the recurrent campaigns developed the psyche of being "fearful of the masses" (*pai qunzhong*), because whenever a campaign took place it was up to the workers to expose the "wrongdoings" of the cadres; keeping a good relationship with the vast majority of the workers was the surest way for cadres to survive these events. Administratively, they had little leverage to demand the personal submission and loyalty from most of the workers, given the secured employment and fixed wages of the latter; quite the reverse, the cadres counted on the workers' cooperation to ensure the timely completion of production tasks, which was essential to keeping their positions and eventually being promoted. Economically, the cadres were not too different from the rank and file, especially senior workers, given the narrow gap between their income levels and living conditions.

Therefore, there was an overall symmetry—or an equilibrium—in the relations between the cadres and the workers, when the political, ideological, administrative, and economic factors outlined above were all taken into account. This equilibrium in turn reflected the Maoist approach to labor management and factory governance. As full members of a state firm with lifetime employment, the workers no doubt depended upon their work unit for livelihood, but it was less likely for them to develop personal dependence on the cadres for subsistence. Quite the contrary, whenever the cadres were suspected of practicing favoritism, those who suffered unfair treatment would be in a position to protest. This protest could be expressed in an informal, traditional manner that was grounded on the subsistence ethic inherited from pre-1949 Chinese society, such as picking a quarrel, cursing, or even beating up the cadres when the workers believed that these individuals had hurt their rights or interests. They could also protest in a formal manner, as shown in the previous chapter; their growing consciousness of themselves as the "masters" (*zhurenweng*) of the factory certainly emboldened them.

All these should not lead one to assume, however, that the relationship between the cadres and workers was equal, as claimed by the Maoist rhetoric.

Nor should one deny the existence of personal patron-client ties between some cadres and the few workers who were politically motivated in seeking promotion from the rank and file. This, however, should not be equated with the clientelist explanation that assumes on the one hand the cadres' unrestrained power in determining workers' wages and jobs and on the other the personal dependence of the latter on the former, hence the predominance of patron-client networks in factory politics and the split between the activists and non-activists among the workers (Walder 1986, 162–189). The prevalence of clientelism became possible only in the late 1970s and afterward, as will be shown in Chapter 6, when the reform of state-owned enterprises resulted in the devolution of power to individual enterprises in production and marketing and when the contract system was widely introduced; the factory leaders eventually had autonomy in hiring and firing workers, determining the workers' wage levels and bonus payments, and building housing units and allocating them by their own policies. At the same time, the workers remained dependent on their work unit for livelihood before they were able to freely change their jobs without losing their welfare benefits. It was likely that the patron-client networks sprang between factory managers and workers under these circumstances, as our interviewees frequently complained. These personalized networks were also likely to develop in the small collectively owned firms where the cadres had greater control over production and labor management than their counterparts in state firms. All in all, the clientelist relations were less likely to prevail in the state firms of the Maoist era, because their preconditions (i.e., the cadres' autonomy in employment and labor remuneration, *and* the workers' personal dependence on the cadres rather than the work unit) did not exist. Nor was there sufficient evidence to show a split of workers into two separate and confrontational groups of activists and non-activists as the most salient consequence of the patron-client ties.

Therefore, much of the disjunction between the clientelist explanations in past studies and the findings in this chapter can be attributed to the fact that most of the workers interviewed in the late 1970s and early 1980s still had a "fresh" memory of their recent experiences in the state firms, where the factory leadership had just obtained a degree of autonomy in labor management and where material incentives were recently introduced, much of which were at the cadres' discretion; clientelist networks thus were likely to sprawl at the beginning of the post-Mao era as a result of economic reform that centered on distributing power to individual enterprises. In contrast, our informants recalled their past experiences from a distance; they were better able to disconnect their experiences in the high Mao era from what happened right after Mao. There might be also a psychological factor among the retirees; some of them indeed appeared to be nostalgic for the "glorious" old days when the workers were hailed as the masters of their factories, which contrasted sharply with their strong resentment toward the prevalence of personal ties and favoritism in the post-Mao years. This nostalgia undoubtedly tinted their narratives, but nevertheless the sharp contrast in factory politics between the Mao and post-Mao years as represented in this study is unmistakable, eclipsing the possible distortions inherent to any representation based on oral history.

To recapitulate, an equilibrium prevailed in power relations in the state firms of Maoist China. Underlying this equilibrium was a set of economic, social, and political institutions characteristic of the industrial enterprises under the socialist state. As intermediaries between the state and workers, the cadres at different levels of a factory did have a degree of discretion in making decisions that could directly affect workers' opportunities, and cultivating activists among the workers was indeed an effective tool for the cadres to keep the firms running smoothly. However, this should not lead one to assume that the activists were selected only based on personal loyalty to the cadres or that the cadres only awarded their supporters with wage raises, bonus payments, promotions, and other opportunities. After all, the cadres did not own the enterprises they supervised, and they were subject to both the formal supervision from above and the informal constraints from within the unit in their charge. Their limited power in employment and labor remuneration and their dependence on the workers in production on the one hand, and the workers' security of living guaranteed by the state on the other, made the relationship between the cadres and workers of a state firm very different from that between the owner of a private firm and its employees before and after the Mao era. The relationship between cadres and workers in the state firms of socialist China, in the final analysis, was neither the one of equality and intimacy, as the Maoist rhetoric claimed, nor the one of "extreme dependency and arbitrariness" (Whyte 1999, 178). It was characterized by an equilibrium, or an overall symmetry in power relations between cadres and workers, which grew out of their shared identity with the work unit and mutual subordination to the state.

4 | WORKER PERFORMANCE IN EVERYDAY PRODUCTION

"ECONOMISM," AS PIERRE BOURDIEU terms it, is an inclination to interpret the motivations and choices of individuals in non-Western or precapitalist societies by using the categories, concepts, or methods derived from the experiences of Western societies. As "the historical product of capitalism" and "a form of ethnocentrism," Bourdieu writes, economism "recognizes no other forms of interest than that which capitalism has produced"; it denies "non-economic interests" as well as "a set of mechanisms tending to limit and disguise the play of (narrowly) 'economic' interest and calculation" widely seen in precapitalist "good-faith" economies; instead, economism only considers what Marx calls "naked self-interest" and "the remorseless logic" or "egoistic calculation" behind it (Bourdieu 1990, 112–115). The same problem is found in the literature on the behavior of individual workers in the socialist economy of Maoist China. The labor force in state-owned factories is often depicted as sensitive only to material incentives; whether the material incentive exists or to what extent it functions is believed to be the most critical factor determining worker morale and performance. For decades since the inception of economic reforms in the late 1970s, therefore, the official media and pro-reform economists in China have assumed the widespread existence of inefficiency and low productivity in state firms in the Mao era, attributing this problem to egalitarianism or the lack of material incentives in labor remuneration.[1]

In the English-language literature on the Chinese economy, the most explicit statement is made in the work of Justin Yifu Lin and his collaborators. In the absence of state-firm autonomy in labor management, they argue, "workers' income level cannot be set in accordance with their performance. Thus, they had little incentive to work hard. Since incentive to work is proportional to the rewards gained from working, to enhance workers' incentive, managers must adopt a system whereby hard work is rewarded. However, under the traditional economic system, a business could neither choose nor fire its workers. Moreover, urban employees were paid a fixed wage, irrespective of their performance. The incentive to work was thus suppressed" (Lin et al. 2003, 87).

Likewise, Andrew Walder observes a marked decline in individual performance, work discipline, and attendance in the early 1970s and attributes it to the cancellation of bonuses, the decline of real wages, the worsening of housing shortages, and the deterioration of overall living conditions in the preceding two decades (Walder 1986, 193–219). Other scholars writing on China's state enterprises do not readily accept this explanation (e.g., Howard 1991, 94; Sheehan 1998, 197; Hassard et al. 2007, 154), nor do they offer in-depth research on the issue of work incentives in state firms, other than sketchy descriptions of the official institutions and policies on wage and bonus systems and non-material incentives (e.g., Hoffmann 1974, 93–122; Lee 1987, 31–40; Henley and Nyaw 1987; Pegels 1987, 147–158). By and large, however, egalitarianism in resource allocation and labor remuneration in industrial enterprises, remaining largely intact in the 1980s, is believed to be at the root of inefficiency in China's industry before the reform era.[2]

Departing from neoclassical assumptions about the centrality of individuals' rational choice in their pursuit of profit maximization and the subsequent belittlement of the institutional environment in which they think and act, evident in the above interpretations of Chinese workers, a more nuanced perspective in social sciences, dubbed "new institutionalism," foregrounds the key role of institutions in regulating economic and social activities. While economists of this school are concerned primarily with the formal aspects of the institutional context, particularly the firm system, the state apparatus, and its enforcement of a whole set of laws and regulations on property rights (e.g., Coase 1960; North 1981), sociologists in this paradigm call for attention to both formal *and* informal elements that inform one's social behavior. For the new institutionalists, the social and economic activities of individuals are subject to the constraints of an institutional web comprising formal systems and organizations as well as informal practices, customs, norms, values, public opinions, and so forth within a given community. Compliance with the rules and norms of the community enables the group to provide certain benefits that cannot be produced individually by its members; shared by all members, these benefits constitute a "collective good" that serves the interest of the group as a whole but might be in conflict with the short-term goals or preferences of some individuals in the group. Whether or not the individuals abide by the rules and practices, however, directly affects the solidarity of the group, which in turn determines the group's ability to produce the collective good. Conforming to the formal and informal institutions, therefore, forms the most important basis on which one maintains their standing and reputation within the group, the most important aspect of one's social capital; for most of the group members, this is also the strategy that best serves their interests, given the fact that the long-term benefits brought by a person's social capital can outweigh the short-term material gain of breaking the rules. Situated in this institutional context, one's motivation and choice of action are complex, and the neoclassical conception of rational choice cannot fully explain the complexity. While the maximization of self-interest, be it social capital or the narrowly defined economic capital, remains ultimately the most important driver behind one's choice of action, this calculation is subject to the constraint of formal and informal institutions. The rationality embodied in one's choice of action, therefore, can be termed as "context-bound rationality" (Nee 1998, 1–12), which is best explained by a "thick" description that takes into account a full array of formal and informal elements informing the social context in which the choice is made, rather than a thin description that recognizes only the rationality represented by one's simple calculation of self-interest in the narrow economic sense.

Needless to say, the new institutionalists share with neoclassical economists their faith in the fundamental importance of the free market and the rational choice of individuals in the efficient allocation of resources and production of goods, but their emphasis on institutions can nevertheless serve as a point of departure for us to contextualize the behavior of Chinese workers. Past studies on worker performance in Maoist China, to their credit, have also taken institutions into account when explaining the inefficiency in factory production. But their analysis is often limited to the formal institutions, and among these, they single out the egalitarian practices in labor payment as the most decisive factor, assuming a direct link between this and the low morale in production; missing in their description are other components of the formal institutions as well as the whole set of informal institutions. This chapter shows, however, that there were many formal institutions in microeconomic organizations, and these changed over time during the Mao era; in addition to the labor payment system, other formal institutions also came to influence workers' motives and performance on the shop floor, including, among others, the composition and social status of the labor force itself, the enforcement of work disciplines and regulations, and political organizations and activities. No less important in shaping the workers' behavior are the hidden, invisible or informal institutions, such as the workers' identity with the factory that employed them, their self-consciousness in relation to other social groups, the cohesion of the group in which the workers performed their tasks together, everyday work norms that prevailed within the group, collective sanctioning against deviations from the norms, and so forth. In order to fully comprehend the behaviors of Chinese workers, therefore, we need a thick description that places them in the historical context in which the various formal and informal institutions interwove to motivate and constrain them as individuals and as a group in the workplace.

WORKER PERFORMANCE IN RETROSPECT

One of the central questions in our interviews concerns the workers' morale and performance. Almost all of our informants stressed that the workers performed largely well in the Mao era; they generally described themselves or their co-workers as "motivated" (*you jijixing*) or "highly motivated" (*jijixing gao*), "enthusiastic" (*ganjing da*) or "working with all strength" (*ganhuo pinming*) in production, who cared little about labor remuneration (*buji baochou*) and voluntarily worked extra hours or shifts (*yiwu jiaban jiadian*). In actuality, however, the workers' morale varied during different periods of the Mao era. Many of the interviewees agreed that their performance was the best before the Cultural Revolution.[3] During the seventeen years between 1949 and 1966, there were a few moments when people appeared to be particularly zealous to work. One was the early 1950s, when a large portion of urban workers, who had suffered unemployment and price inflation in the last few years of the Guomindang rule, experienced "emancipation" (*fanshen*, literally turning upside down) in one form or another after they became employees of state firms and enjoyed the security of their livelihood after 1949 (H7).[4] Another wave of workers' rising enthusiasm occurred during the Socialist Transformation of Private Industry and Commerce in the mid-1950s, when many of those who had worked in private businesses and were subject to their bosses' exploitation believed that they became "the masters of the new society" after the Transformation (N2, N3). The three years of the Great Leap Forward (1958–1960) saw an unprecedented boost of workers' efforts in production. "So motivated were the workers during the Great Leap Forward," a retiree from Renfeng Fabric Factory of Ningbo recalled, "that we labored day and night, without caring about monetary reward or time input. After finishing the day shift, we continued the night shift—we were young and able to stand it. The Great Leap Forward was the most fanatic moment, and we worked the hardest. We worked day and night, for twelve hours, from six o'clock in the evening to six o'clock in the early morning" (N6). An informant from the Xi'an Instrument Factory made a similar comment: "During the Great Leap Forward, workers were particularly enthusiastic. No one complained of working extra shifts or hours; people worked long and hard without grudge. They were all happy to work an extra nightshift without an extra-shift pay at all, though the factory only distributed two steamed buns to each of them" (S10; see also B8, H3).

There were also moments when the workers' morale plummeted. The first was the later phase of the Great Leap Forward and the few years afterward, when they suffered hunger and physical exhaustion on the one hand and ideological disillusion on the other. "By the end of 1959," recalled the former vice director of Guangzhou Fountain Pen Factory, "the situation had completely changed, and everyone was in panic, workers had lost much of their energy, and production declined. By the beginning of 1960, hunger began to strike, and everyone felt starved. We cadres were rationed 2.5 to 3 *liang* of rice a day, and workers 3 to 4 *liang*" (N9). A former workshop head of Shanghai Compressor Factory also noted that "during the three years of economic adjustment from 1961 to 1963, the economy of the country was in extreme difficulty, people's living standard declined, and their physical condition deteriorated, so the workers' zeal to work decreased" (S11).

The workers' morale was at rock bottom almost everywhere during the first few years of the Cultural Revolution, when they were split into different factions and engaged in conflicts and even armed struggles, causing the removal of experienced personnel from management and a standstill in production in a large number of state firms. Our informants all noted that the years from 1966 to 1967 or 1968 were when their performance was "the sloppiest" (*zui mahu*) (S4, S9). At Wuhan Rubber Plant, for instance, workers continued to arrive and leave on schedule, but they "did little while on shift" (*shangban bu zuoshi*). As a former employee recollected, "While on duty, we did it only perfunctorily, for the task was not up to me alone. Whenever anyone suggested a break, dozens of us quit. Those who were good at playing poker had fun among themselves, while we who had children did not join them but we would do our own needlework and would not leave until the end of our shift" (W2). At the Special Product Factory of the No. 1 Metallurgical Ministry in Wuhan, in another instance, a factional struggle among the workers caused suspension of operation in 1968, and the workers typically "arrived at 7:00 a.m., went off duty at 8:00 a.m., and disappeared completely by 9:00 a.m." (*qishang baxia jiuzouguang*) (H9). So was the situation at the Wuhan Steel and Iron Work, where most of the employees went to work late and off duty early, and some of them returned home right after they checked in, only leaving party members and "backbone" workers to stay on duty (H14).[5] The situation improved after the large firms came under "military control" (*junguan*) in 1969, when a company of PLA soldiers was dispatched to each of these factories to curb armed struggles and ensure the recovery of production. By 1972, production had become largely normal nationwide, when the party-state leadership gradually shifted its emphasis from mass mobilization to stabilizing and increasing production.

Except for these moments of mass agitation and disorder, however, our informants generally described the rest of the 1960s and the 1970s as a time when workers performed normally and dutifully. They all agreed that shirking remained a problem during these years, but they stressed that it was limited to a small number of workers and far from being a common phenomenon before the late 1970s. According to an estimate by a retiree from the Shanghai Light Bulb Factory, for example, in his work unit those who did a sloppy job were limited to "two or three out of every ten individuals"

(S4). Another informant from Shanghai Yimin Food Factory gauged that only about "five to six out of one hundred individuals" in her factory had the problem of loafing on the job (S8). Most of our interviewees, however, emphasized that shirking was limited to the "very few" (*henshao* or *feichang shao*) or was "extremely rare" (*ji gebie*) (L2).⁶ The reasons behind their poor performance varied. Some workers were slow in finishing their tasks not because they slacked deliberately but simply because, they said, they were "unskilled" (*bu shulian*) (H3) or "slow-paced by nature" (*shoujiao man*) (S6) and "cannot speed up no matter what" (*zuobukuai, meibanfa*) (S8); others were likely to be late to their shift simply because they were mothers in maternity or because they had a sick child to take care of (S8, L6). There were, however, indeed workers who shirked on purpose. Being "lazy" and despised by co-workers, they shirked their duties using whatever excuses, such as going to the restroom more frequently than others, fetching boiled water for people in their group, or asking for sick leave by pretending to be ill and thus getting a note from the factory's clinic (B7). There were also workers who slowed down because they had failed to compete with others for the nomination of "advanced individual" (*xianjin fenzi*) or model worker and therefore were resentful throughout the rest of the year (B7, H18). Finally, there were a few who counted on their good background and paid less attention to their everyday performance than others, such as the employees who were children of "revolutionary martyrs" (*geming lieshi*) or veterans of the Korean War (B8), a background that ensured their good standing in society and in the workplace no matter how badly they did their jobs.

These results from our interviews suggest that the lack of material incentives alone cannot fully explain workers' morale, or lack of it, in the Mao era. Aside from the short period around 1960, when the exceptional hardship in the wake of the Great Leap Forward caused the momentary dampening of workers' enthusiasm, and except for the first few years of the Cultural Revolution, when factional struggles caused disorder and standstill in production, the vast majority of the workers in state-owned factories routinely and dutifully performed their tasks in the Mao era. It was only after 1978, as our informants all pointed out, that shirking did become a prevalent problem, an issue to be addressed in the last section of this chapter. So why is there a disjunction between the myth of low performance that was central to the post-Mao discourse on economic reform and workers' own experiences?

If our informants' recollections of their past are creditable, what exactly were the mechanisms that kept the workers performing reasonably well in factory production when there was no direct link between labor input and remuneration?

"NAIVE AND SIMPLE"? THE POLITICIZATION OF FACTORY LIFE

One word that the interviewees frequently used to explain why they had been positive and responsible in factory production in the Mao era was *danchun*, literally, simple-minded and naive in thinking; they typically compared their *danchun* in the Mao era to workers' preoccupation with self-interest and material gain in the reform era. Here are a few typical comments from our informants on their experiences before 1978:

> "People at that time were indeed obedient, naive, and super naive! So much has changed nowadays that the difference is like that between heaven and earth" (C3, a retiree from the Nanjing Clock Factory);
> "The ethos of that era was such that people should work as hard as possible. It was as if one would be disgraced if he or she did not work extra hours and extra shifts. What people valued at that time was a sort of honor and pride, and they were all serious about 'Serving the People' and making contribution as much as they could. No one talked about money. It was such a kind of mentality" (N10, a technician from Huaqiao Sugar Plant in Guangzhou);
> "There was no bargaining at all. People did whatever the supervisor instructed, and they just obeyed; no one talked about compensation . . . They were just concerned with how to increase production. They thought about nothing but work, and wanted to work more" (B1, a worker from an aerospace instruments factory in Beijing);
> "From today's point of view, people at that time indeed appeared to be a bit silly and idiotic! . . . Workers gave priority to the interests of the state and the public instead of their own; everybody thought this way, and no one thought about himself or herself first" (C5, a retired trade union cadre from the Nanjing Precast Concrete Plant);
> "The mood of the society influenced us a lot. Everyone was enthusiastic, competing for doing everything without thinking about reward, and no one worked in a slipshod manner; they all believed that they worked for

the country and therefore made an all-out effort. Being late and leaving early, a common phenomenon in the factories nowadays, did not exist at all, and no one thought about shirking. Work is work, and it has to be done wholeheartedly, and no exception was allowed for anyone." (B2, a worker from Shijiazhuang Chemical Fertilizer Plant)

The easiest explanation of, and indeed an obvious reason behind, the workers' *danchun* can be found in the party-state's efforts in ideological education and political propaganda, which shaped in part the workers' attitudes toward the workplace. Propaganda was especially important in the recurrent waves of mass mobilization for the state's goals of industrialization and social transformation. During the Great Leap Forward, for instance, people throughout rural collectives and urban units worked extremely hard without expecting proportional and immediate reward; this was precisely due to the intensive propaganda that aroused their patriotic zeal to build a strong nation by catching up with the leading capitalist powers and kindled their dream of quickly entering Communism and thereby living in unprecedented material affluence. Thus, at Nanjing Steel and Iron Work, according to one of its retirees, workers were "obedient" (*tinghua*) to their superiors and worked hard at that time because they truly "aspired to live the fancy life of having 'multi-story buildings with electric lights and telephones' (*loushang louxia, diandeng dianhua*)" (L8)—the hallmark of Communism, as the official propaganda wanted ordinary people to believe.

In addition to the goal-directed propaganda, the state's ideological indoctrination through school education and the media also played a part in shaping the political and moral consciousness of the public. Central to its efforts in this regard was promoting the revolutionary spirits of self-denial for the interests of the collective (*dagong wusi*) and other altruistic values. A quality-control worker from the Ningbo Port Machinery Factory thus described the situation in his work unit: "People at that time had a strong motive to work mainly because they were not so concerned with self-interest. The leaders as well as the workers were not so selfish. To say that they were not selfish at all is an exaggeration, but selfishness was indeed limited. The main reason lay in education. There were lots of education in the 1950s and 1960s, such as Learning from Lei Feng, Learning from Chen Yonggui, and the like" (N4). The examiner himself suffered a severe injury to his feet when he risked his safety to remove a flaming part from a vehicle he was inspecting.

Another worker from a dockyard in Guangzhou under the No. 4 Navigation Engineering Bureau of the Ministry of Communication explained the importance of propaganda this way: "We worked really hard. That's because we were led by political slogans at that time. There were campaigns one after another, such as 'a major battle for thirty days' or 'a major battle for ninety days' to finish the yearly tasks beyond the quotas, hence these kinds of battles. These slogans made our thinking militarized. Now you cannot imagine that kind of atmosphere. People at that time did not care about eating, drinking, or entertainment. We stressed revolution, learning from Lei Feng, and later learning from Wang the Iron Man, and later there was Jiao Yulu. So there were such heroic figures, one after another, that inspired us. The idealism among the people at that time, as well as the potential tapped by the idealism, were truly strong" (N7). Similarly, a retiree from the Shengli Oil Field in Shandong province recalled that people were so motivated at the time of a "major battle for oil" (*shiyou dahuizhan*) that "they worked for three weeks in a row without going home for a good sleep, although their homes were just next to the work site; they only took a nap right in the plant and then continued to work. . . ." "Other times," he went on, "they wanted to be an 'anonymous Lei Feng' by sneaking into the plant at midnight to work for hours without letting others know. The reason? I believe political education at that time made people simple-minded and naive. All they knew about was work, and they worked so hard. Chairman Mao was truly terrific—he knew how to make people united" (Y2).

Aside from ideological indoctrination and political mobilization, workers were also subject to pressure produced by recurrent political campaigns, regular study sessions, and everyday discourse on correct thinking and behavior. At the Xingyuan Silk Factory in Nanjing, for instance, "ideological work was an everyday routine" (*tiantian zhua sixiang*), as a worker recalled. After completing an eight-hour shift, the team leader ritualistically called together members of the same team for a study session (L2). At Wuhan Steelworks, "politics was above everything else" (*zhengzhi dayu yiqie*) as in all other state enterprises during the Cultural Revolution. Therefore, at least two study sessions were conducted each week, involving every worker. Sometimes workers had to participate in the "spare time study" on Sunday. For them, "political performance" (*zhengzhi biaoxian*) was very important, linked to one's chances for career advancement, so they all appeared to be engaged on these occasions (H10).

Political pressure reached a climax during the Cultural Revolution, especially in military enterprises or state enterprises under the PLA's military control. At a microwave radio equipment factory in Beijing, workers had to work hard or they would be charged with "sabotage against military production" (*pohuai jungong shengchan*) by the factory's "council for military control" (B9). The aforementioned Gedian Chemical Factory in Wuhan was under military control until the end of the Cultural Revolution. Workers, therefore, were organized into military units and subject to tight control. Our informant thus described how political pressure affected their performance:

> "Late arrival and early leaving were impossible. The factory's management was in the hands of the military, which used several methods that you don't readily know. One was the recitation every day in the early morning, reading aloud the *Selected Works of Mao* every day. If you were late, they would look for ideological reasons and be mean to you, saying that you didn't understand Mao Zedong Thought. So do you dare to be late? When they did so, they made it a matter of principle and great magnitude that you could not bear with. In the evening, once again, you had to study every day for an entire week, from Monday to Sunday. It would be either a meeting or a study session. Everyone thus came under high pressure under this circumstance. No freedom. No ideas. No way to think freely. Late arrival or early leaving? You don't dare to do it at all." (W1)

Other interviewees witnessed the same kind of pressure in their workplaces. They had to work hard, be on time, and make sure that no accidents happened to them, or they would be suspected of sabotaging public properties and undermining socialism; for those who had "bad class labels" (*chushen buhao*), any mistakes or accidents that involved them could be interpreted as hostility from class enemies and signs of class struggle (W1, W2, W3). Not surprisingly, workers had the fear of "being backward" (*luohou*), which meant lagging behind others in everyday production, political study, or any other public occasions (H17).⁷ Those who had a bad family background worked exceptionally hard to prove their correctness, at least before the Cultural Revolution; during the Cultural Revolution, they had no chance at all for promotion or being considered advanced workers, as a retired worker from the No. 1 Company of the No. 1 Metallurgical Ministry confirmed (H18). Political pressure thus had an obvious effect on workers' morale.

The politicization of factory life produced not only pressure and anxiety among the workers but also opportunity and motivation. Arriving and leaving on time, doing a good job while on duty, working extra hours or shifts without pay, or helping co-workers, participating in innovative activities, and so on—all these were believed to be manifestation of one's commitment to the enterprise and love of socialism and were linked with opportunities for upward mobility, such as obtaining membership in the Communist Party or the Youth League, being nominated as an Advanced Producer or Model Laborer, going to college as a Worker-Peasant-Soldier Student, or being promoted from an ordinary worker to a team or section leader and further to a workshop head or even higher positions (e.g., H9, H16). Each year, the workers were particularly motivated in May, a month known to them as the "Red May" because of the May Day, the Youth Day on May 4th, and other historic events in the party's revolutionary history. Various competitions centered on work quality and quantity, therefore, were organized around those festivals. Winners were praised and put on the Honors List, displayed on the wall of a building (H4). At the Xiangtan Electric Machinery Factory, during the peak of the Cultural Revolution, the most active of the workers organized themselves into a "Loyalty Team" (*zhongziban*) who worked extra hours and shifts voluntarily as a way to "express their loyalty to the Party." Doing otherwise, as a retiree from this factory admitted, would be too costly: "If workers did a poor job, were irresponsible, or arrived late and left early, they would be penalized and would suffer a lot when it came to nominating the advanced workers or recommending a raise. The cost was too huge, so no one acted carelessly" (H19). At the radio equipment factory in Beijing, workers "competed with one another" for opportunities to do extra tasks. "If you don't rush, then the opportunities will be gone, they will be seized by others. But people who were veterans like us were eager for progress. So you have to rush, or no opportunities are left for you. If you don't do extra tasks, you have no achievements" (B7).

BEYOND DANCHUN: SOCIAL STANDING AND SELF-IDENTITY

Education and propaganda were indeed powerful tools to mobilize people during the campaigns, and they were particularly effective on those who were political motivated. However, these methods alone could not sustain the morale of the entire labor force in state enterprises for an extended period, especially in everyday production. Other factors came into play here to influence the workers. One had to do with workers' changing circumstances, which forged their cognition of their current standing in the factory in relation to their past experiences. Some of our informants said that they were committed to work because they were "the people who had lived through the days before Liberation" (*jiefang yiqian guolai de ren*) and they had the mentality of "repaying a debt of gratitude" (*bao'en*); therefore, a worker would take on "whatever tasks" assigned to them, and "he would get his job done even if he had to work extra shifts or hours without pay. He was naive and simple-minded to such a degree" (W5). A female worker from Renfeng Fabric Factory in Ningbo had a similar view: "People like me came over from the old society. Back then we worked just like slaves for the private boss ... for twelve hours a day, with little payment. It was really, really very hard, and very pitiful. Therefore, after entering the state factory, workers in the factory all worked responsibly and did not care about remuneration, and we all hoped the factory would grow" (N6).[8]

The feeling of gratitude was also strong among workers recruited from the rural area. Given the barrier of the household registration system preventing the free flow of rural populations into the cities, the sharp contrast between the registered urban residents and their rural counterparts in their entitlement to the benefits offered by their respective production units, and the extremely rare opportunities for villagers to become state-enterprise employees, those who "jumped out of the farmers' gate" (*tiao chu nongmen*) felt themselves to be truly lucky, compared to the large number of young villagers left behind them. They felt that working hard was the only means to preserve their status as state employees and seek further opportunities for upward mobility. At the aforementioned dockyard in Guangzhou, many of the workers making concrete preforms were recruited from the countryside and thus felt "satisfied" about their living condition. For them, "having moved from the countryside to the city, entered a large state enterprise, and become workers and urban residents, all these meant that their livelihood would be guaranteed by the state, and that they would have higher political standing. So they had a sense of honor. Most of them thus were highly motivated—this was very different from the materialism nowadays." The informant himself, receiving thirty-one catties of rice a month like others, felt so grateful that he sincerely noted in his diary: "Thanks to the Party Central, and thanks to Chairman Mao" (N7). Likewise, the three female interviewees who had been villagers and later recruited by the Filature of Huanggang Region in Hubei province in 1966, 1960, and 1971, respectively, all said that they felt "very proud," "very glorious," and "very happy" for having moved "from the countryside to the city" and changed their status "from a peasant to a worker" after three months of apprenticeship (H1, H3, H4). As a worker at Shijiazhuang Chemical Fertilizer Plant, Mr. Cui (b. 1936) felt "particularly proud" of his change from a villager to a worker of a state firm in 1957, which, as he put it, "appeared to be even more spectacular than having a child going to college nowadays from the villagers' point of view" (B2). The same was true about the miners at the Shitouzui Mine of the Mining Industry Bureau of Wuhan Municipality, who were mostly recruited from the rural area. According to one of the miners, to "jump out of the farmers' gate" and become a miner, hence a state-firm employee, "was very difficult" because the recruitment involved strict investigation of candidates' political background. Once hired, all the young miners were highly enthusiastic, and everyone "wanted to perform well" (H13).

Entering a state enterprise also meant a lot to urban residents. In the 1960s and 1970s, as the urban population grew quickly, employment in state firms became increasingly competitive. Alternatively, more and more job candidates accepted positions in collective firms funded and run by local government authorities. The collective-enterprise employees accounted for 26.5 percent of the entire working force in 1957, 30 to 33 percent in the 1960s, and 27 to 30 percent in the 1970s because state firms were unable to absorb many job seekers (Guojia tongjiju 1983, 123). The differences between state and collective enterprises in wage levels and fringe benefits were stark. Our interviewees pointed out that, as workers of state enterprises, their wages were higher than workers of the same grade in the collective enterprises by three to four yuan in Nanjing (L7) and up to ten yuan in Shanghai (N3). When it came to getting a raise, there was a difference of only about one yuan for workers of the same grade between the two types of enterprises, but "one yuan was very valuable at that time" (N4).⁹ The difference was even more pronounced in fringe benefits, especially healthcare. In Shanghai, for instance, employees of state firms under the No. 1 Bureau of Commerce paid nothing to see a doctor, whereas those of the collective firms under the No. 2 Bureau of Commerce had to pay 0.1 yuan as a registration fee for each visit (S13). In Wuhan, likewise, healthcare for workers of state firms was completely free, while collective firms under the No. 2 Bureau of Commerce reimbursed only 50 to 80 percent of their workers' medical expenses, and the remainder had to be deducted from their wage payments (W4, W5). Furthermore, unlike workers of state firms who received full pay regardless of how much they had done for the month, those of collective firms received full pay only when they finished all their monthly assignments; otherwise, they were paid according to how much they had finished. And unlike female workers of state firms whose wage was paid in full for their fifty-six-day maternity leave, those in collective firms received only 50 percent of their wages. To perpetuate the gap between the two groups, the state's policy further prohibited workers at a collective firm to switch their employment to a state firm or vice versa; changes in jobs were allowed only between enterprises of the same type (N7, S13, W5). All these institutional discriminations worked to demoralize collective workers and made them socially inferior; they "considered themselves unlucky" (*ziren daomei*), as a retiree from the Gongnong Garment Factory in Wuhan admitted (W5).

In sharp contrast, workers of state enterprises had a strong sense of pride. "Being a regular employee of the state enterprise," said a worker of Jiangning Lathe Factory of Shanghai, "lent us an exceptionally strong sense of honor and pride, when compared to other types of workers or other groups in society." Workers of state enterprises felt themselves to be "superior to all others" (*gaoren yideng*) (S18). Other interviewees made similar comments. They stressed that they felt "very glorious and proud" or had "a special sense of honor" for their jobs in state firms (H6, S8, S10). This feeling was particularly strong among workers of large-scale enterprises under the direct administration of the central government, or those of the military. A worker of the No. 768 Factory of the military thus described how proud he was when traveling around the country, carrying a letter of introduction that bore the seal of the No. 4 Ministry of Machinery Industry of the People's Republic of China; he invariably received warm treatment upon showing the letter (B6).

Workers of oil fields were widely respected in society because of the key role oil production played in the nation's industrialization (L4, Y1, Y4). Behind the feeling of superiority and pride, however, were "the real benefits" (*shizai de haochu*) that the employees of the large firms received, such as more opportunities for them to be college students or to be assigned an apartment, as a cadre of the Ministry of Communication's local bureau in Guangzhou pointed out (N7). Oil field workers' wages, for instance, were significantly higher than those in other vocations, as witnessed by one of our informants (Y1) and confirmed by nationwide statistic.[10]

Therefore, behind the façade of the party-state's rhetoric on the equality and liberation of the laboring people, there was a stark inequality in its economic and social institutions that split the society and formalized a newly forged social hierarchy. It was evident not only in the mandatory segregation of the rural population from urban residents and the compulsory procurement system that benefited the latter, but also in the separation of the workers of state enterprises from their counterparts in collective enterprises. The different treatments of these types of workers in job assignments, wages, fringe benefits, and vocational mobility created invisible yet entrenched social and psychological barriers between them that shaped their respective identities and mutual attitudes. The remark by Mr. Yang (b. 1933), a retiree from the Nanjing Carrier Equipment Factory, best illustrates the bias of state-firm workers against those of local collective firms: "Don't mention it! Workers from state-owned units are after all a bit more civilized. Look at those from small factories and collectives, what a mix of people from all backgrounds, just like what you find on the street. Those of us from the state-owned unit, in terms of their integrity (*sushi*), are indeed superior in all aspects" (C1). Thus, alongside the strong consciousness of different class labels assigned to each of the workers, which was determined by family origin (*chushen*) and persistently underscored by the state discourse on class struggle, there was also a strong consciousness of social inequality between people of different status (*chengfen*), which was determined by one's residential registration status as well as the state-owned or collective type of their work unit—an inequality that was more substantial to everyone than class labels, but was denied and obscured by the state's egalitarian rhetoric. Intermarriage, for instance, almost impossible between rural and urban residents because of the huge gap in benefits associated with their different residential statuses and the institutional barrier in rural-to-urban migration, was also very difficult between workers of state and collective enterprises. Our interviewees repeatedly noted that, when dating, women tended to avoid workers from collective factories because the latter were poorly paid and accommodated in housing and other benefits (N2). On the other hand, male workers at state enterprises had an obvious advantage. Our informants cheerfully claimed that "it was easy for the boys in our work unit to find a partner in marriage, because girls were willing to marry them" (B6) or that "we are a state enterprise in large size and with good benefits and higher wages ... so it is easy to find a partner in marriage" (L2). A female worker of the state-owned Jiefang Plastic Product Factory in Shanghai felt so privileged that she declined the proposal from a policeman because "his conditions were not that good" compared to hers (S3).

This hierarchy and gross inequality, while impeding social integration, proved to be an advantage for state enterprises. The workers' sense of pride and superiority, compounded with their complete dependence on the factories for livelihood, allowed them to develop a strong identity with their *danwei* or work unit. This identity, to be sure, was not the same as group cohesiveness in sociological sense, because the workers did not have a choice between staying in the group or leaving it for higher compensation and better treatments; they also were not necessarily attracted to one another's shared goals and commitments, as is often the case for members of a group that displays high level of cohesiveness (Hogg 1992, 11–30). Nevertheless, the *danwei* identity functioned in a similar fashion as group cohesiveness in cultivating workers' conformity to factory norms and ethics, maintaining their morale, keeping them satisfied with their jobs, and improving their productivity and performance in factory production. The importance of identity to the functionality of organizations has been well noted in sociological literature. The identity that workers developed with their jobs and/or organizations is believed to be "the only source of intentional efforts" (White 2008, 291), or as important as monetary compensation to make these organizations work (Akerlof and Kranton 2005, 11, 202). Identity, in essence, served as another form of incentive, or an alternative tool of control to keep group members engaged. In the context of state enterprises in Maoist China, where monetary incentives were almost nonexistent, workers' identity, in the form of their pride in their jobs and satisfaction with their current status, was more important than any other motivating factor.

"TREATING THE FACTORY AS HOME"?
WORKERS' LOYALTY IN QUESTION

While the workers' pride and sense of honor could be real, as our interviewees have frequently confirmed, whether they developed true loyalty to their enterprises remains a question that has to be further investigated in order to make a plausible assessment of the morale and incentives in state firms. Needless to say, whether or not a group or organization succeeds depends in large measure on its members' loyalty, which is defined as "adherence to a social unit to which one belongs, as well as its goals, symbols, and beliefs," or "adherence to ingroup norms and trustworthiness in dealings with fellow ingroup members" (Brewer and Brown 1998, 560), or even as a commitment that "involves greater concern for group welfare than for personal welfare" (Zdaniuk and Levine 2001, 502). To what extent, then, did Chinese workers develop loyalty to their work units?

Throughout the Mao era, the state and all its enterprises made efforts to indoctrinate the workers with a consciousness of being the "masters" (*zhurenweng*) of the enterprise. A popular slogan in all factories thus was "treating the factory as home" (*yi cang wei jia*). "The meaning of this slogan," as a maintenance worker at the Zhenjiang Mine explained, "is to love the factory just as if it is your home, to take care of the things at the factory just as the things of your home, and to think of the factory first when it comes to production and work. If there is any accident or emergency that happens to the factory, then you should treat it just like it is happening to your home; you should be anxious about it and do whatever you can to solve the problems or difficulties that the factory encountered, such as join a voluntary task and the like." When asked about who were loyal to the factory and who were not, he commented: "It all depends. Some people were indeed loyal, loving the factory as a home; but there were also some who were not. No matter how the factory ran, it did not matter to them. There were indeed people who thought like this. So it depends. For instance, some were motivated and they would go to work for extra shifts whenever the factory was in a particular situation, no matter how difficult it was for his family. He would overcome whatever difficulties to do extra shifts. A lot of people were like this. Those who were sluggish and indifferent were relatively rare, after all. People's thinking was simple and naive back then. All those of our generation were relatively simple and naive" (N2).

Attributing the workers' loyalty to purity and simple-mindedness, as discussed earlier, does not really answer the question. To judge the level to which the workers were loyal to their enterprises, to be sure, requires a systematic survey involving a large number of workers spanning different age groups from different sectors of manufacturing and service. The results of our limited number of interviews, however, nevertheless offer some clues. By and large, we can safely say that loyalty was more likely among the following three groups. The first, of course, included the leaders of state firms, ranging from the directors, party secretaries, and trade union presidents at the top, to workshop heads in the middle, and some of the group or section heads at the bottom level. Also included were some of the workers who had been party members, advanced individuals, activists, or model workers. Members of this group were largely satisfied with their positions and achievements.

The second group included senior employees who had worked for the enterprise for decades. Their seniority and experiences certainly contributed to their standing and reputation among the workers. Their wage levels, which were linked with their seniority, were also likely some of the highest. All these factors made them the privileged minority, whose emotional attachment to the enterprise was particularly strong. A good example here is a retiree from the Shanghai No. 1 Artistic Carving Factory. "Having worked for twenty-nine years from 1973 to 2002," he recalled, "we still had the feeling of being the factory's masters even when we were to be laid off. Those who had been laid off would complain of the worsening situation in the factory.... I truly treated the factory as my home before I got married. It was fine for me to work long hours. Later, as a salesman, I was earnest on my job and worked extra hours endlessly and voluntarily" (S6). At the Gongnong Garment Factory of Wuhan, an informant said, "those old workers performed exceptionally well. They treated the factory as their own homes. This was basically the case. They were all the elderly who had lived through the old society and truly saw the factory as their own home" (W5).

The third group was those who had been marginalized in society before they entered the factory. They included female workers in the cities who had suffered unemployment and later succeeded in competition for the jobs in state firms; they also included those who were recruited from the countryside and changed their status from peasant to worker. Members of this group could be easily satisfied with their current standing as state-firm workers, performed well on the shop floor, and remained loyal to their firms until they retired. Mr. Cui (b. 1936), a peasant-turned-worker at the Shijiazhuang Chemical Fertilizer Plant, thus said that, though "an ordinary worker," he "truly treated the factory as [his] own home, and almost wanted to stay there all day" (B2).

The workers' loyalty was further linked with their dependence on the factory for their livelihood, as the following comment depicts: "Despite the low level of material well-being back then, the employees did not worry about their food. When they got sick, there was a workers' hospital for treatment. So everyone was worry-free, and they had a deep emotional tie with the enterprise. They treated the factory's properties as those of their own homes and took good care of them" (H9).[11] A former manager of a transportation company in Tianmen, Hubei province, whose career as a worker started as early as in 1948, estimated that "95 percent of the ordinary employees" in his company "had the feeling of being masters" and that "the notion of treating the factory as home was strong among the vast majority of the employees because it was what they depended on for survival" (H23). To explain his loyalty, a driver of the transportation team of Liaohe Oil Field mentioned an anecdote: "When an earthquake stroke Liaohe in 1974, what I thought about first was the vehicle and the assets of our work unit. So I waited in my vehicle for possible rescue tasks without thinking of any problems occurring to my wife and children. I looked for my wife and children only after I finished my tasks" (Y4).

In sharp contrast, those who denied that they had loyalty to their firms were individuals of the following three groups. The first was those who had had high expectations of themselves but failed to fulfill their ambitions for various reasons and thus felt dissatisfied with where and what they were. Consider the following two examples. A repair worker at the Gedian Chemical Plant, who joined the factory in 1970 when it was still under PLA's military control, thus recalled: "Politically the masses were the masters at that time, but we did not have such an idea of being the master. No ideas like that when working. We only did our job and got paid." He denied that the workers in his plant had the "willingness or the idea" to make the factory better, "because people were faced with high pressure at that time, and, being oppressed, it was difficult for them to have any ideas." He further decried the aforementioned propaganda as "cheating" and "false," affirming that "I myself just muddled along from day to day, and did so only for survival, and only for the pay" (W1). The repair worker's resentment was understandable, for he was a high-school graduate in 1968 and was sent down from Wuhan to the countryside together with his parent for one and half years before being recruited into the plant, a small one in the suburb of the city; there he remained an ordinary worker for nine years without promotion. Similarly, a PLA veteran who joined the Nanjing Steel and Iron Work in 1965 failed to become a CCP member, remained an ordinary worker before his appointment as an officer of the plant's Material Section (thanks to his high school diploma), and saw no further promotion for the rest of his career at the factory. He thus denied that he had any sense of being the master; what he thought about was "just get the job done and live a life" (*jiu xiang ganhuo chifan*) (L1).

The second was those who were persistently delinquent, negligent, or indolent, bringing annoyance to co-workers or troubles to the factory from time to time, and subject to the leaders' censure and peers' ridicule before they became "rotten" enough to warrant a dismissal from the factory (B3). And the third group included those who were at the bottom of the labor force, struggling with the hardships of life and toiling all day. A miner from Shitouzui Mine of Wuhan, who started his job in 1971, explained that his "feeling as the master" was "not quite clear" because "at that time we mined on the ground every day and the job was very hard and backbreaking, so we did not have much time to think about anything else" (H13).

Finally, there was a considerable number of ordinary workers as well as some of the lower-ranking cadres who, short of motivations for upward mobility, were neither frustrated nor satisfied with what they were. Their attitudes to the factory thus fell between the two opposites of being explicitly grateful or loyal and being resentful or disloyal. The attitudes of the retiree from the Shanghai Light Bulb Factory best illustrate this. He said that his feeling of being the master of the factory was momentary, occurring only when the workers were stirred up at a factory-wide meeting of mobilization, and that feeling "gradually vanished as time went on." "It was just like a wind. Only for a moment, I felt the factory was like my home" (S4). A retiree from the Shanghai Silicon Steel Factory thus described himself: "After entering the factory, I just wanted to stay there for life, but I did not feel that it was my home. Home is home, factory is factory. At that time we thought different from now: We never thought of job-hopping. I join the factory and work for you, and you should take care of me all the way until my death, and that's it!" (S2).

In addition to the reasons specific to individual workers as outlined above, there was also an institutional factor behind the lack of the master's consciousness among the workers. Since 1960, workers had been encouraged to participate in the "democratic management" (*minzhu guanli*) of the enterprise, in response to the party's call for "two participations, one change, and three-way unity" (*liangcan yigai sanjiehe*) (i.e., for cadres to participate in production and for workers to participate in management, changing the irrational regulations and practices and uniting cadres, technicians, and workers in technological renovations) (*WXXB*, 13: 626). From time to time, many of our informants were indeed involved in various activities to solve technical issues or improve tools or machines,[12] but few had a chance to play a substantial role in management, a task up to the cadres above them and quality controllers (S2).[13] Both the trade unions and the workers' congress, the two major venues for worker participation, were subject to the factory leader's and party secretary's control, and their functions were limited to handling issues pertaining to workers' welfare benefits rather than their rights in the workplace (see Chapter 2); in other words, there were no institutional channels whereby the workers could develop a real sense of being the master of state firms or feel strong loyalty to them.[14]

BETWEEN THE PUBLIC AND THE PRIVATE

To further gauge the degree of workers' loyalty to their firms, let us look at how our informants responded to the question of whether nor not they had experienced or witnessed any instances of "seeking private gain at public expense" (*sungong feisi*), a phrase commonly used in the Maoist discourse to depict the opposite of workers' selfless devotion and full commitment to the public good as masters of the factory. About half of our interviewees denied that this phenomenon was a severe problem in their enterprises, and the reasons they offered fell largely into the following three categories. The first was again the workers' "purity and simple-mindedness." As they explained, no one took home the factory's products or other objects because they "cherished the state's properties" (S3). "No one pocketed the lost money or other things that they picked up, instead they tried their best to find the owner and assuage the owner's anxiety. People's minds back then were truly very pure" (L3). The second reason was that the factory's property was useless to themselves or their families, as reported by a textile factory worker (S7), a miner (H11), and a service management officer (S9). The third reason was the mutual surveillance among the workers coupled with severe disciplinary measures and consequences for the offenders. A chef at the No. 1 Factory of Shanghai Steelworks said that anyone in his kitchen who took anything home, once caught, had to pay a fine that was one hundred times the value of the object being taken, or they would be fired if it was a more severe offense (S1). At the Port Machinery Factory in Ningbo, a female janitor collected bits of abandoned solder wires while she was cleaning the grounds and sold them to a recycling station; she was then investigated by police officers, an instance suggesting how difficult it was for people to make profits by illegally taking and selling public goods (N4). At the No. 2 Automobile Works in Hubei, a veteran-turned-worker committed suicide after he was humiliated at a public struggle meeting for his pocketing only a few yuan of public funds. "Once stolen," an informant from this enterprise explained, "public properties could be easily identified. So is the saying, 'one hole for each radish.' Once a person made this mistake, he could no longer face the society" (H2; also Y2).

Most of the informants who admitted the problem of "seeking private gain at public expense" in their work units explained that this was limited to only a few and involved taking trivial amounts of small objects (L1, S5). It was possible, for example, for a textile factory worker to take home a small bunch of yarn, but this was "very rare" because the worker could not really make money from it (N1). It was also likely for a miner to bring home a few pieces of coal for fuel if he had a family (L7). Excessive and frequent infractions, on the other hand, would likely incur criticism from factory leaders and ridicule from peers. At the Shanghai No. 1 Artistic Carving Factory, for instance, a worker took objects from the factory so often that later a cartoon poster was displayed at an exhibition depicting the person crawling through the hole of a traditional Chinese copper coin, thus condemning the offender by innuendo because his surname was Kong (literally, "the hole") (S6).

There were, however, also activities that involved a group of employees and fell into the gray area between right and wrong. A former employee from a military enterprise in Beijing admitted that, whenever any of the workers wanted to add a small kitchen to their crowded apartment, they and their buddies would first let their team leader know; the leader would allow them to put together the needed materials such as wires and nails for the task, and they would keep the entrance guard away before taking the objects from the factory yard. For them, this was only a "minor mistake" and a right thing justified by their survival needs (B7). In another instance, in the early 1960s when people suffered from hunger everywhere, the art troupe of a military enterprise making clothing and bedding products divided among its members the pumpkins they had received as rewards from one of their shows; for this, its leader was pardoned because she had once shaken hands and danced with Chairman Mao (H5)! At the Yimin Food Factory in Shanghai, warehouse workers were asked to save any leftover sugar, red beans, almonds, and the like that they picked up from the floor of the warehouse, and at the end of the year the head of the warehouse clandestinely divided the saved leftovers among the members of his group. This scandal remained a secret until one of the workers was unhappy with their small raise and reported the transgression to factory management, forcing the head to resign (S8).

The problem of "seeking private gain at public expense" was the severest in food processing factories and public canteens. At the Beijing No. 2 Food Processing Factory, a retired worker recalled, employees were free to eat candies and fruits "as much as they liked," and the informant himself admitted that he never bought sugar since he was hired in 1971, although there was a great shortage of sugar in the market and it was rationed to Beijing residents (B3). At the aforementioned Yimin Food Factory, our informant, a newcomer to the factory at the time, was shocked upon seeing that the workers threw away ice cream bars or other foods after only taking one bite; she soon realized that this "wasteful" manner was "just too common" there. She said that "there were too many instances" in which workers took things home; "edible things were everywhere in our factory, so theft was prevalent. Many workers lived in poverty just outside the factory compound. They could not help but steal upon seeing those things, and they were good at stealing." Those who made canned lunch meat, for example, cut pork into long slices and put them into a thermos bottle to take home, so it was difficult to catch them (S8). The same trick was done by the cook of the workers' canteen at Gedian Chemical Factory in Wuhan, who poured the canteen's cooking oil into his own thermos bottle; that was when every resident was rationed only 250 grams of oil per month (W1). At one of the construction divisions of the PLA, likewise, a driver who transported foods for three canteens of the division witnessed how a canteen chief gave eggs, fish, and meat to people of his circle or brought the canteen's foods home (H17).

These facts suggest that, during severe shortages of food, housing, and other resources, people were likely to engage in self-profiteering activities wherever the objective conditions in their workplaces permitted. Not surprisingly, food processing factories and public canteens were places where theft of public goods happened more often than in other places. In other words, most of the workers in state enterprises appeared to be committed to their firms not necessarily because they were "naive and simple-minded" under the influence of state propaganda but more likely because of two basic reasons, as the examples have shown. First, there was little room for both the cadres and ordinary workers to profit from illegally possessing and selling the goods from their work units, nor could many of them consume the products they made. Second, the risk for doing so was much higher than the potential gain. Once uncovered, the offenders had to face not just simply paying a fine but also losing their social and political standing in a society where one's face mattered more than anything else. Therefore, it is true that most workers and cadres of state firms did not engage in these self-enriching activities during the Mao era, as many of the nostalgic retirees claimed. But the reasons for this were not so much about the asserted purity and loyalty of the workers as the institutional circumstances that limited their choices of action.

DISCIPLINING THE WORKERS: RULES, PRODUCTION LINE, AND PEER PRESSURE

In addition to the ideological and political tools outlined so far, the use of regulations and other disciplinary measures was equally important to constrain the workers. Under the "militarized management" (*buduishi guanli*) at the No. 2 Automobile Works in Hubei, for example, roll call happened daily in every workshop at 8:00 a.m. Those who failed to appear were excused the first time, censured for the second offense, and penalized by a pay deduction for the third, and so on (H2). To receive full pay, therefore, workers had to make every effort to show up on time; normally they had to arrive fifteen minutes before their shift started (S3, S6, S7, S8). At the Xinghuo Cotton Mill in Nanjing, a worker who had arrived late, left early, or been absent twice a month or more had to make a "self-examination" before members of the same group; those who had to be absent for one or two days had to seek approval from the group leader, and longer absences had to be approved by the factory leader (L6). It was very difficult to get a request for a leave of absence: A worker at a food processing factory in Tianmen had to wait for three months after his wife gave birth to their child, and he was allowed only a one-day leave to see his wife and newborn (H24). Likewise, those who did a poor job or failed to finish the required number of tasks on time were also subject to a deduction from their monthly bonus, which ranged from as little as 0.80 to 2 yuan before the Cultural Revolution (N9) to more than 10 yuan in the late 1970s (N3). To finish their tasks in a timely manner, female workers at the Xinghuo Cotton Mill in Nanjing had to eat lunch as quickly as possible and avoid drinking water before their shift to reduce the trips to the toilet, and they had to rush to the restroom when they had to do so while on duty (L6). Apprentices had to work particularly hard and carefully to guarantee the quality of their jobs, or they ran the risk of failing to obtain a permanent job (N2).

Another factor conducive to workers' performance was quality control in production, which was strict in state firms during the Mao era. Consider the following two textile factories. At the bedding and clothing factory in Wuhan, our informants thus described quality control there: "Superior quality was a requirement in our factory as a military enterprise. Quality was a top priority. We paid meticulous attention to details in the production of bedding and clothing products for the military supply department. Our production is characteristically handmade in a streamline, and every worker has her unique code. So it can be immediately identified if any problem occurred at any link of production" (H6). "Quality control was conducted at every link, including the last one before the product left the factory. No matter it was ordinary textile goods or bedding and clothing products, once a minor mistake occurred, an examination meeting would follow, and we won't leave the problem unsolved before dismissal" (H5). Strict measures of quality control were also common in ordinary factories. At Hefeng Yarn Mill in Ningbo, a quality-control group from the factory's lab routinely patrolled the workshop; its examiners frequently pulled out yarn to take a close look when it came out from the spinning unit. A worker's wage grade was directly linked with the quality of the yarn they produced. "If you are a worker of fine yarn, for example," our interviewee explained, "he [the examiner] would stand next to you and keep watching while you were working. How much you produced, what percent of defective product, and what percent of finished product, all these were evaluated. The examiners were selected from the most qualified workers, not elected by vote. . . . They were chosen solely because of their skills. Your skills must be particularly outstanding [to be an examiner]. . . . For example, we connect broken yarns. Yarns can be broken and have to be linked together. If you did a poor job, the connecting knot looks thicker and visible, and the cloth thus woven will look uneven. If you are skilled, the knot would be invisible and smooth. This is a masterly skill, and it has to be practiced with a tremendous amount of effort, practiced even during your spare time." A worker's wage grade was thus determined. "If you did a poor job, your grade would be lower, so was your wage. . . . You could be a first-grade worker, if you attended many [spinning units] or a second-grade worker for fewer [units] or a third-grade workers for even fewer" (N1).

Finally, we have to take into account the machine factor and the human factor in understanding workers' performance in production. In most factories, manufacturing took the form of a production line or an assembly line, with each worker performing a specific task or with a group of workers doing the same job as a link of the entire production process. Under this circumstance, it was almost impossible for the workers to be late or to leave early or to slow down, thus affecting the progress of the entire line. There were, to be sure, always a few who tended to dillydally while working or who were slow-paced by nature; in this case, the factory leader had to remove them from the line and assign them a different task, such as distributing equipment and uniforms or cleaning the work floor (S8). For those working on the line, however, "there was no way to slack," as a retiree from the Shanghai Silicon Steel Factory commented, "because each of the many steps of the whole process was fixed. It was impossible to slack even if one had the intention to do so" (S2). Another retiree from the Shanghai Light Bulb Factory made a similar comment: "Every group had its own production target. If you failed to finish [your own task], then others had to do it for you, but everyone had his or her own task . . . therefore, it was almost impossible for someone else to work for you. This was true for us working on a production line" (S4). Nor was it tolerable for workers to be late or to leave early in factories where production involved three shifts, with eight hours for each shift, because one's late arrival would mean the preceding worker's delayed leaving, and one's early leaving would mean the next workers' early arrival, which was nearly impossible unless the incumbent worker had requested an early exit and a prearrangement was made for an early handover (N1). Early leaving happened occasionally to workers who performed auxiliary tasks for the line, only when a worker had to leave early for a particular reason and only after they had entrusted their duties to someone else (S8).

The nature of production in some factories also led to strict prohibition against dereliction. For instance, in chemical factories, our informant recalled, "if you showed the slightest degree of irresponsibility, there could be leaking of gas and thus explosion at any moment. You can't afford to be careless in any case. If you did something wrong by mistake, there could be accidents to follow" (W2). At the Wuhan Pharmaceutical Factory, workers had to pay close attention to the time and temperature of the drugs being made. If the temperature was too high, the drug would be carbonized and useless. "Therefore," a retiree from the factory emphasized, "workers in our factory had to have a strong sense of responsibility. Accidents could happen when you slacked just a little" (W4).

Given that workers in state firms typically performed as a group for the same task or for the same production line, that their synchronized efforts were essential for the smooth operation of the line, and that workers of the same group or the same line were usually held liable collectively for any consequences of dereliction in production, they tended to develop a form of collective surveillance over each member of the group and a mechanism of group sanctioning against flagrant slacking. Our informants from different factories repeatedly confirmed this:

"Slacking was quite difficult because we worked as a group at that time, and each person's performance was obvious to everyone else" (H13);

"We worked together every day and we could instantly notice whoever was shirking; therefore, there was basically no one who arrived late or left early or slacked" (H16);

"Every day we worked together for hard tasks. Everyone kept looking at each other, and no one shirked and idled" (H17);

"Most workers at that time . . . worked extremely hard for the sake of saving face. . . . People looked at one another and competed mutually before 1978, no matter whether or not the supervisor was present and whether or not their tasks were to be inspected" (Y1);

"Eighty to ninety percent of workers in our factory were female, and we were all motivated. There were a few who wanted to slack, but they had to act more positively when the rest of us were highly motivated." (L2)

Peer pressure had an effective check on slacking. Our informants often talked about the "extent of tolerance" (*rongrendu*) which the workers as a group allowed for derelict behavior within the group. Sporadic shirking by an individual was tolerable, as a retired fiscal officer in Shanghai explained; if late arrival and early leaving or other forms of shirking happened too often for the same person, however, that person "would feel embarrassed" (S9). Another informant from Shanghai confirmed: "Every group had its own extent of tolerance. It's okay if it involved only a minor problem and occurred infrequently. However, if it happened repeatedly, people won't tolerate (*renjia ye hui kan bu xia qu de*), and there would be an adverse consequence" (S4). Given the presence of peer pressure, even the most careless individuals had to make sure that their performance would be "largely acceptable to others" (*datishang kan de guoqu*)" and knew that they "had to get the job done" (*huo yao zuo wan*) (W1). Though limited in number, the slackers were nevertheless subject to group sanctioning in the form of ridicule and open criticism. In the words of the retired oil worker from the Shengli Oil Field in Shandong, "they were the people that we looked down upon" (*doushi naxie women kanbuqi de ren*) (Y2).

THE EQUILIBRIUM IN LABOR RELATIONS

State-firm workers were subject to a whole set of formal and informal institutions during the Mao era. To assume that the Chinese workers lacked motivation and slacked on the shop floor because of the nonexistence of immediate monetary rewards or other forms of material gain oversimplifies the realities of factory production. On the other hand, however, it is equally simplistic to claim that the workers were "naive and simple," fully committed to the public and downplaying private interest. This chapter, instead, interprets the workers' performance by putting them into a historical context in which multiple factors, formal and informal, worked together to motivate as well as constrain them. The workers' choices cannot be fully understood without taking into account the following four sets of institutional realities and practices central to the context in which they lived and worked.

(1) *The absence of material incentives for individuals.* During most of the Maoist years, workers saw no wage increases, and when a wage adjustment did happen, one's upgrading of wage level was based primarily on seniority rather than performance. The pay difference between workers of different wage grades, age cohorts, and skill levels was narrow. Bonuses were banned during the Cultural Revolution, and when they were in use, as seen in some years before 1966 and again in the late 1970s, they were paid to almost all workers at the same rate as a necessary supplement to their wages, rather than as an incentive linked with their labor input. Tied to a specific state firm for life once hired, the workers also lacked the opportunity to switch jobs for higher pay; and when a worker did change their job, which was rare, their wage grade remained the same no matter where they worked. Therefore, there was indeed no direct link between one's labor effort and monetary reward in most of the Maoist era, and throughout the rest of the era, the link was weak. Behind this policy of labor remuneration was the mounting population pressure over limited economic resources, a reality that compelled the socialist state to provide all adults in the cities with job opportunities but minimize their wage differences to ensure subsistence for all; this meant freezing wage grades and levels for years and even decades, having a preference for time rates over piece rates in labor remuneration, and providing little freedom for workers to change their jobs. All these contrasted sharply with persistent labor shortages, high labor turnover rates, the wide use of progressive piece rates, and the widened gap between the so-called shock workers and ordinary workers in the Soviet Union from the 1930s to the 1950s (Kirsch 1972, 31–33; Lane 1985, 146–148; Filtzer 1986, 50–55, 96–97, 188).

(2) *Social cleavage and inequality.* Given the limited job opportunities in the cities, especially in state-owned factories, the state had to block the flow of the rural population into the cities and limit the number of workers hired by state firms. The result was stark inequality under the newly created, rigid, and institutionalized social hierarchy in post-1949 urban China, with formal workers of the state firms at the top, those of collective firms in the middle, and the millions of informal workers at the bottom, as shown in Chapter 1. To properly understand the morale of the labor force in state firms, therefore, we should consider how its three basic sources affected the workers' self-perception and collective consciousness: Workers who had suffered unemployment and poverty before 1949 witnessed a striking difference

between their past and their secured livelihood after becoming state-firm employees, a situation that was especially true in the early and mid-1950s; workers who were recruited from the countryside, in large number during the Great Leap Forward and on a limited scale afterward, were also aware of the sharp contrast between their past experiences as peasants and their new status as urban workers; in most of the Mao era, however, the new employees in state firms were recruited from the urban youth, who luckily shunned employment in collective firms. All these workers thus had a good reason to feel proud and grateful for their status as the privileged minority in relation to the entire labor force of the nation and for the difficulty and the luck behind their successful entrance into state firms. The sharp contrast with collective and informal workers, the strong sense of honor and privilege, and the identity they developed with their own work units functioned to offset the lack of material incentives to some degree and accounted for part of their motivation for good or acceptable performance in the workplace.

(3) *Formal incentives and constraints.* In the absence of material stimuli, the strongest incentive for workers to perform well came from the political realm. To be named an Advanced Producer, a Model Laborer, or a woman pace-setter; to be a member of the party or the Youth League; or to be promoted from the rank and file to a cadre or a white-collar officer—all these meant a lot to the workers. These honors and opportunities distinguished the most motivated individuals from the rest of the workforce, satisfied their pursuit of fame and respect, and, to some degree, brought them the material benefits of their new positions, no matter how limited these benefits might be. Workers were encouraged to compete with one another individually or as a group, although not all workers were equally motivated by these opportunities. On the other hand, no workers wanted to be labeled as a "backward element" because of poor performance in production and political activities. The other side of control in factory production, therefore, was the imposition of high pressure for conformity as well as various disciplinary measures. Failure to arrive or leave on time and poor performance were not only linked with one's political attitude but also subject to punishment under formal regulations and rules of the factory.

(4) *Informal institutions.* Aside from the formal means of motivation and control, informal institutions were also important in shaping workers' behavior. Central to such informal constraints were peer pressure or group

surveillance and sanctioning against dereliction among the workers of the same workshop or the same team, and the different leadership styles and abilities of factory managers and supervisors. Needless to say, these factors were context specific and varied from factory to factory, depending on who the workers were and how the management operated. The leaders' role was particularly important. As a miner from Zhenjiang explained, "Labor productivity depends primarily on the leaders. Whether or not a leader worked hard mattered a lot. If the leader gave up his duties, workers would be surely lazy. When the superiors monitored closely, those below them would work hard. People were so passive" (N2). Other informants explained how the workers responded to their supervisors; they had to work more hours if their team leader instructed so (W3), or they could also leave a bit earlier if the team leader was willing to "pass it off" (or "gloss it over") (*da mafuyan*) (B9). These informal elements worked together to form the norms of the workplace, or the unwritten "conventions and codes of behavior," as Douglass North terms it (1990, 4, 91), which interacted with the formal rules to guide the workers in production.

Together, these factors, more than anything else, constituted the essential features of an enterprise as the very "work unit" (*danwei*) in which its members interacted with one another as a group. It was in this context that the workers experienced their everyday lives inside and outside the factory. For most of them, there were largely three choices of action at the workplace. The first was shirking, in the forms of consistent failure to observe one's work shift or schedule, poor performance, or sabotage of machines and other public property. This was obviously the least feasible option, given the strict work disciplines of the factory, mutual surveillance, and group pressure among co-workers, and, more important, the risk of losing one's job and hence the security of their livelihood and standing in society. Contrary to this was the second option, by which a politically motivated worker performed exceptionally well, showing full commitment to the factory at the expense of their own self-interest. This choice was indeed attractive to many workers at the times of intense mobilization. In the end, however, only a minority of workers stuck to this option, not only because mass mobilization could never last long, but also because the opportunities awarded to the most dedicated workers were few. Therefore, for the vast majority of workers, the third and most likely option was to observe the factory's regulations; avoid mistakes, accidents, and other problems of delinquency; and perform one's routine duties in a manner that met the norms of the workplace. This was a choice for any worker who wished to remain "normal" and to save face in and outside the workplace, hence the prevalence of an equilibrium in worker performance in everyday production.

Needless to say, this equilibrium was not always present in state firms. It came into being only when a whole set of factory institutions was established to regulate labor relations within a state-owned enterprise. Among these institutions were the permanent employment of formal workers, their entitlement to a comprehensive package of fringe benefits, their participation in mass organizations and factory governing bodies, and the regulations and policies regarding labor remuneration. These institutions were first established in the early to mid-1950s by borrowing the factory system from the Soviet Union and inheriting some of the business practices that had been implemented in government-owned or large private enterprises under the Nationalist state (Yeh 1997; Frazier 2002; Bian 2009). The Great Leap Forward in 1958 undermined some of these institutions, as seen in the rapid increase of informal workers and the abandonment of the piece-rate wage system for the time-rate system; these radical policies, however, soon resulted in a severe shortage of resources to support the rapidly expanding urban population and a significant decline in labor productivity. To accelerate the recovery from the chaos of the Great Leap Forward, the state laid off a large number of informal workers, reintroduced the piece-rate system, or combined piece rates with time rates in the wage system in the early 1960s (Lin Pan 2019, 2021). After the outbreak of the Cultural Revolution in 1966, when radical students and workers rebelled against the establishments in urban China, the formal institutions of state firms also came under their attack, and many factory institutions ceased to function or were completely abandoned (see Chapter 5). But they were reintroduced or reestablished by and large after the death of Lin Biao in 1971, when the state implemented a series of new policies to end political disorder and boost economic growth; except for a short moment of disruption in late 1975 and 1976 when Mao tried to defend his legacies by launching a campaign against "rightist deviations," all of the factory institutions that had been established in the 1950s, reestablished in the early 1960s, and rebuilt in the early 1970s continued throughout the 1970s and even into the early years of the reform era. It was these formal institutions on workers' rights in employment, labor remuneration, and factory governance that interacted with a set of informal institutions outlined earlier, to motivate as well as constrain the rank and file on an everyday basis and give rise to the equilibrium in the workplace.

It is worth emphasizing that this equilibrium existed as long as (1) the workers maintained their status as permanent and privileged employees, (2) they had no opportunities to change jobs or work outside the factory for more income, (3) they were economically least differentiated in the absence of strong material incentives, and (4) they maintained a strong sense of group identity and performed under moral incentives and peer pressure. In other words, the features that characterized a work unit also constituted the key pillars sustaining the equilibrium in labor politics within the work unit. The equilibrium and the work unit went hand in hand. The equilibrium came into being only when a work unit was well established and tightly insulated from outside; the loss of these features would necessarily mean the collapse of a traditional work unit, the disappearance of the equilibrium, and a change of worker identity and behavior.

It is from this perspective that worker performance in factory production can be properly understood. The workers were undoubtedly rational actors, but their rationality was never based on the "naked self-interest" or their sheer calculation of immediate material gain or loss; instead, it was based on their consideration of all factors affecting their standing and well-being in the state firms. This way of thinking and choice of action thus can be best termed as "context-bound rationality," to borrow from Victor Nee (1998, 10). Unless there existed better jobs and higher pay outside their factory, or unless they were politically ambitious and motivated, for most of the workers who wanted to keep their job, live a decent life, and be respected by their peers and leaders, the best choice was to abide by the factory's regulations, work on schedule, and perform their duties in a manner that satisfied themselves and their peers' and leaders' expectations, hence the prevalence of an equilibrium in the workplace in which both overt shirking and full commitment to work were rare; instead, what prevailed among the vast majority of the workforce was an attitude between the two extremes. The workers of state firms, in other words, were not as self-disciplined or morally committed as the nostalgic retirees of the post-Mao era claimed. The workers appeared to be "naive and simple" because they could not act otherwise in the social and historical context in which they worked and lived their everyday lives.

To conclude, the state firms of Maoist China were far from a moralist heaven. To see the workers of the Mao era as naive and simple-minded is misleading, reflecting more or less a nostalgia of the older generation of the working class in response to the striking disparity in wealth distribution and rampant corruption in the post-Mao era. On the other hand, however, it is equally oversimplified to conclude that slacking was commonplace and that the Maoist factories were necessarily inefficient because of the lack of material incentives. As a matter of fact, labor productivity in state firms increased steadily throughout the Mao era (Guojia tongjiju 1983, 297), not only because of capital investment and technological progress, but also because of the functioning of the work unit equilibrium that effectively regulated the labor force. Many of the problems that are often attributed to the workers of the Maoist era actually became severe only after 1976, when the pressure for conformity was gone and material incentives were widely used as the only stimulus to boost productivity, causing irreversible damage to the workplace equilibrium (as will be demonstrated in Chapter 6). To grasp the operational realities of the state firms and the actual experiences of Chinese workers, we have to avoid idealizing the factory institutions and worker performance as did the nostalgic retirees, or taking for granted the official discourse in post-1978 China, which attributed the new problems of the reform era solely to the institutions inherited from the Maoist past and magnified the problems and failures of the Mao era to legitimate the reform agenda.

5 THE FRUSTRATED MASTERS

Workers before and during the Cultural Revolution

THE WORK UNIT EQUILIBRIUM, as shown in the preceding two chapters, resulted from a particular set of formal institutions interacting with various informal factors in everyday factory politics and production activities. Key to the normal functioning of these formal institutions were the following two features that distinguished state firms from all other types of enterprises during or after the Maoist era. The first was the exclusiveness of factory institutions in labor relations. The most important institutions in a state firm, including permanent employment, comprehensive fringe benefits, membership in trade unions, and participation in the staff and workers' congress (SWC), were open only to the full-time, regular workers; informal workers, who constituted roughly 13 to 14 percent of the labor force in the first two years of the Cultural Revolution and 14 to 15 percent in the late 1970s (Guojia tongjiju 1987, 26, 33), were largely denied eligibility to these rights and privileges. Therefore, a second feature of factory institutions in Maoist China, derived from the first, was the striking disparity in workers' economic, social, and political standings. This is seen not only between formal and informal workers in state firms and among workers between state-owned and collectively owned firms, but also among the formal workers within a state firm. Depending on their family statuses and political backgrounds, formal workers in a state firm were differentiated into four groups as explained in

Chapter 1, namely: (1) a small group of activists, who were eligible for various honorary titles, party membership, and promotion to the rank of cadre; (2) the vast majority of ordinary workers, who were disinterested in, and ineligible for, such opportunities, but nevertheless performed reasonably well in everyday production; (3) a small number of "backward elements" who were poor performers in production and even troublemakers in the eyes of factory cadres; and (4) the few pariahs or individuals of the "Five Categories." In a nutshell, a state-owned factory, as well as the entire Chinese society under Mao, was by no means a socialist utopia promising to deliver equality for all; stark inequalities existed throughout the country and within every factory, despite Mao's personal obsession with egalitarian ideals (Bianco 2018, 65, 71).

As a result, huge tensions existed among workers of different standings within and outside the state firms, and this undermined the equilibrium in labor relations and factory politics. First, informal workers were unhappy with their second-class status and exclusion from the benefits and opportunities enjoyed by formal workers. Second, workers of collective firms competed for opportunities in state firms or wanted their own firm to be converted into a state-owned entity. Third, among the formal workers of a state firm, the sharp contrast between the activists and backward elements in political opportunities also resulted in disgruntlement among the latter and their resultant hostility toward those who discriminated against them. Fourth, tensions heightened particularly in factories where the cadres of different levels engaged in various forms of corruption and thus alienated themselves from the rank and file. All these constituted the environment in which the Cultural Revolution took place in the factories and explained, directly or indirectly, why the workers were split into different factions.

This chapter, therefore, begins with a survey of workers' social and economic conditions as well as a look at the problems of corruption among factory elites before the Cultural Revolution, in order to understand the different attitudes among the workers toward rebellions by Red Guards after 1966. It then examines how workers of different backgrounds developed various strategies for participating in the movement, how the state responded to their demands, and to what extent the workers of different factions achieved their respective goals. The chapter ends with a deliberation on the impact of the Cultural Revolution on the equilibrium in labor relations, the vulnerability of the rebuilt equilibrium in the last years of the Cultural Revolution, and its implications for understanding the inception of post-Mao reforms in state-owned enterprises.

A FAILED REVOLUTION: SOCIAL AND POLITICAL REALITIES BEFORE 1966
Power Relations in Private Firms

The new government that the CCP established in 1949 defined itself as a "state of people's democracy" under the leadership of the working class and based on the alliance between workers and farmers (*Renmin ribao*, 1949-10-01). To build its legitimacy among the urban working population, the state attempted to reshape workers' political consciousness. In the 1950s, the state began using its media to propagate the idea that, under the rule of the Communist Party, the oppression and exploitation people had suffered in the "old society" were over, and they had finally "stood up and become masters of their fate" (*fanshen zuo zhuren*). The realities that confronted the workers in the 1950s, however, were rather complicated. Following the CCP's takeover, some industrial cities witnessed workers of private factories taking violent actions against their bosses (Sheehan 1998, 24, 55; Perry 2007). In response, the government quickly carried out measures to stabilize the situation and prevent factory owners from abandoning their businesses. Under the coordination of local governments and trade union organizations, workers at many factories tolerated lower wages, more work hours, and even unemployment in order to speed up the recovery of production. Traditional power relations and practices on the shop floor continued by and large in private businesses, where more than 70 percent of workers were employed in the early 1950s; workers there saw no improvement in their livelihood and social standing in the first few years following the Communist takeover.

A turning point in power relations in private firms was the "Five-Anti" (*wufan*) Campaign, which started in January 1952 against businessowners who were charged with any of the following five types of crimes: bribery, theft of state property, tax evasion, cheating on a government contract, and stealing state economic intelligence. By that time, the Korean War was almost over, and the task of economic recovery was nearing completion. Therefore, the eradication of "lawless capitalists" was finally on the state's agenda. Along with the Five-Anti Campaign came the "Democratic Reform" (*minzhu gaige*), which aimed to stamp out any anti-government elements and terminate personal dependence or patronage networks among the workers in private firms (Lin Chaochao 2010). In Shanghai, for instance, grassroots trade union organizations organized meetings of "speaking bitterness" (*suku*) in almost every factory, where worker activists recounted their sufferings in the factory, revealed the crimes that the management personnel had committed, and forced the "lawless capitalists to make a thorough confession" (Huo 2015). Their actions resulted in the arrest of more than two hundred individuals; forty-nine capitalists attempted suicide and thirty-four died. As a result, some private businessowners had to suspend production, cancel the provision of meals for employees, and even stop wage payment, known together as "three terminations" (*santing*), causing the unemployment of as many as 130,000 workers in the city. In response, workers became even more radical; some surrounded factory office buildings for days and humiliated the owners or managers by tying them up, starving them, or removing their hats and clothes in front of a crowd. By early May when the campaign was over, as many as 163,400 private businessowners in Shanghai had been subject to the investigations of the aforementioned "five offenses" (*wudu*), and it was reported that "class relations underwent a profound change, whereby the working class established its leading role in the relationship between management and labor" (Huo 2009, 2015).

Workers' influences in private businesses after the Five-Anti Campaign culminated in the wide establishment of the Committee for Increasing Production and Saving Costs (*zengchan jieyue weiyuanhui*) in private factories. Comprised of representatives from the CCP, the trade union, workers, and management, the committee was intended to supervise the management's decision making on budgets and procurement of raw materials for the production of goods contracted by the government, and to prevent the management from engaging in tax evasion and other illegal activities. The trade union inside each private business also enhanced its interference with the firm's management, especially over administrative, fiscal, and personnel issues. For instance, without the trade union's endorsement, shown by affixing its seal, any check from a private factory would likely be rejected by the bank. The factory management also had to seek the trade union's approval when making any change to its personnel. The trade union thus actually controlled the factory's accounts and decision-making process in many private firms (Huo 2009).

But the growing power of the trade union and worker representatives also resulted in a phenomenon known as "economism" (*jingjizhuyi*), or demands for increasing workers' income in private businesses at the cost of the government's tax revenue. Under pressure from workers, private firms had to increase wages or bonuses. In some factories in Shanghai, for example, bonuses increased to a third or even two-thirds of workers' incomes (Zhang Jiancai 2017); in some extreme cases, bonuses skyrocketed to "an astonishing level so as to be several times workers' basic wages" (Huo 2015). Workers of different firms competed with one another for higher wages and more stipends so as to cover "all kinds of needs in clothing, food, residence, and transportation" (Huo 2015). But the higher income failed to incentivize the workers; quite the contrary, slacking became increasingly common in private firms, as seen in workers' inclinations to arrive late, leave early, or be absent entirely. Local governments suffered a significant loss of income taxes from private firms as the latter paid too much to workers and therefore lowered their profit rates. The state thus had to implement a series of measures in 1953 and 1954 to curb economism, such as increasing the income tax rates for targeted private firms or revising contracts with them so as to increase the quota of production while reducing the price of products procured by the government (Zhang Jiancai 2017). As a result, workers' real income decreased in 1954 and 1955 (Lin Chaochao 2019).

The reduced willingness of private firms to continue their businesses and the state's growing need to establish its centralized control of the national economy eventually led to the Socialist Transformation of Private Industry and Commerce in 1956, whereby all private industrial and commercial firms were swiftly (in a matter of roughly six months) turned into businesses of "public-private joint ownership" (*gongsi heying*) or state-owned factories. This ended not only the former capitalists' decision-making power in the firms of joint ownership, but also the autonomy of workers (or the trade unions) to speak for themselves over wages and benefits, as all factories were now completely subject to the state's control in every aspect of production and management. Throughout the country, a wage reform was implemented in all factories in 1956, which divided workers into eight grades in terms of wage levels. The scales of the eight-grade wage system varied in different regions and industrial sectors. The monthly wages for workers in the iron and steel industry in Shanghai, for instance, ranged from 42.4 yuan for the first grade to 123 yuan for the eighth grade (Yuan and Wang 2008).

Economic Differentiation and Social Stratification

Together, the Three-Anti Campaign of 1952, the Socialist Transformation movement, and the wage reform of 1956 worked to forge a new hierarchy in urban China that continued into the early 1960s. At the top were the "retained personnel" (*baoliu renyuan*) who had served as managers, engineers, technicians, and skilled workers in government-owned, private, or foreign enterprises before 1949 and, after the Communist takeover of these enterprises, were allowed by the new government to keep their original positions and salaries. As many as 750,000 individuals in industrial enterprises in the early 1950s fell into this category (Lin Pan 2018). Understandably, many of them were considered problematic in terms of family relations and political backgrounds, as they had joined the Guomindang or served the Nationalist government before 1949; yet they were indispensable for the new state to keep the enterprises running, which was key to economic rehabilitation and social stability. After the Socialist Transformation of 1956, many former owners, managers, and clerks in the newly reorganized firms under public-private joint ownership continued to receive their salaries at the original level, hence known as "retained wages" (*baoliu gongzi*); this constituted a major part of their incomes after the wage reform of 1956. A survey conducted in 1964 by the Shanghai Municipal Party Committee shows that, among the 1.6 million surveyed individuals in Shanghai and some cities of Zhejiang and Jiangsu provinces, 140,000 received retained wages. One accountant of Shanghai Electrical Bureau who had worked for an enterprise of the Nationalist government, for instance, received a retained wage of 561 yuan per month, which was nearly six times his "standard wage" (*biaozhun gongzi*, that is, the wage level after the introduction of the eight-grade wage system in 1956) of 94 yuan per month. Retained wages also applied to ordinary clerks of former private firms. Zhu Erjie, a gatekeeper at Dacheng Factory in Changzhou, for instance, was paid 320 yuan monthly. Qiu Xianzhang, a mailroom worker at Jiuhua Socks Factory in Shanghai, received a monthly wage of 374 yuan. Yang Ge, a clerk at a real estate company that had been a foreign firm before 1949, was paid a retained wage of 351 yuan per month, which was in addition to his standard wage of 49 yuan per month (Lin Chaochao 2019).[1]

Their high income allowed the retained personnel to live a luxurious lifestyle. According to the same survey, a former factory owner in Shanghai spent about 5,000 US dollars to buy a new car, riding it every day to the factory; when workers were in awe of his monthly wage of more than 600 yuan, he replied, "This amount is less than my wife's monthly pocket money." In another instance, an engineer named Wei, who worked at Yonglijiu Chemical Factory in Tianjin, had a family of three and lived in an independent house equipped with all kinds of electric home appliances available at that time, such as a vacuum, television, recorder, stereo speakers, and more than a dozen radio receivers. To put on a show of chrysanthemums at home, he bought more than 100 different varieties of the flower and shipped them from Beijing. Bored by the food cooked by the two nannies it hired, his family frequented local upper-scale restaurants, spending "as much as 30 to 40 yuan" for each meal (it was not uncommon, the survey added, for senior engineers in Shanghai and other cities to hire two or three nannies, although normally they had only a few family members). The aforementioned Wu of Dazhonghua Rubber Factory had a budget of 50 yuan each day for food, and his nanny found it difficult to use this whole amount on groceries for cooking. The extravagant consumption of food remained unchanged at the times of famine during the Great Leap Forward. An engineer at Dacheng Textile Factory, with a monthly salary of 402 yuan (including 276 yuan as a retained wage), "ate a chicken every two or three days" and sometimes "spent as much as 100 yuan on two chickens" during the time of "temporary hardship" (namely 1959–1961). Zhou Xiaotian, an actor with the Tianjin Peking Opera Troupe who had a monthly wage of 750 yuan, fed his pets, including two dogs and one cat, "with refined grain, eggs, milk, and pork liver" during the same period (Shanghai shiwei 1964).

Ordinary workers also saw a hike in their income level during the time of economism from 1952 to 1953 (Riskin 1987, 62–63). With the generous payment of bonuses under different names, which could be several times their basic wages, workers in private firms could easily make more than 100 yuan per month. The average income of all workers in five private paper mills in Shanghai, for example, was 145 yuan per month. Overall, workers in private firms earned 50 percent more than their counterparts in state-owned factories because of the payment of various bonuses in this city. The high income allowed some workers to indulge in luxurious lifestyles, as well. They hired nannies at home, rode a taxi for daily outings, and frequented nightclubs, skating rinks, and entertainment venues. Some of them even engaged in gambling, prostitution, and concubinage (Huo 2015). But the golden age of the privileged workers came to an end as a result of the state's ban on economism. The cancellation or reduction of bonuses and other incentives in both private and state firms led to a decline in workers' income in 1954. In 1955, the average annual wage of all workers in Shanghai was 802 yuan, which was 3.84 percent less than the level of the previous year. The wage reform of 1956 resulted in an overall improvement of workers' income nationwide, but the cancellation of piece-rate wages for certain tasks and the chaos in production during the Great Leap Forward caused a decline in workers' wage income, which was 64.7 yuan per month on average in Shanghai in 1961 (Lin Chaochao 2019). Throughout the whole country, workers' average annual wage declined from 637 yuan in 1957 to 592 yuan in 1962, remaining around 700 yuan in the 1970s (Guojia tongjiju 1983, 490).

While workers' wage levels stagnated and even declined during the Maoist years, the price of essential commodities for livelihood increased moderately. For instance, the average retail price of grain was 0.10 yuan per catty in 1953, 0.12 yuan in 1965, and 0.14 yuan in 1976; the price of pork was 0.47 yuan per catty in 1953, increased to 0.81 yuan in 1965, and remained 0.81 yuan in 1976 (Guojia tongjiju 1983, 470). Meanwhile, the average size of urban households grew, from 4.37 persons per household in 1957 to 5.30 in 1964, and the number of family members for each worker to support also increased from 3.29 to 3.40 during the same period (Guojia tongjiju 1983, 492). This led to a deterioration in workers' living standards in most of the 1950s and 1960s. On the whole, the monthly living expenses of an urban worker's family decreased from 18.50 yuan per person in 1957 to 18.39 yuan in 1964 across the entire country (Guojia tongjiju 1983, 492). In Shanghai, with a monthly income between 60 and 80 yuan, a typical worker's household of four to six members earned just enough for their daily expenses, of which the spending on food accounted for 50 to 60 percent, or roughly 1 to 1.6 yuan per day for the entire family. As a result, workers' daily meals consisted primarily of staple foods (rice or wheat) and vegetables, with only a very limited amount of meat, which was 1.12 catties (or 1.23 pounds) per month for each person on average in 1957 and 1.37 catties (or 1.51 pounds) in 1964 (Song 2011). Life was even harder for households whose monthly income was under 60 yuan in Shanghai; they had to spend about 75 percent of their income on food and count on their work unit's subsidies to make ends meet. For instance, a survey of more than a thousand workers in Shanghai Diesel Factory in 1955 showed that 35 percent of workers fell into the category of "workers in difficulty" (*kunnan zhigong*) who received subsidies from the factory; the most disadvantaged of them could only eat two meals of porridge each day. In the same city, about 40 percent of workers' families lived in slum areas crammed with straw-mat shacks (*penghu*) or "simple sheds" (*jianwu*) (Lin Chaochao 2019). These shelters were dark and humid inside, leaked in raining days, and were often plagued with diseases and epidemics. Usually a slum area had only one or two tap-water faucets for all families to share. In the 1950s and 1960s, it was not uncommon for all members of a worker's family to share a single bed in the filthy and dangerous shelter. The slum areas did not disappear in Shanghai until the early 1970s (Yuan and Wang 2008).

A stark disjunction thus prevailed in the 1950s and early 1960s between the state's propaganda of a "new society," in which the working class was exalted to the status of masters, and the grim realities of social stratification and polarization. Social inequality and cleavage continued to characterize urban China despite the revolution that promised to deliver "equality for all" (*renren pingdeng*). This is clearly seen in the Yonglining Chemical Factory in Nanjing in the 1950s. According to a report from 1957, among the 276 households in the No. 2 Village of the factory's residential area, 68 belonged to the factory's engineering and technical personnel, 110 belonged to the factory's staff members, and only 98 belonged to ordinary workers. Among the households of engineers, technicians, and staff members, 115 hired a home maid, and their living expenses were about 20 yuan per person per month, whereas the "households in difficulty" (*kunnanhu*) had only about 10 yuan per person each month. According to the report,

> "because of historical reasons, there has been a schism between the families of factory personnel with a higher education [i.e., engineers, technicians, and senior staff members] and the families of workers. These two groups look down on each other, and are resentful of each other. The housewives of staff families address themselves mutually as 'Madam Zhang' or 'Madam Li' and the like, but they would call the wives of worker's families as 'Zhang's mother' or "Li's mother' and so on. When all

of them attended a newspaper-reading meeting, the worker's wives sit together as a group, and the staff's wives formed another group. Even the children of the two groups would not play together with each other." (NJ6001-3-329)

Problematic Cadres and Party Members

Workers' disillusion grew in the late 1950s and early 1960s not only because much of their expectation of *fanshen* in social standing and living conditions did not fully come true, but also because the actual performance of the party members and cadres around them was disappointing. Reports on the "rectification of the party" (*zhengdang*) campaign in the factories in Nanjing, which swept through rural and urban China in 1965 as the final phase of the longer Socialist Education Movement that had begun in late 1962, reveal the real situation of the party members and local cadres in the city on the eve of the Cultural Revolution.

One report found that most of the party members in the surveyed factories obtained their membership after 1949. At the Military Factory No. 741, for example, of the 360 party members, there were only 60 who joined the party before 1949; and among the recent party members, 112 obtained party membership after 1958. Because of their relative lack of experience, the report continued, these party members "did not receive systematic education of Marxism and Leninism, and fell short of revolutionary trials and rigorous tests." With "impure motives" for joining the party, some of them committed various crimes, such as "embezzlement and theft" (*tanwu daoqi*), "moral degeneration" (*fuhua duoluo*), or "breach of laws and disciplines" (*weifa luanji*). A party member named Yang Genfa was arrested because he seduced and had sex with a thirteen-year-old girl. Still more party members, the report pointed out, had problems including "giving up the motive to progress, indulging in eating and drinking, losing the willingness to fight, and even trying to quit party membership," and since 1963 four or five individuals verbally requested to withdraw from the party. Some party members were known as "standard clocks" (*biaozhunzhong*), for their daily routines were nothing less than "going to work for eight hours, and doing home chores afterward." And "they failed to act as role models. Instead, they came to blows easily over trivial matters, thus having very bad influences. Some party members were superstitious, so as to seek advice from a diviner or practice witchcraft at home for sick children instead of seeing a doctor" (NJ4045-3-35).

Another report from the Military Factory No. 513 in Nanjing classified the 321 party members in this unit into five categories: 95 members (30 percent) were "good"; 167 (50 percent) were "fair"; 39 (12.15 percent) were "problematic"; 6 (1.8 percent) had "many problems in severe nature, including moral degeneration"; and finally, 14 were "ordinary party members who failed to play the role as a party member." The report went on to list five major problems found among the party members and grassroots cadres:

1) "Failure to act exemplarily in carrying out the party's policies, as seen in their engagement in illegal construction of infrastructural projects";
2) "Compromises during the times of hardship [meaning the years of the Great Leap Forward], such as eating and taking exceedingly; engaging in back-door deals and barter to benefit a small group at the cost of the public; doing money-making jobs or small businesses after hours, and even engaging in petty theft";
3) "Violation of party disciplines and state laws, as seen in the repeated engagement in graft, theft, and market speculations";
4) "Dallying with women and engaging in illicit sex"; and
5) "Having the various problems of individualism, such as being conceited and complacent, losing the revolutionary will, caring too much about one's own status, ignoring the well-being of the masses, boasting about one's own achievements in the past and recklessly bullying others, seeking unearned gains, being obsessed exclusively with one's own duties [without caring about politics], seeking material incentives and prioritizing the earning of bonuses, seeking upward mobility but refusing downward one, causing disputes and divisions, and equating oneself with ordinary people (*laobaixing dangyuan*)." (NJ4045-3-35)

Likewise, the work team for socialist education (*shejiao gongzuodui*) in the Military Factory No. 772 identified eight symptoms of "individualism" (*gerenzhuyi*) among the party members of the factory, including:

1) "Asking for a better treatment when assigned a new job or demanding more pay during a wage upgrade by talking to the leaders or comrades around them and submitting a written request";

2) "Caring about nothing else but earning bonuses" and "loving money as much as their life." For instance, when receiving a bonus payment, "they got so excited that they kept counting the money all the way from the factory back to home." However, when there was no bonus for a certain task, "they appeared to be disinterested and tired"; "a certain person argued with the small production group leader only because he wanted to get a few more cents of bonus, and so angry he became that he even threw the money to the ground, and did not stop the quarrel until he was paid a bit more";

3) "Being picky in job assignment," as evidenced by the statement of a certain party member: "I will not accept a new job if it does not satisfy four criteria: good working environment, high wage, comparable status, and light duty";

4) "Choosing a task only according to one's own interest" and refusing assignment to a new factory in a different city in Northwest China; one person even openly claimed: "I won't go there! I'd prefer to be degraded and die in Nanjing and even go back home and be a farmer";

5) "Focusing on vocational expertise at the cost of political commitment" (*zhi zhuan bu hong*), as evident in a party member's remark: "One has to be solid in technical skills in order to live a good life. As for politics, you just need to do a passable job." He thus was inactive in political activities and was "at a loss and sleepy" during political study sessions;

6) "Being resentful of others who got a promotion when one himself did not";

7) "Being indulgent in an easy life and content with things as they are"; and

8) "Doing money-making jobs for oneself during work hours, spending time on tourism during a business trip," and so forth. (NJ4045-3-36)

The same report further listed eight problems among the cadres of the No. 772 Factory:

1) "Overlooking the boundary and mixing oneself with bad people by eating and drinking together with the latter or addressing each other as brothers. Some of them trust capitalists more than they trust their own comrades, and they only talk about uniting with the capitalists instead of the ideological transformation of the latter. They marry the children of landlords, rich peasants, and reactionaries, subject themselves to their influences, and become their captives. Some extol the bourgeois style of courtship and corrupt the mind of adolescents by saying 'first, kneel down and court sincerely; and second, write a love letter and get it done forever'";
2) "Eating and taking exceedingly during the times of hardship. They cut down the ration coupons for distribution to the masses, embezzle public funds and steal public goods, engage in market speculation, and lend high-interest loans";
3) "When promoting cadres, they care only about the candidates' vocational competence without looking at their political performance, investigating their family backgrounds, or looking into their political history. They overlook the candidates' moral qualifications, ignore the opinions of the masses, pay no attention to the candidates' actual performances. Instead, they only seek those who are good at flattering, have the gift of gab, curry favor with their superior, and cater to their tastes. They trust such candidates with important tasks and put them into the leader's position and even to the key posts";
4) "Becoming morally degenerated under the influences of corrupt bourgeois ideas. They engage in illicit sexual relations. Some of them threaten and seduce the other side by all kinds of means. For example, one would warn the other side: 'If you agree, you'll get a promotion or a reward; if not, you'll be sent down.' Pretending to care about a woman and express his tender feeling, one would bring her to a movie theater, a park, or a restaurant, so that the latter would be corrupted in the long run. Some of them are addicted to the bourgeois lifestyle so as to wear bizarre cloths, look like a weirdo, dance in the dark, listen to obscene phonograph records, sing erotic songs, say vulgar words, and make coarse jokes";
5) "Having the severe problem of capitalist thinking in business management. They deceive the superior in order to win honors and awards,

report falsely on production, pay no attention to product quality, equate defective products with quality ones, allow the defective products to leave the factory, deceive customers, cause severe losses to the state and huge damages to national defense";

6) "Being detached from the masses. They are arrogant and arbitrary when making a decision, and revenge those who disagree with them, making the masses in silent fury and causing severe tensions in the relationship between the party and the masses";

7) "Indulging in family life and seeking no progress. So goes the saying among some cadres: 'Small wok, small stove, and small happiness; petty husband, petty wife, and petty amusement (*xiaoguo, xiaozao, xiaolequ, xiaofu xiaoqi xiaobaxi*),' and 'beat the bell for one day as long as you are still a monk for a day' and even fail to beat the bell at all when you are still a monk [meaning adopting a passive attitude toward one's duty or overlooking one's duty at all]. A certain cadre used several work hours only to change his seat so that he could sit together with his wife in a movie theater. Some cadres killed their time in office in such a way that they spent hours on a cup of tea, a cigarette, and a newspaper, while lying on a sofa, sitting cross-legged, keeping adding water to a teacup, and chatting endlessly"; and

8) "Wavering in one's ideological commitment when Chiang Kai-shek threatened an invasion from Taiwan into the mainland, so as to request a withdrawal from the party and give up party membership." (NJ4045-3-36)

Obviously, despite the Maoist state's rhetoric of creating a new society, delivering equality for all, and turning all individuals into "the socialist new men" (*shehuizhuyi xinren*), the 1950s and early 1960s witnessed huge problems arising from the stark polarization in wealth distribution and a profound cleavage between the privileged, be they the retained personnel of former private businesses or the cadres with a revolutionary background and those at the bottom of society who remained as marginalized as before. Beneath the surface of an ostensibly stable political order, therefore, was a mounting tension that could easily turn into violent upheaval when the disgruntled were allowed a chance to challenge the status quo while their memories about the revolutionary past remained fresh. The outbreak of the Cultural Revolution in 1966 offered them a perfect opportunity to do so.

TO REBEL OR NOT TO REBEL?

Like all prior political campaigns, the Cultural Revolution in 1966 started because of Mao's planning and initiation. Mao's aim was to remove from the party's leadership the so-called "power-holders taking the capitalist road" represented by Liu Shaoqi, the head of the state and vice chair of the CCP who had been widely known within the party as Mao's designated successor since the late 1940s. The reasons behind Mao's actions were complex and subject to controversy. They had to do, at least in part, with the different approaches of Mao and Liu to reconstructing the economy and correcting the perceived problems on many fronts of state affairs. While Liu was obsessed with the immediate effects of his practical policies in recovering the economy, Mao was more concerned with the ideological implications and long-term consequences of such policies for building socialism in China (Schram 1989, 125–171). A more profound reason, however, was Mao's growing concern with Liu's defiance of, and challenge to, his supremacy within the party. For Mao, Liu's growing popularity in correcting the radicalism of the Great Leap Forward (GLF) and rehabilitating the devastated economy in the early 1960s constituted a threat to Mao's own influence within the party, and he knew well that a tacit consensus existed among the senior cadres of the party that held Mao ultimately responsible for the failure of the GLF. Mao thus was determined to defend his position and perpetuate his policy lines by ousting Liu and his followers from party leadership at all levels. This goal could be achieved only through a mass movement from the bottom up, rather than a top-down campaign through the party-state's bureaucratic organs, which were controlled by the very targets he wanted to attack (see also MacFarquhar and Schoenhals 2006, 3–13; Walder 2015, 180–199).

Who Were the Rebels, and Why Did They Rebel?

As it turned out, however, the mass movement, once started, quickly went rampant with a momentum of its own that was out of Mao's control. Participants in the grassroots movement soon developed into different factions and competed fiercely with one another, often violently. Past studies have offered different interpretations on why worker participation evolved into factional conflicts. While many of them underscored the correlation between participants' interests and networks before 1966 and their choice of action after the outbreak of the Cultural Revolution (Lee 1978; Perry and Li 1997; Meisner 1999; Andreas 2009; Wu 2014), others have paid more attention to manipulations by the top leadership of the party-state and the subsequent unpredictable tactical maneuvers by various factions that had no ideological basis (Walder 2009, 2019), or to a mix of preexisting identities, personalities, and subcultures that shaped the leadership of rebels (Perry and Li 1997).

Our interviews with those who joined various Red Guard organizations suggest that one's personal standing and experiences before the Cultural Revolution directly influenced their initial responses to mass mobilization at the beginning of the Cultural Revolution. Just like in the preceding movements, local cadres, party members, and worker activists were among the first to respond to Mao's call for action against capitalist power-holders by creating their own "Red Guard" organizations under the patronage of the existing local government and party authorities. But the members of these organizations soon came under attack from radical participants who called themselves "rebels" (*zaofanpai*) while labeling the former as "loyalists" (*baohuangpai*)—loyal to the existing leaders of local government and party organizations. When asked about the background of rebel leaders, our informants frequently described them as those who were "eloquent, educated, and popular" (L2), or "good at speech and organizing skills" (L1), or "active and radical in thinking" (N1); and they were all the "young people" who "dared to speak and dared to act" (*ganshuo gangan*) (H14). In other words, the rebel leaders were usually those who distinguished themselves from the rest of the workforce by their propensity to speak out and ability to affect those around them, by their unconventional thinking and noncompliance to those above them, and by their willingness to risk doing so. The rebels, therefore, were different from the officially recognized "activists" (*jiji fenzi*), who were supposed to be loyal to the factory, excellent in production, and subservient to the factory management; being outspoken and competent members of the organization were never part of the criteria in selecting model workers and activists, though it was not impossible that some of them were also eloquent and popular on the shop floor.

A common reason for these individuals to take the lead in rebelling against factory leaders was that they were dissatisfied with their current position or discontent with the way they were treated in the workplace. The rebel leader at the Huaqiao Sugar Plant in Guangzhou, for instance, was a low-rank cadre of the factory's security department who had long wanted a promotion from his incumbent position as the head of the factory's security guards, but he never succeeded and therefore "felt frustrated for years." He saw the Cultural Revolution as an opportunity for him to achieve his personal goal and therefore started a rebellion against factory leaders, counting on his background as "a person of good class status, a veteran, a man of poor-peasant origin, and a party member." As a rebel leader, he was active in the factory and beyond, in the actions of "beating, smashing, and looting" (*dazaqiang*), as his wife's sister's husband recalled it (N10). Another example was Xu Shengnian in Hefeng Yarn Mill in Ningbo, who lost his cadre status because of an "economic problem" and was sent down to this factory to be an ordinary worker. He therefore was "very frustrated" and once attempted to commit suicide by slashing his wrists before the Cultural Revolution. In the factory, again he found himself isolated from his co-workers because he was from the northern part of China and unable to speak the local dialect; he became the object of workers' "ridicules and satires," who kept asking him: "How come you got demoted? What's wrong with you?" Therefore he was among the first to join the rebels and quickly became the leader of a rebel group because of his former experience as a cadre that made him "well informed, able to mobilize, and eloquent;" he eventually became a member of the local prefecture's Revolutionary Committee (N1). Other informants, too, described the rebel leaders in their factories as having been "marginalized" (H15) or "unfairly treated" (S6), or as having been "censured by the leader for poor performance and therefore resentful to the leader" (C1), or simply as "an opportunist who wants to be an official and climb upward" (S8; see also S20). Likewise, Fang Hao (b. 1938), a former cadre of the Xi'an Instrument Factory, described the rebel leaders in his work unit as those who were "resentful of the society and the cadres above them because of the punishments they had received, or dissatisfied with themselves or their own families because of their landlord or capitalist class status" (S10).

In addition to ambitious but frustrated individuals, another source of rebels was those who had been notorious in their work units for being disobedient and troublemaking before the Cultural Revolution. As a retiree from the Shanghai Medical Equipment Factory described, those who led the rebellion in his work unit were "mostly the ones who moped about all day and usually did a bad job in production;" for them, the Cultural Revolution was "a good opportunity to travel outside and free themselves from work duties, while receiving wages as usual and even having the possibility of getting promoted to the leader's position" (N3). So too is the impression of a former machinery repairer from a mine in Zhenjiang about the rebels in his work unit: "The leaders of rebels were all those who were the most careless and slovenly (*zui diaoerlangdang*) during working hours; they were often summoned by the leaders for castigation but they never reformed and instead became very resentful. When the Cultural Revolution arrived, they jumped out and became the most active" (N2). Yang Xiaofeng (b. 1943), a female retiree from Yimin Food Factory in Shanghai, has the same observation of the rebels: "Many of the rebels were those who had been accused of offenses such as blackmailing and looting. In fact, I believe that many of them belonged to the dregs of society" (S8).

The fact that most of the rebel leaders came from the unconventional and noncompliant part of the workforce was not surprising. Since the completion of "socialist transformation of industry and commerce" in 1956 that eliminated private economy in the cities, workers in both state-owned and collectively owned businesses had depended on their work units for income and provision of welfare benefits and public services; they also developed a culture of political conformity under the influence of both the residual Confucian values and the party's ideological indoctrination. They learned from the recurrent political campaigns—in particular, the Anti-Rightist Campaign and the Socialist Education Movement—the risk of openly criticizing the cadres or the party-state per se. Therefore, it was unlikely for the vast majority of ordinary workers or grassroots cadres to initiate a rebellion against the leadership of their work units or the authorities above them. Only the disadvantaged, marginalized, or discontented among the workers, who did not have as much at stake as the rest of the workforce, were likely to take the first step in rising against factory leaders, of whom they had been most resentful. Mao Yuanxin (b. 1941), the nephew of Mao Zedong, thus correctly described the background of most rebels throughout the country at the outset of the Cultural Revolution:

"Everywhere the rebels are those who have been 'misbehaving' (*tiaopi daodan*) in the past; they are the masses that have been led. They live a life that is somewhat careless, which is a shortcoming. However, they also have many merits: they look at problems with a sharp eye, dare to express themselves, and dare to rebel against their own mistakes. They have no standing, no reputation, and have never received serious attention; therefore, they have nothing to lose, nor do they want to gain anything. They dare to think, dare to speak, and dare to rebel. Once armed with Mao Zedong Thought, they will be true (Marxist) materialists." (Xu Jingxian 2013, 309)

It was not surprising, therefore, that those who took the lead in rebelling against factory authorities and beyond belonged to the minority of the working class throughout the cities. Mr. Yi (b. 1943), a former fitter at the Wuhan Light Industrial Machinery Factory from 1972 to 1994, noted that only about one-sixth or one-seventh of the approximately one thousand workers in his factory actively participated in the rebellions in and outside his work unit (W6). Over time, workers were split between those who challenged the authorities, hence known as the "rebels," and those who spoke for and defended the current leadership of their work units, hence known as the "loyalists." While the loyalists formed the majority at the beginning of the Cultural Revolution, the rebels expanded quickly in the following years by absorbing more and more ordinary workers, as their actions received endorsement from Mao and as rebellion against the incumbent leadership of one's work unit or locality became politically correct and even necessary for one to protect themselves and survive the Cultural Revolution. In other words, it was the fear of losing that drove many workers to participate in factional struggles (Walder 2009, 260).

The Loyalists and the Onlookers

A basic fact about the Cultural Revolution is that most factory workers were divided into two factions: the rebels and the loyalists. This division, to be sure, was not all that clear when we look at the Red Guard organizations beyond the factories, especially the groupings of Red Guards at the city or regional level. In Nanjing, for instance, the most influential organizations during the height of the Cultural Revolution were the following two: the

"Provincial Red Headquarters" (Shenghongzong or Hongzong), established on November 1, 1966, which was based on Nanjing University's "Red Rebels' Team" and known for its radicalism; and the mainstream "Nanjing 8-27," established on December 20, 1966 and backed by the party and military authorities of Jiangsu province. Nanjing 8-27 originated from a radical student organization at Nanjing University, once received Premier Zhou Enlai's open support, and based all of its decisions on the instructions of the CCP central committee or the editorials of the party's leading newspapers. Both the Hongzong and the 8-27 appeared to be radical organizations who worked together to defeat the workers' Red Guards mentioned earlier; the latter was known for being conservative in its rebellion against the existing party and government authorities. The divide between the Hongzong and the 8-27, however, soon surfaced because of the different attitudes of their top leaders toward "seizure of power" (*duoquan*). On January 28, 1967, at the instruction of Premier Zhou, who saw the seizure of power as a means to end the chaos of Red Guard agitations nationwide, and in collaboration with the local PLA authorities, the Hongzong together with other radical organizations successfully took power from the existing government offices at all levels in Nanjing. In response, the 8-27 leaders, who had been hesitant about seizing power from the government, denounced Hongzong's unilateral action as "nonsensical" (*haogepi*), henceforth known as the "faction of nonsense" (*pipai*), while Hongzong hailed its success as "really good" (*haodehen*), hence the "faction of goodness" (*haopai*). Obviously, this divide among the rebels had little to do with family backgrounds or economic status, and it was difficult to distinguish between the radicals or conservatives among the members of either the Hongzong or the 8-27 (C2; Dong and Walder 2010, 2011a, 2011b).

Nevertheless, within a factory, the division of workers into the conflicting groups of rebels and loyalists was the norm rather than the exception. The rebels, as noted earlier, were usually the disobedient, resentful, and marginalized workers or the grassroots cadres who had been frustrated in their quest for upward mobility. The loyalists, by contrast, were normally members of the party or the Youth League, labor models, activists, senior workers, or lower- and middle-ranking cadres; all of them had been more or less the beneficiaries of the preexisting institutional arrangements in their work unit and therefore identified with the leaders of their factory. The following three interviewees described the differences between the two groups of workers in their own work units. According to a former driver who was once a leader of rebels at the Ningbo Port Machinery Factory during the Cultural Revolution, "there were always two factions" in his factory; "the loyalists were usually the activists, siding with the leaders. And those who had been criticized and penalized by the leaders would oppose the leaders and become rebels" (N4). At the Wuhan Pharmaceutical Factory, Mr. Yue, a retiree, recalled, "the conservatives were those who supported the party; they wanted to preserve their own interests when the power holders were subject to a struggle. As for the rebels, they were all workers. Ordinary people joined the rebels, unlike the ordinary cadres, supervisors, secretaries, and the like, who supported the factory leader" (W4). At a military bedding and clothing factory in Wuhan, workers again were divided between the faction of "Mighty Army" (*baiwan xiongshi*) and the Revolutionaries. According to a former workshop head, "most of the Mighty Army were conservatives, who wanted to protect the factory. The Revolutionaries, on the other hand, were involved in the activities of beating, smashing, and plundering outside the factory. The conservatives were active in production, and the Revolutionaries were interested only in the struggle against good people" (H7).

Further analysis is needed to ascertain the attitude of most factory workers. As shown earlier, it was very rare for ordinary workers to take the lead rebelling against their supervisors or factory leaders at the beginning of the Cultural Revolution; after all, they could not foresee the rebels' rise to power or the incumbent leaders' removal from office, which did actually happen later to most factories. Before the rebels successfully seized power, most workers chose to do what they used to do in production or, if production was suspended because of the armed struggles between conflicting factions, chose to be onlookers, if they did not have to openly join the loyalists in defending the current factory leaders, which appeared to be politically correct in the early stage of the Cultural Revolution. When they did join the loyalists, they did not take any radical or violent actions as the rebels likely did. Mr. Yang (b. 1942), a worker at the Qingyun Aeronautical Instruments Factory in Beijing from 1960, thus claimed: "I was a loyalist, but what we did was only attending the meetings or things like that; we could not do otherwise. ... We shouted slogans, but we did not specify the names. We differed from the rebels in that when they shouted slogans, they directly said, 'down with so-and-so,' but we had no severe conflict with them" (B1). After the rebels took power and organized the Revolutionary Committee as a new form of government at every level, however, most workers naturally asserted their allegiance to the new authorities in their factory and beyond.

All in all, the majority of ordinary workers were largely apolitical, and most avoided siding openly with either the rebels or the loyalists when the factional struggle was ongoing and no side prevailed over the other. The aforementioned female worker at Hefeng Yarn Mill in Ningbo thus described her and her co-workers' attitude: "We the people at the bottom only cared about our production, no matter how chaotic the situation was among the people above us. We workers never got involved." When asked if she joined the rebels or the conservatives, she replied: "No, no, we workers belonged to the 'onlookers' (*xiaoyaopai*), and we never joined them. Yes, there were activists, who did. But the majority of workers in our factory were apathetic about politics" (N1). So too was the observation of Zeng Yueqing, a female worker at Xiangtan Electric Machinery Factory from 1958: "There were two organizations in my factory, the Red Workers Headquarters and the Revolutionary Rebels' Alliance. They had armed fights against each other. And everyone in the factory was a member of the revolutionary organizations, but the majority of them only went with the tide; they were not active and they never took the lead. Only those who were active in the rebellions later became the leaders" (H19). Similarly, a former technician of the Huaqiao Sugar Plant thus described the workers in his factory: "There were three factions in our factory during the Cultural Revolution: the onlookers, the loyalists, and the rebels. I followed the loyalists in my mind and hoped to maintain the status quo, because we felt that we had done fairly well. Nevertheless, I appeared to be someone unaffiliated.... Being a member of the onlookers, I cared about neither side. No matter what you two sides did, I did not care; after all, I was free from work duties (when production was suspended due to armed factional struggles). I was concerned only with receiving my wages in a timely manner" (N10).[2]

POWER HOLDERS AND THE FIVE CATEGORIES UNDER ATTACK
Revenge on "Power Holders"
As suggested earlier, worker rebels at the beginning of the Cultural Revolution invariably targeted the so-called "capitalist power holders" or "capitalist

roaders" (*zouzipai*) in their factories. As Yang Xiaofeng of the Shanghai Yimin Food Factory put it: "At that time, if you were a party secretary, a factory head, or something like that, you were a capitalist roader, no matter whether or not that was true. As long as you were a cadre, you were a capitalist roader, and you had to step down. You'd be subject to criticism and struggle as long as you were a cadre; this was especially true in factories and schools" (S8). Luo Guiling (b. 1936) of Shanghai Compressor Factory, too, observed that, in his work unit, "cadres from the factory level to the intermediary level in the workshops and administrative offices suffered criticism, persecution, and even beating. Their positions were invariably yielded to the rebels" (S11). So too was the situation of Fang Hao (b. 1938), who was a cadre of the party committee at Xi'an Instruments Factory from 1959 to 1998. "During the Cultural Revolution," he said, "the cadres in my factory suffered the most, including almost all cadres at the middle level and above. Some of them were struggled almost to death, and I was one of them. All of the cadres stepped aside and went down to bottom-level units for labor under surveillance" (S10).

The struggle against power holders usually came with physical abuse and humiliation. At the Specialty Company in Wuhan, for instance, struggle meetings against the cadres of different levels were repeated in the second half of 1967. At the meetings, recalled Yan Shanfa (b. 1948), who worked there from 1965, "the cadres, while being struggled, had to hang an iron-made plague on the neck and bend over, with the two arms held backward, in a style known as 'riding the airplane.' If someone did not bend over enough to form a ninety-degree angle, or if he stumbled, [the Red Guards] would hit him with a rifle butt or kick him. Standing in the heat of the sun in July or August, the cadres' sweat trickled all the way down to their feet, making the floor wet. Some of them were put on a parade on the street while wearing a high hat or locked in a room for a beating" (H9; see B1 for a similar account of struggle meetings at the Qingyun Aeronautical Instruments Factory in Beijing). Unable to bear the humiliation and torture, some cadres committed suicide or attempted it, such as the factory head of the Yimin Food Factory in Shanghai, who jumped from the office building to the ground, breaking his foot and thus needing a wheelchair for the rest of his life (S8).

To take revenge on the cadres who had punished or upset them was a common reason why the rebels treated the power holders with brutality. At the Carrier Equipment Factory in Nanjing, the worker Red Guards forced the factory head to crawl backward on the stairs in the office building while wearing an iron circle on his neck, because, according to Mr. Yang, "these workers had long been resentful of the leader and now they took advantage of this opportunity" (C1). One of the victims of the rebels' revenge was Mr. Huang, who was appointed in 1969 as the section chief in charge of material supplies and sales at the Huaqiao Sugar Plant in Guangzhou. During the movement of "cleansing the class ranks" in the Cultural Revolution, however, he was accused of being a hidden spy engaging in espionage for foreign agencies because of his background as a family member of a former Nationalist official with overseas connections. He was locked in a room in the factory for investigation for eighty-seven days, and he was targeted for public denouncement at a mass meeting, where he kneeled on the stage with his arms tied behind his back. During the meeting, one of the workers from his workshop came forward to him, taking off his leather shoe and beating Huang's head while yelling: "You deserve it today!" Huang quickly lost consciousness. After he woke up, the workers kept denouncing him, complaining that Huang had failed to provide them with a meal during their night shift or had canceled their bonus because they were late to their shift, all of which Huang admitted. But the real reason behind the beating was because Huang rejected one worker's request to help him relocate his wife to Guangzhou, on the ground that the city was chaotic at that time and his factory was already burdened with more than one thousand workers. The workers thus hated Huang, and the struggle meeting offered them an opportunity to vent their anger (N10).

Mr. Chen, a former lathe worker at the Ningbo Port Machinery Factory, told a story about himself as a rebel leader. Chen entered the factory in 1964 and retired in 1992. In 1967, he joined the factory's Revolutionary Committee as a rebel leader but continued to participate in production every day. Later he was held responsible for an accident, in which he forgot to turn off the lathe he operated, causing the machine to break on a night when he was working alone in the factory. Chen immediately went to the home of the party secretary of the factory and reported the accident, and the secretary said nothing at that moment. A few days later, however, Chen received a notice from the city's industrial bureau, blaming him for "being lax about discipline in production and damaging the lathe on purpose." It was obvious to him that if he admitted the accusation, he would lose his membership in the Revolutionary Committee. So he refused to sign the notice, insisting that it was his negligence, not deliberate action, that caused the accident. The next day, he broke into a meeting of the bureau's party committee and distributed his appeal, which surprised everyone. Afterward, Chen "became pugnacious every day toward the secretary and even shouted abuse at him." His hostility culminated in gathering more than ten of his followers to beat up the secretary (N5).

Violence by Outsiders

It is worth noting that while confrontation between rebels and loyalists was common in almost every factory, the direct use of violence against each other was the exception rather than the norm. After all, both the rebels and loyalists were employees of the same work unit, the same workshop, or even the same production group; they worked side by side every day and knew each other well. It was not uncommon that even members of the same family and indeed many wives and husbands belonged to different factions. Therefore, when the factional confrontation within a work unit did develop to such a level as to necessitate a fight, which was usually initiated by the rebels, the rebels rarely took violent actions directly against the loyalists within their factory; instead, they often asked rebels from outside to attack their enemies at home; deaths likely occurred in these armed conflicts simply because the outsiders were less lenient and discreet than their peers within the factory when attacking the loyalists or because they failed to identify the right targets, whom they did not know at all. To quote again Mr. Huang of the Huaqiao Sugar Plant in Guangzhou:

> "The armed fight started in 1967 and, as a result, the Sugar Plant suspended production for a year or two. One person died of armed fight in the Cultural Revolution, who was the vice factory head of our sugar plant. Frustrated with having always been a vice head and never had a chance of promotion to the full factory head position, he joined the rebels. One day when we had a factory-wide meeting, the rebels wanted to teach the loyalists a lesson but they couldn't do so by themselves. So they asked the Red Guards from a school outside the factory to come in and surround the site of our meeting. The rebels originally had wanted the Red Guards to beat one of the loyalists who was tall, thin, and wearing a pair of eyeglasses; unfortunately the vice factory head had the same features. Therefore, right after the meeting ended, a Red Guard came forward and hit the head of the vice factory head with a rod. The vice head, a wrong

target, thus died. Upon seeing the death, all of the rebels ran away, hiding themselves together with their family members in the Military School of Physical Education for about a month. They did not come back until a negotiation was done and the loyalists agreed that no revenge would be taken on the rebels since both sides belonged to the working class, something that was also emphasized by the authority at higher levels." (N10)

Almost the same story occurred to Zhang Genbao, a rebel from the Zhenjiang Mine under the Shanghai municipal bureau of metallurgical industry. In an armed fight with the loyalists one night, he was mistakenly beaten to death by the rebels from outside who did not know him. The mine's rebels, however, blamed the loyalists of the same work unit for Zhang's death and paraded his corpse on the street in protest (N2).

Searching one's home and confiscating property was another common action taken by the rebels. But again, some worker rebels would avoid doing so directly by themselves if the target was from the same unit. Mrs. Yang, once a Red Guard from a school in Shanghai before she began working at the Yimin Food Factory in 1968, thus described her experiences as a school student and Red Guard: "We were utilized by others at that time. For instance, when the Cultural Revolution took place in a factory, the workers would feel embarrassed to search the home of someone of their own factory. Therefore, they always came to our school and asked us, the Red Guards, for help, believing that we the Red Guards could do the job well. But it was so violent that you could not bear with it."

"So did you witness it?" asked our interviewer.

"Witness it? No! I participated in it. I was just curious and therefore went there. After arriving there, however, we forced all members of the family, young and old, into a bathroom. We then searched every room and made it a big mess. We climbed to the roof and knocked everywhere, and we dug the floors, just trying to find something. I didn't know if anything was found. But I can tell you the whole process was horrifying, if you experience it in person" (S8).

Targeting the "Five Categories"

Aside from factory cadres, another group subject to the violence of worker rebels was the so-called "Elements of Five Categories" (*wulei fenzi*), including former landlords, rich peasants, counterrevolutionaries, bad elements, and rightists (see Chapter 1). In the cities where rich peasants were rare, former businessowners or capitalists (*zibenjia*) were substituted in as one of the Five Categories. People of the Five Categories surfaced as the targets of Red Guard attacks especially after factory leaders (party committee secretaries and factory heads, and sometimes also workshop directors and party branch secretaries) stepped down, or where the factory leaders survived the Cultural Revolution and even joined the rebels but a target was nevertheless needed for the rebels' collective actions. If the factory had been a private business before 1956, the former owner was a likely target. The Nine Dragon Hotel in Nanjing, for instance, was a business under "joint state-private ownership" (*gongsi heying*) after 1956. During the Cultural Revolution, the former owners of the property became the targets of Red Guards' attacks, who "poured black ink on their faces, searched and looted their homes, paraded them on the street by force, put a tall paper hat on their heads and a board on their necks with the sign of 'monsters and demons' (*niugui sheshen*), and forced them to 'squeeze the toothpaste' or admit their additional wrongdoings bit by bit." Nevertheless, as Mrs. Yang (b. 1938), a retiree from this company, clarified, "those who beat them were the people from outside, and, whenever this happened, we workers shouted our slogan: Engage in the struggle with words, but not physical attack! After a struggle meeting, we provided the capitalists with some food—it was primarily to reform their thoughts after all" (L8). Likewise, Mrs. Yang Ren, a former small-business owner and an accountant at Nanjing Vegetable Company, became the target of "students from the outside," who took her onto the street for a parade by "taking off her shoes and pouring black ink on her body, from her head all the way down to her feet" (C5). At the Xingyuan Silk Mill in Nanjing, after ousting the factory head and party secretary, the rebels, who were mainly female workers, directed their attack at the mill's former owner and searched his home; among the objects they confiscated were gold and a painting by Tang Bohu, a famous artist of the Ming dynasty. Later when the Cultural Revolution was over, the former capitalist was compensated 56 yuan for each *liang* of gold that had been confiscated (L2). Similarly, at Renfeng Fabric Mill in Ningbo, a factory under joint state-private ownership, worker rebels (again mainly women) targeted the few former small-business owners "who had been harsh to workers before the transition to joined ownership" at the repeated struggle meetings, but "never beat them" (N6).

Individuals from the families of former landlords could also easily become targets of suspicion and persecution during the Cultural Revolution. A case in point here is Mr. Sun (b. 1942), who became a worker at the Heshun County Chemical Fertilizer Factory in 1958. By the time the Cultural Revolution started, he had been promoted to the position of workshop director supervising dozens of workers, but he soon lost his position because of his family background. The person who made this happen was Zhang Fulai, a new worker in Sun's workshop who had been recently demobilized from the army. When he was asked to get some work attendance sheets from Sun's home, Zhang happened to find a book of Sun's family genealogy, and he looked at it for a long time, as Sun's mother later told her son. The book showed the history of Sun's ancestors as local landlords. The next day, Zhang put up a big-character poster, condemning Sun as "a descendant of landlords" and calling for "serious caution against class enemy." As a result, Sun lost not only his position as a workshop director but also his fiancée, who had been ready to marry him (B13). Another example is a worker named Gu at the Ningbo Port Machinery Factory. Before he joined the factory in 1960, Gu, as a landlord's son, had lost his job as a navigator of a ship owned by the Ningbo Port, because of the suspicion among port leaders that he would likely steer the ship to Taiwan in response to Chiang Kai-shek's call for "retaking the mainland." When the Cultural Revolution broke out, he naturally became a target of workers' attack because of his "historical and family problems." Gu protested and argued with port leaders, insisting that he had already confessed and clarified everything about his family and himself during the "Four Clean-ups" movement. Nevertheless, he was determined a "counterrevolutionary" and imprisoned for seven years (N5).

The counterrevolutionaries (*fangeming*), as one of the Five Categories, included "historical" (*lishi*) and "active" (*xianxing*) subtypes. Historical counterrevolutionaries were those who had served the Guomindang regime before 1949, such as the former head of the Xiaguan railway station in Nanjing who was once a member of the Nationalist Party. As a "historical counterrevolutionary," he had to stand on a table at a struggle meeting against him in the winter during the Cultural Revolution (C4). "Active counterrevolutionaries," on the other hand, were those who did something wrong politically, right before they were prosecuted, such as Mr. Meng (b. 1936), who worked for Beijing Gear Factory from 1961 to 1971. One day in December 1968, when he was back home from his shift and chatting with his co-workers, he commented on Mao's latest call for urban youth to go "up to the mountains and down to the countryside" (*shangshan xiaxiang*), saying: "Chairman Mao's words are just like a fart—it makes the entire country stinky." To his surprise, his co-workers soon reported this to factory leaders. Subsequently, at a struggle meeting attended by more than seven thousand people, he was condemned as an active counterrevolutionary (B3).

In fact, before he became a counterrevolutionary, Meng had been accused as a rightist during the Great Leap Forward, when he, as an active serviceman in the army, honestly talked about what he had just witnessed during a visit to his home village at the meetings of his platoon, company, and battalion, respectively, for two hours each time. On that visit, he found that his mother, in order to survive the famine, had remarried in another village, and many in his village, still in their forties or younger, had died of hunger; all the villagers ate were soups made of potato leaves. His witness statements were later reported to higher levels of the military, and he was determined a rightist. Because of this, he was criticized and denounced "almost every day" for nearly a year at various meetings in his factory until his son was born in June 1967; in fact, he was one of the thirty-odd "bad elements" (*huaifenzi*) in his factory who received the same kind of treatment during the Cultural Revolution (B3). The bad elements, for their part, were those who did not necessarily do anything for the Guomindang regime or against the Communist state; instead, they were "bad" because they did something that was considered morally wrong, such as adultery, as in the case of a female worker at the Xiaguan Railway Station in Nanjing, who was punished by cutting her hair in the style of "half-shaved head" (*yin yang tou*) (C4), or because they committed crimes such as petty theft (*xiaotou xiaomo*) and thus frequently served as the targets of struggle meetings, as what happened at the Zhongshan Mine in Nanjing (L7).

WORKERS EMPOWERED
Seizure of Power

The hallmark of the Cultural Revolution, and the focal point of conflicts between rebels and loyalists, was the seizure of power by Red Guard organizations from the existing party-state authorities, following months of mobilization and armed struggles between different factions. Beginning with the "January Revolution" in Shanghai in 1967 (Perry and Li 1997, 18), the seizure of power swept across the entire country throughout the following year, resulting in the establishment of a new form of government called the Revolutionary Committee (*geming weiyuanhui*) at every level, from individual factories in the cities and people's communes in the countryside all the way up to the provincial level by the summer of 1968. The most important—and also highly symbolic—action in the seizure of power was to take away the seals of the government and party committee being attacked and the dossier files of their personnel (L6). Mrs. Huang (b. 1928), then a rebel at the Nanjing Petrochemical Refinery, thus described the event in her factory: "Everything went haywire at that time. To seize power, the rebels wanted the party committee's seal, and they took it by force and also checked the dossiers. We were the pawns and feared nothing! We didn't even care about death at that time, so I really had no fear at all! After all, we were not the officials" (C6).

The dossier files were particularly important for the worker rebels because they contained the details about the history of every factory leader and party member as well as personal information on ordinary workers. These details, never disclosed to any individuals involved, had been the most mysterious and fatal weapon for factory authorities to deal with problematic workers before the Cultural Revolution. Lacking access to these dossiers, ordinary workers had always been vulnerable to the cadres. As a retiree of the Ningbo Port Machinery Factory put it: "When the masses engaged in a struggle against the leaders, they could only put together some materials that were actually useless. However, if the leaders wanted to punish someone, they could be really formidable. How did they know that the person [the aforementioned Gu] was the son of a landlord and a counterrevolutionary? All these were found by the leaders from his dossier. So if a leader wanted to punish someone, that could be easily done. But how could ordinary people get to know these materials?" (N5). Not surprisingly, the dossier files of all personnel of a factory also became the most important objects that the worker rebels wanted to control during the seizure of power. Mrs. Huang thus mentioned that the rebels at her factory "kept hand-copying the dossiers, and examined them day and night, hoping to find something they needed" (C6).

The Revolutionary Committee as a "Tripartite Combination"

The Revolutionary Committee, established everywhere after the seizure of power, was organized by the "three-in-one" (*sanjiehe*) principle, consisting of the following three components in a given factory: (1) "revolutionary cadres," or some of the preexisting factory and party leaders, who had been supportive of the rebels during the Cultural Revolution and remained responsible for the factory's routine production activities; (2) "representatives of revolutionary mass organizations," or the leaders of worker rebels, who continued to work every day but attended committee meetings, thus playing a key role in the factory's decision making; and (3) the representatives of the military, usually the commanders of the troops who had been dispatched to a factory or a locality to end the armed fights between different factions under the name of "supporting the leftists" (*zhi zuo*) and who continued to serve as a stabilizing factor afterward (Perry and Li 1997, 151; MacFarquhar and Schoenhals 2006, 202, 241).

Our informant's account of the formation of the revolutionary committee at the Ningbo Port Machinery Factory illustrates the process of seizure of power and the subsequent roles of rebel leaders and preexisting cadres in the new government:

> "We rebels started the seizure of power only after the January Storm in Shanghai. Before that, we never thought of seizure of power, and the leaders continued to manage production as usual; we brought them to a struggle meeting for a round of criticism only when we organized such a meeting. It was after the seizure of power in Shanghai that the two organizations of rebels in our factory worked together to have the seizure of power done. If the leaders had appeared to be fine for us, they would be incorporated [into the committee]; if they had behaved badly, we would deprive them of power, forcing them to give up. There was no armed fight between the two rebel organizations in our factory, nor did our factory head step down because of a struggle—he was incorporated. The reason was because we couldn't find a reason to take him down; the Twelve Articles made it clear: The seizure of power could only be done toward capitalist power holders; if a leader only made some mistakes in his work, then no power could be taken away from him; he had to be incorporated [into the committee]." (N4)

Comments by other informants on the respective role of each of the three components in the committee are also worth mentioning here. At Hefeng Yarn Mill in Ningbo, for instance, the committee consisted of "the people from the troops, the original factory head, and a representative of the masses, named Xu Shengnian, who also participated in the factory's revolutionary committee." Of the three elements, Xu was the most influential, for he "had the ability to lead a group of people" (N1). At the military bedding and clothing factory in Wuhan, however, the leader of worker rebels, named Wu Fuxi, "could only be the vice director [of the factory's revolutionary committee]," and the director position was usually filled by the representative of the army; therefore, "the real power lay in the hands of the military" (H7). The least powerful of the three components of a revolutionary committee seemed to be the preexisting factory leaders who had survived the Cultural Revolution. At the Shanghai Medical Equipment Factory, for instance, "the rebel leaders overthrew the original leaders but later put them back to power, because Chairman Mao said, of the cadres, more than 90 percent were good. So the rebels had to call back and hold up the old leaders, but they would not allow the old leaders to have real power—the latter could only be puppets and do what they were instructed to do" (N3). It was likely that in many factories, of the three components of a revolutionary committee, the most powerful would be the rebel leader, since the preexisting factory leaders had lost their original prestige and influence after several rounds of struggle meetings against them, and because the military representative was neither as familiar with the workers as the rebel leaders nor as knowledgeable about production as the preexisting factory leaders.

However, rebel leaders, as key members of a factory revolutionary committee, had their own weaknesses. While they were extremely popular and influential among the radical workers during the phases of mass mobilization and seizure of power, their influence inevitably dwindled after the establishment of the Revolutionary Committee, when the chaos of factional struggles subsided and production resurfaced as the most important task in the factory. Arising from the rank and file, the rebel leaders had little knowledge about production management, and they had no idea how to run the factory. In some factories, production was paralyzed because of their mismanagement (H19). Therefore, they had to yield to the original factory leaders in managing the factory's routine production. Without substantial administrative duties, they had to participate in everyday production as ordinary workers. At the Zhenjiang Mine, for instance, the rebels, who became the leaders of the mine through seizure of power, "all walked away ignominiously [from the positions they had held] during the later phase [of the Cultural Revolution]. When they were in power, production verged on a paralysis.... These people only cared about rebellion and knew nothing about production" (N2). Mr. Li (b. 1944), a worker at the No. 768 Factory in Beijing for thirty-four years since 1965, described the rebels in a similar way: "The rebels were good at rebellion but incompetent at managing an enterprise. Later they all lost their influences, couldn't keep their current positions, and walked away" (B9).

Not surprisingly, by the time the Cultural Revolution was over and the Gang of Four, who represented a new generation of leadership that came to power during the Cultural Revolution at the top level, was arrested, the rebel leaders who had joined and led the revolutionary committees in factories all stepped down, yielding their positions to those who had led the factories before the Cultural Revolution or led the loyalists at the beginning of the Cultural Revolution.[3]

ECONOMISM SUPPRESSED AND FULFILLED

So far our examination of the Cultural Revolution in the factories has focused on the activities of formal workers from state firms, be they rebels, loyalists, or onlookers. To have a complete picture of worker participation in the movement, however, we need to further look at how the informal workers were involved. Despite their second-class status in the factories, the activists among contract and temporary workers played an important role in shaping the Cultural Revolution in its early stages. This is best seen in the "wind of economism," a conspicuous phenomenon at the beginning of the Cultural Revolution that had a prolonged impact on the composition and well-being of factory workers.

Unlike the rebel organizations of students and formal workers, whose rallying cries were largely political and focused on their demands for official recognition of their organizations as legitimate and revolutionary at the beginning, and later for sharing of power in the newly established revolutionary committee, the requests from informal workers were characteristically economic and social: They demanded the conversion of their status from contract or temporary workers into regular workers and an increase in their wages. The informal workers in Shanghai were among the first to establish a rebel organization of their own, named "Shanghai General Headquarters for Red Workers' Revolutionary Rebellion" (*Shanghai shi hongse gongren geming zaofan zongsilingbu*). Their demands included: ensuring their job security and protecting them from being laid off; abolishing the systems of contract and temporary workers; increasing their wage levels and welfare benefits; and allowing them to join the trade union and other mass organizations. Workers of collectively owned firms, for their part, requested conversion of their work units into state-owned firms so as to improve their status and income; intern workers and other low-wage workers in many factories also demanded a wage hike, better fringe benefits, and more free goods. To assuage worker disgruntlement after the outbreak of the Cultural Revolution, some firms did concede to these requests, hence the rampancy of the "wind of economism" in Shanghai (Perry and Li 1997, 97–117; Li Xun 1998).

The most influential organization of informal workers, however, was the "National General Corps of Rebellion for Red Laborers" (*Quanguo hongse laodongzhe zaofan zongtuan*, or *Quanhongzong*), established in Beijing in November 1966, which quickly grew to have its chapters in most provinces. In Beijing alone it rallied more than fifty thousand supporters to besiege and occupy the buildings of the Ministry of Labor and the General Trade Union on December 25 and 27, 1966, respectively. Their demands included: ensuring their right to participate in the Cultural Revolution; preventing layoffs of informal workers; and allowing those who had been laid off after June 1966 to return to their work units and repaying the wages they had lost. Unfortunately, while these requests were endorsed by Jiang Qing, Mao's wife and a key member of the party central's Cultural Revolution Group, the party's Political Bureau did not approve them; instead, it ordered that the *Quanhongzong* be dismantled together with all other national-level rebel organizations (Li Bote 2003). Obviously, the informal workers' demands went well beyond the government's fiscal affordability and political tolerance, for not only did the conversion of informal workers into regular workers in large number constitute a huge financial burden on the government, but the fast expansion of nationwide rebel organizations also threatened and squeezed the authority of the Communist state per se. Not surprisingly, the state's propaganda machines unanimously denounced the wind of economism, condemning any concessions made by local governments to workers' requests as counterrevolutionary steps taken by capitalist power holders to divert the Cultural Revolution from the right direction.

It should be noted, however, that the Maoist state, while resolute in curbing economism at the beginning of the movement, did not completely reject workers' economic requests. In its "notice against economism" on January 11, 1967, the party's central committee stated that "the central committee will conduct an investigative study during the Proletarian Cultural Revolution about economic issues that involved unreasonable elements and will set forth solutions by adopting the reasonable opinions of the masses" (Zhonggong zhongyang 1967). In another notice about "further attack on counterrevolutionary economism" announced on January 18, 1968, the central committee again promised that it would carry out reforms on the use of informal workers on the basis of an investigation as well as reforms regarding wages, fringe benefits, bonuses, stipends, and labor protection goods "in the latter phase of the movement" (Zhonggong zhongyang 1968). Subsequently, three years later, in November 1971, when the chaos of mass mobilization and factional struggles subsided, upon Mao's approval the party central committee announced that more than 6 million long-term contract workers would be converted into formal workers and that a wage hike would be allowed for more than 13.4 million formal workers (Wenxian yanjiushi 2013, 6: 388). As a result, most long-term contract workers became formal workers. In Shanghai alone, more than 100,000 informal workers were turned into formal workers in 1971; by 1975, informal workers accounted for only 1.5 percent of the entire labor force in state-owned factories in this city (Lin Chaochao 2014). Many of workers' economic requests materialized in large industrial cities by the end of the Cultural Revolution.

THE FRAGILITY OF THE REBUILT EQUILIBRIUM

The Cultural Revolution had a severe impact on the fundamental institutions that had sustained the work unit equilibrium in state-owned factories before 1966. Under the wind of economism, low-wage workers demanded an increase in their pay and improvements in their working and living conditions, and informal workers requested their conversion into formal employees. All these requests challenged the social hierarchy and economic inequality that were central to the equilibrium. The Cultural Revolution also caused the paralysis of the traditional means of worker participation in factory governance; both the staff and workers' congress and the trade unions ceased to function after 1966 because of the mass mobilization and factional struggle that involved almost all workers. In most factories, worker elites and technocrats, who mostly joined the faction of the loyalists or conservatives, lost their dominance in the work unit and yielded to the supremacy of rebel factions consisting primarily of the ordinary and the marginalized of the labor force. The use of piece rates and payment of bonuses were denounced as "material stimuli" and completely banned in the most radical years of the late 1960s and early 1970s. As a result of these developments, the equilibrium that had characterized the socioeconomic hierarchy and power relations in state firms was greatly undermined and even disappeared during the height of the Cultural Revolution.

When the fervor of radicalism was over in the 1970s, however, the state's efforts to restore order and boost production also resulted, more or less, in the reestablishment of the equilibrium in industrial enterprises. Most factory cadres and technical elites resumed their original positions after the establishment of the Revolutionary Committee as the new governing body of the work unit. The massive conversion of contemporary and contract workers into the formal labor force worked to enhance the traditional system of permanent employment. The momentum of restoring pre–Cultural Revolution practices in factory governance accelerated after 1973, when Deng Xiaoping was reappointed by Mao to lead the efforts of economic reconstruction and political stabilization. As a result, many institutions that had been widely used in the 1950s and early 1960s but abolished after 1966 were somehow reintroduced, such as the piece-rate wage system, regulations to enforce working discipline, the staff and workers' congress, the trade union, and other mass organizations. Once again, an equilibrium resurfaced to regulate socioeconomic activities and power relations in every work unit. The reassurance of permanent employment and the all-encompassing fringe benefits made the enlarged formal working force completely dependent on their work unit for meeting their subsistence needs, making the work unit a tight-knit community in which the workers strongly identified with the workplace. This group identity within the work unit and the wide use of non-material incentives, coupled with the complete absence of income-making opportunities outside the work unit and the nonexistence or very limited use of material incentives, gave rise to a work norm that effectively prevented individual workers from overt shirking but failed to stimulate them to work hard. Likewise, in their everyday interactions with factory cadres, ordinary workers saw no reason to develop personal dependence to the latter, given the security of their job, the fixed level of their wages (determined by one's work age in line with the state's universal policies), and the availability of various channels for them to express their complaints and seek improvements of their living and working conditions. But their influence stopped there, and no avenues were made accessible for them to effectively participate in their factory's decision-making process, despite their presumed status as the masters of the workplace. In a nutshell, despite its unprecedented impact on factory institutions at its beginning, the Cultural Revolution did little to transform the socioeconomic and political orders as it had promised.

But the equilibrium that was reestablished in the last years of the Cultural Revolution was more vulnerable than it had been before because of the Maoist state's two contradictory objectives in factory governance: its pragmatic need to end political chaos and stabilize production on the one hand, and its commitment to the Maoist ideology that had fueled the Cultural Revolution on the other. Thus, while the state had to reappoint the experienced cadres and technical elites who had been ousted from factory leadership at the beginning of the Cultural Revolution back to their original positions after 1969, it nevertheless emphasized preserving the "new things" (*xinsheng shiwu*) that had emerged during the Cultural Revolution—most importantly, the key administrative positions at every level occupied by rebel leaders, hence the continued factional struggles between the old and new elites that went on throughout the 1970s and plagued political stability in many localities (Dong and Walder 2021). In labor management, while the state promoted the use of a piece-rate wage system wherever it was applicable, it constantly cautioned against the excessive use of "material stimuli" (*wuzhi ciji*) and the widening gap in income distribution among the labor force. Likewise, while the state made unprecedented efforts to convert a large number of informal workers into the formal and permanent labor force in 1971, thus ending the massive employment of contract workers in state-owned factories in large industrial cities, the last years of the Maoist era nevertheless witnessed a new wave of hiring informal workers in enterprises of "local state-ownership" (*difang guoying*) at the county or township level. This was a result of rural industrialization in the 1970s, particularly the mushrooming of small-scale mines, fertilizer plants, and agricultural machinery manufacturing and repair factories. The total number of informal workers thus skyrocketed from 3.45 million in 1972 (the lowest level during the decade of the Cultural Revolution) to 11.7 million in 1979 (Guojia tongjiju 1987, 26, 33). Striking inequality between formal and informal workers in social status and material well-being once against prevailed in the final years of the Cultural Revolution.

Behind the changing and conflicting policies in factory governance and labor management in the last years of the Maoist era were Mao's own ambiguous and shifting attitudes toward the radicalism of the Cultural Revolution. Mao was eager to rebuild his popularity as the leader of the party-state after the death of Lin Biao, his hand-picked successor, who had died in an airplane crash on September 13, 1971, after Lin Biao's supporters failed to assassinate Mao. As a result, Mao allowed Premier Zhou Enlai to take the lead in correcting the "ultra-leftist line" in economic policies in order to placate the people who had been shocked by the Lin Biao incident and were growing discontent with the radical policies of the Cultural Revolution. Later in 1973, Mao further reappointed Deng Xiaoping, who had been ousted in 1966, to key positions in the central government to assume much of Zhou's duties in leading the country's economic rehabilitation when the latter was hospitalized. It was under the stewardship of Zhou and more importantly Deng that much of the radical policies of the Cultural Revolution were halted or reversed, as seen in the "liberation" and rehabilitation of a large number of political and intellectual elites who had stepped down in the previous years, the use of piece-rate wages to incentivize workers, the reinforcement of workplace discipline to regulate worker performance in production, and the removal of notorious rebel leaders from local leadership to curb the rampancy of factionalism that had plagued the government system at every level. Unfortunately, Deng's vigorous measures of "all-around rectification" (*quanmian zhengdun*) caused Mao's concern with the possible prospect of a complete negation of the Cultural Revolution, which mattered so much to Mao's political heritage; hence Mao launched a campaign against Deng to "fight back the wind of rightist deviationism" in November 1975 (Pang and Jin 2011, 6:2687–2729). The death of Mao in 1976 and the subsequent arrest of the Gang of Four paved the way for Deng's eventual rise to the paramount leadership of the party-state in December 1978. Exactly how Deng's inception of economic reforms in the 1980s led to drastic changes in factory institutions and the loss of the equilibrium in factory politics is the subject of the Chapter 6.

6 | THE MASTER OF ONE'S OWN LABOR ONLY

Workers in the Reform Era

STATE-OWNED ENTERPRISES in China underwent a series of institutional reforms from the late 1970s through the 2000s. Before the reform era, China had a planned economy under the state's centralized control; state firms dominated the nation's industry while private businesses were nearly nonexistent. Three decades later, when the most critical phase of economic reforms was over, the number of state-controlled enterprises decreased from 83,700 in 1978 to 20,680 in 2007; their contribution to the nation's total industrial output also declined from 77.63 percent to 29.54 percent during the same period. On the other hand, private firms increased to more than 303,100 by 2007, and their contribution to China's industrial output accounted for more than 70 percent (Guojia tongjiju 2008, 16). The various non-state sectors hired 229 million workers, or 78 percent of the entire employment in urban China.[1] China, in a word, transitioned from a socialist economy based on state and collective ownership to a market economy based largely on private ownership.

Given the prevalence of a dual equilibrium in labor relations and shop floor politics in state-owned enterprises during most of the Maoist era, and given the importance of this equilibrium in sustaining the necessary level of efficiency in state-firm production to ensure the steady growth of China's industrial output throughout most of the pre-reform years, why then did the post-Mao state implement enterprise reforms one after another that resulted in the undoing of the Maoist factory system and the eventual loss of the equilibrium? More importantly, how did the reforms affect workers' social standing and economic well-being? And how did workers redefine their roles in the workplace, rebuild their relations with enterprise management, and reshape their strategies in everyday production as the reforms unfolded over the decades? Finally, did enterprise reforms result in the emergence of a new equilibrium in the workplace? These are among the questions to be explored in the rest of this study.

"MONEY COMES FIRST": WORKER RESPONSE TO INITIAL ENTERPRISE REFORMS, 1978-1985
Initiation of Enterprise Reforms

As mentioned in the Introduction, in order to justify the reforms of state-owned enterprises, the post-Mao state's propaganda in the late 1970s and 1980s assumed the prevalence of shirking and inefficiency in industrial production during the Maoist years and further attributed these presumed problems to the policies of egalitarianism (*daguofan*, literally, "eating from one big pot") in labor remuneration and permanent employment (*tiefanwan* or "the iron rice bowl") in labor relations. Without denying the existence of these problems in the most radical years under Mao, the preceding chapters have revealed the realities of worker performance in production that run counter to the post-Mao state's distorted representation. In fact, the real reasons for the reforms of industrial enterprises had little to do with worker performance. Instead, most of the reform measures were introduced one after another from the late 1970s through the 1990s as a result of the post-Mao leadership's responses to a set of complex and emergent challenges. By and large, these challenges fell into the following two categories.

One was external to the enterprises, namely the fiscal challenges that confronted the central government. In most of the Mao era, the state pursued the policy of fiscal self-sufficiency and, as a result, maintained an overall balance between its revenue and expenditures. In 1977, for example, the state's revenue were 87 billion yuan and its expenditures were 84 billion yuan, thus resulting in a surplus of 3 billion yuan. For decades, the Maoist state, therefore, was proud of its being free of both foreign and domestic debts (*ji wu neizhai*, *you wu waizhai*). But the post-Mao leadership's decision to embark on the construction of large-scale modern industrial and infrastructural projects (mostly based on imported equipment and technologies), to increase the procurement prices of agricultural produces, and to allow the twenty million "sent-down youth" to return to their home cities drained much of the state's fiscal resources. Its expenditure increased to 112 billion yuan in 1978 and 128 billion yuan in 1979, hence a huge fiscal deficit, which reached 13.5 billion yuan in 1979, or nearly 12 percent of its revenue (Guojia tongjiju 2005, 104). With the debt-free principle continuing to guide its fiscal policy at the beginning of the post-Mao era, the state did not consider the use of financial levers, such as issuing government bonds, borrowing from foreign banks, or inflation, to be an option in dealing with the deficit. The only way to offset the deficit, therefore, was to increase its revenue from the existing sources. Of these, the most important were profits generated by state-owned enterprises, which had to be completely remitted to the central government; these accounted for about half of the state's annual revenue. In 1978, for instance, revenue from industrial enterprises amounted to 57 billion yuan, or 50.5 percent of the state's total revenue (113 billion yuan) (Guojia tongjiju 2003, 282). Obviously, the most important measure for the state to meet its growing expenditures was to find a way for such enterprises to increase their profits. This brings us to the next factor leading to the reforms of industrial enterprises: the lack of incentives for local enterprises to seek the maximization of profits.

For decades since the 1950s, all state-owned enterprises in China operated as merely "factories" under the individual ministries of the central government or its local agencies, and they were completely subject to their respective ministry's planning and orders in each and every aspect of enterprise management, ranging from the hiring of workers and appointment of factory leaders to the procurement or provision of raw materials and the sales or allocations of finished products. More specifically, the state imposed on individual factories various "mandatory requirements" that they had to meet each year, including a factory's total output, the quantity of its major products, the levels of major economic and technological input, the types of new products to be tested, the rate of cost reduction, the total number of employees, the total wage payments and the average wages per person, the level of labor productivity, and the rate of profits, etc. Fiscally, the state implemented the policy of "unified revenue and unified expenditures" that allowed individual factories no autonomy in this regard. The factories had to completely turn over their profits to the state and counted on the latter for the allocation of funds for each of their planned activities. In a word, a state-owned enterprise was nothing less than an affiliate of the central or local government, lacking autonomy in every aspect of enterprise management. To be sure, to incentivize the individual factories and boost production, the state did once try to offer them a degree of autonomy in the Maoist era. In 1958, for instance, the central government implemented two measures in this direction. The first was to devolve its power of enterprise management to provincial governments, who were believed to be more sensitive than itself in responding to local conditions in the supply of raw materials and demand for products. As a result, the number of enterprises affiliated with the individual ministries of the central government decreased by 88 percent, from 9,300 to 1,200. The same measure was later repeated in 1969, resulting in the devolution of 2,400 enterprises (78 percent) from the central to provincial governments. The second and even more significant measure implemented in 1958 was to allow individual enterprises more power to manage themselves, including: (1) reducing the twelve mandatory targets to only four, namely a factory's total output, total employment, total wage payment, and total profit, leaving the remaining eight as "non-mandatory," which meant that individual factories were allowed to adjust them as needed; (2) allowing the factories to retain a portion of profits for various purposes, including using them for bonuses and welfare programs for workers (which, however, had to be limited to 5 percent of a factory's total wage payment); and (3) allowing these factories to make adjustments to their own institutions and personnel as long as the total employment remained the same. But these measures soon resulted in chaos in enterprise management, rapid expansion of local investments, and shortages in the supply of raw materials and products, hence the huge problems of inflation and fiscal deficits. The central government thus suspended most of the measures in early 1959 and would never try them again during the Maoist era (Zhao Lingyun 1999).

To incentivize industrial enterprises to increase production and hence generate more profits to satisfy the central government's growing need for revenue, industrial reforms in 1979 and 1980 again centered on the devolution of management power from the central government to individual enterprises. Likewise, the state allowed these firms a degree of autonomy in the planning of production, sales of products, determination of their prices, employment of workers, and, most importantly, sharing of profits between the state and individual firms. These measures did offer the firms greater incentive to boost production, but they also caused an unexpected decrease in the state's revenue from these firms, which declined year after year, from 49.5 billion yuan in 1979 to only 29.6 billion yuan in 1982, primarily because of the firms' growing share of profits at the cost of the central government.[2] Therefore, as a second step of industrial enterprise reform, the state introduced the policy of "taxation in lieu of profit sharing" (*ligaishui*) in 1983. Individual firms were no longer required to share most of their profits with the state, but they had to pay the state a tax that was initially 55 percent of their profits and was adjustable and specific for different products after 1985 (Zhao Lingyun 1999). As a result, the most profitable enterprises were also burdened with the highest tax rates, hence the so-called phenomenon of "whip the fast-walking ox" (*bianda kuai niu*), which in turn reduced their willingness to maximize profits. Nevertheless, under the new policy of taxation, individual firms were allowed full autonomy in using their profits as bonuses to incentivize workers, and unlike its practice in the past, the state imposed no maximum or minimum limits (*shangbu fengding, xiabu baodi*) on the percentage of profits for this use.

Impact on Worker Performance

These reforms immediately led to changes in labor management within individual enterprises. Unlike the Maoist practices of the past that had prioritized political pressure as well as various political rewards to ensure conformity, factory managers of the 1980s increasingly emphasized the use of material incentives to motivate workers, particularly bonus payments. These had been excessively used before the Great Leap Forward, greatly reduced in the early 1960s, and eliminated during the Cultural Revolution. When bonus payments were reintroduced after 1978, workers' attitude toward production quickly changed. Before 1978, as shown in the preceding chapters, there was no direct link between workers' labor input and income level. Nevertheless, most workers performed reasonably well during most of the Maoist years when a set of formal institutions interacted with informal practices to shape the work norms that effectively constrained them. Working extra hours or shifts was a way for workers to show their unselfishness and commitment to the collective; workers routinely did so without question, especially when the pressure for political conformity was tense and the political rewards were attractive. However, once the pressure was gone and doing extra tasks became linked with the payment of bonus, workers were no longer willing to labor more or longer without compensation; to perform extra duties, "you have to pay more," said a retiree from a military enterprise in Beijing (B8).

Under the bonus payment policy, workers' income was directly linked with their skill level, labor intensity, and quantity of tasks performed. When they had a chance to choose a job or decide how they would perform or how long they would work, the workers would first ask whether the job came with a bonus and how the bonus was determined. They avoided or shirked tasks that offered no bonuses and preferred those that came with generous rewards, hence the cultivation and prevalence of the "money comes first" (*yiqie xiang qian kan*) mentality. This was especially true in the early 1980s, when political campaigns and the daily routines of political study were gone. The payment of a bonus thus became the only effective tool for factory managers to incentivize workers; for the latter, to earn more bonus was also the most important reason to work hard. A former transportation worker at the Liaohe Oil Field put the change in their attitude bluntly: "After the reform and opening-up, people began to care only about money (*kaishi renqian*), and they no long worked as enthusiastically as before. While working, they only thought about whether or not the job was rewarded" (Y4). "Before 1978," another oil field worker admitted, "everyone worked hard. Afterward, their morale deteriorated year after year" (Y1). The reform leaders of the post-Mao era as well as enterprise managers did not realize that the reintroduction of bonuses did not always produce the expected results. Psychological studies have shown that the use of monetary incentives could "backfire and reduce the performance of agents or their compliance with rules" (Fehr and Falk 2002, 687), which was especially true for in-group members with a strong desire to avoid social disapproval and who therefore saw the monetary incentives as distrust and a violation of a psychological contract (Sliwka 2007; Ellingsen and Johannesson 2008; Gneezy et al. 2011). Chinese workers of the once tight-knit *danwei* of state firms were no exception.

Equally damaging to the workers' morale was their reduced identity with their factories. The increase in opportunities for extra income or a better job outside the factory reduced their dependence on the work unit in the 1980s. In Shanghai, for instance, workers "did private tasks (*gan sihuo*)" outside their enterprise for extra income during weekends or holidays. Some of them pretended to be sick during weekdays and went to the so-called "township and village enterprises" (TVEs), which mushroomed in the countryside, helping them set up equipment or train workers; there were also workers who "asked for sick leave and went to Wenzhou to do small business such as selling cigarettes" (S4). As more and more individuals profited from these activities and became "households of ten thousand yuan" (*wanyuanhu*) or millionaires, the workers of the state firms, who had been proud of their "iron rice bowl" (*tiefanwan*), lost their sense of honor and privilege; working for the increasingly inefficient and unprofitable state firms became less and less attractive.

This all took place at a time when Chinese society was undergoing political relaxation under Deng Xiaoping's new leadership, especially in the few years of the late 1970s and the early 1980s (Goldman 1994, 62–82). Gone was the excessive politicization of factory life; the political pressure on workers vanished. Those who had refrained from shirking out of fear before tended to act freely in pursuit of self-interest when they found opportunities within or outside the factory. On the other hand, the traditional political rewards that had motivated workers prior to 1978 lost much of their appeal. The nomination of Advanced Producers or Model Laborers, for example, gave priority to those who made a "special contribution" or "invention and renovation," which usually meant the engineers, technicians, or management personnel of a factory; ordinary blue-collar workers had no chance to compete with them (B9). Party membership had been the ladder for workers to move upward before, but the introduction of the contract system changed the traditional mechanism of mobility; personal connections with the factory leader, who had greater control of the work force after contracting with the government for a fixed target of output and profit, mattered more than one's political performance. In some factories, party membership became almost worthless. A retiree from the machinery factory of Shengli Oil Field recalled that when he tried to apply for party membership in 1992, his supervisor made fun of him: "So you wanted to be a party member? Okay, I'd like to sell my membership to you for 500 yuan. Don't apply, forget it. It is useless" (Y2).

"BECOMING HIRED LABOR": WORKERS UNDER THE RESPONSIBILITY SYSTEM, 1986-1995

It should be noted, however, that except for the introduction of bonus payments and the growing income-making opportunities outside the work unit that altered the work norms in state firms, much of the Maoist systems and practices in factory governance remained unchanged by the mid-1980s. It was the next two major reforms, namely the introduction of the contracted responsibility system in 1986 and, more importantly, the transition to the modern corporate system in 1995, that fundamentally transformed labor relations in China's industries. The immediate reason behind the introduction of the contracted management responsibility system (*chengbao jingying zerenzhi*) in 1986 remained fiscal. As mentioned above, the reform of "taxation in lieu of profit sharing" resulted in ever-growing taxes on the most profitable firms, which explained their gradual loss of incentive to increase profits. Beginning in the second half of 1985, large- and medium-size enterprises witnessed a steady decline in profits for twenty-two consecutive months (Wu Li 2010, 781). As a result, the state's revenue from the income taxes of enterprises declined from 69.6 billion yuan in 1985 to 69.2 billion yuan in 1986 and 66.5 billion yuan in 1987. Once again, the state suffered a deficit in its fiscal balance, which increased to 8.3 billion in 1986, compared to a surplus of 57 million yuan in 1985 (Guojia tongjiju 2005, 104). The solution to this fiscal mire was to substitute the taxation system with the contracted responsibility system, which was first proposed by the central government in December 1986 and applied to 80 percent of large- and medium-scale enterprises by the end of 1987.

The goal of enterprise reforms in this phase was to fully separate the state's "right of ownership" (*suoyouquan*) of an enterprise from the enterprise's "right of management" (*jingyingquan*), thus breaking from the practice of a planned economy in which the state was both the owner and manager of its enterprises. Key to the reform was the policy of "two guarantees and one link" (*shuangbao yigua*), namely, for the enterprise under contract to guarantee its remission to the central government of its pre-negotiated amounts of taxes and profits that would increase year by year, guarantee its implementation of projects on technological upgrades approved by the central government, and link the total amount of its wage payment with the profits and taxes it materialized. After fulfilling their obligations of profit sharing and tax payment, the enterprises under contract were allowed to keep the remainder of the profits; and those who signed a contract with the government to run the enterprises were fully responsible for the management of their personnel and all activities in relation to the production and marketing of products.

The Loss of the Equilibrium in Power Relations

An immediate impact of the reform on the institutions of factory governance was the dramatically increased power of the leader of a factory (*changzhang*), who was above everyone else in making decisions over the factory's personnel and financial issues. The factory head was no longer subject to supervision by the factory's party secretary, whose role was reduced to overseeing the activities of the party's organization in the factory and who was no longer allowed to intervene with the factory head's decision-making process; and the factory leader was also free of the constraints imposed by the factory's SWC or trade union, whose functions deteriorated under the responsibility system. Thus, instead of appointing factory cadres according to the established practices that had been based largely on candidates' merits, the head under contract tended to appoint only those whom they personally trusted and favored; most of the newly appointed cadres, especially the cadres in key positions, thus were the factory head's family members, relatives, or friends who owed their personal loyalty to the factory leader only, hence the prevalence of "patriarchal style" leadership (*jiazhangzhi*) and the dominance of patron-client networks in many state-owned enterprises. A survey of three thousand workers from sixty state-owned enterprises conducted in the early 1990s showed that among the seven factors influencing one's chances of getting a factory leader's favorable consideration, "having a good personal relationship with the leader" and "strong social networks" were ranked as the top two, whereas one's education ranked at the bottom (Zhang Yongshan 1992).

All these developments further paved the way for unprecedented corruption among factory leaders. This took various forms, such as fabricating accounts so that the expenses on wages, transportation, business travel, and the like were inflated and the difference between the fabricated and actual amounts were pocketed; secretly selling the factory's products or properties and pocketing the revenue by hiding them from the account; bribing business partners or taking kickbacks and bribes from the latter; embezzling the factory's funds under the excuse of sponsoring a program or donating to another entity; wasting the factory's funds on extravagant meals, hotels, and cars; and illegally transferring the factory's funds to personal accounts at foreign banks. Instead of "getting an appointment by competition and making income by efforts" (*shanggang kao jingzheng, shouru kao gongxian*) as the official media made people believe, workers were frustrated by the phenomenon of "unfairness in appointments" (*jingzheng bugongping*) and "abuse of power for private gain" (*yiquanmousi*) among the cadres (Zhang Yunxiao 1995). All these contrasted sharply with the traditional image of factory cadres who had to refrain from engaging in flagrant corruption, live a life not too different from the rank and file, and even yield their opportunities in housing and wage upgrades to ordinary workers, as the preceding chapters have shown.

The end result of the reforms in labor management by the 1980s and 1990s, therefore, was the loss of the equilibrium in power relations within a factory; workers completely lost their discursive and institutional leverages to counterbalance the power of the factory management. Gone was their status as the masters of the enterprise and as the leading class in society who had possessed the inherent power to supervise the corruptible cadres, according to the Maoist ideology. Unlike their relationship before the reform that had been largely symmetrical, as shown in earlier chapters, workers became increasingly disadvantaged in relation to the cadres under the contracted responsibility system, as this system often came with the implementation of a "labor contract system" (*laodong hetong zhi*). A growing number of workers signed a contract with the new management of their factories for a fixed term of employment; in certain sectors, such as textile, building, and coal mining, contracted workers accounted for 50 to 70 percent of the labor force by 1990. Instead of their shared identity with the *danwei* or work unit and the interdependence with each other as seen in most of the Maoist past, tensions developed between the workers and cadres. Workers were disgruntled with the cadres' overt practice of favoritism toward family members and friends in hiring, promotion, and task assignment in everyday production. They resented the unbridled corruption among the cadres of all levels at the cost of the factory and their own interests. And they were frustrated in particular by the widening gap between themselves and the cadres in income level, as the latter typically earned an annual income that was six to twenty-six times theirs and on average nine times, as an investigation in Henan province indicated (Cui Yi 1991).

The Loss of the Equilibrium in Labor Relations

Enterprise reforms in the 1980s and early 1990s further resulted in the loss of the equilibrium in labor relations that had prevailed in the Maoist era. Unlike the situation before 1986, when a factory leader had no right to fire a worker no matter how badly they performed, the factory under the responsibility system was allowed to fire any worker who failed to fulfill the requirements of the contract. Moreover, in sharp contrast with the past, when bonuses were usually paid at the same rate to all workers of the same unit (the so-called *maomaoyu dajiasa* or "drizzles on all") regardless of differences in individual performance, factory managers under the responsibility system were able to apply different bonus amounts to different workers, and they were able to punish those who performed poorly by cancelling or reducing the payment of bonuses and even wages. Gone was the "iron rice bowl" or permanent employment and the mentality of being "masters" of their enterprises; instead, contract workers developed a sense of "being hired" (*bei guyong*) and belonging to "second-class workers" (*erdeng gongren*), who "work for money" (*ganhuo zhengqian*) or "work as much as how much is paid" (*gei duoshao qian, gan duoshao huo*) (Cui Yi 1991; Xie Deming et al. 1997).

All these factors largely explain the significant decline in workers' morale after the introduction of the responsibility system in 1986, as evidenced in the investigations of different localities. From its survey of 4,300 workers of twelve state-owned enterprises conducted in 1986, for example, the General Trade Union of Shanghai Municipality found that 50 percent of the workers believed that they lacked the incentive to work hard (Zhang Yunxiao 1995); its survey of another 10,000 workers from twenty-five enterprises in different sectors in 1988 further showed that while 84.6 percent of the workers approved of the responsibility system, 62 percent of them believed that their incentives to work had remained unchanged or declined, compared to the 38 percent of workers who were more incentivized than before to work hard (Gong Xinxin 1989). Another report on the industrial enterprises of sixteen different sectors in Shanghai found that 97.5 percent of the factory leaders surveyed in 1987 were disappointed about the low morale of workers in their enterprises, while 97.3 percent of the workers in those enterprises also admitted that they lacked the incentive to work (Mu Liangping 1990). Similarly, the General Trade Union of Wuhan Municipality found that, of the 1,097 workers it polled in 1991, 72 percent admitted that they were "not fully incentivized to work" (Cui Yi 1991).

Workers' low morale in production, as these surveys reveal, manifested in many ways, such as lower attendance, late arrival and early leave, shirking or working for only three or four hours on average per day, and paying less attention to the quality of products and the maintenance of equipment, hence a decline in labor productivity in certain enterprises (Tangshanshi zonggonghui diaochazu 1988). According to an investigation of two factories in Hangzhou conducted by researchers from the Party Central's Department of Propaganda in 1990, work norms had changed so much in these firms that workers there generally accepted finishing two-thirds of required workload as "satisfactory"; this contrasted sharply with the norm before the introduction of the responsibility system, when finishing two-thirds of work had been considered a sign of "poor performance" (Zhongxuanbu yanjiushi diaoyanzu 1992).

Aside from the marginalization of their status under the responsibility system and their troubled relationship with the management after 1986, workers' reduced willingness to perform well in production also had to do with economic and social factors. One was the unprecedented inflation that caused an annual increase in workers' living cost by 7.55 percent from 1984 to 1987 and a further increase of 17.7 percent in the first nine months of 1988 across the entire country. As a result, despite increases in their nominal incomes, 36.7 percent of workers in Shanghai complained of a decline in their real standard of living in the first half of 1988, and 75.84 percent of workers expressed their economic and psychological inability to tolerate the inflation (Gong Xinxin 1989). In the whole country, 35.8 percent of urban households saw a continued decline in their real incomes in 1989 (Mu Liangping 1990).

Equally frustrating to the workers was the fact that their income level also declined in comparison to those who found new opportunities outside the state-owned enterprises. Among the groups who became rich quickly were the so-called "self-employed individuals" (*getihu*), who had been marginalized because of their failure to get hired by a state-owned enterprise but now earned much more than factory workers by engaging in peddling or a small business. Others chose to be on a leave of absence from, or simply quit their jobs at, a state-owned enterprise, so that they could "jump into the sea" (*xiahai*), that is, find a high-income job, such as being a taxi driver, an employee of a foreign company or a joint venture, or a private business owner. Still, there was a growing number of workers who kept their jobs at a state-owned factory but accepted invitations from the mushrooming TVEs to work during weekends and holidays, where they earned much more than the wages from the factories. In a typical instance, the most skilled workers and tuners at the Shanghai Piano Factory quit their jobs and found employment at the TVEs on the outskirts of the city, where they received a payment of 20,000 to 30,000 yuan as the "expense on security of livelihood" in addition to a monthly wage that was much higher than what they had earned before (Gong Xinxin 1989). All these economic and social factors thus worked together to foster a "sense of relative deprivation" (*xiangdui boduo gan*) among the workers of state-owned enterprises and dampen their morale at the workplace. The equilibrium in labor relations that had characterized the state firms and sustained worker morale had largely vanished by the early 1990s.

MASTERHOOD LOST: WORKERS IN ENTERPRISE RESTRUCTURING, 1995-2008

The responsibility system did not last long. Beginning in 1995, the state vigorously promoted the establishment of the "modern corporate system" (*xiandai qiye zhidu*) on the basis of shareholding, a process known as "institutional transformation" (*gaizhi*). The aggravated fiscal difficulty remained an important impetus for the state to take this new step of enterprise reform. Compared to its level in preceding years, which ranged from 23.7 billion yuan in 1991 to 29.3 billion yuan in 1993, the state's deficit increased to 57.4 billion yuan in 1994 and 58.1 billion yuan in 1995 (Guojia tongjiju 2005, 105). One of the factors contributing to the state's growing deficits had to do with the state-owned enterprises under the contracted management responsibility system, whose income taxes declined from 62.8 billion in 1991 to 62.5 billion in 1992 and 58.3 billion in 1993 (Guojia tongjiju 2003, 282). This in turn led to a more fundamental reason behind the state's decision to transform state-owned enterprises into shareholding or private firms. The responsibility system, while offering enterprise managers a strong incentive to increase productivity and maximize profits, also resulted in two major problems: (1) their prioritization of short-term goals by maximizing the use of existing equipment and exploiting contract workers without long-term investment in technological innovation and upgrades and workers' protection and welfare; and (2) their entitlement to the full monetary compensation guaranteed by the contract when the enterprise made profits but immunity from the full liability for the enterprise's loss, or the so-called "contract for profit but not for loss" (*fuying bu fukui*). Obviously, the contracted management responsibility system, like the preceding experiments, could only be temporary and transitional; for policymakers and economists, the only long-term solution to the growing debts and other problems of state-owned enterprises was to completely privatize them or transform them into shareholding firms open to private investors.

The Institutional Transformation

The state's strategy for establishing the modern corporate system was to "grasp the big and release the small" (*zhuada fangxiao*); that is, the state would retain its control of the largest enterprises in the most critical sectors by holding all or most of their shares after these firms were turned into shareholding companies; to improve the solvency of some of the enterprises that had been burdened with too much debt, much of their liabilities would be converted into shares to be owned by the debtors (*zhai zhuan gu*). At the same time, the state allowed small- and medium-size state-owned enterprises to be sold to private investors or turned into shareholding companies without limiting the percentage of shares owned by private investors. As it turned out, most of these firms were "sold" to their existing managers at a price much lower than the actual values of these firms' assets. For instance, the nine state-owned enterprises of one city were sold for 1.72 million yuan in the end, which was only 0.41 percent of their total assets that were appraised at 420 million yuan in total before the sale, or 1.7 percent of their net assets that were appraised at 100 million yuan. In another city, the 236 state-owned enterprises, which had a total net asset of 730 million yuan before privatization, owed a debt of 661 million yuan in the end after many deductions and offsets when they were appraised for sales. Even when the enterprise to be sold had a net asset, the buyers did not have to pay the full price in cash during the transaction; instead, most of the buyers paid through installations for five or more years, and the installations would be paid from the annual profits the buyers made from the firms. As a result, most of the state-owned enterprises were privatized in the way of "half given out and half sold out" (*ban song ban mai*) or "sold in name and given out in reality" (*ming mai shi song*), as Premier Zhu Rongji complained (Chen Guoheng 1999).

The restructuring had huge impact on workers. By and large, the privatized firms handled their relationship with the workers of former state-owned enterprises in two ways. One was to completely cease their ties with them by "buying off seniority" (*maiduan gongling*), that is, offering them a one-time severance package on the basis of years served so that the firm would no longer be responsible for the workers' reemployment or retirement and welfare benefits. Typically, all workers in the same factory would be paid a base amount at the same rate, to be supplemented with a specific payment to each worker based on their years of employment in the factory at the rate of between 200 and 500 yuan per year (Wang Mingcai 1997; Shan Zhufei 1999). The other method was to retain the workers from the former state-owned enterprises and allow them to buy and hold the shares of the privatized firm, which usually accounted for 5 to 20 percent of its total shares and even up to more than 50 percent in small firms (You Lixin 1995; Yu Ji 2004); this would incentivize the workers to grow identity and concern with the firm, as the policymakers expected, though in reality the worker shareholders owned the shares usually for short-term gain only and showed little concern with the firm's long-term goals, as some researchers found (Wang Yanbin 2002). In some factories, the paternalistic practices continued after the restructuring, as seen in the priority given to senior workers in housing allocation (Unger and Chan 2007).

Workers' Status and Identity Redefined

The biggest impact of the reform on workers, however, was a fundamental change to their legal status and social standing in relation to enterprise management and other groups in society. Before the institutional transformation, workers of state-owned enterprises remained legally the "masters" of their work units as long as these enterprises were under "ownership by the whole people" (*quanmin suoyou*), and they were still entitled to a full range of rights and benefits as long as they performed their duties under the responsibility system. More importantly, the traditional mechanisms of worker participation, including the trade union, workers' congress, and appeals by letter and visit, remained in place to satisfy workers' needs at the workplace, despite the growing power of the factory managers that curtailed the use of these institutions in small factories.

After the transition to the modern corporate system (i.e., privatization in most cases), however, workers' legal status was completely subverted. A researcher thus observed the changes to workers: "This is the present reality of the enterprises' institutional restructuring: the existing factory leaders and managers of state-owned and collectively owned enterprises became owners of capital almost overnight, by the means of 'buying-off' and by taking advantage of their privileged status and their high-incomes and opportunities made available to them by the state's policies in the past twenty years. At the same time, the vast masses of workers remained proletariat who owned nearly nothing." He further described the actual relationship between workers and owners of privatized firms: "Once they became the 'bosses' (*laoban*), those who had recently maneuvered enterprise reforms and institutional transformation would flagrantly manage to weaken the working class's status and violated their personal interests. They either fired the workers who had worked with them for decades in developing the enterprises by forcing the workers to sign an agreement that was no different from an unequal treaty, or forced them to work for more than ten hours a day, arbitrarily cut down their benefits, and paid them only a small fraction—one hundredth or even one thousandth—of their own earnings; they were indifferent to workers' illness and plight; and they were free to make a body search and even corporal punishment on workers, without treating them as human beings. Even more miserable, of course, were those who were laid off, thus unable to see a doctor, buy a housing unit, or pay their children's tuitions, and even unable to maintain the minimum level of subsistence" (Chen Zuwei 2004). Another observer notes that the workers eventually became the "masters in real sense"—to the extent that they became the owners of their own labor and nothing else (Liu and Gao 2002). Thus, after two decades of enterprise reforms, workers' labor was completely commodified; market forces came to determine labor relations in lieu of the "socialist social contract" that had defined workers' rights and duties for decades before the reform (Tang and Parish 2000, 3–16; Lee 2007a, 3–33).

The workers who felt most frustrated and helpless in the transformation were those in their forties and fifties, who had been at their work units for many years or even decades but had great difficulty finding a new job after being laid off. Here are some of their typical laments:

- "Having contributed to the enterprise's growth for so many years, now we are getting old and became 'useless.' We are being kicked away from the enterprise at the moment when we count on it for the rest of our lives! How can we bear with it!" (Wei Dongning 2006);
- "Having done the revolutionary work for decades to build socialism, we suddenly found ourselves descended from the masters to hired labor, as the state-owned enterprise is turned into a shareholding firm" (Luo Tianwen 1994); or
- "We have worked in the enterprise for decades, and it was us who had built its assets that are worth tens of millions of yuan. We have nowhere to go if we were forced to leave. Enterprise reform is bound to take place, but the interests of elder workers should be taken care of. By no means should the elder workers be thrown away as a burden" (Huang and Lu 1996).

Not surprisingly, nostalgia for the Maoist past prevailed among them, as reflected in the following remarks:

- "I cannot help but burst into tears when watching a chorus of the song 'We Workers Have the Power' on a TV show on May Day. How proud we were as iron-and-steel workers and as oil field workers at that time; all others envied us. Now something is wrong, and we earn too little—less than the entry-level pay for young people in the service sector" (Huang and Lu 1996); and
- "In the past we all belonged to one family, ate from the same pot, shared joys and sorrows together. Now, the enterprise has to be reorganized. How vexed we are and how unfair it is!" (Luo Tianwen 1994).

Those who were fortunate enough to keep their jobs in the restructured firms did not fare as well as they had hoped. They were subjected to regulations and disciplines that were much more demanding than before. Reorganized from a state-owned enterprise in 1996, Guangzhou Iron & Steel Group Corporation, for instance, gave each worker a copy of an *Employees'*

Handbook, which stipulated in detail employees' duties and linked their different levels of performance with specific amounts of reward or penalty. In another instance, Guangzhong Enterprise Group Corporation, restructured in the same year, would fire any employee responsible for an accident that incurred a loss of more than 5,000 yuan. A 2002 survey of workers in large state-controlled companies in Guangzhou, including these two firms, thus found that 71 percent of them believed that labor management was more restrictive than prior to 1996. While they worked harder than before, however, workers' income and benefits did not improve as much as they expected. The same survey shows that although 51.7 percent of workers did earn more than before, more than 60 percent of the workers saw no changes in their benefits and 34 percent of them received the same wages as before; 14 percent of workers earned less than before and 15.5 percent of them suffered a reduction of benefits (Liu and Gao 2002). In Wuhan, a major industrial city in central China, a 1999 survey of workers of state-controlled firms showed that while there were 43.5 percent of worker households who "earned slightly more than their spending," there were also 31.5 percent of households who could only "make ends meet," and 13 percent lived in "hardship" or "exceptional hardship" (Li Jun et al. 2001). In Changchun, a large industrial city in Northeast China, a survey of 1,400 workers in 1999 showed that 50.8 percent of them saw no significant changes in their wage levels after the institutional transformation, and 16.2 percent of them earned less than before (Wu Xiaoming 1999). A nationwide survey of workers conducted by the All China General Trade Union in 2007 further revealed that 84.3 percent of the polled workers were "very dissatisfied" with their income, and 33.1 percent believed that their income had declined compared to five years earlier (Su Linsen 2011).

As a result, workers throughout the country found that their standing in society had significantly deteriorated after decades of reforms. In the countrywide survey of 2007 mentioned above, 69.5 percent of workers were "dissatisfied" with where they were in society and averse to the obsolete sayings of "the working class is the leading class" or "wholeheartedly rely on the working class" (Su Linsen 2011). In Wuhan, 61.1 percent of the surveyed workers were disappointed with their lowered social standing and 44.4 percent felt "inferior" about themselves (Li Jun et al. 2001). In Changchun, 38.9 percent of the polled workers believed that they were less respected than before and 48.4 percent believed that they belonged to the average in society (Wu Xiaoming 1999). A worker from the Nanjing Handicraft Equipment Factory thus compared workers' social standing before and after the reforms: "When I was a child, my parents taught us to receive a good education so that we could be skilled workers after we grew up; now we try our best for our child to receive a good education only for the purpose of not to be a worker any more in the future" (Huang and Lu 1996).

Stronger Incentives and Better Performance

While industrial workers of the reform era lost forever their status as the "masters" of their factories or as the leading class in society, most of them actually performed better in production after the institutional transformation than they did before. This was especially true in private firms, where 73 percent of employees were satisfied with their jobs, according to an investigation of 247 employees from five companies in Sichuan province and Shenzhen of Guangdong province in 2001; this contrasted sharply with the situation in state-controlled companies and state-owned enterprises, where only 41 percent and 12 percent of workers were interested in their jobs, respectively (Zhu Min et al. 2001).[3] As for the reasons why workers performed better in private firms, when they were interviewed in 2005, the workers at a privatized firm gave different answers, often referring to their experiences in the early stages of enterprise reforms:

- "At a state-owned enterprise, those who earn more do not work a lot, and those who work a lot do not earn more. Sometimes those who earn more do not work at all. At the private firm, however, the more you work, the more you earn, so it's fairer here";
- "[At the private firm] workers' morale is higher, because under the piece-rate system, the more you work, the more you earn. So, this is where workers of a private firm are different from workers of a state firm: you have to work and think about nothing else when you are on duty. Only when you work hard, the firm runs well and you are better off, too";
- "The biggest difference I sensed for working at a private firm is that, though my job is more demanding, I earn much more, and feel much better";

- "Since I entered the private firm, the anger that I had always had when working in a state-owned enterprise has gone. I am no longer angry. Of course, I still have the sense of responsibility and I still have to do a good job. But I am no longer angry. Earlier, when working at the state-owned enterprise, the unfairness, injustice, wastefulness, and mistakes in management always annoyed me. Now, the angry mode is completely gone. At a private firm, it makes no sense to talk about being fair or unfair. It is just about being willing or unwilling. You may continue to work, if you want to keep your job here; otherwise, you may choose to leave";
- "I was always resentful over the unfairness and chaos in management before when working at a state firm. Now everyone is a hired laborer working for his boss; you make money for yourself and you have nothing to do with anyone else";
- "At the state-owned enterprise, we loafed around every day, because no matter how hardworking you were, you worked for the leaders who earned much more, not for the factory that could never be run well. Now working for the private firm, I am paid according to my effort. If I perform well, the factory will be better, which will also benefit us. If I do a bad job, I will lose my rice bowl." (You Zhenglin 2007)

Privatization, as these remarks suggest, did indeed give workers the freedom that they had never had in the past and a strong reason to work harder than before, a fact that contrasted sharply with their experiences in the Maoist past, when they were exalted as the masters of the country and guaranteed a security of livelihood yet deprived the freedom to make a choice in employment. Private firms were also much less infected by the problem of cadre corruption and favoritism that had plagued many state firms in the early stages of enterprise reforms in the 1980s and early 1990s, as discussed earlier. But the freedom that the workers obtained in the reform was also accompanied with a strong sense of insecurity in employment and a lack of identity with the workplace. While laboring harder and therefore earning much more than before, few workers achieved the same level of emotional attachment to the jobs they performed or developed the sense of group solidarity among their co-workers or mutual trust with the cadres that they had experienced in the state firms of the Maoist era. The only purpose for them to willingly work hard in the private firms was to earn more and nothing else. The equilibrium in labor relations and the workers' subsequent commitment to the workplace that had characterized the factories of the Maoist past were rarely found in the private firms of the 1990s and thereafter.

FACTORY GOVERNANCE RESTRUCTURED
The SWC in the 1980s

Needless to say, the marginalization of state-firm workers during industrial reforms incurred widespread resentment and resistance. Depending on the circumstances in which they were situated, workers of different firms struggled for distinct objectives and employed various strategies. By and large, three patterns emerged countrywide. First, in localities where large-scale state firms concentrated, such as the northeastern provinces, and where these firms' restructuring resulted in a large number of laid-off workers but limited opportunities for reemployment, workers tended to be particularly nostalgic about their glorious past and therefore justified their claims in the language of Maoist morality that centered on social equity, economic security, and political equality between cadres and workers (Lee 2007b). While directing their complaints to the local government, mainly in the form of a collective petition, their ultimate target was the central government, whose decision to restructure the firms and let most of them go bankrupt or be privatized was responsible for their plight.

In sharp contrast, in areas where the economic structure was diversified and the job market was developed, such as Shanghai and other coastal cities, the laid-off workers tended to embrace the opportunities offered by the market; their disgruntlement, mostly directed toward their work unit rather than the local or central government, thus focused on the terms of compensation for leaving the work unit or about the implementation of such terms. Finally, in between these two patterns, there were many medium- and small-size firms in the cities of interior provinces that underwent restructuring or privatization as well. While the workers of these firms struggled to find reemployment opportunities on their own, and many suffered unprecedented hardship in making ends meet, factory leaders as well as local government officials were the biggest beneficiaries by becoming new owners of the restructured firms or profiting from colluding with external buyers in privatizing the firm at the cost of the workers. The laid-off workers thus directed their grievances chiefly to the abusive factory leaders and corrupt government officials, and their protests, mostly spontaneous and poorly organized, could develop into violent actions. Of course, these three patterns could be found in any industrial city, given the vast differences between individual enterprises in size, kind, management, and profitability, but each of them did indeed show a regional concentration, as a recent study has revealed (Hurst 2009, 108–132).

What, then, was the role of the traditional organizations of mass participation in workers' struggles against marginalization? Throughout the 1980s and 1990s, the staff and workers' congress and the trade union continued to exist in state-owned enterprises before they were converted into private firms. In certain areas, the SWC appeared to be more active than before, especially when it came to making decisions that directly affected workers' well-being, such as constructing dormitory buildings and pooling funds for the construction project (B13; N1; N2). For instance, it was usually up to the SWC to propose a plan for the allocation of newly built apartments by ranking the needs of qualified employees, that is, assigning to each of them a score based on their years of employment and existing housing conditions (i.e., per capita square meters of the current living space) (S13). At Xi'an Instruments Factory, the factory management suspended its plan of housing construction and allocation reform precisely because of objection from the SWC in 1992 (S10). The workers' congress also played a part in decisions about the compensation and reappointment of workers who were laid off, as Sun Aiting (b. 1955) witnessed at her factory of more than three hundred workers (S6).

On the other hand, however, enterprise reforms ended in the growing power of factory leaders in the management of production and employment at the expense of workers. Ms. Fan (b. 1948) thus compared the situation at her work unit, Nanjing Telecommunication Equipment Factory, before and after the reform: "Before the reform, the SWC at our factory did have a certain degree of power; all of the worker representatives were elected from grassroots workers and the election was competitive. Later, however, the factory head and other leaders also attended the congress, and none of us dared to speak out. Earlier, the workers' congress discussed and voted on major issues about production, construction, and personnel, but none of its influences existed after the reform and by the time I retired" (L5). Our interviewees at other factories had similar views: "The SWC did not really have much to do! It's not really something. It didn't work!" (C2); "The SWC is nothing more than a formality. Everything was up to the leaders no matter whether there was a vote or not. Yes, the workers' congress could make proposals, but it was up to the leader to make a decision in the end. The factory head had a final say" (H1); "The SWC had no real power. It's only a matter of formality" (S2).

Similarly, workers of the 1980s and early 1990s tended to compare the roles of the trade union in their factories before and after the reform. In general, our informants had positive memories of the trade union in the decades prior to the reform. A retiree who worked for Renfeng Fabric Mill in Ningbo from 1950 thus described the trade union there: "Whenever the workers encountered anything that they were unhappy with, they would first talk to the trade union, and the trade union would then report it to higher levels, though its influence was not that big." He added, "In the first few years after the Liberation, the trade union did have real power, and the president of the trade union in the city of Ningbo even carried a gun with him" (N6). Ding Shuhua (b. 1941), who joined the Huanggang Region Filature in 1960, observed that the trade union in her factory "did have power in the 1960s and 1970s, and it was indeed able to speak and act for workers. Later, however, it lost such abilities and failed to pass on accurately government information from top down" (H3). Yang Xiaofeng (b. 1943), a female retiree from Yimin Food Factory in Shanghai, had a similar remark: "Earlier on, the trade union was surely able to speak for workers. Later, it gradually lost its abilities over the years. After 1990, they only copied the words of the factory head" (S8). At the bedding factory in Wuhan, according to Zhang Qishan (b. 1942), who joined the factory in 1963, "the trade union spoke for workers and actively helped those in difficulties. Therefore, some of the elderly workers still have emotional attachment to it even nowadays" (H6).

The reason that a sharp contrast between the Mao and reform eras existed in our informants' memories of the trade union is not difficult to understand. Since the 1990s, most of the state-owned enterprises have undergone a fundamental transformation from a "work unit" running under the socialist state to a modern corporation competing in a market economy. Workers' identity or self-perception also changed, from the "masters" of the factory to nothing less than wage workers. In a similar vein, the trade union also underwent substantial changes, from acting more or less on behalf of the workers in a paternalistic style to subserviently implementing the purposes of the corporate management and showing much less care for the workers' interests as a group or their personal needs.

The Deterioration of "Three Old Bodies"

An important consequence of the institutional transformation in the second half of the 1990s and the 2000s was the restructuring of the governance framework within the reorganized enterprises, best seen in the deterioration of the functions of the preexisting governing organs including the party committee, the SWC, and the trade union, together known as the "three old bodies" (*laosanhui*), and in their stead the rise of "three new bodies" (*xinsanhui*), namely the shareholders' meeting, the executive board, and the supervisory board. The party committee, which had been the core decision-making body within a state-owned enterprise, continued to exist in state-controlled companies and, from time to time, tried to habitually influence the appointment of senior managers in these firms, thus inevitably conflicting with the firm's executive board. In most enterprises where the party committee existed, however, it had to limit itself to the nominal roles of ensuring the firm's compliance with state laws and policies, assisting the firm management in administrative affairs, and overseeing worker participation in political organizations and events, etc. The executive board of a shareholding company, for its part, was in full charge of the company's businesses and answered to the shareholders' meeting, which had the ultimate power in making key decisions for the firm and electing its executive board members.

What, then, were the new roles and functions of the SWC and the trade union in a shareholding company? According to the Company Law enacted in 1993 and amended in 2005, the SWC had the following rights: to elect employees' representatives as members of the executive board; to elect employees' representatives as members of the supervisory board, who should constitute at least a third of the board's membership; and to participate in discussions on major issues concerning the company's institutional transformation or management and the introduction of important regulations. The trade union, by the law, had the right to represent employees to sign with the company a collective contract about labor remuneration, work hours, benefits, insurance, and labor security and health protection. Likewise, the trade union also had the right to make suggestions on major issues concerning the company's reorganization or management and the creation of regulations and institutions.

The actual situations of the SWC and the trade union varied widely in firms of different sizes and shareholding structures. While they continued to exist in state-controlled companies, the functionality of both organizations deteriorated. The trade union typically suffered a downsizing of its personnel and downgrading of its standing in the governance structure of these firms. As a result, the workers of state-controlled companies tended to turn to their supervisors and co-workers directly about issues they encountered on the shop floor; less than 10 percent of them showed their willingness to consult the trade union in this regard, as a research of state firms in Hubei province revealed. The same research found that for personal problems they encountered in daily life, most workers turned to their friends or parents for help rather than the trade union cadres or supervisors (Zhao Lijiang et al. 2013). In private firms, the SWC and the trade union were either perfunctory or nonexistent. In Beijing, for example, only 37 percent of private firms reported the establishment of a workers' congress by the end of 2007 (Wang and Zhang 2008). In Hunan province, 12.6 percent of the workers who were surveyed in 2008 denied the existence of a trade union in their firms, and 29.3 percent claimed that no workers' congress ever existed in their companies (Xie Yuhua 2009). Where these organizations did exist, they often had problems such as having "no personnel, no office space, no funds, and no activities" (Zhou Shengzhan 2011).

The malfunctioning or nonexistence of the SWC and the trade union in private and shareholding companies were part of the reason behind the worsening working conditions and maltreatment of workers in these firms, which in turn led to the growing incidents of worker protests in the late 1990s and 2000s. In the absence of a trade union, for instance, many private firms avoided signing a labor contract with employees, who were mostly migrant workers from rural areas newly coming to the cities for employment opportunities. A 2007 survey of private firms in Shanghai and other nine cities showed that only 63.7 percent of them signed a contract with their employees, and most of the contracts were for short terms of one or two years. The lack of a labor contract made it possible for private employers to delay or deduct wage payments to migrant workers. A 2005 survey of 800 migrant workers in five cities of Hunan province showed, for example, that 30 percent of the workers failed to receive pay on time, and those who received a payment often found many deductions under various excuses, not to mention that they were paid at a rate much lower than urban workers in state firms (Han Bing 2008).

Nor did the SWC play its role as expected in the institutional transformation of most state-owned enterprises. A good case in point is the failed reorganization of Tonghua Steel and Iron Corporation, or Tonggang, in 2009. Established in 1958, Tonggang was the largest steel and iron firm in Jilin province. In 2005, it was transformed from a state-owned enterprise into a state-controlled shareholding company, with the private Jianlong Group as its second largest shareholder, who possessed nearly 40 percent of the company's shares and thus controlled its management. As a result of the transformation, the new management downsized the company's employment from 22,000 to 14,000 workers, forcing about 7,000 workers who were fifty-two or older to "retire internally" with a monthly stipend of less than 500 yuan. But this measure did not help the company survive the global recession in 2008, when workers' monthly wages were reduced to about 300 yuan, while the managers of the company received an annual salary of 400,000 to one million yuan. Having lost more than a billion yuan in that year, Jianlong withdrew from Tonggang. However, the recovery of the market in the second half of 2008 quickly made Tonggang profitable, and Jianlong joined it again under the auspices of the provincial government and became its largest shareholder after injecting one billion yuan, thus possessing 66 percent of the company's shares in July 2009. But workers at Tonggang fiercely resisted this move. Upon the announcement of Jianlong's control of Tonggang on July 24, about ten thousand workers surrounded the office building, took out the newly appointed general manager, named Chen Guojun, from the building, and beat him for hours, forcing the provincial government to make an announcement at 5:15 p.m. to permanently terminate Tonggang's reorganization with Jianlong. Chen died later the same day (Tang and Sun 2012).

The immediate reason leading to workers' protests was of course their disappointment with the performance of the managers from Jianlong in the preceding years, whose only concern turned out to be the maximization of profits from Tonggang without considering the well-being of the workers. But the eruption of workers' anger in July 2009 also had to do with the fact that their "democratic rights" (*minzhu quanli*) were totally ignored in the second round of restructuring. By the aforementioned Company Law as well as "Opinions on Regulating the Work Relating to the Restructuring of State-Owned Enterprises," a document released by the central government in 2003, any proposition about turning a state-owned enterprise into a non-state-owned enterprise had to be submitted to the SWC for deliberation and workers' opinions had to be fully respected before the proposition could be approved; and any plan about the placement of current employees of an enterprise to be restructured had to be first discussed and approved by its SWC before the plan could be implemented. Unfortunately, Tonggang announced its plan for workers' placement on July 22 without first seeking input and approval from the SWC; from the workers' point of view, therefore, the whole process of restructuring was a deal under the table that completely excluded them. Equally disappointing to them was the malfunctioning of the appeal system in the previous years, when the workers who had been forced to retire early saw no results despite their collective petitions and repeated visits to government offices at the city, provincial, and national levels. The trade union at Tonggang, which had never been independent and able to represent the workers before the restructuring, turned out to be even less helpful after 2005, when its organization was limited to the workshop level and its full-time personnel were eliminated under Jianlong's management; it failed to represent workers and mediate between the workers and the management when tensions mounted between the two sides (Tang and Sun 2012).

The Last Stand of Maoist Workers
While the examples of weakened or malfunctioning SWCs and trade unions were abundant in the late 1990s and the 2000s, there was no lack of instances in which the grieved workers used the preexisting platforms of mass participation as a weapon to defend their interests in enterprise restructuring or privatization. Let us look at an instance of worker resistance in a paper mill in Zhengzhou of Henan province.

Established in 1958, Zhengzhou Paper Mill had about 690 workers and 170 retirees in the late 1990s. With a history of contributing to the state a tax of more than a million yuan and profits of more than two million yuan each year until the late 1980s, the factory began to lose money annually after 1989, incurring a debt of more than 20 million yuan by 1995 when it completely suspended production because of the local government's environment protection policy; all workers therefore were furloughed. To ensure the factory's survival, factory head Cheng Wenkui tried to sell part of the factory's premises in vain in 1996 because of workers' protests and the local government's insistence that any sales of the factory's property had to be approved by its SWC. In November 1997, the factory eventually made a deal with the private Fenghua Company Limited for the latter to purchase it. The factory's SWC quickly approved the merger because of Fenghua's commitment to fully restoring the paper mill's production, paying off the wages and stipends that the mill owed to its workers, making up the payment of retirement funds, and reemploying all furloughed workers. As it turned out, however, Fenghua's real intention to annex the paper mill was to use its premises for development of real estate projects; it never delivered what it had promised to the paper mill workers, except for paying them a monthly stipend of 170 yuan for two months only, which was less than the minimum monthly pay of 235 yuan required by the local government. Disappointed, a number of SWC representatives petitioned four times to the municipal government for the termination of the merger but to no avail in 1999.

The workers thus started a movement under the slogan of "opposing deceptive merger, rescuing the factory and protecting the home" (*fan qizha jianbing, jiuchang hu jiayuan*), which culminated in their occupation of the factory for a week and holding a special SWC meeting on October 28, 1999, in which fifty of the fifty-five representatives voted for the paper mill's withdrawal from Fenghua; the municipal government refused to endorse the result, on the ground that "no retrogression from the reform is allowed" (*gaige buzou huitou lu*). In response, the workers once again occupied the paper mill and expelled the personnel that had been appointed by Fenghua on June 7, 2000, for the alleged purpose of carrying out the special SWC resolution. A month later, the city government sent hundreds of armed police to the paper mill and succeeded in ending the occupation and arresting Li Jiaqing, vice director and associate general engineer of the mill who had organized the occupation.

To end the stalemate, another SWC meeting was held in September 2000 under the city's general trade union's auspices, and a new group of workers' representatives and the paper mill's trade union committee members were elected, headed by forty-year-old Liu Yurui, to negotiate with Fenghua. As a result of the repeated petitions by Liu and her trade union, the city government allowed the paper mill to be separated from Fenghua. On January 7,

2001, the three sides (local government, paper mill, and Fenghua) reached an agreement that ended the merger and allowed the paper mill to form a separate shareholding company, with all workers as its shareholders. Because of Liu Yurui and her comrades' efforts, Li Jiaqing, who had been detained and charged with "single-handedly organizing the SWC meeting" and "instigating the mob to disturb social order," was released on bail on May 23, 2001, and would never be tried again. The next two years saw a stalemate between the workers and the local government, with the former insisting on recovering their status as state-firm workers and the later adhering to its stance of restructuring the factory into a shareholding company. The government prevailed in August 2003, as the shareholding company was eventually established, with its management board members elected by the company's SWC.

This instance is worth noting because of the unusual and indeed unprecedented roles that the SWC and the trade union played at the paper mill. As mentioned earlier, the state allowed the SWC to play a critical part in the institutional transformation of state firms, as seen in the congress's newly granted rights to elect worker representatives for the management board and supervisory board and to participate in discussions of key decisions concerning a state firm's restructuring. In practice, local governments pushed these policies even further as to require approval by the SWC before any decisions about a state firm's privatization or sales of its properties, not so much because of their respect to workers' rights as their concerns with the risk of worker unrest and threat to social stability, which mattered more than anything else in evaluating government officials' performance. Workers, too, used the SWC and trade union as legal weapons to defend their interests. In the case of the paper mill, the SWC first vetoed the factory director's proposition to use part of its lot as a lien for a mortgage from a local bank in April 1995. Later the congress further voted for approving the merger with Fenghua in 1998 and voted again for terminating the merger in 2000. Unlike its predecessors before the mid-1990s whose functions had been limited to perfunctorily endorsing whatever decisions made by the factory management or only making suggestions that directly pertained to workers' working or living conditions, the SWC for the first time played a decisive role in changing the factory's fate and, along with it, workers' treatment. Much of the same can be said about the paper mill's trade union, which, likewise, played a key role in representing its workers to petition the local government and negotiate with Fenghua for the factory's separation from the latter. Equally unusual was the fact that the chair of the paper mill's labor union was elected by the workers rather than appointed by Fenghua, and the chair spoke forcefully for workers in their struggle against Fenghua instead of serving as an intermediary between the two as a labor union leader had typically done before.

It is also worth mentioning that what inspired and empowered the workers were the values and ideas dating back to the Maoist era that were ingrained in their minds. Central to their appeals was the notion that the paper mill was a state firm and, having worked there for years and even decades, they had the inalienable right to protect it from misappropriation. If the factory had to be restructured into a private or shareholding firm, their rights as workers had to be fully respected, and they had the power to take it back and restore its original status as a state firm if its new owner failed to deliver what they had promised. In other words, they believed that they remained the true masters of the factory. The moral principles of the Maoist enterprises still held true to the discontented state-firm workers; in fact, some of the leaders of worker protests had been activists during the Cultural Revolution (Feng Chen 2003, 2008). While in the Maoist era, the saying "being the master of the factory" sounded like empty rhetoric carrying no substantial and tangible meaning for most workers, here they realized that "being the master" meant a lot, and they eventually had a chance to practice it in reality. Seemingly, while the old slogan of "love the factory as one's home" (*aichang rujia*) sounded irrelevant to them when the factory's survival as well as their positions in it were secured before the reform, the workers suddenly understood the real meaning of the factory as their "home" (*jia* or *jiayuan*). "Protecting the factory and rescue the home" thus became the rallying cry for workers who were marginalized during the reform. Wang Gong, who had worked in the paper mill for more than three decades (1972–2004), thus explained why he and his co-workers had to resist the merger: "This is my idea: we have to get the factory back. Only when it's back, can we restore our status as its masters. If it is sold, you'll lose it and become homeless." In its report to the city government, the paper mill's SWC also stated: "The factory is a state firm, and its properties belong to the whole people. As part of the whole people, the workers of the paper mill have the unshakable duty as its masters to supervise the merger and check whether or not the transfer of ownership is legal" (Tong Xin 2006).

Unfortunately, as government officials admonished and as the workers eventually realized, economic reform was a trend that no one could reverse. Although the workers succeeded in getting the paper mill back from Fenghua, this instance itself was an exception rather than the norm during the nationwide drive of enterprise restructuring in the second half of the 1990s and into the 2000s, and it was possible only in factories where the workers had a strong consensus and concerted action to resist restructuring and when they felt the result of the restructuring seriously infringed on their personal rights and interests. Fenghua eventually conceded and gave up the merger not because the amalgamation itself was procedurally illegal, but only because it was unable and unwilling to deal with the workers who showed an exceptional level of solidarity and bellicosity. No wonder an advisor to Fenghua lamented: "How come a merger that had been finalized under a contract and implemented for more than a year had to be renounced in the end? This is just unthinkable in Western countries and also impossible in coastal cities such as Guangzhou or Shanghai. It should not happen in a market economy. The workers of this factory have their own tradition. Their notions are too backward. This is why reforms have been so difficult and sluggish in this city" (Tong Xin 2006).

To the extent that the paper mill workers who participated in the resistance were all regular state-firm workers and that they justified their struggle against the merger by resorting to the old notions of the Maoist era, we may define this type of collective action as the last stand of the Maoist workers. As it turned out, most of such protests by state-firm workers were responsive and spontaneous, limited to specific issues within an enterprise. And much of the workers' claims remained corrective, aiming to restore what they had lost during the reform, rather than creative and adaptive to the emerging market economy (Feng Chen 2000, 2010). This goal was doomed in the age of irreversible enterprise restructuring. Not surprisingly, while the workers succeeded in separating the paper mill from Fenghua, they could never turn it back into a state firm and restore their old status there. The paper mill was eventually transformed into a shareholding company. As Liu Yurui, the chair of the newly reorganized labor union, warned the workers who became the company's shareholders: "The old days are gone. No lazy guy is allowed. Everyone has to work hard" (Tong Xin 2006).

THE RISE OF A NEW GENERATION OF INDUSTRIAL WORKERS

What happened to the Zhengzhou Paper Mill only reflects the experiences of traditional state-firm workers with urban residential status. To fully understand how labor relations evolved in industrial enterprises in the first two decades of the twenty-first century and in which direction factory politics will develop in the future, we have to take into account another category of workers who have come to dominate the manufacturing industries in China: migrant workers, or *nongmingong* ("peasant workers"), who had been rural residents under the traditional household registration system before coming to the cities for employment opportunities.

Rural Migrant Workers

The first generation of migrant workers emerged in the 1980s, when the dissolution of the collective system in agriculture at the beginning of the 1980s made it possible for them to migrate freely and seek off-farm jobs mostly in local areas, and many entered the so-called township-and-village enterprises. Their numbers increased from roughly two million in the early 1980s to about thirty million by the end of the decade, of which only about 23 percent migrated out of province. The wave of rural-to-urban migration surged in the following two decades, causing the number of migrant workers to expand to about 70 million by 1995 and 140 million by 2008. After a slowdown during the global economic recession in 2008, the number expanded further to about 170 million in 2019. They accounted for more than two-thirds of the entire rank of workers in China and dominated the labor-intensive sectors where the tasks were known for being "dirty, dangerous, and strenuous" (90 percent in construction, 80 percent in mining, 60 percent in textile and garment, and 50 percent in urban service sectors) (Ketizu 2010).

Given their rural residential status and the many disadvantages associated with it—in education, social networking, job opportunities, and access to legal protection—migrant workers suffered a huge amount of discrimination at the workplace for years compared to their urban counterparts. In 2002, for instance, they earned only 640 yuan per month on average (Zhou and Yuan 2014), or half the monthly wages of urban workers; their average hourly wage (2.85 yuan in large cities and 2.65 yuan in medium and small cities) was also about half of the hourly rate for urban workers (Li and Wu 2020). A 2006 report showed that migrant workers labored 6.3 days per week and 8.9 hours per day on average, and 46.9 percent of them worked seven days a week. Migrant workers suffered vocational illnesses and injuries more frequently than urban workers because of the insufficient provision or lack of equipment for safety and environmental protection in the sectors where they were concentrated. They were unable to send their children to local public schools for free education and had to pay a tuition for their children to study at schools specifically established for them. Without access to the urban public medical system, two-thirds of migrant workers chose to receive simple treatments from private clinics or buy medicines themselves instead of seeking hospitalization. Living in congested dormitories or shelters provided by employers or rented apartments, three-fourths of married migrant workers suffered separation from their family members who remained in home villages, causing the growth of the so-called "left-behind" children to more than 58 million by 2005 (Han Jun et al. 2009). And migrant workers were officially excluded from trade union organizations, which were open only to workers of urban residential status before 2003. Staying outside the formal institutional framework for legal protection, they were vulnerable to various forms of maltreatment by employers, who were mostly private business owners (only 9.66 percent of migrant workers were hired in public sectors in 2007 and 10.85 percent in 2016; see Li and Wu 2020).

Some positive changes have happened for migrant workers more recently. A series of government regulations were introduced from 2003 to 2006 to expand the coverage of worksite injury insurance, medical service, and retirement benefits to migrant workers and promote their equal treatment in employment, vocational training, wage payment, and children's education (Han Jun et al. 2009). As a result, white-collar employees increased from 8.59 percent in 2007 to 31.11 percent of the entire population of migrant workers in 2016 (Li and Wu 2020). The annual and hourly wages of migrant workers increased from 8,115 yuan and 2.72 yuan, respectively, in 2002, to 30,464 yuan and 13.30 yuan in 2014, thus greatly narrowing their gap with urban workers from 50.8 percent of the latter's hourly rate in 2002 to 87.44 percent in 2014. By 2019, migrant workers' monthly wages had increased to 3,962 yuan on average, and 4,567 yuan and 4,667 yuan in the sectors of construction and transportation, respectively (Guojia tongjiju 2019). The migrant workers who participated in medical, retirement, and injury insurance increased from 4.80 percent, 6.93 percent, and none, respectively, in 2002 to 37.96 percent,

37.09 percent, and 33.84 percent in 2014 (of course, still significantly lagging behind urban workers, who had coverage of 82.10 percent, 63.42 percent, and 43.40 percent, respectively, in 2014) (Li and Wu 2020). In 2016, the central government planned to have up to 100 million rural residents officially settled in cities; in 2019 it removed all barriers against rural residents' settlement and household registration in cities whose populations were under three million. As a result, 19 percent of migrant workers had owned an apartment in the cities where they worked by 2018; those who rented an apartment also increased to 61.3 percent (Guojia tongjiju 2019). Combined, 83.7 percent of their housing units had a shower and 94.8 percent had access to the internet. The migrant workers who owned refrigerators, washing machines, and cars increased to 65.7 percent, 66.1 percent, and 28.2 percent, respectively, in 2019. Furthermore, 99.5 percent of the school-age children of migrant workers received an education in the cities where their parents worked; among these children, 83.4 percent and 85.2 percent went to local public elementary and middle schools, and the rest attended private schools that received government funding. All these, needless to say, contributed to migrant workers' identifying with the cities where they lived, as seen by the fact that 40 percent of them believed themselves to be local townspeople, and 80.6 percent of them confirmed that they were comfortable living in the cities by 2019 (Guojia tongjiju 2020).

Behind these improvements were the striking changes in the composition, ability, and expectations of the migrant workers themselves over the past four decades. Back in the early 1980s, the villagers who sought jobs in the cities were mostly born in the late 1950s or 1960s, thus having been farmers for years who earned very little under the collective system of the Maoist era. The introduction of the household responsibility system around 1980 enabled them to migrate freely, and the primary reason for them to leave the village and work in the factories was for subsistence, or earning extra money in addition to the income from farming to make ends meet. Therefore, as migrant workers, they tended to accept pay at any level as long as it was higher than working at home on the farm. In sharp contrast, the migrant workers who entered factories in the 2000s and 2010s were mostly born after 1980 and even after 1990; without experiences in farming at home, they went to the cities for jobs immediately after graduating from school. Compared to the first generation of migrant workers, they were much better educated, with 56 percent graduating from middle school, 16.6 percent from high school, and 11.1 percent from college in 2019 (Guojia tongjiju 2020), averaging 9.13 years of education in 2007 and 9.78 years in 2016 (Li and Wu 2020). They also paid more attention to vocational training, participating in various classes in preparation for a desirable job, and most of them were able to speak standard Mandarin, unlike the earlier generation, whose Mandarin typically had an accent. Therefore, they had higher expectations of the jobs they were looking for, mostly eschewing jobs that were believed to be "dirty, strenuous, or heavy" and favoring positions in the service sectors such as marketing, housekeeping, food service, entertainment, and the beauty industry. Furthermore, unlike the first generation of migrant workers who took for granted their rural resident status and kept many of their habits as peasants, most of the new-generation migrant workers identified themselves as chiefly urban residents who never intended to go back to their home villages for a living, after working in the cities for years or growing up in the cities as the children of the first generation of migrant workers; only 38.6 percent of them still considered themselves rural residents, as a 2017–2018 survey revealed (Yin Jianbing et al. 2020).

Workers as Rightful Protesters

It is against this background that the actions taken by the new-generation migrant workers in the 2000s and 2020s can be properly understood. Compared to their predecessors one or two decades ago who tended to give up when confronted with injustice and abuse on the shop floor, the workers of the new millennium were more confident in their abilities and more willing to defend themselves (Ngai and Lu 2010). The wide use of cell phones and easy access to the internet made them more informed of the events going on in their factories and beyond and more connected to each other through social apps (most notably, QQ and WeChat). Therefore, these workers could easily organize into various informal "circles of friends" (*pengyouquan*), mostly on the basis of shared geographic origins (*laoxiang* or *tongxiang*), which allowed them to take action as a group quickly and easily. With a growing awareness of their legal rights as factory employees and familiarity with relevant laws and regulations, these workers showed a strong willingness to defend their rights and interests, and most of them chose to do so tactically within the existing legal framework, particularly the Labor Contract Law enacted by the central state in 2008 (Gallagher 2017). Their biggest concern was fair and equal treatment at the workplace. They would act together against the factory management when they could no longer tolerate the low pay or poor working conditions. Unlike the unemployed workers of state firms who suffered deprivation in enterprise restructuring and acted violently out of desperation (Lee 2007a, 159–161), migrant workers struggled primarily against discrimination from private employers.

One example to illustrate this point was a strike that took place at SNS Company in 2003. Founded by an investor from Taiwan in 1994 in the suburban Putuo district of Shanghai to manufacture industrial metal filters, this firm hired about two hundred workers who typically joined the factory because of introduction by, and connection with, senior employees; they thus formed different groups and QQ clusters on the basis of shared friendship, kinship, or hometown. For years, the workers had been unhappy with the factory's practice of withholding new employees' first month's wages, which the company would consider forfeit if the worker left the firm before their contract expired. They were also frequently annoyed by the firm's harsh treatment of workers, such as imposing a fine of 100 yuan on a certain employee for taking a nap by the machine after working extra hours for three days in a row and thus being extremely tired; the fine was more than the compensation he had received for the extra hours in the previous three days. Their conflict with the management started in July 2003 when the Shanghai Municipal Government raised the minimum monthly wage to 570 yuan but the company cut it to 540 instead. The person who initiated the action was Xiao Ding, who was popular among the workers. Ding and two other worker representatives first requested a face-to-face discussion with the firm's manager on the issues. Rejected, they began a three-day stoppage and at the same time submitted to the local township government a petition to organize their own labor union in August. In response, the trade union of the township's industrial park sent a cadre to assist them in establishing the labor union and recommended the chair of the industrial park's trade union to be the temporary head of the firm's labor union, which the workers refused, believing that the chair would side with the factory rather than with themselves. After winning more than two-thirds of the votes, Ding became the head of the factory's labor union, with an office room allocated by the factory and three paid days of union work in accordance with national law. Ding soon succeeded in getting back the wages that the firm owed them and increasing their minimum wage to the new level mandated by the government.

Four years later, in Spring 2007, Ding led another confrontation with the factory management. After realizing that the factory's method of calculating the rate of overtime payment did not conform to the municipal government's regulation and, as a result, the factory had paid the workers 3.70 yuan less per hour for overtime work, the workers held a meeting at Ding's suggestion and decided to request an adjustment of the overtime rate to the level required by the government. In response, the factory first rejected the request, but then, under the pressure from the trade union of the township government, the manager of the factory agreed to correct the method of overtime payment calculation. To their disappointment, however, the workers soon found that the manager increased their dormitory fee from 50 yuan to 100 yuan per month, canceled the 4-yuan stipend for the second work shift, and reduced the 6-yuan stipend for the third shift to 3 yuan. The cafeteria also canceled the daily free supply of fruits and a bag of instant noodles per worker for weekend overtime work. Their actual income thus was less than before the adjustment. This put Ding and his co-workers in an awkward situation, because all these benefits had resulted from the workers' repeated bargaining with the management over the years rather than based on any government regulations; there was no legal ground for them to demand the recovery of these benefits. To fight back, however, Ding convened another meeting of workers, where more than 80 percent of them voted for the decision to get back what the factory had owed them in the previous years because of the incorrect calculation of overtime pay. With the help of the Legal Support Center under the district-level trade union as well as the district's Labor and Social Security Bureau, the workers eventually received compensation from the factory for underpaid overtime work.

As it turned out, the actions by the employees of the SNS company foreshadowed the arrival of a new wave of worker activism in twenty-first century China, which culminated in the strike of 2,000 workers from a factory of the Honda Company in Shishan township of Hainan district of Foshan, Guangdong province. Lasting from May 17 to June 4, 2010, this strike ended in the factory's agreement to increase workers' monthly wages by 33 percent. Worker disgruntlement in the 2000s and 2010s, as these instances suggest, showed several commonalities. First, most of the participants belonged to the new generation of migrant workers, who were brought together by social media via the internet. Therefore, most of the collective actions by these workers took the form of "cellular activism" (Lee 2007a, 5–30). Second, what triggered their collective actions was typically the workers' intolerance of low wages that barely allowed them to make ends meet. In other words, workers' requests remained largely about their economic interest, unlike state-firm workers, whose appeals centered on their rights (Chan and Ngai 2009; Elfstrom and Kuruvilla 2014). In the case of the Honda factory, most workers received the level-one wage of 1,510 yuan per month; after deducting insurance and paying rent, meals, utilities, and groceries, an average worker could only save about 450 yuan. Demanding an increase of wages or proper compensation of overtime pay thus was common to all these protests (Feng Chen 2010).

Third and most important, instead of rioting on the street, blocking factory entrances, damaging the machines, beating up the management personnel, or other forms of violence, the workers turned out to be very tactical by limiting their actions to those largely within the scope allowed by laws and regulations and by taking advantage of existing government institutions. To make their actions organized and legal, the workers frequently resorted to state laws, primarily the Labor Law and the Labor Contract Law (Gallagher 2005, 113; Gallagher 2017, 131–145). Some of them established their own labor union by first seeking guidance and assistance from the trade union at the township or district level; where a trade union was already established in the factory but controlled by the employer, they transformed it into a more autonomous organization with the trade union leaders directly elected by themselves, and the union leaders thus produced turned out to be capable of representing the workers and truly engaging in "collective bargaining" (Quan 2016). Instead of an open and organized strike, which remained illegal and banned by the government, the workers turned to the informal means of stoppage or slacking in production that were acknowledged, if not allowed, by the Law of Trade Union. In the absence of an industry-wide trade union to back them and with little resources at their disposal, worker activists and the grassroots labor unions they led also sought help from the trade union and relevant government agencies at higher levels and even experts or lawyers who specialized in labor relations and social security; this turned out to be critical in making the workers' protests successful, as seen in the above cases, although high-level trade union cadres tended to act as intermediaries between the protesters and factory management, hence the so-called "bureaucratic collective bargaining" in which workers played little part (Chan 2013; Chan and Hui 2013; Estlund 2017, 135–137). Obviously, despite the surging of strikes and protests after 2000, worker activism remained in a rudimentary stage. The workers had yet to organize themselves into a unified group, cultivate a class consciousness of their own, or develop their subjectivity to a level that would enable them to fully represent themselves (Lee 2016).

All in all, the decades of enterprise reforms after 1979 resulted in not only a sweeping transformation of most state firms into private or shareholding companies but also a fundamental change in workers' status, from the "masters" of their factory who were entitled to a full range of rights and privileges to nothing more than hired laborers. Along with the demise of the work unit as a community of the privileged workers was the loss of the dual equilibrium in labor relations and shop floor politics that had functioned to constrain the workers as well as the cadres. Equally noticeable was the deterioration of the traditional institutions of factory governance, chiefly the SWC and the trade union. Workers who were disadvantaged and marginalized in enterprise reforms could no longer count on those means to address their grievances over working and living conditions as they had done in the Maoist past. There were indeed instances in which the disgruntled workers turned the SWC into an effective weapon for defending their rights and interests in the privatization of state firms, but this was the first and also the last time when the workers could exercise their power as the true masters of their factory before it was finally privatized.

After privatization, workers in China enjoyed economic freedom that they never had before. They were free to change their jobs and shop around for the best price for their labor, and many indeed succeeded, finding a job of their own choice and earning much more than before. But they could no longer treat the workplace as their *danwei*, develop a strong sense of identity with it, or cultivate a social bond with their co-workers. Nor did they have any discursive or institutional leverage to bargain with the owners or supervisors of the workplace; their relationship with the latter was simplified into that between the boss and hired laborers. The dual equilibrium that had been intrinsic to the work unit of the Maoist era never reemerged. For the new generation of industrial workers who just left their villages, owned nothing else but their labor, and jumped frequently from factory to factory, what mattered was not the freedom to sell their labor, but being treated fairly and equally in the workplace. Despite the state's recent legislation on workers' minimum wages, safety protection, fringe benefits, and residential rights in the cities, the workers' quest for full citizenship at the workplace depends ultimately on their collective endeavor to organize and express themselves legally and independently.

CONCLUSION

WORKERS' MASTERHOOD AND SUBSTANTIVE GOVERNANCE

To make sense of factory politics in Maoist China, this study uses the term "substantive governance" to distinguish the reality of worker participation in factory management from the Maoist state's rhetoric about the political rights of Chinese workers. By the Communist Party's ideology and the constitution of the PRC, the industrial workers in post-1949 China were the leading class of the socialist society. The party's propaganda further portrayed the workers as the masters of state-owned factories who had the inalienable rights to participate in their firm's decision-making process, elect factory leaders, and supervise management activities; these "democratic management" practices were further believed to be part of the very foundation on which "socialist democracy" was to be established in China. In the same vein, as the masters of their enterprises, workers were expected to "treat the factory as home," take good care of it, and work hard; moral and political awards alone should be enough incentive.

In at least three aspects, this study reveals the realities of the labor force in the socialist factories that contradict the state's representation of it. First, not all workers were equal and could be called the masters of their factories. There was a striking differentiation and subsequent inequality between workers of different statuses and employment terms throughout the Maoist era. Only the formal workers of permanent employment in a state firm were entitled to a full package of welfare benefits and full membership in the mass organizations for participation in factory governance, and they therefore could call themselves the masters of the factory. Excluded from their rank were the informal workers of rural residential status who worked for a short term, were paid much less than formal workers, and were denied eligibility for fringe benefits; and at the bottom were the stigmatized individuals known as members of the Five Categories, who served as political targets in the recurrent campaigns. Second, even the masters, or the formal workers of a state firm, were excluded from the actual process of factory management despite their membership in the SWC, the trade union, and other grassroots organizations. Key decisions regarding a factory's production and personnel were always made by government authorities above the factory under the highly centralized system of economic planning; ordinary workers had little chance of getting involved in enterprise management. Third, there was indeed a brief moment in the history of Maoist China when the most disgruntled and ambitious workers did get a chance to seize power from factory management, as seen during the initial phase of the Cultural Revolution, when their rebellion caused the paralysis of the existing factory institutions. But their "masterhood" turned out to be fragile and short-lived; they were quickly marginalized in the reestablished factory leadership in the early 1970s and then completely excluded from it when the Cultural Revolution ended in 1976.

These facts, however, should not lead to the conclusion that the Maoist state's rhetoric naming industrial workers the masters of the factory was empty and that the institutions for worker participation in factory governance failed to work at all. To properly understand the purpose and functionality of these institutions and the state's representation of them, this study has adopted a substantive approach. Instead of a formalist perspective that judges the functionality of factory institutions by asking whether these institutions succeeded or failed in serving their official purposes, this study asks how they functioned to meet their real-world objectives. It is from this perspective that I use the term "substantive governance" to distinguish the actual purposes of factory institutions from their official descriptions.

This perspective allows us to view factory institutions differently from how they would appear in the formalist perspective. For instance, the various means of identity building, such as classification of family backgrounds, application for party membership, political study sessions, and the awarding of honors and titles, while ostensibly serving the purpose of promoting the workers' correct consciousness and cultivating their socialist morality, actually functioned as nothing more than tools to discipline the labor force. Not surprisingly, while these means failed by and large to indoctrinate the workers with socialist moral codes, they nevertheless functioned effectively to prevent workers from overtly breaching the rules and regulations of their work units. Likewise, the organizations and practices of participation in factory governance, chiefly the SWC and the trade union, though officially designated as channels for workers to exercise their rights and as tools to promote democracy at the grassroots level, in reality functioned as venues for workers to express their day-to-day concerns and grievances about production and family life. Thus, while these institutions failed to include workers in the factory's decision-making processes, they did turn out to be more or less effective in accommodating the workers' needs in the workplace and beyond. The gap between the de facto objectives and the actual performance of these institutions, therefore, was much narrower than their official representation would suggest.

It is important to note, however, that despite the state's claim that industrial workers were the masters of state firms, their participation in factory governance was limited as long as these factories were subject to the state's centralized planning. Under the socialist system of command economy, it was up to government authorities at the central or provincial level to make decisions about production and employment for every factory. The tasks left for the leaders of a factory or a workshop within it thus were limited to the mundane routines of how to discipline the labor force and ensure the timely and complete fulfillment of production orders imposed from above. It was in these regards that the workers' subjectivity mattered, for their performance directly determined whether those orders could be filled. While factory leaders used a set of political tools to regulate the workers, the latter also had various means, formal or informal, to express their concerns and grievances. The workers' status as the masters in the workplace was real in this regard: not only because they were entitled to permanent employment, a fixed wage rate, and a full package of welfare benefits, over which the factory cadres had little control, but also because of their ability to articulate their discontent over living and working conditions, and to have their requests often heard and properly accommodated.

In the final analysis, the Maoist approach to factory governance was substantive in essence. Behind the state's prioritizing of identity building and moral cultivation was the real purpose of turning the workers into a well-disciplined labor force; and behind the rhetoric of promoting grassroots democracy and honoring industrial workers as the masters of the factory was the real purpose of keeping the labor force content by addressing issues concerning their well-being and subsistence but nothing else. Compared to the use of coercion or material incentives, this approach was cost-effective. Instead of disciplining the workers with the use of terror, punishment, or close surveillance, as the totalitarian model would assume, or with the use of material stimuli as seen in a free market economy, the Maoist factories controlled their workers with a rather sophisticated set of tools that minimized factory spending yet turned out to be no less effective.

THE DUAL EQUILIBRIUM IN THE SOCIALIST WORKPLACE

This study further reveals the existence of a dual equilibrium in labor relations and power politics in state firms. To be sure, in their everyday production activities, few workers lived up to the image of the masters of the factory so as to treat the factory as their home, take good care of its property, and work diligently, as the state's propaganda advocated. Nor is it true, however, that the workers totally lacked a sense of responsibility in production and that shirking was everywhere, thus making production inefficient, as the propaganda of the post-Mao leadership would make people believe in order to justify its policies of enterprise reform in the late 1970s and the 1980s. In reality, workers' daily performance on the shop floor depended on how the formal institutions in labor management interacted with the informal institutions to motivate as well as constrain them both as individuals and as a group. On the surface of it, there seemed to be no reason for them to work hard when labor reward was disconnected from labor input for most of the Maoist era: Wage levels were fixed and unchanging for years, and a bonus, if any, was paid to everyone at the same rate as a temporary augment to the fixed wage. Nevertheless, overt shirking and negligence were indeed rare among the workers, as our informants have widely observed. After all, the workers of a state firm were subject to the constraints of a full set of formal institutions encompassing workplace disciplines and regulations, cadres' supervision and quality-control measures, as well as the incentives of political honors and promotions. Equally important was the functioning of various informal factors, such as peer pressure that worked against excessive shirking as well as working exceedingly hard, the workers' identity with the workplace and necessary level of commitment to their duties, and their pride or sense of self-satisfaction over each job they completed (which was especially true for senior workers, whose experience and reputation won them respect from their peers).

Therefore, under normal circumstances when both the formal and informal factors were at work, neither outright shirking nor full dedication to production was a wise choice for most ordinary workers. What prevailed among them was instead a group norm by which they performed to a level in between the two extremes. In other words, while they did not have to work extra hours voluntarily or do a superior job if they were not politically motivated, they did need to complete their shift on schedule and make sure that the quantity and quality of their work met the minimum level of requirements, hence the rise of a workplace equilibrium. This equilibrium in turn explained in large measure the necessary level of efficiency in state firms that made the steady growth of China's industrial output throughout the Maoist era possible.

Our study also sheds light on an equilibrium in power relations between factory cadres and ordinary workers. It was true that maintaining a good relationship with the cadres was critical for workers seeking party membership or promotion from the rank and file. The few who were politically motivated were likely to develop a certain degree of personal dependence on the abusive cadres, and the patron-client network did exist to some extent between them. But this should not lead us to assume that the clientelist ties were so pervasive on the shop floor as to cause the splitting of workers into two mutually antagonistic groups of clients, who monopolized the channels of upward mobility, and the non-clients, who were excluded from such opportunities. There were two basic reasons why the patron-client network was not as pervasive as previously assumed. First, the cadres' abuse of power in determining workers' eligibility for a wage upgrade, job assignment, or distribution of bonuses, housing, or other material goods was limited and had to be disguised in a justifiable manner due to close monitoring by the public and strict enforcement of clear-cut policies or regulations at the national or local level; overt discrimination or favoritism would immediately result in an open challenge, a written petition, or a visit to superior government authorities, as this study has shown. Second and more important, because all formal state-firm workers were guaranteed a permanent job, a fixed wage commensurate with their seniority in employment, and a full package of benefits, no factory leader could deprive them of these rights without the approval of government authorities above the factory workers. Therefore, most workers found it unnecessary to cultivate a particular personal tie with those above them, nor would they deem it a wise choice to openly confront the cadres unless the latter seriously hurt them. When it came to nominating a worker for political honors, cadres usually based their nomination on the nominee's performance in production and popularity among their peers. The cadres' discretion in finalizing the nominees mattered, but their decision had to be based on a careful balance between their personal preferences and workers' consensus, without compromising their own creditability and reputation.

Two more reasons account for the advantages on the workers' side in their everyday interactions with the cadres. First, by the Maoist ideology, as the leading class with correct political consciousness, industrial workers in socialist China had the innate right to supervise and criticize the corruptible cadres; the latter, for their part, were disadvantaged in the Maoist discourse of class struggle and always served as the targets of recurrent political campaigns from the 1950s through the 1970s. This discursive disparity in the workers' favor explained in large measure their readiness to speak out and combat the cadres when they suffered abuses by the latter. Second, the cadres of different levels depended on workers' collaboration to ensure the timely and full completion of production tasks. Maintaining a good relationship with the labor force and keeping the latter happy were key to achieving the necessary level of productivity and thus securing cadres' own positions. Therefore, instead of workers' one-sided dependence on the presumably all-powerful cadres, what prevailed on the shop floor was an equilibrium in power relations. Empowered by a set of formal factory systems that safeguarded their livelihood and by the political discourse that prioritized their rights, the workers as an entity were no less powerful than the cadres in the workplace.

Needless to say, the precondition for the prevalence of the dual equilibrium was the existence and functioning of a set of institutional components that worked together to turn the work unit or *danwei*—a factory or a workshop within it—into a relatively isolated, exclusive space in which the workers engaged in everyday production and power relations. Central to these components were the state's employment policy that guaranteed all formal workers a permanent job and full coverage of welfare benefits; their privileged status in relation to other groups in society and their discursive advantage as the leading class, hence their supervisory power over factory cadres; the use of political honors instead of material rewards to incentivize workers in production and participation in factory governance; and the absence of opportunities for workers to find a job or earn extra income outside their work unit. Together, these institutions served as the key pillars bolstering the *danwei* as not only a workplace but also a closed community with which the workers strongly identified. They cultivated the collective consciousness of being the masters of the workplace with the unalienable rights to fight against cadre abuse, yet at the same time they came under the tight control of the state, lacking any leverage to change their jobs or bargain for a raise; they were subject to the everyday constraints of both the formal regulations of the factory and the informal norms among the workers themselves. It is in this sense that the factory workers in Maoist China are characterized as "the master in bondage" in this study.

ENTERPRISE REFORM AND IDENTITY REBUILDING

This study's findings offer a new vantage point from which to consider the dynamics of industrial enterprise reforms in post-Mao China. Unlike agricultural reforms that started in 1979 and proceeded quickly, finishing by 1981 when the household responsibility system replaced the collective system and remained the dominant way of farming in the following decades, industrial reforms lasted much longer, from the 1980s to the 2000s. Contrary to the post-Mao neoliberal discourse that blamed the Maoist institutions of labor management for inefficiency in production, the preceding chapters have shown that inefficiency was not so much a problem for most enterprises in the Maoist era as has been widely assumed; a significant decline in labor productivity took place not before the reform but under the responsibility system from the mid-1980s to the mid-1990s. The major driving force behind industrial reforms in the post-Mao era was the worsening fiscal situation of the central government due to its rapidly increased spending in the late 1970s and early 1980s. During this time, the new leadership after Mao was eager to win popular support and establish its legitimacy by increasing the state procurement prices of agricultural products, raising the wage levels for all employees of urban residency, and investing massively in new industrial projects. To offset its rapidly growing deficit, the state had to find a new way to generate more income from its factories that had traditionally contributed half of its revenue, hence the implementation of various reform measures to boost production and revenue. As it turned out, throughout the 1980s and 1990s fiscal difficulties remained the most important driver behind the state's introduction of reform measures, one after another, for the purpose of satisfying its financial needs, as the state's spending always outweighed its revenue.

Equally important to understanding the logic of industrial reforms, however, is the unique nature of the dual equilibrium that sustained the productivity of state firms in Maoist China. That equilibrium was fragile to the extent that its existence hinged on the support of a set of institutional pillars that were interlinked and interdependent to turn every factory into a sealed "ecosystem." A very essential precondition for this equilibrium was the complete insulation and isolation of the ecosystem; the absence of any one of these pillars would leave the ecosystem open to the invasion of elements alien to it and detrimental to its viability, hence damaging the other pillars one after another, which in turn forced the state to take further measures to correct the problems arising during, rather than before, the reforms. The end result of these chain reactions was the eventual collapse of the entire ecosystem and the destruction of the dual equilibrium, a consequence that defied the reformers' original planning and intention; the entire process of economic reform itself was indeed like navigating uncharted waters or, in the words of Deng Xiaoping, "crossing the river by groping for stepping stones" (*mozhe shitou guohe*), ending in the privatization of most state-owned enterprises—a result that was far beyond the reformers' imagination at the beginning.

Workers' identity, values, and behavior changed accordingly as the reforms unfolded through different phases. As the first step, the devolution of power from the central government to individual enterprises in the last years of the 1970s and the first half of the 1980s allowed factory leaders to link production with remuneration for workers, thus causing a change to work norms from the one centering on group solidarity, peer pressure, and collective sanctioning to the one emphasizing the use of material incentives and competition among group members, thus weakening the validity of political pressure and rewards that had been key to disciplining the workers before. The implementation of the contracted management responsibility system from the mid-1980s to the mid-1990s, as the second step of enterprise reforms, further reversed power relations between cadres and workers. Instead of a symmetric relationship in which the workers' discursive and institutional leverages effectively counterbalanced the administrative power of the cadres, the latter established their firm dominance over the former under the contract system that allowed them greater autonomy than before in both employment and labor remuneration; the rigid hierarchy in power and stark disparity in income between cades and workers greatly undermined workers' identity with the enterprise. Equally damaging to workers' identity with, and willingness to work hard for, the enterprise was the growth of opportunities for people to earn more income outside the factory during this phase; the traditional pride workers felt about belonging to a state firm yielded to a feeling of being marginalized.

The final blow to workers' traditional identity was of course the third step of enterprise reform, namely the transformation of all state firms into shareholding or private companies in the second half of the 1990s and the early 2000s. The legal and ideological grounds for workers to consider themselves as "masters" of their factories were completely lost; they were once again proletarianized, becoming the "masters of their own labor" only. The absence or malfunctioning of the SWC and the trade union made them even more vulnerable and helpless than before. The trauma was particularly acute for middle-aged workers who had the burden of supporting their families but experienced a sudden change to their jobs, making them less secure and less paid than before; many even suffered a layoff without reasonable compensation, hence the eruption of protests in large numbers throughout the country in the 1990s and 2000s. Interestingly, it was during the last days of the state-owned enterprises that the SWC and the trade union in them functioned, for the first and last time, as the true weapons for the workers involved to exercise their rights as the masters of their factories before the latter were privatized. For most state-firm workers, economic reforms were at once a process of liberalization that opened them to more opportunities and freedom than before and an experience of deprivation, or "disenfranchisement" (Andreas 2019), in which they lost forever the rights and privileges that had made them identify so closely with their workplaces for decades under Maoism.

CHINESE WORKERS AT THE INTERSECTION

Chinese industrial workers, as well as the institutional circumstances in which they are situated, have experienced huge changes in recent decades. As the main labor force in the traditional sectors of manufacturing, construction, transportation, and services, their rank has transitioned from primarily the privileged workers of state firms with an urban residential status to predominantly migrant workers hired mostly by private firms. The migrant workers have further transitioned from the first generation of the 1980s and the 1990s, who endured disadvantages and discriminations in every aspect of work and life, to the second generation of the 2000s and 2010s, whose social, educational, and economic gaps with workers of urban backgrounds have been quickly narrowing. As a result of migrant workers' persistent protests against maltreatment and marginalization in and outside the workplace, the state kept adjusting its policies in a wide array of areas, ranging from their residential registration and settlement in the cities and legal protection of their personal safety and rights in the workplace to their entitlement to social security, health insurance, and children's education. Therefore, the strong sense of marginalization and helplessness that had prevailed among the migrant workers in the early years of the reform era has quickly yielded to their relentless pursuit of integration into the city in which they and their family members have lived.

The Maoist heritages of labor politics could be both an impediment to and a facilitator in the new-generation workers' quest for full citizenship in the places where they work and live. Gone is the notion of workers as the masters of their factory, which has completely lost its appeal to most of the workers of the twenty-first century who are nothing more than the employees of private firms. Their lack of the right to strike under the existing laws and the inability of enterprise-level trade unions to represent them made defending their rights and interests on a legal ground and in an open, organized manner particularly difficult. Nevertheless, the strong sense of social equity and justice that they inherited from the Maoist past and the education that they universally received for years have made them readily receptive to the new notions about individual rights in the workplace, and they are willing to fight for these rights. The multilayered trade-union organization and its corresponding law, which have their origins in the Maoist era and have survived into the twenty-first century, have played multifaceted and complex roles in this regard. Where the labor union continued to exist and came into being from the top down (i.e., created and controlled by the factory management itself), workers rarely turned to it for assistance, since the enterprise-level labor union sided more often with the management than with the workers. Unlike the state firms of the Maoist era, where workers' well-being was inextricably linked with their work unit and where the workers did count on the labor union for their needs in production and everyday life, the institutional transformation since the mid-1990s has completely separated the interests of workers from those of their employers. The enterprise-level labor union controlled by the private firm thus necessarily represented the interests of factory owners and managers rather than that of workers. So too is the labor union authority at the level immediately above the enterprise, which in most cases means the township-level trade union organization; as part of the township government, its primary goal is to ensure that the enterprises under it operate normally and thus generate the tax revenue it desperately needs. Instead of supporting the workers, the township-level trade union tends to collude with private business managers to deal with the disgruntled workers. This contrasts sharply with the trade union at higher (district, municipal, or provincial) levels. As we have seen in the cases cited in the last chapter as well as in the cases from the Maoist era in earlier chapters, the higher the level of the trade union, the more tenuous the link between its interests and those of the enterprises involved, and the more likely it acted independently and neutrally, speaking for workers rather than the enterprise. It is also under the auspices of the higher-level trade unions that the workers of private firms establish their own labor unions or reorganize the existing labor union to make it autonomous and representative of their own interests.

To sum up, in contrast with the workers of state firms during the Maoist era who were entitled to a full range of rights and privileges as the masters of their factories at the ideological level yet subject to strict control by the state and deprived of any opportunities outside their work unit, labor relations in the restructured enterprises in twenty-first-century China have been far from achieving a new equilibrium despite decades of economic reforms that have destroyed the old one. The new generation of workers has obtained the freedom to control their own labor force but at the cost of the security of employment and livelihood. Until they can protect themselves against abuses in the workplace, the new generation of industrial workers cannot be the true masters of their own labor. Their quest for citizenship with full rights as employees in the factory and as legal residents in the city awaits their further actions to speak for themselves, the full functioning of organizations that truly represent them, and the further enactment and implementation of a wide spectrum of laws and regulations in their interests.

Glossary

aichang rujia	爱厂如家
baiping	摆平
baiwan xiongshi	百万雄师
ban song ban mai	半送半卖
baocaitou	包菜头
bao'en	报恩
baohuangpai	保皇派
baoliu gongzi	保留工资
baoliu renyuan	保留人员
bei guyong	被雇佣
beiyonggong	备用工
bi	比
bianda kuainiu	鞭打快牛
biaozhunzhong	标准钟
bijiao gongkai touming	比较公开透明
bijiaogongzheng, meiyou baobiwubi de xingwei	比较公正，没有包庇舞弊的行为
bijiao pingdeng	比较平等
bu fuqi, kanbuqi	不服气、看不起
bu shulian	不熟练

buduishi guanli	部队式管理
bufu	不服
buheli yaoqiu	不合理要求
buji baochou	不计报酬
changzhang	厂长
chejian zhuren	车间主任
chengbao jingying zerenzhi	承包经营责任制
chengfen	成分
chengshi pinmin	城市贫民
chikui	吃亏
chongfeng zai qianmian	冲锋在前
chushen	出身
chushen buhao	出身不好
dage baobuping	打个抱不平
dagongwusi	大公无私
dajiejie	大姐姐
dajiti	大集体
danchun	单纯
dangjia zuozhu	当家作主
dangyuan	党员
danwei	单位
datishang kan de guoqu	大体上看得过去
dazaqiang	打砸抢
dazibao	大字报
difang guoying	地方国营
dingban	顶班
dou hen fuqi	都很服气
dou hen peifu tamen	都很佩服他们
duochi duozhan	多吃多占
duoquan	夺权
doushi bi chulai de	都是比出来的
doushi futie de	都是服帖的
doushi gan chulai de, zhen gan	都是干出来的，真干
doushi naxie women kanbuqi de ren	都是那些我们看不起的人
dousi pixiu	斗私批修

erdeng gongren	二等工人
fan cuowu	犯错误
fan qizha jianbing, jiuchang hu jiayuan	反欺诈兼并，救厂护家园
fangeming	反革命
fanshen	翻身
fanshen zuo zhuren	翻身做主人
feichang shao	非常少
feipin dawang	废品大王
fuhua duoluo	腐化堕落
fuying bu fukui	负赢不负亏
gaige buzou huitou lu	改革不走回头路
gaizhi	改制
gan yazi guohe	赶鸭子过河
ganbu shi sazi	干部是傻子
ganhuo pinming	干活拼命
ganhuo zhengqian	干活挣钱
gan sihuo	干私活
ganshuo gangan	能说敢干
gaoren yideng	高人一等
gei duoshao qian, gan duoshao huo	给多少钱，干多少活
geming lieshi	革命烈士
geming weiyuanhui	革命委员会
gen xianzai wanquan bu yiyang	跟现在完全不一样
genban	跟班
genben bu xialai	根本不下来
geren zongjie	个人总结
gerenzhuyi	个人主义
getihu	个体户
gongdaihui	工代会
gongduanzhang	工段长
gonghui	工会
gongkai touming	公开透明
gongling	工龄
gongren	公认
gongsi heying	公私合营

gongxuandui	工宣队
gongzuo hao, renyuan hao	工作好、人缘好
gongzuo jiji, qunzhong jichu hao	工作积极，群众基础好
gongzuo yao na de qilai	工作要拿得起来
guanliaozhuyi	官僚主义
guanxi	关系
guanxi bijiao yiban	关系比较一般
guanxi feichang rongqia	关系非常融洽
guanxi manhao	关系蛮好
hai bucuo	还不错
haipa qunzhong	害怕群众
haodehen	好得很
haopai	好派
he gongren bu daga	和工人不搭嘎
hen minzhu	很民主
hen tiliang	很体谅
hen touming, meiyou baobi wubi de kongjian	很透明，没有包庇舞弊的空间
henshao	很少
hetonggong	合同工
hong	红
huaifenzi	坏分子
huairen huaishi	坏人坏事
huixiang zhinong	回乡支农
huo yao zuo wan	活要做完
ji gebie	极个别
ji wu neizhai, you wu waizhai	既无内债，又无外债
jia	家
jiayuan	家园
jiaban	加班
jian jian you dafu, tiao tiao you jiaodai	件件有答复，条条有交代
jiang suihe	讲随和
jianwu	简屋
jiating chushen	家庭出身
jiazhangzhi	家长制

jibenshang meiyou shenme kaihoumen	基本上没有什么开后门
jie'an lü	结案率
jiefang yiqian guolai de ren	解放以前过来的人
jigebie	极个别
jijifenzi	积极分子
jijixing gao	积极性高
jingda xisuan	精打细算
jingjian xiafang	精简下放
jingjizhuyi	经济主义
jingyingquan	经营权
jingzheng bugongping	竞争不公平
jiti suoyou	集体所有
jiujiliang	救济粮
jiu xiang ganhuo chifan	就想干活吃饭
junguan	军管
kaishi renqian	开始认钱
kao gongren xuan chulai de	靠工人选出来的
kao guanxi shangqu de	靠关系上去的
kaochaqi	考察期
ken chiku, jishuhao, biaoxianhao	肯吃苦、技术好、表现好
kuanggong	旷工
kunnan zhigong	困难职工
kunnanhu	困难户
kuoda minzhu	扩大民主
la guanxi zou houmen	拉关系走后门
laobaixing dangyuan	老百姓党员
laoban	老板
laodong hetong zhi	劳动合同制
laodong mofan	劳动模范
laojiao	劳教
laosanhui	老三会
laoxiang	老乡
lengyanlengyu	冷言冷语
liang	两
liangcan yigai sanjiehe	两参一改三结合

liangdian yixian	两点一线
ligaishui	利改税
lilun	理论
lingdao	领导
lingdao jieji	领导阶级
lingdao kanzhong ni	领导看重你
lingshigong	临时工
lishi	历史
loushang louxia, diandeng dianhua	楼上楼下，电灯电话
luohou	落后
luohou fenzi	落后分子
maiduan gongling	买断工龄
Mao Zedong sixiang	毛泽东思想
maomaoyu dajiasa	毛毛雨大家洒
meishi	没事
meiyou baobi xingwei	没有包庇行为
mingling	命令
ming mai shi song	名卖实送
minzhu banchang	民主办厂
minzhu gaige	民主改革
minzhu guanli	民主管理
minzhu quanli	民主权利
mozhe shitou guohe	摸着石头过河
Nanjing shi zonggonghui	南京市总工会
nannu guanxi	男女关系
nashi buxuyao taohao lingdao	那时不需要讨好领导
neng zai taimian shang jiajian guang	能在台面上见见光
nengshou	能手
niugui sheshen	牛鬼蛇神
nongmingong	农民工
pai qunzhong	怕群众
paimapi	拍马屁
paimapi shangqu de	拍马屁上去的
penghu	棚户
pengtouhui	碰头会

pengyouquan	朋友圈
ping	评
pingdeng	平等
pingqi pingzuo	平起平坐
pinmin	贫民
pinxia zhongnong	贫下中农
pipai	屁派
pohuai jungong shengchan	破坏军工生产
qianrang	谦让
qinjian banchang	勤俭办厂
qinzagong	勤杂工
qishang baxia jiuzouguang	七上八下九走光
qu nao qu chao	去闹去吵
Quanguo hongse laodongzhe zaofan zongtuan	全国红色劳动者造反总团
Quanhongzong	全红总
quanmian zhengdun	全面整顿
quanmin suoyou	全民所有
queshi you zhen benshi, queshi gande bucuo	确实有真本事，确实干得不错
qungongzu	群工组
qunzhong	群众
qunzhong guanxi	群众关系
qunzhong guanxi hao	群众关系好
qunzhong yaoyou yijian	群众要有意见
qunzhong yijian da	群众意见大
renjia ye hui kan bu xia qu de	人家也会看不下去的
renmin laixin	人民来信
renmin laixin laifang	人民来信来访
renqi tunsheng	忍气吞声
renren pingdeng	人人平等
rongrendu	容忍度
shangliang	商量
shehui fengqi bijiao hao	社会风气比较好
shiji biaoxian	实际表现

sanjiehe	三结合
sanshang sanxia	三上三下
santing	三停
shangban bu zuoshi	上班不做事
shangbu fengding, xiabu baodi	上不封顶，下不保底
Shanghai shi hongse gongren geming zaofan zongsilingbu	上海市红色工人革命造反总司令部
shanggai kao jingzheng, shouru kao gongxian	上岗靠竞争，收入靠贡献
shangshan xiaxiang	上山下乡
shaobufen	少部分
shaoshu	少数
shehuizhuyi xinren	社会主义新人
shejiao gongzuodui	社教工作队
shengchan xiaozu	生产小组
shengguan bu facai, liangshi jian xialai	升官不发财，粮食减下来
shenxianshizu	身先士卒
shiqu minxin	失去民心事事有人管
shishi you ren guan, renren you shi guan	事事有人管，人人有事管
shiyou dahuizhan	石油大会战
shizai de haochu	实在的好处
shoujiao man	手脚慢
shuangbao yigua	双保一挂
si tao banzi	四套班子
silei fenzi	四类分子
sirenbang	四人帮
sixiang biaoxian	思想表现
sixiang huibao	思想汇报
sizuo	死做
suku	诉苦
sungong feisi	损公肥私
suo zhe tou zuo	缩着头做
suoyouquan	所有权
sushi	素质
tanwu daoqi	贪污盗窃

tiantian zhua sixiang	天天抓思想
tiao chu nongmen	跳出农门
tiaopi daodan	调皮捣蛋
tiefanwan	铁饭碗
tinghua	听话
tingtian youming	听天由命
tongxiang	同乡
toumingde	透明的
tuochan ganbu	脱产干部
wanyuanhu	万元户
weifa luanji	违法乱纪
wudu	五毒
wufan	五反
wuhao banzu	五好班组
wuhao gongren	五好工人
wulei fenzi	五类分子
wuzhi ciji	物质刺激
xiahai	下海
xiandai qiye zhidu	现代企业制度
xiangdui boduo gan	相对剥夺感
xianjin geren	先进个人
xianjin fenzi	先进分子
xianjin shengchanzhe	先进生产者
xianxing	现行
xiaoguo, xiaozao, xiaolequ, xiaofu xiaoqi xiaobaxi	小锅小灶小乐趣，小夫小妻小把戏
xiaojiti	小集体
xiaoshang xiaofan	小商小贩
xiaotou xiaomo	小偷小摸
xiaoyaopai	逍遥派
xinfu koufu	心服口服
xinsanhui	新三会
xinsheng shiwu	新生事物
xuexi xianjin	学习先进
yao baiping renjia	要摆平人家

yao neng cheng de qilai de	要能撑得起来的
yao zhen de zhu xiamian de gongren	要镇得住下面的工人
yaoyou nadechu de shuju	要有拿得出的数据
yi cang wei jia	以厂为家
yilu pingdeng	一律平等
yin yang tou	阴阳头
yiqie xiang qian kan	一切向钱看
yiquanmousi	以权谋私
yitiaolong	一条龙
yiwu jiaban jiadian	义务加班加点
yizhangzhi	一长制
yongbuzhao taohao	用不着讨好
you jijixing	有积极性
you xia er shang de jiandu	由下而上的监督
youmin	游民
yu qunzhong da cheng yipian	与群众打成一片
zaofanpai	造反派
zengchan jieyue weiyuanhui	增产节约委员会
zhai zhuan gu	债转股
zhanfang	占房
zhengdang	整党
zhengzhi biaoxian	政治表现
zhengzhi dayu yiqie	政治压倒一切
zhibanzhang	值班长
zhigong daibiao dahui	职工代表大会
zhigong daibiao huiyi	职工代表会议
zhi zhuan bu hong	只专不红
zhibanzhang	值班长
zhishifenzi	知识分子
zhixinren	知心人
zhiyuan	职员
zhongdian peiyang	重点培养
zhongziban	忠字班
zhuada fangxia	抓大放小
zhua geming, cu shengchan	抓革命，促生产

zhuan	专
zhurenweng	主人翁
zibenjia	资本家
zichanjieji minzhupai	资产阶级民主派
zigan duoluo	自甘堕落
ziren daomei	自认倒霉
ziwo jiantao	自我检讨
zouzipai	走资派
zuikude	最苦的
zui mahu	最马虎
zuinenggan, zuichikui	最能干、最吃亏
zuochulai de laomo	做出来的劳模
zuobukuai, meibanfa	做不快，没办法
zuzhang	组长

List of Interviewees

No.	Name	Sex	Born	Work unit	Job	Since	Interview transcribed
B1	Yang	M	1942	Beijing Qingyun Aeronautical Instruments Factory	Warehouse director	1960	7/4/2012
B2	Cui Runxiang	M	1936	Shijiazhuang Chemical Fertilizer Plant	Instrument repair worker	1957	7/2012
B3	Meng	M	1936	Beijing Gear Factory; Beijing No. 2 Food Processing Factory	Worker	1961	7/12–14/2012
B4							
B5							
B6	Tan	M	1932	Dahua Electronic Co. (formerly Factory No. 768)	Staff member	1958	7/15/2012
B7	Guo	M	1942	Dahua Electronic Co. (formerly Factory No. 768)	Worker	1961	7/15/2012
B8	Han	M	1938	Dahua Electronic Co. (formerly Factory No. 768)	Staff member, vice factory head	1960	7/19–23/2012

272 LIST OF INTERVIEWEES

No.	Name	Sex	Born	Work unit	Job	Since	Interview transcribed
B9	Li	M	1944	Dahua Electronic Co. (formerly Factory No. 768)	Worker	1965	7/19/2012
B10	Anonymous	M	1949	Affiliated factory of Chinese Academy of Sciences	Worker	1963	7/25/2012
B11	Anonymous	F	1942	Taiyuan Steel and Iron Work	Technician	1963	7/25/2012
B12	Li	F	1956	Longhua County Garment Factory	Worker	1974	7/4/2012
B13	Sun	M	1942	Heshun County Chemical Fertilizer Plant	Worker	1958	2/9/2013
C1	Yang	M	1933	The Carrier Equipment Factory of Nanjing Telecommunication Bureau	Worker	1958	8/26/2013
C2	Cao	M	1939	Chongqing Changshou Chemical Plant; Nanjing Oil Refinery	Technician Engineer	1967 1984	8/25/2013
C3	Zhao	M	1935	Jiangnan Clock Factory	Worker	1956	9/1/2013
C4	Chen	F	1927	Nanjing Xiaguan Railway Station	Worker	1958	8/25/2013
C5	Yang Wanru	F	1933	Nanjing Precast Concrete Plant	Trade union staff	1956	9/1/2013
C6	Huang	F	1928	Jinzhou No. 6 Petroleum Plant; Nanjing Oil Refinery	Staff member	1954	8/31/2013

LIST OF INTERVIEWEES 273

No.	Name	Sex	Born	Work unit	Job	Since	Interview transcribed
C7	Qiu Baohua	M	1956	Chao County Agricultural Machinery Factory; Hongwei Machinery Factory	Worker Worker	1970 1973	9/1/2013
H1	Dai Zhenhua	M	1942	Huanggang Region Filature	Warehouse/ canteen manager	1966	2/11/2013
H2	Chen Yinzu	M	1947	No. 2 Automobile Work	Plumber	1971	12/8/2012
H3	Ding Shuhua	F	1941	Huanggang Region Filature	Worker	1960	2/11/2013
H4	Ni Juhua	F	1953	Huanggang Region Filature	Worker	1971	2/11/2013
H5	Zhou Meizhen	F	1936	Zhengzhou Cotton Mill; Bedding and Clothing Factory of Central China Military Zone	Worker	1956	2/15/2013
H6	Zhang Qishan	M	1942	Bedding and Clothing Factory of Central China Military Zone	Propaganda secretary	1963	2/15/2013
H7	Wang Zhiwan	M	1932	Bedding and Clothing Factory of Central China Military Zone	Worker/ workshop director	1950	2/15/2013
H8	Wu Binquan	M	1942	Huanggang Region Bedding Factory; Huanggang Region Filature	Worker/ workshop director	1967	2/11/2013
H9	Yan Shanfa	M	1948	Specialty Co. of No. 1 Metallurgical Ministry	Electrician	1965	2/1/2013

No.	Name	Sex	Born	Work unit	Job	Since	Interview transcribed
H10	Li Changjian	M	1952	General Machinery Factory of Wuhan Steel and Iron Work	Worker	1970	12/2012
H11	Le Shuiyuan	M	1951	Daye Shitouzui Mine	Miner	1971	12/22/2012
H12	Zhao Li	M	1951	General Machinery Factory of Wuhan Steel and Iron Work	Worker	1968	12/9/2012
H13	Zhou Dexian	M	1950	Daye Shitouzui Mine	Miner	1971	12/15/2012
H14	Chang Shouzhong	M	1933	Transportation Co. of Wuhan Steel and Iron Work	Worker	1956	1/10/2013
H15	Tian Chunsheng	M	1951	General Machinery Factory of Wuhan Steel and Iron Work	Worker/ safety inspector	1969	1/5/2013
H16	Hu Shixiang	M	1950	Daye Jinhu Steel and Iron Work	Miner/ engineer	1971	12/23/2012
H17	Hu Congsheng	M	1943	No. 6 Engineering Bureau of China Construction Corp.	Driver	1970	1/17/2013
H18	Wang Jianping	M	1950	No. 1 Co. of No. 1 Metallurgical Ministry	Worker	1971	1/12/2013
H19	Zeng Yueqing	F	1937	Xiangtan Electric Machinery Factory	Electrician	1958	2/15/2013
H20	Yang Zhixiong	M	1929	Electric Power Bureau of Dangyang City	Worker	1959	2/6/2013
H21	Xue Xiaokai	M	1934	Automobile Repair Factory of Renqiu City	Worker	1955	2/13/2013

LIST OF INTERVIEWEES   275

No.	Name	Sex	Born	Work unit	Job	Since	Interview transcribed
H22	Chen Minting	F	1937	Printing Factory of Renqiu City	Workshop director	1967	2/13/2013
H23	Zeng Fanqing	M	1931	Automobile Transportation Co. of Tianmen City	Manager	1948	12/2/2012
H24	Liu Mingsheng	M	1945	Food Management Office of Jiuzheng Township of Tianmen City	Office head	1962	12/2/2012
L1	Liu	M	1941	Nanjing Steel and Iron Work	Worker/technician	1965	11/2012
L2	Fan	M	1941	Nanjing Zhongxingyuan Silk Mill	Worker	1958	11/2012
L3	Sun	M	1958	Housing Management Bureau of Nanjing City	Worker	1975	11/2012
L4	An	M	1930	Shengli Oil Field; No. 2 Co. of Petroleum Industry Ministry	Doctor	1956	11/2012
L5	Fan	F	1948	Nanjing Telecommunication Equipment Factory	Staff member	1967	11/2012
L6	Song	F	1937	Nanjing Xinghuo Cotton Mill; Datong Bedding Factory	Worker/doctor	1956	10/2012
L7	Yao	M	1957	Nanjing Zhongshan Mine	Miner	1972	10/2012
L8	Yang	F	1938	Nanjing Steel and Iron Work; Nanjing Textile Co.	Worker	1958	10/2012
N1	Anonymous	F	?	Ningbo Hefeng Yarn Mill	Worker	1958	1/2013

LIST OF INTERVIEWEES

No.	Name	Sex	Born	Work unit	Job	Since	Interview transcribed
N2	Anonymous	M	1937	Shanghai Printer Factory; Zhenjiang Mine of Shanghai Metallurgical Bureau	Worker	1952	1/2013
N3	Anonymous	M	1935	Shanghai Medical Equipment Factory; Ningbo Port Machinery Factory	Welder	1953	1/2013
N4	Anonymous	M	?	Ningbo Port Machinery Factory	Worker	1958	1/2013
N5	Anonymous	M	1941	Ningbo Steel and Iron Factory; Ningbo Port Machinery Factory	Worker	1958	1/2013
N6	Anonymous	M	1930	Ningbo Renfeng Fabric Mill	Machine repairer	1950	1/2013
	Anonymous	F	1930	Ningbo Renfeng Fabric Mill	Weaver	1950	
N7	Anonymous	M	1953	Precast Concrete Plant of Guangzhou Lijiao Dockyard	Worker	1969	1/2013
N9	Anonymous	M	1928	Guangzhou Fountain Pen Factory	Manager; section leader	1954	1/2013
N10	Anonymous	M	?	Guangzhou Huaqiao Sugar Mill	Technician	1955	1/2013
S1	Shen Ning	M	1952	Shanghai Steel and Iron Work No. 1 Factory	Worker	1976	12/16/2012
S2	Wang Gang	M	1956	Shanghai Silicon Steel Factory	Worker/ group leader	1975	12/16/2012

No.	Name	Sex	Born	Work unit	Job	Since	Interview transcribed
S3	Jiang Jiaqiang	F	?	Jiefang Plastic Product Factory	Worker	1972	12/28/2012
S4	Chen Zhiping	M	1946	Shanghai Light Bulb Factory	Worker	1963	12/15/2012
S5	Zhang Yanmiao	M	1953	Xingan County Electronic Instrument Factory	Worker	1970	12/27/2012
S6	Sun Aiting	F	1955	Shanghai No. 1 Artistic Carving Factory	Carver	1973	12/27/2012
S7	Zhang Yiping	F	1955	Shanghai No. 17 Cotton Textile Factory	Worker/ group leader/ trade union chair	1971	12/27/2012
S8	Yang Xiaofeng	F	1943	Shanghai Yimin Food Factory	Worker/ group leader	1968	12/27/2012
S9	Zhong Yunping	F	1954	Shanghai Putuo District Labor Service Co.	Staff member	1972	12/15/2012
S10	Fang Hao; Zhang Aiyun	M F	1938 1931	Xi'an Instrument and Meter Factory	Staff member Worker	1959 1958	12/11/2012
S11	Luo Guiling	M	1936	Shanghai Compressor Factory	Worker/ workshop director	1956	12/22/2012
S12	Wang Jiabing	M	1942	Jiangsu Yizheng Steel and Iron Work	Worker/ factory director	1958	12/11/2012
S13	Gong Gendi	F	1953	Shanghai Huangpu District Fuel Co.	Worker	1979	12/27/2012
S14	Sun Guolong	M	1952	Huaibei Power Plant	Worker	1968	12/2012
S15	Wang Wenyun	M	1948	No. 1 Division of Shanghai Port Affairs Bureau	Driver	1965	12/10/2012

No.	Name	Sex	Born	Work unit	Job	Since	Interview transcribed
S16	Wang Chunsheng	M	1956	Shanghai Petrochemical General Plant	Worker/ group leader	1974	12/2012
S18	Ni Heqiao	M	1941	Shanghai Jiangning Machine Tool Factory	Worker	1966	12/10/2012
S19	Liu Zhongpei	F	1942	Shanghai Port Affairs Bureau	Loader driver	1976	12/12/2012
S20	Zhang Zhongbo	M	1935	Shanghai Petrochemical General Plant	Engineer	1952	12/10/2012
S21	Chen Jiexiang	M	1932	Shanghai Jiading Jingyi Repair Workshop	Vice director	1960	12/10/2012
W1	Xiong	M	1943	Hubei Gedian Chemical Plant	Worker	1970	9/2013
W2	Anonymous	F	1935	Wuhan Rubber Plant	Worker	1958	9/2013
W3	Feng	M	1940	Wuhan Pharmaceutical Factory	Worker	1958	9/2013
W4	Feng	M	1940	Wuhan Pharmaceutical Factory	Worker	1958	9/2013
	Yue	M	?	Wuhan Pharmaceutical Factory	Worker	?	
W5	Yue	M	1949	Wuhan Gongnong Garment Factory	Worker	1965	9/2013
W6	Yi	M	1943	Wuhan Light Industrial Machinery Factory	Worker	1972	9/2013
Y1	Zhu Delong	M	1948	Shandong Shengli Oil Field	Worker	1965	9/2013
Y2	Wang Lixin	M	1946	Shandong Shengli Oil Field	Worker	1966	9/2013

LIST OF INTERVIEWEES 279

No.	Name	Sex	Born	Work unit	Job	Since	Interview transcribed
Y3	Huang Zenggui	M	1947	Shandong Shengli Oil Field	Worker	1967	9/2013
Y4	Yan Longyou	M	1949	Liaohe Oil Field	Worker	1971	9/2013
Y5	Sun Jianguo	M	1940	Baotou City Cotton Textile Mill	Worker	1963	9/2013
Y6	Li Shengtang	M	1940	Hohhot Machine Tool Factory	Worker	1958	9/2013
Y7a	Zhou	F	1940	Jinchuan Trading Co.	Staff member	1960	9/2013
Y7b	Li	F	1943	Linyi Chemical Fertilizer Plant	Technician	1965	9/2013
Y7c	Wang Ting'ai	M	1944	Linyi Chemical Fertilizer Plant	Manager	1965	9/2013

Notes

INTRODUCTION

1. Throughout this book, the files from the Nanjing Municipal Archives are cited by their *quanzonghao* (sectional number), *muluhao* (catalogue serial number), and *anjuanhao* (file number).

2. See, for example, Meisner 1972; Lee 1973; Bettelheim 1974; Hoffmann 1974, 1977; Riskin 1975; Nee 1975; and Prybyla 1975, 1977.

3. See, for example, Taylor 1956; Lewis 1963; Barnett 1967; and Townsend 1967. It is worth noting that some of the most perceptive works during the Cold War period also identified the aspects of Maoist politics that differed from the totalitarianism in Russia and its East European satellite states. Franz Schurmann, for instance, noticed that, unlike the use of mass terror and prevalence of external controls (primarily through the secret police) in the Soviet Union, Maoist China emphasized internal controls through party organizations (1968, 311–315; see also Bianco 2018, 63). For Lucian W. Pye, totalitarianism was a product of industrialized societies able to build large-scale and highly disciplined organizations; to create an extreme form of totalitarianism in an agrarian society such as China could only help its leadership achieve the appearance rather than the substance of development (1968, 234–240).

4. See, for instance, Dernberger 1972 and Weisskopf 1980.

5. To name only a few, Eyferth 2009; Li 2009; Hershatter 2011; Smith 2012; Wu 2014; DeMare 2015; Schmalzer 2016; Ho 2018; Wang 2018; Wemheuer 2019; Cliver 2020; and Meyskens 2020.

6. The Maoist state, in other words, was no exception in undergoing a transition from an organization under a charismatic leadership to a routinized bureaucracy that was based on specialization and professionalism, just like all other modern societies, as Max Weber perceptively observed (2009, 196–244).

7. See, for example, Chan 2001; Gallagher 2005, 2017; Lee 2007a; Gold et al. 2009; Hurst 2009; Zhang 2015; Estlund 2017; Andreas 2019; and Elfstrom 2021.

CHAPTER 1

1. See, e.g., H11; H12; H13; L5; N7.

CHAPTER 2

1. For a more detailed discussion of the one-man system, see Brugger 1976, 188–191; Zhang Zhanbin 1988, 65–75; Wang and Li 1992, 50–59; and Cliver 2009.

2. See Gongren ribao she 1982, 72, 80; Zhang Jing 2001, 46–47; and An Miao 1990, 121–125.

3. See also H24; S9.

4. See also H7; H8; S10.

5. See also, e.g., C2; C6; H5; H7; H10; H17; S2; S3; S5; S10; Y1.

6. See also L1; L2; N5.

CHAPTER 3

1. See, e.g., Wolf 1966; Power 1970; Strickon and Greenfield 1972; and Eisenstadt and Roniger 1984.

2. Studies of the more advanced societies identify a new type of clientelism, as seen in the relationship between a mass party and voters, which is more impersonal, symmetric, bureaucratized, rational-instrumental, and short-term than the old clientelism in traditional societies, which involves face-to-face interactions, diffuse moral obligations, and enduring emotional ties (e.g., Weingrod 1968; Caciagli and Belloni 1981; Hopkin and Mastropaolo 2001).

3. See also L6; H4; W2.

4. See also N1 for a similar comment.

5. Also, e.g., L8; N2; S20.

6. See also H10; H13; H15; L3.

7. See also H4; S10; S18; W4.

8. See also S11; S18; Y1; Y4.

9. See also, e.g., H15; L6; N4.

10. See also L5; N4; S7; Y2.
11. See also L5; L6; L8; S19.
12. See also L4; L5; L3; N2; W2; W4.
13. See also W4 for similar comments.

CHAPTER 4

1. See, for instance, Liu Guoguang and Zhao Renwei 1979; Xue Muqiao 1992; and Wu Jinglian 2007.

2. See, for example, Pang and De Boer 1983, 659; Helburn and Shearer 1984, 8–9; Dollar 1990, 91–92; Putterman 1992, 472; Zhu et al. 1998, 68; Whyte 1999, 176; Zhang and Yuan 2008, 3; and Kuruvilla et el. 2011, 3–4.

3. See, e.g., S4; S15; W3; H14.
4. See also H20; L4; N6; W5.
5. See also H25; L2; L5; S15.
6. See also L4; L8; H4; H5; H7; S10; S11; etc.
7. See also H18; Y1; Y3; Y4.
8. For similar comments, see H7; H20; L4; N2; N3; N9; N10.
9. Nationwide statistics confirm the difference in wage levels between workers of state and collective enterprises. As late as 1982, for instance, the average wage of all collective-enterprise workers remained about 80 percent of the average wages of all state-enterprise workers in the country (Guojia tongjiju 1983, 488).

10. The average wage of workers in construction and energy exploration was the highest during most of the 1950s through the 1970s, compared to the earnings of workers in all other sectors (Guojia tongjiju 1983, 490).

11. See also S5; S7; S19; W2; N3; B2.
12. See, e.g., S4; S10; S11; W1.
13. See also S6; S8; S15; H13; H19.
14. For a discussion about the reality of "democratic management" (*minzhu guanli*) in Chinese industry during the Mao era and its impact on the transformation of state firms into market-oriented ones in the reform era, see Philion 2009.

CHAPTER 5

1. At the very top, of course, were the famous opera actors or actresses, such as Ma Lianliang, whose total monthly wage reached 1,700 yuan (including 1,366 yuan as retained wage), and Zhou Xinfang, who received 1,760 yuan per month. Still higher were the income levels of former businessowners, who received periodic payments of interest or bonuses from the government after their private firms were purchased by the state or converted into joint-ownership businesses. Wu, the former owner of Dazhonghua Rubber Factory in Shanghai, for instance,

284   NOTES TO CHAPTER 5 AND 6

received 47,000 yuan annually as fixed interest, in addition to his wages that totaled 7,600 yuan a year (Lin Chaochao 2019).

2. For similar comments, see C1; C4; C5; H14; L3; S6.

3. See, e.g., L5; S1; S7; S8.

CHAPTER 6

1. See Guojia tongjiju 2009, Table 4-2, "Annual employments in urban and rural enterprises."

2. See Guojia tongjiju 2000, Table 8-3, "The itemized revenues of the state's finance."

3. Another survey of 693 employees from seven firms in Suzhou of Jiangsu province found that 51 percent of the workers were more incentivized to perform well in production, whereas 49 percent believed that they worked the same way or were less motivated than before (Tong Zhihong 2002). Similarly, a survey of 300 workers from the companies in Jiaxing of Zhejiang province showed that 54 percent of them felt more incentivized to work (Du Shoujia 1996).

References

Akerlof, George A., and Rachel E. Kranton. 2005. "Identity and the Economics of Organizations." *Journal of Economic Perspectives* 19, no. 1: 9–32.

Andreas, Joel. 2009. *Rise of the Red Engineers: The Cultural Revolution and the Origins of China's New Class*. Stanford: Stanford University Press.

———. 2019. *Disenfranchised: The Rise and Fall of Industrial Citizenship in China*. New York: Oxford University Press.

An Miao桉苗. 1990. *Gongren jieji xianzhuang yu zhigong daibiao dahui zhidu yanjiu*工人阶级现状与职工代表大会制度研究 (A Study on the Condition of the Working Class and the System of Staff and Workers' Congress). Shenyang: Liaoning Renmin Chubanshe.

Barnett, Doak. 1967. *Cadres, Bureaucracy, and Political Power in Communist China*. New York: Columbia University Press.

Bettelheim, Charles. 1974. *Cultural Revolution and Industrial Organization in China*. New York: Monthly Review Press.

Bian, Morris L. 2009. *The Making of the State Enterprise System in Modern China*. Cambridge, Mass.: Harvard University Press.

Bianco, Lucien. 2018. *Stalin and Mao: A Comparison of the Russian and Chinese Revolutions*. Hong Kong: The Chinese University of Hong Kong Press.

Blecher, Marc. 1987. "Communist Neo-Traditionalism: Worth and Authority in Chinese Industry" (book review). *Pacific Affairs* 60, no. 4: 657–659.

Bourdieu, Pierre. 1976. "Marriage Strategies as Strategies of Social Reproduction." In *Family and Society: Selections from the Annales Economies, Societes, Civilisations*, edited by Robert Foster and Orest Ranum, 117–144. Baltimore: John Hopkins University Press.

———. 1977. *Outline of a Theory of Practice.* Cambridge, UK: Cambridge University Press.

———. 1990. *The Logic of Practice.* Stanford: Stanford University Press.

Brewer, Marilynn B., and Rupert J. Brown. 1998. "Intergroup Relations." In *The Handbook of Social Psychology*, vol. 2, edited by Daniel T. Gilbert, Susan T. Fiske, and Gardner Lindzey, 554–594. Boston: McGraw-Hill.

Brugger, William. 1976. *Democracy & Organization in the Chinese Industrial Enterprise, 1948–1953.* Cambridge, UK: Cambridge University Press.

Burns, John. 1989. "China's Governance: Political Reform in a Turbulent Environment." *The China Quarterly* 119: 481–518.

Caciagli, Mario, and Frank Belloni. 1981. "The 'New' Clientelism in Southern Italy: The Christian Democratic Party in Catania." In *Political Clientelism, Patronage and Development*, edited by S. N. Eisenstadt and Rene Lamarchand, 35–56. Beverly Hills, CA: Sage.

CBJY. *Guoying qiye jianli zhigong daibiao dahui de chubu jingyan* 国营企业建立职工代表大会的初步经验 (Preliminary Lessons about the Establishment of Staff and Workers' Congress in State-owned Enterprises), edited by Zhonggong zhongyang gongye gongzuobu chengce yanjiushi 中共中央工业工作部政策研究室, 1957. Beijing: Gongren Chubanshe.

Chan, Anita. 2001. *China's Workers under Assault: Exploitation and Abuse in a Globalizing Economy.* Armonk: Sharpe.

Chan, Chris. 2013. "Contesting Class Organization: Migrant Workers' Strikes in China's Pearl River Delta, 1978–2010." *International Labor and Working-Class History* 83: 112–136.

Chan, Chris, and Elaine Hui. 2013. "The Development of Collective Bargaining in China: From 'Collective Bargaining by Riot' to 'Party State-led Wage Bargaining.'" *The China Quarterly* 217: 221–242.

Chan, Chris, and Pun Ngai. 2009. "The Making of a New Working Class? A Study of Collective Actions of Migrant Workers in South China." *The China Quarterly* 198: 287–303.

Chen, Feng. 2000. "Subsistence Crises, Managerial Corruption and Labor Protests in China." *The China Journal* 44: 41–63.

———. 2003. "Industrial Restructuring and Workers' Resistance in China." *Modern China* 29, no. 2: 237–262.

———. 2008. "Worker Leaders and Framing Factory-Based Resistance." In *Popular Protest in China*, edited by Keven O'Brien, 88–107. Cambridge, Mass.: Harvard University Press.

———. 2010. "Trade Unions and the Quadripartite Interactions in Strike Settlement in China." *The China Quarterly* 201: 104–124.

Chen Guoheng 陈国恒. 1999. "Ping 'Maiqi' feng de lilun yu Shijian 评"卖企"风的理论与实践" (On the Theory and Practice of the Drive of "The Enterprises on Sale"). *Qingdao Haiyang daxue xuebao* 青岛海洋大学学报 2: 25–32.

Chen Zuwei 陈祖慰. 2004. "Qiye gaizhi Zhong zhigong zhurenweng diwei de ruogan sikao 企业改制中职工主人翁地位的若干思考" (Thoughts on Workers' Status as Masters in Enterprise Restructuring). *Xiandai qiye* 现代企业 7: 51–52.

Chi Heng 池恒. 1976. "Cong zichan jieji minzhupai dao zouzipai" 从资产阶级民主派到走资派 (From the Bourgeois Democrats to Capitalist Roaders). *Renmin Ribao*, March 2, 1976.

Chow, Tse-tsung. 1960. *The May 4th Movement: Intellectual Revolution in Modern China*. Cambridge, Mass.: Harvard University Press.

Cliver, Robert. 2009. "Minzhu Guanli: the Democratization of Factory Management in the Chinese Revolution." *Labor History* 50, no. 4: 409–435.

———. 2020. *Red Silk: Class, Gender, and Revolution in China's Yangzi Delta Silk Industry*. Cambridge, Mass.: Harvard University Asia Center.

Coase, Ronald. 1960. "The Problem of Social Cost." *Journal of Law and Economics* 3: 1–44.

Coase, Ronald, and Ning Wang. 2012. *How China Became Capitalist*. New York: Palgrave.

Cui Yi 崔义. 1991. "Guanyu guoyou qiye zhigong jijixing de diaocha yanjiu 关于国有企业职工积极性的调查研究" (An Investigation of Workers' Incentives in State-owned Enterprises). *Gaige* 改革 5: 73–77.

Davis, Deborah. 1988. "Patrons and Clients in Chinese Industry." *Modern China* 14, no. 4: 487–497.

DeMare, Brian. 2015. *Mao's Cultural Army: Drama Troupes in China's Rural Revolution*. Cambridge, UK: Cambridge University Press.

Dernberger, Robert. 1972. "Radical Ideology and Economic Development in China: The Cultural Revolution and Its Impact on the Economy." *Asian Survey* 12, no. 12: 1048–1065.

Diao Chengjie 刁成杰. 1996. *Renmin xinfang shilue*人民信访史略 (A Brief History of People's Appeal by Letter and Visit), 1949–1995. Beijing: Beijing Jingji Xueyuan Chubanshe.

Dollar, David. 1990. "Economic Reform and Allocative Efficiency in China's State-owned Industry." *Economic Development and Cultural Change* 39, no. 1: 89–105.

Dong, Guoqiang, and Andrew Walder. 2010. "Nanjing's Failed 'January Revolution' of 1967: The Inner Politics of a Provincial Power Seizure." *The China Quarterly* 203: 675–692.

———. 2011a. "Local Politics in the Chinese Cultural Revolution: Nanjing under Military Control." *The Journal of Asian Studies* 70, no. 2: 425–447.

———. 2011b. "Factions in a Bureaucratic Setting: The Origins of Cultural Revolution Conflict in Nanjing." *The China Journal* 65: 1–25.

———. 2021. *A Decade of Upheaval: The Cultural Revolution in Rural China*. Princeton: Princeton University Press.

Du Shoujia杜守嘉. 1996. "Qiye gaizhi: Zhigong shuo changduan企业改制: 职工说长短" (Enterprise Restructuring: Employees thus Spoke). *Jingji Gongzuo Daokan*经济工作导刊 12: 17–18.

Eisenstadt, S. N., and Luis Roniger. 1984. *Patrons, Clients and Friends: Interpersonal Relations and the Structures of Trust in Society*. Cambridge, UK: Cambridge University Press.

Elfstrom, Manfred. 2021. *Workers and Change in China: Resistance, Repression, Responsiveness*. Cambridge, UK: Cambridge University Press.

Elfstrom, Manfred, and Sarosh Kuruvilla. 2014. "The Changing Nature of Labor Unrest in China." *ILR Review* 67, no. 2: 453–480.

Ellingsen, Tore, and Magnus Johannesson. 2008. "Pride and Prejudice: The Human Side of Incentive Theory." *The American Economic Review* 98, no. 3: 990–1008.

Estlund, Cynthia. 2017. *A New Deal for China's Workers?* Cambridge, Mass.: Harvard University Press.

Eyferth, Jacob. 2009. *Eating Rice from Bamboo Roots: The Social History of a Community of Handicraft Papermakers in Rural Sichuan, 1920–2000*. Cambridge, Mass.: Harvard University Press.

Fehr, Ernst, and Armin Falk. 2002. "Psychological Foundations of Incentives." *European Economic Review* 46, nos. 4–5: 687–724.

Filtzer, Donald. 1986. *Soviet Workers and Stalinist Industrialization: The Formation of Modern Soviet Production Relations, 1928–1941*. London: Pluto Press.

———. 1992. *Soviet Workers and De-Stalinization: The Consolidation of the Modern System of Soviet Production Relations, 1953–1964*. Cambridge, UK: Cambridge University Press.

———. 2002. *Soviet Workers and Late Stalinism: Labor and the Restoration of the Stalinist System after World War II*. Cambridge, UK: Cambridge University Press.

Frazier, Mark W. 2002. *The Making of the Chinese Industrial Workplace: State, Revolution, and Labor Management*. Cambridge, UK: Cambridge University Press.

Fudge, Judy. 2005. "After Industrial Citizenship: Market Citizenship or Citizenship at Work?" *Industrial Relations* 60, no. 4: 631–656.

Fung, Edmund. 2010. *The Intellectual Foundations of Chinese Modernity: Cultural and Political Thoughts in the Republican Era*. Cambridge, UK: Cambridge University Press.

Gallagher, Mary. 2005. *Contagious Capitalism: Globalization and the Politics of Labor in China*. Princeton: Princeton University Press.

———. 2017. *Authoritarian Legality in China: Law, Workers, and the State*. Cambridge, UK: Cambridge University Press.

GHZC. *Zhonghua renmin gongheguo gonghui zhangcheng*中华人民共和国工会章程 (The Constitution of the Trade Union in the People's Republic of China), 1953. Beijing: Gongren Chubanshe.

Gilman, Nils. 2003. *Mandarins of the Future: Modernization Theory in Cold War America*. Baltimore: The Johns Hopkins University Press.

Gneezy, Uri, Stephan Meier, and Pedro Rey-Biel. 2011. "When and Why Incentives (Don't) Work to Modify Behavior." *Journal of Economic Perspectives* 25, no. 4: 1–21.

Gold, Thomas, William Hurst, Jaeyoun Won, and Li Qiang. 2009. *Laid-Off Workers in a Workers' State: Unemployment with Chinese Characteristics*. New York: Palgrave.

Goldman, Merle. 1994. *Sowing the Seeds of Democracy in China: Political Reform in the Deng Xiaoping Era*. Cambridge, Mass.: Harvard University Press.

Gong Xinxin龚馨馨. 1989. "Dui Shanghaishi qiye zhigong laodong jijixing xianzhuang de diaocha对上海市企业职工劳动积极性现状的调查" (An Investigation on Work Attitudes of Enterprise Employees in the City of Shanghai). *Jingji guanli*经济管理 5: 23–27.

Gongren ribao she 工人日报社工会工作部. 1982. *Guoying gongye qiye zhigong daibiao dahui zhanxing tiaoli jianghua* 国营工业企业职工代表大会暂行条例讲话 (Speeches on the Provisional Regulations on the Staff and Workers' Congress in State-owned Industrial Enterprises). Beijing: Gongren Chubanshe.

GZJY. *Zhigong daibiao dahui zhong de gonghui gongzuo jingyan*职工代表大会中的工会工作经验 (Working Experiences of the Trade Union in the Staff and Workers Congress), edited by Gongren Chubanshe工人出版社,1958. Beijing: Gongren Chubanshe.

Gramsci, Antonio. 1976. *Selections from the Prison Notebooks*. New York: International Publishers.

Guojia tongjiju国家统计局. 1983. *Zhongguo tongji nianjian*中国统计年鉴 (China statistic yearbook), 1983. Beijing: Zhongguo Tongji Chubanshe.

———. 1987. *Zhongguo laodong gongzi tongji ziliao*中国劳动工资统计资料 1949–1985. Beijing: Zhongguo Tongji Chubanshe.

———. 2000. *Zhongguo tongji nianjian*中国统计年鉴 (China statistic yearbook), 2000. Beijing: Zhongguo Tongji Chubanshe.

———. 2003. *Zhongguo tongji nianjian*中国统计年鉴 (China statistic yearbook), 2003. Beijing: Zhongguo Tongji Chubanshe.

———. 2005. *Xin Zhongguo wushiwunian tongji ziliao huibian*新中国五十五年统计资料汇编 (China Compendium of Statistics) 1949–2004. Beijing: Zhongguo Tongji Chubanshe.

———. 2008. *Zhongguo gongye jingji tongji nianjian*中国工业经济统计年鉴 (China Statistic Yearbook of Industrial Economy), 2008. Beijing: Zhongguo Tongji Chubanshe.

———. 2009. *Zhongguo tongji nianjian*中国统计年鉴 (China Statistic Yearbook), 2009. Beijing: Zhongguo Tongji Chubanshe.

———. 2019. "2018 nian nongmingong jiance diaocha baogao 2018年农民工监测调查报告" (Report on Investigation and Monitoring of Migrant Workers in 2018). *Jianzhu*建筑 11: 30–32.

———. 2020. "2019 nian nongmingong jiance diaocha baogao 2019年农民工监测调查报告" (Report on Investigation and Monitoring of Migrant Workers in 2018). *Jianzhu*建筑 11: 28–31.

Han Bing韩冰. 2008. "Dangqian qiye gonghui weiquan de kunjing ji falu duice当前企业工会维权的困境及法律对策" (Legal Solutions to Current Difficulties of Enterprise Trade Unions in Protecting Worker Rights). *Xingzheng yu fa* 行政与法 8: 31–34.

Han Jun韩俊, Wang Zhihong汪志洪, Cui Chuanyi崔传义, Jin Sanlin金三林, Qin Zhongchun秦中春, and Li Qing李青. 2009. "Zhongguo nongmingong xianzhuang jiqi fazhan qushi zongbaogao中国农民工现状及其发展趋势总报告" (General Report on the Current Condition and Future Development of Migrant Workers in China). *Gaige*改革 2: 5–27.

Hassard, John, Jackie Sheehan, Meixiang Zhou, Jane Terpstra-Tong, and Jonathan Morris. 2007. *China's State Enterprise Reform: From Marx to the Market*. Oxon: Routledge.

Helburn, I. B., and John C. Shearer. 1984. "Human Resources and Industrial Relations in China: A Time of Ferment." *Industrial and Labor Relations Review* 38, no. 1: 3–15.

Henley, John S., and Nyaw Mee-Kau. 1987. "The Development of Work Incentives in Chinese Industrial Enterprises: Material versus Non-Material Incentives." In *Management Reforms in China*, edited by Malcolm Warner, 127–148. New York: St. Martin's Press.

Hershatter, Gail. 2011. *The Gender of Memory: Rural Women and China's Collective Past*. Berkeley: University of California Press.

Ho, Denise. 2018. *Curating Revolution: Politics on Display in Mao's China*. Cambridge, UK: Cambridge University Press.

Hoffmann, Charles. 1974. *The Chinese Worker*. Albany: SUNY Press.

———. 1977. "Worker Participation in Chinese Factories." *Modern China* 3: 291–320.

Hogg, Michael A. 1992. *The Social Psychology of Group Cohesiveness: From Attraction to Social Identity*. New York: Harvester Wheatsheaf.

Hopkin, Jonathan, and Alfio Mastropaolo. 2001. "From Patronage to Clientelism: Comparing the Italian and Spanish Experiences." In *Clientelism, Interests, and Democratic Representation*, edited by Simona Piattoni, 152–171. Cambridge, UK: Cambridge University Press.

Howard, Pat. 1991. "Rice Bowls and Job Security: The Urban Contract Labor System." *The Australian Journal of Chinese Affairs* 25: 93–114.

Hu Qiaomu 胡乔木. 1978. "Anzhao jingji guilü banshi, jiakuai shixian sige xiandaihua" 按照经济规律办事, 加快实现四个现代化 (Act by Economic Laws and Speed up the Four Modernizations). *Renmin Ribao*, October 6.

Huang Jian 黄健, and Lu Xiangdong 卢向东. 1996. "Guanyu gongren shenghuo diwei he xintai de diaocha 关于工人生活地位和心态的调查" (An Investigation on the Living Conditions and Mentality of Workers). *Qiye guanli* 企业管理 178: 16–17.

Huang Xin 黄辛. 1958. "Lun shehuizhuyi de minzhu he ziyou" 论社会主义的民主与自由 (On Socialist Democracy and Liberty). *Lilun yu shijian* 理论与实践 Z1: 43–47.

Huo Xinbing 霍新宾. 2009. "Laozi guanxi yu shehui zhuanxing: xin Zhongguo chengli qianhou Shanghai de laoxi guanxi biandong" 劳资关系与社会转型——新中国成立前后上海的劳资关系变动 (Labor-capital Relations and Social Transformation: Changes in Labor-capital Relations in Shanghai before and after 1949). *Zhonggong dangshi yanjiu* 中共党史研究 9: 41–51.

———. 2015. "Xinminzhuzhuyi laoxi guanxi zhi mingyun: wufan yundong qianhou Shanghai de laozi guanxi biandong" 新民主主义劳资关系之命运——五反运动前后上海的劳资关系变动 (The Fate of Labor-capital Relations under New Democracy: Changes in Labor-capital Relations in Shanghai during the Five-Anti Campaign). *Shili* 史林 2: 150–165.

Hurst, William. 2009. *The Chinese Worker after Socialism*. Cambridge, UK: Cambridge University Press.

Ketizu (Woguo nongmingong gongzuo shierwu fazhan guihua gangyao yanjiu ketizu 《我国农民工工作"十二五"发展规划纲要研究》课题组). 2010. "Zhongguo nongmingong wenti zongti qushi: guance shierwu 中国农民工问题总体趋势: 观测十二五" (The General Trend in Issues Concerning

Chinese Migrant Workers: The Twelfth Five-year Plan in Perspective). *Gaige* 改革 8: 5–29.

Kirsch, Leonard Joel. 1972. *Soviet Wages: Changes in Structure and Administration Since 1956*. Cambridge, Mass.: The MIT Press.

Kraus, Richard. 1983. "The Chinese State and Its Bureaucrats." In *State and Society in Contemporary China*, edited by Victor Nee and David Mozingo, 132–147. Ithaca: Cornell University Press.

Kuruvilla, Sarosh, Ching Kwan Lee, and Mary E. Gallagher. 2011. *From Iron Rice Bowl to Informalization: Markets, Workers, and the State in a Changing China*. Ithaca: ILR Press.

Lane, David. 1985. *Soviet Economy and Society*. New York: New York University Press.

Latham, Michael. 2000. *Modernization as Ideology: American Social Science and "Nation Building" in the Kennedy Era*. Chapel Hill: The University of North Carolina Press.

Lee, Ching Kwan. 2007a. *Against the Law: Labor Protests in China's Rustbelt and Sunbelt*. Berkeley: University of California Press.

———. 2007b. "What Was Socialism to Chinese Workers? Collective Memories and Labor Politics in an Age of Reform." In *Re-envisioning the Chinese Revolution: The Politics and Poetics of Collective Memories in Reform China*, edited by Ching Kwan Lee and Guobin Yang, 141–165. Stanford: Stanford University Press.

———. 2016. "Precarization or Empowerment? Reflections on Recent Labor Unrest in China." *The Journal of Asian Studies* 75, no. 2: 317–333.

Lee, Hong Yung. 1978. *The Politics of the Chinese Cultural Revolution: A Case Study*. Berkeley: University of California Press.

Lee, Peter N. S. 1987. *Industrial Management and Economic Reform in China, 1949–1984*. Hong Kong: Oxford University Press.

Lee, Rensselaer. 1973. "The Politics of Technology in Communist China." *Comparative Politics* 5, no. 2: 237–260.

Lewis, John. 1963. *Leadership in Communist China*. Ithaca: Cornell University Press.

Li Bote 李伯特. 2003. "Quanhongzong shimo" "全红总" 始末 (A Complete History of Quanhongzong). *Huaxia wenzhai zengkan* 华夏文摘增刊, no. 334.

Li, Huaiyin. 2009. *Village China Under Socialism and Reform: A Micro-history, 1948–2008*. Stanford: Stanford University Press.

———. 2013. *Reinventing Modern China: Imagination and Authenticity in Chinese Historical Writing*. Honolulu: University of Hawaii Press.

———. 2016. "Worker Performance in State-Owned Factories in Maoist China: A Reinterpretation." *Modern China* 42, no. 4: 377–414.

———. 2017. "Everyday Power Relations in State Firms in Socialist China: A Reexamination." *Modern China* 43, no. 3: 288–321.

Li Jiaqi 李家齐, ed. 1997. *Shanghai Gongyun Zhi* 上海工运志 (Gazetteer of Shanghai Worker Movements). Shanghai: Shanghai Shuihui Kexueyuan Chubanshe.

Li Jun 李骏, Mao Minghua 毛明华, and Zhao Dandan 赵丹丹. 2001. "Zhuangui shiqi guoqi zhigong gaige xintai yanjiu: dui Wuhanshi guoqi zhigong de yici diaocha 转轨时期过期职工改革心态研究——对武汉市国企职工的一次调查" (A Study of Workers' Attitudes toward Reforms in State-owned Enterprises in Institutional Transformation). *Sheke yu jingji xinxi* 社科与经济信息 2: 89–92.

Li Shi 李实, and Wu Binbin 吴彬彬. 2020. "Zhongguo waichu nongmingong jingji zhuangkuang yanjiu 中国外出农民工经济状况研究" (Study on the Economic Conditions of Migrant Workers in China). *Shehui kexue zhanxian* 社会科学战线 5: 36–52.

Li Xun 李逊. 1998. "Wenge zhong fasheng zai Shanghai de jinjizhuyi feng" "文革"中发生在上海的"经济主义风" (The Wind of Economism in Shanghai during the Cultural Revolution). *Huaxia wenzhai zengkan* 华夏文摘增刊, no. 158.

Lin Chaochao 林超超. 2010. "Xinguojia yu jiugongren: 1952 nian Shanghai saying gongcang de minzhu gaige yundong" 新国家与旧工人: 1952年上海私营工厂的民主改革运动 (New State and Old Workers: The Democratic Reform Movement in Private Factories in Shanghai in 1952). *Shehuixue yanjiu* 社会学研究 2: 67–86.

———. 2014. "Dayuejin hou de channeng guosheng yu chengshi gongye de zengxiao gaige 大跃进后的产能过剩与城市工业的增效改革" (Production Capacity Surplus and Efficiency-promoting Reforms in Urban Industries after the Great Leap Forward). *Shilin* 史林 3: 133–145.

———. 2019. "20 shiji 50 niandai Shanghai gongren jiating shenghuo shuiping de shizheng yanjiu" 20世纪50年代上海工人家庭生活水平的实证研究 (A Study of the Living Standards of Workers' Families in Shanghai in the 1950s). *Zhongguo jingjishi yanjiu* 中国经济史研究 5: 48–62.

Lin, Justin Yifu, Fang Cai, and Zhou Li. 2003. *The China Miracle: Development Strategy and Economic Reform*. Hong Kong: The Chinese University Press.

Lin Pan 林盼. 2018. "Zhidu bianqian, liyi congtu yu guoying qiye jishu jingying diwei huode" 制度变迁、利益冲突于国营企业技术精英地位获得 (1949-1965) (Institutional Change, Interest Conflict, and Achievement of Technical Elite Status in State-owned Enterprises, 1949-1965). *Zhongguo jingjishi yanjiu* 中国经济史研究 2: 82–96.

———. 2019. "Ji yao xiaolu, ye qiu pingdeng: 20 shiji 60 niandai banjijian gongzi zhi de shishi" 既要效率, 也求平等: 20世纪60年代半计件工资制的实施 (Efficiency and Equity Are Both Desired: The Implementation of the Semi-piece-rate Wage System in the 1960s). *Zhongguo jingjishi yanjiu* 中国经济史研究 1: 53–63.

———. 2021. "Jili zhengce de shijian xiaoguo yu jiceng huiying: yi Dayuejin shiqi gongzi zhidu gaige wei zhongxin" 既要效率, 也求平等: 20世纪60年代半计件工资制的实施 (The Effectiveness of, and Grassroots Reactions to, Incentive Policies: The Wage System Reform during the Great Leap Forward Period). *Zhongguo jingjishi yanjiu* 中国经济史研究 6: 162–175.

Liu Guoguang 刘国光 and Zhao Renwei 赵人伟. 1979. "Shehuizhuyi jingji jihua he shichang de guanxi" 社会主义经济计划和市场的关系 (The Relationship between Socialist Economic Planning and the Market). *Renmin ribao*, June 1.

Liu Yuanwen 刘元文 and Gao Hongxia 高红霞. 2002. "Chanquan gaige hou guoyou qiye laodong guanxi jiben zhuangkuang 产权改革后国有企业劳动关系基本状况" (The General Conditions of Labor Relations in State-owned Reform of Property Rights). *Gonghui lilun yu shijian* 工会理论与实践 6: 3–7.

Lü, Xiaobo. 2000a. *Cadres and Corruption: The Organizational Involution of the Chinese Communist Party*. Stanford: Stanford University Press.

———. 2000b. "Booty Socialism, Bureau-Preneurs, and the State in Transition: Organizational Corruption in China." *Comparative Politics* 32, no. 3: 273–294.

Luo Tianwen 罗天文. 1994. "Gufenzhi gaizao zhong de zhigong xintai: Ma'anshan gangtie gongsi de diaocha 股份制改造中的职工心态——马鞍山钢铁公司的

调查" (The Mentality of Employees in Transition to the Shareholding System). *Sixiang zhengzhi gongzuo yanjiu*思想政治工作研究 1: 40–41.

MacFarquhar, Roderick, and Michael Schoenhals. 2006. *Mao's Last Revolution*. Cambridge: Belknap.

McCallum, Ronald. 2006. "Justice at Work: Industrial Citizenship and the Corporatization of Australian Labor Law." *Journal of Industrial Relations* 48, no. 2: 131–153.

Meisner, Maurice. 1999. *Mao's China and After: A History of the People's Republic*. New York: Free Press.

Meisner, Mitch. 1972. "The Shenyang Transformer Factory: A Profile." *The China Quarterly* 52: 717–737.

Meyskens, Covell F. 2020. *Mao's Third Front: The Militarization of Cold War China*. Cambridge, UK: Cambridge University Press.

Mu Liangping穆良平. 1990. "Yingxiang zhigong jijixing de jingji yinsu jiqi shizheng fenxi影响职工积极性的经济因素及其实证分析" (An Empirical Analysis of the Economic Factors Influencing the Work Attitudes of Employees). *Shehui kexuejia*社会科学家 5: 67–74.

MZDWG. *Jianguo yilai Mao Zedong wengao*建国以来毛泽东文稿 (Mao Zedong's Writings since the Founding of the State), vols. 1–13, edited by Zhonggong zhongyang wenxian yanjiushi中共中央文献研究室, 1998. Beijing: Zhongyang Wenxian Chubanshe.

Nee, Victor. 1975. "Revolution and Bureaucracy: Shanghai in the Cultural Revolution." In *China's Uninterrupted Revolution: From 1840 to the Present*, edited by Victor Nee and James Peck, 322–414. New York: Pantheon Books.

———. 1998. "Sources of the New Institutionalism." In *The New Institutionalism in Sociology*, edited by Mary Brinton and Victor Nee. Stanford: Stanford University Press.

Ngai, Pun, and Lu Huilin. 2010. "Unfinished Proletarianization: Self, Anger, and Class Action among the Second Generation of Peasant-Workers in Present-Day China." *Modern China* 36, no. 5: 493–519.

North, Douglass. 1981. *Structure and Change in Economic History*. New York: Norton.

———. 1990. *Institutions, Institutional Change and Economic Performance*. New York: Cambridge University Press.

Pang, Chung Min, and A. John De Boer. 1983. "Management Decentralization on China's State Firms." *American Journal of Agricultural Economics* 65, no. 4: 657–666.

Pang Xianzhi逢先知and Jin Chongji金冲及,eds. 2011. *Mao Zedong Zhuan*毛泽东传 (Mao Zedong: A Biography), vols. 1–6. Beijing: Zhongyang Wenxian Chubanshe.

Pegels, C. Carl. 1987. *Management and Industry in China*. New York: Praeger.

Perry, Elizabeth J. 1989. "State and Society in Contemporary China." *World Politics* 41, no. 4: 579–591.

———. 2002. *Challenging the Mandate of Heaven: Social Protest and State Power in China*. Armonk: Sharpe.

———. 2007. "Masters of the Country? Shanghai Workers in the Early People's Republic." In *Dilemmas of Victory: The Early Years of the People's Republic*, edited by Jeremy Brown and Paul Pickowicz, 59–79. Cambridge, Mass.: Harvard University Press.

Perry, Elizabeth, and Li Xun. 1997. *Proletarian Power: Shanghai in the Cultural Revolution*. Boulder: Westview.

Philion, Stephen E. 2009. *Workers' Democracy in China's Transition from State Socialism*. New York: Routledge.

Power, John D. 1970. "Peasant Society and Clientelist Politics." *American Political Science Review* 64, no. 2: 411–425.

Prybyla, Jan. 1975. "Impressions of the Chinese Economy." *The Virginia Quarterly Review* 51, no. 1: 19–35.

———. 1977. "Some Economic Strengths and Weaknesses of the People's Republic of China." *Asian Survey* 17, no. 12: 1119–1142.

Putterman, Louis. 1992. "Dualism and Reform in China." *Economic Development and Cultural Change* 40, no. 3: 467–493.

Pye, Lucian. 1968. *The Spirit of Chinese Politics: A Psychocultural Study of the Authority Crisis in Political Development*. Cambridge, Mass.: The MIT Press.

Quan, Katie. 2016. "Labor Transformation in China: Voices from the Frontlines." In *Achieving Workers' Rights in the Global Economy*, edited by Richard Appelbaum and Nelson Lichtenstein, 190–208. Ithaca: Cornell University Press.

Renmin ribao (the People's Daily), accessed via http://utpd.twinbridge.com.ezproxy.lib.utexas.edu.

Riskin, Carl. 1975. "Maoism and Motivation: Work Incentives in China." In *China's Uninterrupted Revolution: From 1840 to the Present*, edited by Victor Nee and James Peck, 415–461. New York: Pantheon Books.

———. 1987. *China's Political Economy: The Quest for Development Since 1949*. Oxford: Oxford University Press.

Schmalzer, Sigrid. 2016. *Red Revolution, Green Revolution: Scientific Farming in Socialist China*. Chicago: University of Chicago Press.

Schram, Stuart. 1989. *The Thought of Mao Tse-tung*. Cambridge, UK: Cambridge University Press.

Schurmann, Franz. 1968. *Ideology and Organization in Communist China*. Berkeley: University of California Press.

Scott, James. 1972. "Patron-Client Politics and Political Change in Southeast Asia." *American Political Science Review* 66, no. 1: 91–113.

———. 1976. *The Moral Economy of the Peasant: Rebellion and Subsistence in Southeast Asia*. New Haven: Yale University Press.

———. 1998. *Seeing Like a State: How Certain Schemes to Improve the Human Condition Have Failed*. New Haven: Yale University Press.

Selden, Mark. 1995. *China in Revolution: The Yenan Way Revisited*. Armonk, NY: Sharpe.

Shan Zhufei 单铸飞. 1999. "Guoyou xiaoxing chushou qiye zhigong quanyi baozhang yu gonghui gongzuo: Hunansheng guoyou xiaoxing qiye chushou qiye qingkuang diaocha 国有小型出售企业职工权益保障与工会工作——湖南省国有小型出售企业情况调查" (An Investigation of the Situation of the Sales of Small-size State-owned Enterprises in Hunan Province). *Gonghui lilun yu shijian* 工会理论与实践 1: 60–62.

Shanghai Shiwei 上海市委"高薪阶层"调查组. 1964. "Duiyu gaoxin jieceng de diaochao baogao"对"高薪阶层"的调查报告 (A Report of Investigation on High-income Groups).

Sheehan, Jackie. 1998. *Chinese Workers: A New History*. London: Routledge.

Shen Jianpeng. 2019. "Jiating chusheng yu lishi wenti yingxiang biye fenpei de zaisikao: jiyu 1965 nian Beijingshi jisuo gaoxiao biyesheng fenpei quxiang de kaocha." *Beijing dangshi* 4: 22–27.

Shi Tanjing 史探径. 2002. "Zhongguo gonghui de lishi, xianzhuang ji guanyou wenti tantao 中国工会的历史、现状及有关问题探讨" (An Inquiry into the

History, Current Circumstances, and Relevant Issues about the Trade Union in China). *Huanqiu falu pinglun*环球法律评论, summer issue: 164–171.

Shi, Tianjian. 1999. "Village Committee Election in China: Institutionalist Tactics for Democracy." *World Politics* 51: 385–412.

Sliwka, Dirk. 2007. "Trust as a Signal of a Social Norm and the Hidden Costs of Incentive Schemes." *The American Economic Review* 97, no. 3: 999–1012.

Smith, Aminda. 2012. *Thought Reform and China's Dangerous Classes: Reeducation, Resistance, and the People*. Lanham: Rowman & Littlefield.

Song Xueqin宋学勤. 2011. "Zhidu yu shenghuo zhijian de zhangli: 1956 zhi 1966 nian jian renmin wuzhi shenghuo zhuangkuang shulun"制度与生活之间的张力: 1956至1966年间人民物质生活状况述论 (Tensions between the System and Realities of Everyday Life: The Living Conditions of Chinese People in 1956–1966). *Shehui kexue zhanxian*社会科学战线 4: 187–194.

Song Xueqin宋学勤 and He Chengyun何成云. 2020. "Shenfen yu zhiye: chengxiang guanxi shiyu zhong de yigongyinong身份与职业: 城乡关系视域中的亦工亦农 (1958–1977)" (Status and Profession: Worker-peasants in the Perspective of Urban-rural Relations, 1958–1977). *Zhonggong dangshi yanjiu*中共党史研究 2: 14–25.

Standing, Guy. 2009. *Work After Globalization: Building Occupational Citizenship*. Cheltenham, UK: Edward Elgar.

———. 2010. "The International Labor Organization." *New Political Economy* 15, no. 2: 307–318.

Strickon, Arnold, and Sidney M. Greenfield. 1972. *Structure and Process in Latin America: Patronage, Clientage, and Power Systems*. Albuquerque: University of New Mexico Press.

Su Linsen苏林森. 2011. "Dangqian woguo zhigong yuqing de weenti he yingdui: jiyu lici quanguo zhigong zhuangkuang diaocha de fenxi当前我国职工舆情的问题和应对——基于历次全国职工状况调查的分析" (Current Issues about Public Opinions among the Workers and Proposed Solutions). *Beijingshi gonghui ganbu xueyuan xuebao*北京市工会干部学院学报 3: 11–15.

Tang Kuiyu唐魁玉 and Sun Xinxin孙鑫欣. 2012. "Guoqi zhidu biange zhong gongren weiquan de jiti xingdong fenxi: yi dongbei Tiangang gongren jiti xingdong weili国企制度变革中工人维权的集体行动分析——以东北田钢工人集体行动为例" (An Analysis of Workers' Collective Actions to Protect their Rights in the Restructuring of State-owned Enterprises: The Case of Tiangang Workers). *Gansu xingzheng xueyuan xuebao*甘肃行政学院学报 5: 95–108.

Tang, Wenfang, and William Parish. 2000. *Chinese Urban Life under Reform: The Changing Social Contract*. Cambridge, UK: Cambridge University Press.

Tangshanshi zonggonghui diaochazu唐山市总工会调查组. 1988. "Tangshanshi bufen qiye zhigong laodong jijixing xianzhuang ji fenxi唐山市部分企业职工劳动积极性现状及分析" (An Analysis of Workers' Morale in Production in Some Enterprises in the City of Tangshan). *Zhongguo laodong kexue*中国劳动科学 12: 20–22.

Taylor, George. 1956. "On the Nature of Communist Rule in China." *World Politics* 9, no. 1: 140–147.

Tong Xin佟新. 2006. "Yanxu shehuizhuyi wenhua chuantong: yiqi guoyou qiye gongren jiti xingdong de ge'an fenxi延续社会主义文化传统——一起国有企业工人集体行动的个案分析" (Continuing the Socialist Cultural Tradition: A Case Study of Workers' Collective Action in a State-owned Enterprise). *Shehuixue yanjiu*社会学研究 1: 59–76.

Tong Zhihong童志宏. 2002. "Qiye gaizhi yu ganbu zhigong de sixiang zhuangkuang diaocha企业改制与干部职工的思想状况调查" (The Thinkings of Cadres and Employees in Enterprise Restructuring). *Jidian xinchanpin daobao*机电新产品导报 3–4: 137–138.

Townsend, James. 1967. *Political Participation in Communist China*. Berkeley: University of California Press.

Unger, Jonathan, and Anita Chan. 2007. "Memories and the Moral Economy of a State-Owned Enterprise." In *Re-envisioning the Chinese Revolution: The Politics and Poetics of Collective Memories in Reform China*, edited by Ching Kwan Lee and Guobin Yang, 119–140. Stanford: Stanford University Press.

Walder, Andrew G. 1986. *Communist Neo-Traditionalism: Work and Authority in Chinese Industry*. Berkeley: University of California Press.

———. 1987. "Actually Existing Maoism." *The Australian Journal of Chinese Affairs* 18: 155–166.

———. 1989. "Social Change in Post-Revolutionary China." *Annual Review of Sociology* 15: 405–424.

———. 2009. *Fractured Rebellion: The Beijing Red Guard Movement*. Cambridge, Mass.: Harvard University Press.

———. 2015. *China Under Mao: A Revolution Derailed*. Cambridge, Mass.: Harvard University Press.

———. 2019. *Agents of Disorder: Inside China's Cultural Revolution*. Cambridge, Mass.: Belknap Press of Harvard University Press.

Wang Chidong 王持栋 and Li Ping 李平. 1992. *Zhongguo qiye minzhu guanli fazhan shilue* 中国企业民主管理发展史略 (A Brief History of the Democratic Management of Enterprises in China). Beijing: Zhongguo Gongren Chubanshe.

Wang, Di. 2018. *The Teahouse Under Socialism: The Decline and Renewal of Public Life in Chengdu, 1950–2000*. Ithaca: Cornell University Press.

Wang Jian 王健 and Zhang Ying 张莹. 2008. "Zhidaihui zhi kunhuo 职代会之困惑" (The Puzzling SWC). *Gongyou* 工友 8: 6–9.

Wang Mingcai 王明才. 1997. "Zhongxiao qiye gaige zenshi yige 'mai' zi liaode 中小企业改革怎是一个'卖'字了得" (How Can the Reform of Medium- and Small-size Enterprises be Reduced to "selling out"). *Zhongguo gaige* 中国改革 3: 50–51.

Wang Yanbin 王彦斌. 2002. "Zhigong chigu zhidu de jingji xinli: guanyu woguo qiye putong zhigong chigu zhidu de jingji xinli fenxi 职工持股制度的经济心理——关于我国企业普通职工持股制度的经济心理分析" (The Economic Psychology of the System of Shareholding by Employees). *Shanghai shehui kexueyuan xueshu jikan* 上海社会科学院院刊 1: 123–131.

Weber, Max. 2009. *From Max Weber: Essays in Sociology*, edited by H. H. Gerth and C. Wright Mills. London: Routledge.

Wei Dongning 魏东宁. 2006. "Guanyu Jinzhoushi gaizhi qiye zhigong xingtai fanying de diaocha baogao 关于锦州市改制企业职工心态反映的调查报告" (Report on the Mentality of Employees in Restructured Enterprises in the City of Jinzhou). *Zhongguo zhigong jiaoyu* 中国职工教育: 52–54.

Weingrod, Alex. 1968. "Patrons, Patronage, and Political Parties." *Comparative Studies in Society and History* 10, no. 4: 377–400.

Weisskopf, Thomas E. 1980. "The Relevance of the Chinese Experience for Third World Economic Development." *Theory and Society* 9, no. 2: 283–318.

Wemheuer, Felix. 2019. *A Social History of Maoist China: Conflict and Change, 1949–1976*. Cambridge, UK: Cambridge University Press.

Wenxian Yanjiushi 中共中央文献研究室. 2013. *Mao Zedong Nianpu* 毛泽东年谱 (Mao Zedong: A Chronology), vols. 1–6. Beijing: Renmin Chubanshe.

White, Harrison C. 2008. *Identity and Control: A Structural Theory of Social Action*. Princeton: Princeton University Press.

Whyte, Martin King. 1999. "The Changing Role of Workers." In *The Paradox of China's Post-Mao Reforms*, edited by Merle Goldman and Roderick MacFarquhar, 173–196. Cambridge, Mass.: Harvard University Press.

Whyte, Martin, and William Parish. 1984. *Urban Life in Contemporary China*. Chicago: The University of Chicago Press.

WJXB. *Jianguo yilai Zhonggong Zhongyang guanyu gongren yundong wenjian xianbian*建国以来中共中央关于工人运动文件选编 (Selected Compendium of Documents of the CCP Central Committee on Worker Movements since the Founding of the PRC), edited by Zhonghua quanguo zonggonghui中华全国总工会, 1989. Beijing: Gongren Chubanshe.

Wolf, Eric R. 1966. "Kinship, Friendship and Patron-Client Relations in Complex Societies." In *The Social Anthropology of Complex Societies*, edited by Michael Banton, 1–22. New York: Praeger.

Womack, Brantly. 1991. "Transfigured Community: Neo-Traditionalism and Work Unit Socialism in China." *The China Quarterly* 126: 313–332.

Wu Jinglian吴敬琏. 2007. "Zhongguo fazhan xin jieduan xuyao yanjiu de ruogan zhongda wenti"中国发展新阶段需要研究的若干重大问题 (A Number of Major Issues to Be Studied on China's Development in the Current Stage). *Zhongguo gaige* 9.

———. 2009. *Zhongguo zengzhang moshi jueze*中国增长模式抉择 (The Choice of Growth Mode in China). Shanghai: Shanghai Yuandong Chubanshe.

Wu Li武力. 2010. *Zhonghua renmin gongheguo jingjishi*中华人民共和国经济史 (An Economic History of the People's Republic of China). Beijing: Zhongguo Shidai Jingji Chubanshe.

Wu Xiaoming吴晓明. 1999. "Gaizhi qiye zhigong quanyi, diwei ji shenghuo xintai diaocha改制企业职工权益、地位及生活心态调查" (An Investigation on Workers' Rights, Status, and Everyday Mentality in Restructured Enterprises). *Diaoyan shijie*调研世界 3: 30–43.

Wu, Yiching. 2014. *The Cultural Revolution at the Margins: Chinese Socialism in Crisis*. Cambridge, Mass.: Harvard University Press.

WXXB. *Jianguo yilai zhongyao wenxian xuanbian*建国以来重要文献选编 (Compendium of selected important documents since the founding of the PRC), vols. 1–20, edited by Zhonggong zhongyan wenxian yanjiushi中共中央文献研究室, 1992–1998. Beijing: Zhongyang Wenxian Chubanshe.

XFZ. *Tianjin tongzhi xinfangzhi*天津通志信访志 (The General Gazetteer of Tianjin, Volume on Appeals by Letters and Visits), edited by Tianjinshi difangzhi bianxiu weiyuanhui天津市地方志编修委员会, 1997. Tianjin: Tianjin Shehui Kexueyuan Chubanshe.

Xie Deming谢德明, Li Changgui李长贵, and Xin Guoliang辛国亮. 1997. "Zhigong jijixing yuanhe hualuo职工积极性缘何滑落?" (Why Did Workers' Incentives Dwindle?). *Meitan qiye guanli*煤炭企业管理 8: 50–52.

Xie Yuhua谢玉华. 2009. "Zhongguo gongye minzhu he yuangong canyu zhidu ji gongneng: guoqi minqi waiqi de bijiao中国工业民主和员工参与制度及功能: 国企民企外企的比较——来自湖南的调查" (Industrial Democracy and the Institutions of Employee Participation: A Comparison among State-owned, Private, and Foreign Enterprises). *Jingji shehui tizhi bijiao*经济社会体制比较 1: 129–135.

Xu Jingxian徐景贤. 2013. *Wenge mingren Xu Jingxian zuihou huiyi* 文革名人徐景贤最后回忆 (Xu Jingxian's Last Memoir). Hong Kong: Xing'erke Chuban Gongsi.

Xue Muqiao薛暮桥. 1992. "Gaige jiushi weile jiefang shengchanli"改革就是为了解放生产力" (Reforms Are for the End of Emancipating the Forces of Production). In *Zhongguo zhuming jingji xuejia lun gaige*中国著名经济学家论改革 (China's Famous Economists on Reform), edited by He Wei何伟 and Wei Jie魏杰, 3–22. Beijing: Renmin Chubanshe.

Yang, Mayfair. 1994. *Gifts, Favors, and Banquets: The Art of Social Relationships in China*. Ithaca: Cornell University Press.

Yeh, Wen-Hsin. 1997. "The Republican Origins of the Danwei: The Case of Shanghai's Bank of China." In *Danwei: The Changing Chinese Workplace in Historical and Comparative Perspective*, edited by Xiaobo Lu and Elizabeth J. Perry, 60–88. Armonk, NY: Sharpe.

Yin Jianbing印建兵, Yang Huitong杨慧童, Du He杜赫, and Yu Lin俞林. 2020. "Xinshengdai nongmingong shimin zhuanhua xianzhuang fenxi yu cedu新生代农民工市民转化现状分析与测度" (An Analysis and Estimate of the New-generation Migrant Workers and their Transformation into Urban Residents). *Tongji yu juece*统计与决策 9: 80–83.

You Lixin尤立新. 1995. "Guangyu zhigong geren chigu wenti de diaocha baogao 关于职工个人持股问题的调查报告" (Report on the Issue of Shareholding by Individual Workers). *Gonghui lilun yu shijian*工会理论与实践 4: 60–63.

You Zhenglin游正林. 2007. "Xinli qiyue yu guoyou qiye gongren de bugong-zhenggan: yi Xicang weili心理契约与国有企业工人的不公正感——以西厂为例" (Psychological Contract and the Sense of Unfairness among Workers of State-owned Enterprises: The Case of Xicang). *Hunan shifan daxue shehui kexue xuebao*湖南师范大学社会科学学报 2: 77–82.

Yu Ji于吉. 2004. "Jujiao zhigong chigu聚焦职工持股" (Employees' Holding of Shares in Focus). *Qiye guanli*企业管理 3: 6–13.

Yuan Jin袁进 and Wang Youfu王有富. 2008. "Ku bing xingfu zhe: 20 shiji 50 niandai Shanghai gangtie gongren shenghuo jilu"苦并幸福着——20世纪50年代上海钢铁工人生活记录 (Hardship Mingled with Happiness: The Everyday Life of Workers in the Iron and Steel Industry in Shanghai in the 1950s). *Shuzhai*书摘 11: 46–49.

Zdaniuk, Bozena, and John M. Levine. 2001. "Group Loyalty: Impact of Members' Identification and Contributions." *Journal of Experimental Social Psychology* 37: 502–509.

Zhang Jiancai张建才. 2017. "Jianguo chuqi laozi guanxi wenti de jingji weidu: 1953, 1954 nian Shanghaishi saying qiye zhong fandui jijingzhuyi wenti chutan"建国初期劳资关系问题的"经济"维度 (The Economic Dimension of the Labor-capital Relations in Early PRC Years: The "Anti-economism" Issue in Private Enterprises in Shanghai, 1953–1954). *Jiangsu shehui kexue*江苏社会科学 2: 232–238.

Zhang Jing张静. 2001. *Liyi zuzhihua danwei: qiye zhidaihui anli yanjiu*利益组织化单位：企业职代会案例研究 (The Organized Interest of Work Units: A Case Study of Enterprise Staff and Workers' Congress). Beijing: Zhongguo Shehui Kexue Chubanshe.

Zhang, Lu. 2015. *Inside China's Automobile Factories: The Politics of Labor and Worker Resistance*. Cambridge, UK: Cambridge University Press.

Zhang Wenkui张文魁 and Yuan Dongming袁东明. 2008. *Zhongguo jingji gaige 30 nian: guoyou qiye juan*中国经济改革30年：国有企业卷 (30 Years of Economic Reform in China: The Volume on State-owned Enterprises). Chongqing: Chongqing Chubanshe.

Zhang Xuebing 张学兵. 2014. "Jihua wai yonggong: dangdai Zhongguo shi shang de yizhong ziyuan peizhi xingshi 计划外用工：当代中国史上的一种资源配置形式" (Unplanned Employment: A Form of Resource Relocation in Contemporary China). *Zhonggong dangshi yanjiu* 中共党史研究 1: 57–68.

Zhang Yongshan 张永山. 1992. "Woguo guoyou qiye zhigong de gongping gan jiegou ji chengyin fenxi 我国国有企业职工的公平感结构及成因分析" (An Analysis of the Sense of Fairness among Workers of State-owned Enterprises and its Causes). *Jingjixue dongtai* 经济学动态 3: 23–29.

Zhang Yunxiao 张云霄. 1995. "Guangyu jinyibu diaodong zhigong jijixing de tansuo 关于进一步调动职工积极性的探索" (Exploring the Further Ways to Incentivize Workers). *Shanghai gonghui guanli ganbu xueyuan xuebao* 上海工会管理干部学院学报 1: 22–26.

Zhang Zhanbin 张占斌. 1988. *Xin Zhongguo qiye lingdao zhidu* 新中国企业领导制度 (The Institutions of Enterprise Leadership in New China). Beijing: Chunqiu Chubanshe.

Zhao Lijiang 赵丽江, Wang Xiaoxu 王晓旭, and Xie Jun 谢俊. 2013. "Daxing guoqi shi shixing gongye minzhu de guanjian lingyu: Gongren canyu guanli dee Hubei jingyan ji xiangguan fenxi 大型国企是实行工业民主的关键领域——工人参与管理的湖北经验及相关分析" (Large-size State-owned Enterprises is the Key Domain for Implementing Industrial Democracy). *Zhongnan caijing zhengfa daxue xuebao* 中南财经政法大学学报 6: 96–102.

Zhao Lingyun 赵凌云. 1999. "Nian jian Zhongguo guoyou qiye gaige fasheng yu tuijiin guocheng de lishi fenxi 1978–1998 年间中国国有企业改革发生与推进过程的历史分析" (A Historical Analysis of the Inception and Unfolding of State-owned Enterprises in China in 1978–1998). *Dangdai zhongguoshi yanjiu* 当代中国史研究 5–6: 199–218.

Zhonggong zhongyang 中共中央 (CCP Central Committee). 1967. *Guanyu fandui jingjizhuyi de tongzhi* 关于反对经济主义的通知 (CCP Central Committee Notice against Economism).

———. 1968. *Guanyu jinyibu daji fangeming jijingzhuyi he toujidaoba huodong de tongzhi* 中关于进一步打击反革命经济主义和投机倒把活动的通知 (Notice about Further Attack on Counterrevolutionary Economism and Speculative Activities).

Zhongxuanbu yanjiushi diaoyanzu中宣部研究室调研组. 1992. "Zhigong de fenpei guannian jixu yindao: dui Hanggang, Minfeng zhicang bufen zhigong fenpei guannian de diaocha职工的分配观念亟需引导——对杭钢、民丰纸厂部分职工分配观念的调查" (An Investigation of the Ideas about Income Distribution among Some Workers of Hanggang and Minfeng Paper Mill). *Sixiang zhengzhi gongzuo yanjiu*思想政治工作研究 1: 28–29.

Zhou Bing周冰 and Yuan Desheng袁德胜. 2014. "Nongmingong gongzi shuiping, tongji wucha he chengxiang shouru chaju农民工工资水平、统计误差和城乡收入差距" (Migrant Workers' Wage Levels, Statistical Errors, and Rural-urban Income Gaps). *Nankai xuebao*南开学报 1: 126–133.

Zhou Shengzhan周胜展. 2011. "Qiye gaizhi hou de gonghui weiquan zhineng sikao企业改制后的工会维权职能思考" (Thoughts on the Functions of Trade Unions in Protecting Worker Rights after Enterprise Restructuring). *Zhongwai qiyejia*中外企业家 5: 27–28.

Zhu, Cherrie Jiuhua, Helen De Cieri, and Peter J. Dowling. 1998. "The Reform of Employee Compensation in China's Industrial Enterprises." *Management International Review* 2: 65–87.

Zhu Min朱敏, Wu Xiaoxi伍晓曦, and Feng Lian冯炼. 2001. "Butong suoyouzhi qiye yuangong jijixing shizheng yanjiu不同所有制企业员工积极性实证分析" (An Empirical Study of the Work Morale of Employees in Enterprises of Different Types of Ownership). *Caijing kexue*财经科学 4: 44–49.

Zhu Xiaoyang朱晓阳 and Chen Peihua陈佩华. 2003. "Zhigong daibiao dahui: zhigong liyi de zhiduhua biaoda qudao? 职工代表大会：职工利益的制度化表达渠道" (The Staff and Workers' Congress: A Channel of Institutionalized Articulation of Staff and Workers' Interests?). *Kaifang shidai* 2.

ZYWJ. *Zhongguo gonghui diqici quanguo daibiao dahui zhuyao wenjian*中国工会第七次全国代表大会主要文件 (Major Documents of the Seventh National Congress of the Trade Unions of China), edited by Gongren chubanshe, 1953. Beijing: Gongren Chubanshe.

Index

activists: 3, 10, 29, 30, 56, 60, 102–103, 114, 119–121; relations with workers, 121–124; relations with cadres, 124–127. *See also* Advanced Producer, Five-Good Worker, Model Laborer, model worker
Advanced Producer, 12, 31, 50–53, 58, 94–95, 119, 212
Akerlof, George, 148
An Miao, 66, 67, 282, 285
Andreas, Joel, 4, 28, 30, 64, 93, 182, 255, 282
Anti-Rightist Campaign, 33, 83, 184
appeal by letter and visit, 5, 14, 17, 20, 62, 65, 82–91, 232. *See also* people's letter

backward elements, 12, 31, 93, 114, 142, 162, 168, 189
Bad Elements, 12

Barnett, Doak, 281, 285
Belloni, Frank, 282, 286
Beijing Gear Factory, 195
Beijing No. 2 Food Processing Factory, 155, 271
Beijing Qingyun Aerospace Instrument Factory, 41, 117, 139, 187, 189, 271
Bettelheim, Charles, 281, 285
Bian, Morris, 164, 285
Bianco, Lucien, 59, 168, 281
big-character poster, 36, 47, 108, 118, 194
Blecher, Marc, 103, 285
bonus, 95–96, 106, 107, 112, 119, 130, 131, 133, 157, 178, 190, 210–211, 213, 216, 249. *See also* wage
Bourdieu, Pierre, 20
branch secretary. *See* Chinese Communist Party

Brewer, Marilynn, 149
Brown, Rupert, 149
Brugger, William, 282, 286
Burns, John, 3

Caciagli, Mario, 282, 286
Cadre. *See* factory cadres
capitalist, 34, 35, 90–91, 92, 179, 183, 193
capitalist roader, 34, 189. *See also* capitalist power holder
capitalist power holder, 128, 181, 182, 187–189, 197, 201
CCP. *See* Chinese Communist Party
Chan, Anita, 3, 29, 220, 282. *See also* Chen Peihua
Chan, Chris, 243, 244, 286
Changzhou Dacheng Factory, 172
Chen, Feng, 235, 236, 243, 287
Chen Guoheng, 220, 287
Chen Peihua, 64
Chen Zuwei, 221, 287
Chi Heng, 64, 287
Chiang Kai-shek, 180, 194
Chinese Communist Party, 7, 17; admission into, 5, 12, 14, 29–31, 37–42, 43, 44, 102, 119, 120, 143, 168, 212, 248, 250; branch secretary, 8, 17, 48, 88–90, 92, 94–97, 104, 126, 150, 153, 189, 190, 193, 214; cadres of, 34, 64; central committee of, 201, 217; committee, 66–67, 73–74, 76, 86, 91, 92, 172, 191, 196, 229; and democracy, 80; ideology of, 15, 18; ideology of, 15; leaders of, 63, 82, 181; loyalty to, 143; members of, 51, 55, 60, 68, 88, 116, 137, 150, 162, 176, 182, 183, 186; problems with cadres and members of, 176–180; propaganda of, 46. *See also* party-state
Chinese Communist Youth League, 17, 39, 42, 44, 51, 97, 120, 143, 162, 186
Chow, Tse-tsung, 64
class status, 33–34, 36–37, 98, 168, 183, 199
class struggle, 35, 142, 147, 251
cleansing the class ranks, 190
clientelism, 24, 102, 103, 112, 119, 130, 250, 282. *See also* patron-client relations
Cliver, Robert, 282, 287
Coase, Ronald, 133
Cold War, 6, 7
collective ownership: 30, 206; factories of, 20, 88, 130, 167, 184, 200, 221
Company Law, 229, 231
Contract workers, 21, 24, 31, 65, 201–203, 216. *See also* informal workers
contracted responsibility system, 24, 213–220, 254
Cui Yi, 216, 217, 287
Cultural Revolution: 3, 5, 11, 15, 21, 32, 33, 34, 36, 40, 44–45, 47, 50, 63–64, 76, 105, 108; 114, 120, 124, 129, 135, 137, 138, 141–143, 157, 161, 164, 210,

235, 247; 167–205, *passim*; economic disparity before, 172–176; rebels in, 181–185; loyalists and onlookers in, 185–188; attack on power holders in, 188–191; violence in, 191–192; seizure of power in, 195–197; Revolutionary Committee in, 63, 183, 188, 190, 196, 197–199, 202; economism in, 199–201

danwei, 21, 128, 148, 163, 211, 215, 244, 252. *See also* work unit
Davis, Deborah, 103
De Boer, John, 283, 297
DeMare, Brian, 282, 288
democratic management, 1–2, 3, 4, 14, 16, 58, 64, 153, 246, 283
Deng Xiaoping, 24, 202, 204, 253
Dernberger, Robert, 281, 288
divorce, 79, 105, 126
Dollar, David, 283, 288
Dong, Guoqiang, 186, 203, 288
Du Shoujia, 284, 288
dual equilibrium, 20–21, 23, 206, 244, 249, 252, 253. *See also* equilibrium

economism, 21, 65, 132, 171, 173–174, 199–201, 294, 304, 305
ecosystem, 23, 253
Eisenstadt, S. N., 282, 288
egalitarianism, 2, 12, 19, 132, 133, 135, 147, 168, 204, 207
Elements of Four Categories. *See* Four Categories

Elfstrom, Manfred, 243, 282, 288
Ellingsen, Tore, 211, 288
Equilibrium: 16–24, 27, 167–168, 201–205, 206–207, 214–215, 226, 244, 257; in labor relations, 20, 160–166; in power relations, 20, 128–131; loss of, 205, 207, 214–218. *See also* dual equilibrium
enterprise reform, 24, 25, 26, 207, 213, 216, 221, 224, 225, 227, 244, 252, 254
Estlund, Cynthia, 244, 282, 288
Eyferth, Jacob, 281, 289

factory. *See* state-owned factory, state-owned enterprise, township and village enterprise
factory cadres: 2, 3, 11–12, 23, 24, 57, 64, 68, 71, 73, 80, 87, 88, 92, 99, 103, 168, 192, 202, 203, 214, 215, 248, 250, 252; abuse of power by, 12, 23, 92, 117, 128, 215, 240, 250, 252; costs and privileges of, 105–109; promotion to, 29, 60, 120, 126–127, 130, 152, 168, 178, 179, 183, 191, 215, 250; relations with workers, 109–112; three tiers of, 104–105. *See also* factory head, production group head, workshop director, branch secretary
factory head, 58, 63, 65, 76, 81, 93, 94, 104, 105, 115, 126, 189–190, 191, 193, 197, 198, 214, 227–228, 233
Falk, Armin, 211, 289

family origin, 33–34, 36–37, 147
favoritism, 17, 18, 24, 73, 103, 114–118, 128, 129, 131, 215, 225, 251
female: students, 35; workers, 36, 38, 51, 79, 86, 88, 118, 144, 145, 146, 148, 150, 154, 157, 160, 188, 193, 195; model workers, 120; cadres, 58, 88, 89; retirees, 117, 120, 184, 228
Fehr, Ernst, 211, 289
Filtzer, Donald, 59, 112, 161, 289
Five Categories, 12, 33–37
Four Categories, 12, 33
Five-Good Worker, 51, 52, 55–56
Four Clean-ups, 35, 194. *See also* Socialist Education Movement
Frazier, Mark, 164, 289
Fudge, Judy, 30
Fung, Edmund, 64

Gallagher, Mary, 241, 243, 282, 289
Gang of Four, 2, 199, 205
Gao Hongxia, 221, 295
Gedian Chemical Plant, 124, 142, 151, 155, 278
General Trade Union: All China, 200, 223; in Nanjing, 1, 84–92; in Ningbo, 121; in Shanghai, 216; in Wuhan, 217
Gilman, Nils, 6
Gneezy, Uri, 211, 289
Gold, Thomas, 282, 290
Goldman, Merle, 212, 290, 302
Gong Xinxin, 216, 217, 218, 290
Gramsci, Antonio, 13

Great Leap Forward, 15, 29, 31, 32, 40, 45, 67, 83–87, 107, 136, 138, 140, 162, 164, 173, 174, 177, 181, 195, 210
Greenfield, Sidney, 282, 299
group sanctioning, 23, 159, 160. *See also* peer pressure
Guangzhong Enterprise Group Corporation, 223
Guangzhou Fountain Pen Factory, 114, 116, 136, 276
Guangzhou Huaqiao Sugar Mill, 34, 95, 113, 139, 183, 188, 190, 191, 276
Guangzhou Lijiao Dock, 35
Guangzhou Iron & Steel Group Corporation, 222–223
Guomindang, 136, 172, 194, 195. *See also* Nationalist Party
guanxi, 17, 40, 109, 110, 121, 123

habitus, 19
Han Bing, 231, 291
Han Jun, 238, 291
Hassard, John, 133, 291
He Chengyun, 32
Helburn, I. B., 283, 291
Henley, John, 133, 291
Hershatter, Gail, 281, 291
Heshun County Chemical Fertilizer Factory, 194
high modernism, 12
Ho, Denise, 282, 291
Hoffmann, Charles, 133, 281, 291
Hogg, Michael, 148

Hong Kong, 9
Hopkin, Jonathan, 282, 292
household registration system, 31, 144, 237, 239
household responsibility system, 239, 252
housing, 17, 23, 28, 30, 60, 71, 73, 74, 77, 102, 106, 112, 113, 116–119, 130, 133, 148, 156, 215, 220, 221, 227, 239, 250
Hu Qiaomu, 2
Huaibei Power Plant, 70
Huang Jian, 222, 292
Huang Xin, 65
Huanggang Region Bedding Factory, 70,
Huanggang Region Filature, 48, 118, 121, 145, 228
Hui, Elaine, 244, 286
Hungary, 66, 113
Hurst, William, 227, 282, 290, 292
Huo Xinbing, 170, 171, 174

identity, 5, 17, 22, 24, 28–61 *passim*, 118, 128, 131, 135, 144–148, 162, 165, 202, 211, 215, 220–224, 225, 228, 244, 247, 249, 250, 252–255
ideology: 10, 14, 15, 16, 17, 18, 42–43, 59–61, 62–63, 64, 100, 203, 215, 246, 251. *See also* Maoism, Marxism, Leninism
Industrial 70 Articles, 67, 71, 76,
industrial citizenship, 4, 30
informal workers. *See* workers
iron rice bowl, 207, 212, 216

January Revolution, 196, 197
Jiang Qing, 200
Jin Chongji, 204, 297
Jinzhou No. 6 Oil Refinery, 120, 272
Johannesson, Magnus, 211, 288

Kirsch, Leonard, 161
Korean War, 38, 138, 169
Kranton, Rachel, 148
Kraus, Richard, 3
Kuruvilla, Sarosh, 243, 283, 288

labor camp, 35
Labor Contract Law, 240, 243
labor contract system, 215, 230
labor relations, 4–5; management of, 15;
landlord, 12, 33, 35, 39, 62, 84, 179, 183, 193, 194, 196
Lane, David, 112, 161, 293
Latham, Michael, 6
Lee, Ching Kwan, 3, 29, 133, 182, 221, 226, 241, 243, 244
Lee, Hong Yung, 182, 293
Lee, Peter, 133, 293
Lee, Rensselaer, 281, 293
Leninism, 13, 50, 59, 61, 176
Levine, John, 149
Lewis, John, 281, 293
Li Bote, 200, 293
Li, Huaiyin, 4, 6, 64, 281, 294
Li Jiaqi, 51, 294
Li Jun, 223, 294
Li Ping, 66, 282, 301

Li Shi, 237, 238, 239, 240, 294
Li Xun, 65, 182, 196, 197, 200
Liaohe Oil Field, 41, 151, 211
lifetime employment. *See* permanent employment
Lin Biao, 43, 45, 164, 204
Lin Chaochao, 32, 170, 171, 172, 174, 175, 201, 284
Lin, Justin, 133
Lin Pan, 164, 172, 295
Liu Guoguang, 283, 295
Liu Shaoqi, 181
Liu Yuanwen, 221, 295
Lu, Huilin, 240, 296
Lu Xiangdong, 292
Lü, Xiaobo, 3, 17, 295, 303
Lu Xiangdong, 222, 224, 292
Luo Tianwen, 222, 295

marriage, 55, 116, 126, 148, 150, 179, 194, 238
masters: workers as, 1, 10, 15, 21, 23–26, 28–61 *passim*, 62–63, 65, 75, 99, 100, 129, 131, 136, 149–151, 153, 167, 169, 175, 177, 203, 215, 216, 220–222, 224, 225, 228, 235, 244, 246–249, 252, 254, 255–257
MacFarquhar, Roderick, 181, 197, 296
Mao Zedong: 2, 4, 5, 34, 42, 44, 58, 59, 90, 111, 141, 145, 155, 164; during the Cultural Revolution, 181, 184, 185, 198, 202, 204. *See also* Mao Zedong Thought
Mao Yuanxin, 184

Mao Zedong Thought, 13, 59–60, 142, 185
Maoism, 12–13, 43, 50, 59–61, 203, 215, 255. *See also* Mao Zedong Thought
Marx, 42, 132
Marxism, 13, 50, 59, 61, 176
masses, 15, 35, 37, 40, 51, 55, 66, 67, 68, 73, 91, 95, 106, 108–109, 113–114, 118, 121–122, 125, 129, 151, 177, 179–180, 185, 196, 198, 201
Mastropaolo, Alfio, 282, 292
McCallum, Ronald, 30
Meisner, Mitch, 281, 296
Meisner, Maurice, 182, 296
Meyskens, Covell, 282, 296
migrant workers: 25–26, 27, 230, 237–240, 255; as protesters, 240–245
Military Bedding and Clothing Factory in Wuhan, 38, 97, 98, 120, 155, 157, 187, 198, 228
Military Factory No. 103, 48
Military Factory No. 513, 177
Military Factory No. 741, 176
Military Factory No. 768, 39, 42, 142, 146, 154–155, 211
Military Factory No. 772, 177, 178
Model Laborer. *See* model workers
model workers, 50–51, 93, 119–122, 124, 138, 143, 150, 182
modern corporate system, 213, 218, 219, 221,
Mu Liangping, 217, 296

INDEX 313

Nanjing 8–27, 186
Nanjing Brick and Tile Factory, 85
Nanjing Carrier Machine Factory, 69, 147, 189, 272
Nanjing Clock Factory, 79, 139, 272
Nanjing Cotton Textile Factory, 87
Nanjing Datong Bedding Factory, 34, 36, 39
Nanjing Diaoyutai Textile Factory, 88
Nanjing Farm, 88
Nanjing General Trade Union, 1, 84–93
Nanjing Handicraft Equipment Factory, 224
Nanjing Housing Management Bureau, 71, 77
Nanjing Jinchuan Power Meter Factory, 54, 55
Nanjing Light Bulb and Valve Factory, 53, 56
Nanjing Municipal Archives, 8
Nanjing Nine Dragon Hotel, 193
Nanjing Radio Components Factory, 52
Nanjing Precast Concrete Factory, 47, 115, 139
Nanjing Qinfeng Cigarette Factory, 86
Nanjing Shuguang Cotton Textile Factory, 88–92
Nanjing Steam Navigation and Electric Machinery Factory, 85
Nanjing Steel and Iron Work, 41, 78, 140, 152, 275
Nanjing Taiping Ceramic Factory, 52, 58
Nanjing Telecommunication Equipment Factory, 51, 54, 55, 56, 71, 104, 106, 110, 120, 227
Nanjing Textile Company, 78, 275
Nanjing University, 186
Nanjing Vegetable Company, 193
Nanjing Vegetable Oil Mill, 88
Nanjing Wireless Components Factory, 58
Nanjing Xiaguan Grain Processing Factory, 86
Nanjing Xiaguan Railway Station, 46, 117, 194, 272
Nanjing Xianfeng Hardware Factory, 57
Nanjing Xinghuo Cotton Mill, 36, 45, 46, 47, 107, 114, 156, 157
Nanjing Xingyuan Silk Factory, 141, 193
Nanjing Yonglining Chemical Factory, 175
Nanjing Yuhuatai Park of Revolutionary Martyrs, 88
Nanjing Zhongshan Mine, 39, 195, 275
Nanjing Zhongxingyuan Silk Mill, 38, 111, 275
Nationalist Government, 15, 34, 64, 97, 172,
Nationalist Party, 34, 35, 36, 39, 164, 194. *See also* Guomindang
Nee, Victor, 134, 165, 281, 298
neotraditionalism, 3

Ngai, Pun, 240, 243, 286, 296
Ningbo Hefeng Yarn Mill, 96, 109, 115, 121, 125, 126, 157, 183, 188, 198, 275
Ningbo Port Machinery Factory, 40, 45, 47, 69, 140, 187, 190, 194, 196, 197
Ningbo Renfeng Fabric Mill, 120, 136, 144, 193, 228, 276
No. 2 Automobile Works, 154, 156, 273
North, Douglass, 133, 163
nostalgia. *See* workers
Nyaw Mee-Kau, 133, 291

one-man system, 63, 282
One-Strike, Three-Anti Campaign, 129

Pang, Chung Min, 283, 297
Pang Xianzhi, 204, 297
Parish, William, 3, 28, 29, 221
party membership. *See* Chinese Communist Party
party-state, 2, 13, 17, 18, 26, 42, 59, 65, 137, 140, 147, 181, 182, 184, 196, 204, 205
patrimonialism, 3
patron-client relations, 17, 102–103, 130, 214, 250. *See also* clientelism
peer pressure, 19, 24, 156, 160, 162, 165, 250, 254. *See also* group sanctioning
Pegels, Carl, 133, 297
permanent employment, 4, 11, 17, 18, 19, 80, 99, 111, 128, 129, 164, 167, 202, 207, 216, 246, 248
Perry, Elizabeth, 63, 64, 65, 103, 169, 182, 196, 197, 200
people's letter, 17, 84. *See also* appeal by letter and visit
Philion, Stephen, 283, 297
political study session, 5, 12, 13, 14, 17, 22, 29, 43–45, 46–48, 49, 141, 142, 178, 211, 248
Poor-and-Lower-Middle Peasant, 35, 40, 183
Power, John, 282, 297
power relations, 5, 18–19; equilibrium in, 19
production group, 17, 18, 40, 47, 51, 55, 58, 89, 90, 94–96, 119, 191
production group leader, 34–35, 45, 46, 56, 79, 94, 105–106, 157, 178
Prybyla, Jan, 281, 297
Putterman, Louis, 283, 297
Pye, Lucian, 61, 281, 297

Qiang, Li, 290
Quan, Katie, 243, 297

Red Guard, 34, 168, 182, 185–186, 189, 191–193, 195
retained personnel, 172–173, 180
retained wage, 172, 173, 283
Revolutionary Committee. *See* Cultural Revolution
rich peasant, 12, 33, 36, 39, 84, 179, 193
Riskin, Carl, 173, 281, 298
Roniger, Luis, 282, 288

Schoenhals, Michael, 181, 197, 296
Schmalzer, Sigrid, 282, 298
Schram, Stuart, 108, 181, 298
Schurmann, Franz, 13, 42, 59, 281, 298
Scott, James, 12, 37, 102, 128, 298
Selden, Mark, 108, 298
self-employed individual, 217
sex, 35, 105, 176, 177, 179
Shan Zhufei, 220, 298
Shanghai Artistic Carving Factory, 96, 117, 123, 150, 154
Shanghai Compressor Factory, 71, 97, 107, 114, 136, 189
Shanghai Dacheng Textile Factory, 173
Shanghai Dazhonghua Rubber Factory, 173, 283
Shanghai Electrical Bureau, 172
Shanghai General Petrochemical Plant, 70
Shanghai Jiangning Lathe Factory, 146, 276
Shanghai Jiefang Plastic Factory, 126, 148, 277
Shanghai Jinhua Socks Factory, 172
Shanghai Light Bulb Factory, 57, 97, 137, 152, 158
Shanghai Machine Tool Factory, 74, 75
Shanghai Medical Equipment Factory, 77, 108, 184, 198, 276
Shanghai No.1 Steel Work, 38,
Shanghai No. 17 Cotton Mill, 69, 104, 106, 121
Shanghai Piano Factory, 218
Shanghai Putuo District Labor

Service Company, 96, 117, 277
Shanghai Silicon Steel Factory, 41, 124, 152, 158
Shanghai Yimin Food Factory, 42, 45, 46, 94, 95, 104, 115, 118, 122, 123, 125, 127, 138, 155, 184, 189, 192, 228
Shearer, John, 283, 291
Sheehan, Jackie, 63, 64, 133, 169, 291
Shen Jianpeng,
Shengli Oil Field, 41, 68, 94, 122, 141, 160, 212
Shi Tanjing, 76, 298
Shi, Tianjian, 65, 299
Shijiazhuang Chemical Fertilizer Plant, 121, 140, 145, 151
Shijiazhuang Truck Factory, 72
shirking, 2, 4, 18, 19, 23, 24, 46, 47, 50, 60, 74, 137–138, 140, 159, 160, 163, 165, 166, 171, 203, 207, 212, 217, 243, 249, 250
Shitouzui Mine, 124, 145, 152, 274
slacking. *See* shirking
Sliwka, Dirk, 211, 299
Smith, Aminda, 281, 299
Socialist Education Movement, 84, 87, 129, 176, 177, 184. *See also* Four Clean-ups
Socialist Transformation of Industry and Commerce, 66, 136, 171, 172, 184
SOE. *See* state-owned enterprise
Song Xueqin, 32, 174, 299
Soviet Union: 2, 29, 59, 63, 108, 161, 164, 281; factory system of, 111–112

staff and workers' congress: 5, 12, 14, 17, 21, 25, 26, 31, 62–65, 167, 214, 247, 248, 254; origins of, 66–67; representatives of, 67–70; proposals submitted to and handled by, 70–76; and trade union, 76–81; and appeal by letters and visits, 82; and substantive governance, 98–100; in the 1980s, 226–228; in the 1990s and the 2000s, 229–235

Stalinism, 59, 60, 289

Standing, Guy, 4, 299

state-owned factory, 1, 11, 15, 16, 19, 22, 30, 63, 75, 85, 99, 132, 135, 138, 161, 171, 173, 201, 203, 246. *See also* state-owned factory

state-owned enterprise, 3, 4, 8, 10, 20, 22, 24, 26, 30, 32, 64, 66, 76, 85, 88, 130, 164, 206, 208–209, 214, 216, 217–220, 222, 224–225, 227, 228, 229, 231, 232, 253. *See also* enterprise reform, state-owned factory

Strickon, Arnold, 282, 299

Su Linsen, 223, 299

substantive governance, 11–16, 26, 98–101, 246, 247

Sun Xinxin, 231, 232, 299

SWC. *See* staff and workers' congress

Tang Kuiyu, 231, 232, 299

Tang, Wenfang, 29, 221

Taylor, George, 281, 300l

Tianjin Yonglijiu Chemical Factory, 173

temporary workers, 2, 31–32, 199–200, 216. *See also* informal workers

Three-Anti and Five-Anti Campaign, 83, 129, 172, 184

Tong Xin, 235, 236, 300

Tong Zhihong, 284, 300

Tonghua Steel and Iron Corporation, 231–232

totalitarianism, 2, 3, 6, 12, 61, 102, 249, 281

Townsend, James, 281, 300

township and village enterprise, 24, 212, 218, 237

trade union: 5, 8, 14, 17, 21, 26, 28, 31, 32, 62, 65, 76–82, 95, 98–100, 139, 150, 169, 170, 200, 202, 214, 220, 227, 232, 247, 248, 254; and appeal by letters and visits, 82; in the 1960s, 84–87; and worker grievances, 87–91; at the levels above the factory, 91–93; and economism, 170–171; before and after reforms, 228; in the 1990s and the 2000s, 229–230; in worker protests, 232–234, 240–245; and migrant workers, 238, 255–256; law of, 243. *See also* General Trade Union

TVE. *See* township and village enterprise

unemployment, 1, 3, 135, 150, 161, 169, 170

Unger, Jonathan, 3, 29, 220, 300

Vietnam War, 6

Wage system: 11, 17, 19, 22, 24, 30, 32, 46, 47, 60, 70, 76, 79, 80, 81, 85, 86–91, 93, 95, 106–107, 108, 112–113, 117, 119, 120, 130, 131, 133, 145–146, 150, 157–158, 161, 164, 170, 171–174, 178, 208–209, 210, 213, 215, 218, 223, 230, 237, 238, 241, 242, 243, 248, 249, 250–251, 253; upgrading, 113–116; piece-rate, 17, 87, 164, 174, 202, 203, 204, 224; time-rate, 17, 164, 237, 238; eight grades, 115, 171, 172. *See also* retained wage

Walder, Andrew, 3, 17, 29, 102–103, 112–113, 119, 124, 130 133, 181, 182, 185, 186, 203

Wang Chidong, 66, 282, 301

Wang, Di, 282, 301

Wang Jian, 230, 301

Wang Mingcai, 220, 301

Wang, Ning, 18, 287

Wang Yanbin, 220, 301

Wang Youfu, 172, 175, 304

Weber, Max, 282, 301

Wei Dongning, 222, 301

Weingrod, Alex, 282, 301

Weisskopf, Thomas, 281, 301

welfare benefits. *See* workers

Wemheuer, Felix, 28, 282, 301

Whampoa Military Academy, 39

White, Harrison, 148, 302

Whyte, Martin, 3, 28, 112, 131, 283, 302

Wolf, Eric, 282, 302

Womack, Brantly, 103

women, 35, 36, 38, 51, 54, 58, 75, 79, 86, 88, 89, 117, 118, 120, 144, 145, 146, 148, 150, 154, 157, 160, 162, 177, 179, 184, 188, 193, 195, 228. *See also* female

Won, Jaeyoun, 290

work norms, 17, 19, 135, 203, 210, 213, 217, 254

work unit: 24, 28–29, 31–44, 61, 68, 69, 76, 77, 78, 80, 82, 85, 88, 97, 100, 103, 106, 137, 140, 147–148, 151, 183–184, 185, 186, 189, 191, 192, 201–202, 212, 213, 215, 226–228, 244, 252, 256; as ecosystem, 23, 253; equilibrium of, 16–23, 128–131, 160–166

workers: formal, 21, 28, 30, 161, 164, 167–168, 199, 201, 246–247, 252; informal, 21, 31–32, 161–162, 164, 167–168, 199–201, 203–204, 247; nostalgia among, 3, 10, 11, 25, 131, 156, 166, 222, 226; welfare benefits for, 11, 12, 17, 18, 22, 30, 66, 73–75, 77, 85, 88, 130, 149, 153, 184, 200, 209, 219, 220, 247, 248, 252. *See also* contract workers, temporary workers, migrant workers, model workers, permanent employment, women, female

workshop director, 17, 18, 44, 46, 51, 56, 57, 58, 81, 93, 94, 96, 97, 104–105, 106–107, 114, 116, 194

Wu Binbin, 237, 238, 239, 240, 294

Wu Jinglian, 283, 302

Wu Li, 213, 302
Wu Xiaoming, 223, 224, 302
Wu, Yiching, 182, 281, 302
Wuhan Gongnong Garment Factory, 79, 94, 97, 104, 146, 150, 278
Wuhan Pharmaceutical Factory, 69, 79, 95, 120, 159, 187
Wuhan Rubber Plant, 94, 120, 137, 278
Wuhan Steel Plant, 36, 39, 44, 68, 107, 110, 137, 141

Xia Shuiliu, 1
Xi'an Instrument Factory, 68, 71, 123, 136, 183, 189, 227
Xiangtan Electric Machinery Factory, 143, 188, 274
Xie Deming, 216, 303
Xie Yuhua, 230, 303
Xingan County Electronic Instrument Factory, 125, 277
Xu Jingxian, 185, 303
Xue Muqiao, 283, 303

Yang, Mayfair, 17, 303
Yeh, Wen-Hsin, 164
Yin Jianbing, 240, 303
You Lixin, 220, 304
You Zhenglin, 225, 304
Youth League. *See* Chinese Communist Youth League

Yu Ji, 220, 304
Yuan Desheng, 237, 306
Yuan Dongming, 283, 304
Yuan Jin, 172, 175, 304

Zdaniuk, Bozena, 149
Zhang Jiancai, 171
Zhang Jing, 282, 304
Zhang, Lu, 282, 304
Zhang Ying, 230, 301
Zhao Lingyun, 209, 210,
Zhao Renwei, 283, 295
Zhang Wenkui, 283, 304
Zhang Xuebing, 32
Zhang Yongshan, 214, 305
Zhang Yunxiao, 215, 216, 305
Zhang Zhanbin, 282, 305
Zhao Lijiang, 230, 305
Zhao Lingyun, 209, 210, 305
Zhao Renwei, 283, 295
Zhenjiang Mine, 69, 79, 118, 126, 149, 163, 184, 192, 199, 276
Zhengzhou Paper Mill, 232–237
Zhou Bing, 237, 306
Zhou Enlai, 186, 204
Zhou Shengzhan, 230, 306
Zhu, Cherrie, 283, 306
Zhu Min, 224, 306
Zhu Rongji, 220
Zhu Xiaoyang, 64
zibenjia. See capitalist

The authorized representative in the EU for product safety and compliance is:
Mare Nostrum Group
B.V Doelen 72
4831 GR Breda
The Netherlands